Peasant Rebels under Stalin

You have shot many people
You have driven many to jail
You have sent many into exile
To certain death in the taiga.

To you millions of curses
From old women, cripples, and mothers,
Who you have taken from the warm embraces
Of fathers and unhappy children.

A wife is on the verge of dying
With curses for you on her tongue.
Around her, her family is crying.
In tears are her four little ones.

The family closes her eyes.
Mother will not return from the grave.
We will never know Father's tenderness.
He is dying in the North Urals taiga.

Poor Father, our provider,
Was taken during grain collections.
They took all the grain from our family
And in her grief Mother passed on.

They took all the animals to the kolkhoz.
They sold off our family home.
Now our fate is to wander the earth
With our Grandmother, there are five . . .

Now the old woman wanders through villages
Gathering crumbs in her sack.
Through the storms of the winter she ventures
Cursing the regime of Stalin . . .

You have shot more people than the Tsar.
You have driven more to jail.
You have sent more into exile.
To certain death in the taiga.

—anonymous poem,
translated by Jane Ormrod

Preface

The collectivization of agriculture was a watershed event in the history of the Soviet Union. It was the Communist party's premier effort at social engineering on a mass scale and marked the first of a series of bloody landmarks that would come to characterize and define Stalinism. Collectivization destroyed the peasant commune and left in its place a coercive enterprise, socialist in name only, that the Communist party would use to try to transform the peasantry into a cultural and economic colony. The collective farm was to be an instrument of control: it would enable the state to exact a tribute from the peasantry in the form of grain and other produce and extend political and administrative domination to the countryside. To accomplish its goal of colonization, the party aimed at nothing less than the eradication of peasant culture and independence. It launched a wholesale campaign against such peasant institutions as the *dvor* (household), *skhod* (peasant council), land society, mill (a gathering place for informal politics), market, and even church and traditional holidays in an effort to destroy sources of peasant cultural strength and autonomy. It ordered the closing of village churches and a campaign against religion. Village elites were silenced, priests were arrested, and members of the village intelligentsia who chose not to serve as agents of the state were hounded and harassed. And, under the label of "kulak," prosperous, outspoken, or simply able peasant farmers were subject to arrest and deportation in one of the twentieth century's most horrific episodes of mass repression. Peasants lost control of their means of production and economic destiny. Collectivization was an all-out attack against the peasantry, its culture, and way of life.

This book is, in many ways, a continuation of my earlier work on the mobilization and use of Soviet factory workers—the "25,000ers"—in collectivization (*The Best Sons of the Fatherland: Workers in the Vanguard of Soviet Collectivization*, New York, 1987). That book was a study in the urban social base of Stalinism, a case study, as it were, in Stalinist populism and working-class support for the regime. It was also a study in collectivization and the revolution, broadly defined. The 25,000ers left for the countryside confident in the viability of socialism transplanted to the village. Their confidence quickly evaporated as they became immersed in a hostile and largely alien world resistant to the workers, city, and social-ism in its Stalinist guise. In a sense, the study captured the tremendous irony of the Russian Revolution as these workers—dubbed the cream of the "vanguard class"—became mired in the backwoods of peasant Russia. Their story can be read as a metaphor for an intellectually constructed working-class revolution, fueled by urban instability, power-hungry men, and dreamers, which ran aground, inevitably was bound to run aground, by the realities of Russia's socioeconomic structure—that of an agrarian nation similar in most ways to what would later be called by the "first world," "developing" countries—and its politico-cultural traditions.

This book continues the story by exploring the peasant reality that blocked the revolution, perhaps doomed the revolution from the start. My aim ultimately is to understand something of the politics of the revolution by exploring the politics of the peasantry during the climax of the revolu-tionary experience as it pertained to the countryside, for the main field of contention in revolutionary Russia was never limited to classes (which hardly existed in the Western European sense) but ultimately was a strug-gle between town and countryside, state and peasantry, one in which the outcome was always less clear than apparent. During collectivization, peasant politics were expressed through resistance. This book is a study of peasant resistance, broadly defined, that seeks to document not only the vast struggle waged by the peasantry during collectivization, but also the manifestation in the USSR of universal strategies of peasant resistance in what amounted to a virtual civil war between state and peasantry. In the end and when power and politics are the main criteria, the state surely emerged victorious from its confrontation with the peasantry, an inevita-ble outcome given the enormous repressive powers of the state and the localism of peasant revolt. But it was a Pyrrhic victory, for collectivization had the ultimate effect of unifying the overwhelming majority of the peasantry against the state and its policies. Long after the collectivization campaigns of the Stalin revolution, a peasantry, in some sense of the word, would remain, sometimes embittered and most of the time engaged in a continuing and undeclared war based on the constant and manifold employment of the devices of passive and everyday forms of resistance on the collective farm. The revolution would founder in the very countryside it sought to transform, reminding us once again that the October Revolu-tion and the Stalinist industrial and military infrastructure of the USSR were, from the start, built on a peasant foundation inadequate to sustain a proletarian revolution and too weak to maintain its country's super-power status into the late twentieth century.

Peasant Rebels under Stalin seeks to retrieve a lost chapter from the history of the USSR. This chapter is of immense significance because the peasant revolt against collectivization was the most violent and sustained resistance to the Soviet state after the Russian Civil War. This study pres-ents the history of a peasantry on the brink of destruction. It is a study in peasant culture, politics, and community seen through the prism of resistance. The history of this revolt is also a story of intrinsic human interest. This book is about the women and men who tried to preserve their families, communities, and beliefs from the depredations of Stalinism. Like my first book, this book is concerned with presenting voices from below, allowing, to the extent that it is ever possible, the actors to speak their parts. Not all peasants resisted, but many did and in countless ways. Although their acts were often heroic, this book is not about heroes, but rather about ordinary people driven to acts of heroic desperation by brutal state policies. If in the process of recording their stories we remember the deeds of the people of Nachalova or the women of Butovska, then we will have restored some of the lost voices of Soviet history.

Research for this book began in the mid-1980s, and was completed under the auspices of the Stalin-Era Research and Archive Project of the University of Toronto, funded by an MCRI grant from the Canadian Social Science and Humanities Research Council. Grants from the NEH, the ACLS, the American Philosophical Society, the Social Science Research Council, the Bernadotte E. Schmitt Foundation, IREX, SSHRC, and the Connaught Foundation have made work on this project possible. An earlier version of chapter 6 was first published in *The Russian Review*, vol. 45, no. 1 (January 1985). Copyright © 1986 by *The Russian Review*. All rights reserved. The *Journal of Modern History* granted permission for publication of segments of a previously published article that appeared in 1990.

I would like to thank Barbara Clements, Sheila Fitzpatrick, Stephen Frank, William Husband, Tracy McDonald, and Christine Worobec for reading the manuscript and providing excellent criticism. I am grateful to Kari Bronaugh, Jeffrey Burds, Colleen Craig, V. P. Danilov, Todd Foglesong, Thomas Greene, Nena Hardie, James Harris, Dan Healey, Nancy Lane, Eileen Consey Maniichuk, Jane Ormrod, and Pamela Thomson Verrico for criticism, advice, and support. Tatiana Mironova provided invaluable research assistance, and the director of the Russian State Archive of the Economy, E. A. Tiurina, and her fine staff made my work in Moscow a pleasure. Perhaps most of all, I would like to thank my friend and colleague, Roberta T. Manning, who has generously shared with me her own work on the Soviet countryside in the 1930s and has been a constant source of support. Zoia Viktorovna and Mariia Fedorovna have been a family for me in Moscow, and it is to them that I owe my inspiration. Finally, I mention Sharik, who has made this work possible.

Toronto, Ontario   L. V.
January 1996

Contents

Peasant Rebels under Stalin

Introduction

To all the rules of peasanthood Muravia stays true.
                        —Alexander Tvardovsky, "Land of Muravia"

Collectivization was a violent and bloody clash between two cultures at fatal variance with one another. It was a campaign of domination and destruction, which aimed at nothing less than the internal colonization of the peasantry. Stalinist state building required a "tribute" (grain and other agricultural produce) from the peasantry in order to fill the state's granaries for export and to feed the cities and the Red army—in short, to fulfill the endless demands of primitive socialist accumulation.[1] Collectivization would allow for the extraction of vital resources (grain, soldiers, labor), as well as enable the state to subjugate the peasantry through the imposition of vast and coercive administrative and political controls. To achieve its goals, the state sought the eradication of peasant culture and autonomy, the forced acculturation of the peasantry into the dominant culture. "Depeasantization," a Communist[2] corollary of industrialization, socialism, and the advent of the classless society, would be accelerated as the self-proclaimed forces of "modernity" battled the "darkness" and "backwardness" of the village. Although the Communist party publicly proclaimed collectivization to be the "socialist transformation" of the countryside, it was in reality a war of cultures, a virtual civil war between state and peasantry, town and countryside.

Peasants viewed collectivization as the end of the world and fiercely resisted the onslaught of repression. Weaving a dense web of rumor through the countryside, peasants created a counter-ideology that delegitimized and turned the Communist world upside down by labeling Soviet power the Antichrist and the collective farm his lair. They rebelled against what many called a second serfdom with a vast wave of peasant Luddism, destroying property and leveling wealth that could single out a peasant as a "kulak" or be swallowed up by the rapacious collective farm. Millions fled, taking the traditional route of outmigration to the towns or, in other cases, to the desolate steppe, where families sought refuge and young men joined the ranks of what the state labeled "kulak bandits." Many others looked for justice locally, speaking out boldly at collectivization meetings and writing letters to the central authorities in the vain hope that Stalin, Kalinin, and the Central Committee of the Communist party might defend the peasant against the depredations of a local officialdom implementing central policy. When peaceful means failed, peasants turned to violence. Arson, assault, lynching, and murders of local officials and peasant activists dotted the rural terrain. Rebellion engulfed the countryside, resulting in some 13,000 riots with over two million participants in 1930. Peasant resistance was threatening and pervasive enough for a Commissariat of Agriculture instructor to believe "dark forces" to be at work in the countryside, and for I. M. Vareikis, first secretary of the Central Black Earth regional committee of the Communist party, to conclude that there "probably exists a defined counterrevolutionary SR [Socialist-Revolutionary party] center which is directing this business."[3]

The peasant revolt against collectivization was the most serious episode in popular resistance experienced by the Soviet state after the Russian Civil War. The story of this revolt constitutes one of the many "blank spots"[4] in the history of the former Soviet Union. For decades, Soviet scholars carefully sidestepped the topic, using a fabricated and pseudo-Marxist class language to discuss what became in the truncated historical vision of the Soviet period "class struggle," "kulak insurrection," and "counterrevolutionary terror." Western scholars also avoided the subject, generally focusing on state policies and preferring to leave in place the traditional image of the passive and inert Russian peasant objectified and rendered historically motionless by the totalitarian monolith.[5] More recently, Sheila Fitzpatrick has explored peasant resistance after collectivization, but dismisses peasant resistance during collectivization, concluding that peasants "bore it [collectivization] fatalistically."[6] *Peasant Rebels under Stalin* is mainly, though not exclusively, the story of what happened in 1930, the key year in collectivization. It seeks to demonstrate that the scope and significance of the peasant revolt against collectivization was far greater and more varied than scholars have previously assumed, and that its content and forms grew out of a cultural context specific to peasantries as well as a national context specific to the USSR under Stalin. The book tells only a part of the story of the peasantry during collectivization, but a part that I believe conveys something of the experiences, values, and ways of the peasantry, presenting it as a distinct and meaningful cultural community. The study begins with an analysis of state-peasant relations from the 1917 Revolution to collectivization and then turns to the multilayered dimensions of peasant politics, examining the intricate network of attitudes, beliefs, behaviors, and actions that constitute a peasant culture of resistance.

When peasants engage in acts of resistance, they "speak out loud." That is, this normally silent historical constituency is heard and its actions are recorded, providing the historian with a glimpse of an otherwise often inaccessible sector of society. Resistance serves as a prism, distilling aspects of peasant culture, politics, and community to the historian. The components of resistance—discourse, behavior, and action expressed through rumor, folklore, symbolic inversion, popular culture, passive resistance, violence, and rebellion—form bridges of understanding into the peasant world. As historians of other times and places have suggested, peasant consciousness reveals itself through these components of resistance, thereby allowing values, beliefs, and attitudes rooted in peasant culture to become visible.[7]

In the collectivization era, we see most clearly what might be described as a *culture* of resistance—that is, a specific style of peasant communication, demeanor, and interaction with elites that runs across time and nations and seeks alternately to manipulate, protest, and adapt itself to the prevailing order through subterfuge, rebellion, and other popular forms of resistance, passive and active, as peasants struggle to maintain their identities and lives within and against the dominant culture. The subordinate culture draws upon its own institutions, traditions, values, rituals, and ways to articulate and enunciate its resistance.

Through resistance, the peasantry revealed itself to be separate and distinct, and antithetical to Soviet power during collectivization. The cohesion and solidarity demonstrated by peasant communities at this time was less the result of minimal socioeconomic differentiation, a notion posited in the Western literature,[8] than the result of the state's violation of peasant interests as a whole. Peasants banded together in self-defense as a cultural community struggling for survival in the face of the state's frontal assault on the household economy, peasant customs, and ways of living. Peasant women emerged as natural leaders of revolt, an outcome both predictable and logical given that collectivization impacted most seriously on women's sphere of interest: the domestic economy of private plot and livestock, the care of children, and matters of family subsistence. Peasant political unity during collectivization derived from the violation of the very interests that held the peasantry together as an economic, social, and cultural entity based on small-scale agricultural production, family economies, and community living.[9] The solidarity arising from the assault on peasant interests formed the foundations for the culture of resistance.

The unity exhibited by the Soviet peasantry during collectivization was neither an innate function of socioeconomics nor, indeed, even a necessarily typical feature of peasant communities. Collectivism and community were village ideals or norms, paramount in the value system of the peasantry, but not always or perhaps even generally reflective of reality. In ordinary times, peasant society was characterized by a high degree of segmentation and internal stratification. Within villages, peasants could be divided according to wealth, family networks, gender, generation, factions based on defined interests, and insider-outsider status. Norms of collectivism, unity, and egalitarianism were important values and standards of judgment in the village ethos, as well as, and perhaps more significantly, cudgels of enforcement to be used by the village's patriarchal authority structure on disobedient, dissident, or sometimes simply *different* voices in the community.[10]

Peasant cohesion was situational and contextual. It was most often sustained in confrontations with "outsiders," signifying here agents of the town, officialdom, and dominant classes or groups.[11] An ordinarily conflict-ridden society divided by myriad cleavages was capable of unity and solidarity in action in the face of crisis. In such an instance, the interest of the peasantry as a single entity superseded the usual divisions and ruptures of the community.[12] And here again, the "politics" of collectivism and unity could be turned against those villagers who acted as agents of the state or who sided with the contested practices and policies of the "outsiders." During collectivization, the peasantry engaged in a virtual civil war with the state, yet within this civil war there was another, no less brutal civil war that pitted the village community against a minority of peasant officials and activists who went over to the side of Soviet power.[13]

The 1917 Revolution had the unintended consequence of reinforcing many aspects of peasant culture and, specifically, a number of important features underlying and strengthening community cohesion. Although human and material losses from years of war and the famine that followed in the wake of civil war took a tremendous toll on the peasantry, the revolution, in combination with this time of troubles, had the effect of revitalizing the peasant community. Peasants engaged in massive social leveling. The percentages of poor peasants fell from some 65% to around 25% by the mid-1920s, while the proportion of wealthy peasants declined from roughly 15% (depending upon calculation) to about 3% in the same time span.[14] The middle peasant became the dominant figure in Soviet agriculture as a result of wartime losses, social revolution and redivision of wealth, and the return, often forced, of large numbers of peasants who had quit the commune to establish individual farmsteads in the prewar Stolypin agrarian reforms. Socioeconomic differentiation remained fairly stable through the 1920s, showing only very slight increases at the extremes. Leveling reinforced village homogeneity and cohesion while strengthening the position of the middle peasant who, according to Eric Wolf, represented the most "culturally conservative stratum" of the peasantry and the village force most resistant to change.[15] The commune itself was bolstered as most of the Stolypin peasants returned to communal land tenure, which constituted approximately 95% of all forms of land tenure in the mid-1920s, thereby standardizing the peasant economy.[16] And although peasant households splintered as the liberating effects of the revolution encouraged and enabled peasant sons to free themselves from the authority of the patriarchal household, most peasants, especially women and the weaker members of the community, clung all the more tenaciously to customary and conservative notions of household, family, marriage, and belief in order to survive the crises of the times. While the revolution no doubt dislodged and altered significant aspects of peasant lives, historians increasingly believe that the basic structures and institutions of the village demonstrated considerable continuity over the revolutionary divide, in many cases becoming stronger as a defensive bulwark against economic hardship and the destructive incursions of warring governments and armies, Red and White.[17]

The strengthening of homogeneity and the endurance of peasant culture should not imply that the peasantry was a static, unchanging rustic fixture. Profound processes of change had long been at work in the countryside, accelerating in particular in the late nineteenth and early twentieth centuries. Alternative patterns of socialization appeared as peasant-workers and soldiers returned on visits or permanently to their home villages. Urban patterns of taste and, to a lesser extent, consumption also began to make an appearance in rural Russia as personal contacts between town and countryside became more common. A market economy made inroads into the countryside, altering the economy of the peasant household as well as the internal social dynamics of the commune. Family size declined as extended families slowly began to give way to nuclear families, and marriages began to be based less exclusively on parents' choice. Peasant culture did not stagnate, but evolved over time, absorbing change and pragmatically adapting what was of use.[18] Fundamental structures and institutions of peasant community persisted, demonstrating the durability and adaptability of the peasantry as a culture.

Similar patterns of change persisted into the Soviet period, coexisting, sometimes peacefully, sometimes not, with the prevailing patterns of peasant and community relations and dynamics. Although many interactions between village and town were seriously disrupted during the revolution and civil war,[19] the town and state continued to have an enormous impact on the countryside. Tens of thousands of peasant-workers returned to the village during the civil war, bringing with them new ways and practices not always in line with those of the community. A vast number of peasants served in the army during the world war and civil war, and they, too, returned with new ideas, sometimes at odds with their neighbors. From some of these groups emerged the village's first Communists and Komsomols; the early collective farms and the splintering of households often derived from the aspirations and needs of these prodigal sons. The Communist party, in the meantime, although in practice generally neglectful of the countryside through most of the 1920s and preoccupied with industry and internal party politics, was, in theory, committed to remaking the peasantry, to eliminating it as an antiquated socioeconomic category in an accelerated depeasantization that would transform peasant into proletarian. The party, the Komsomol, peasant-workers home on leave, groups of poor peasants and Red army veterans, and rural correspondents (*sel'kory*) all became dimly lit beacons of Communist sensibility in the village. Efforts at socialization and indoctrination occurred in periodic antireligious campaigns, literacy campaigns, election campaigns, campaigns to recruit party and Komsomol members, campaigns to organize poor peasants or women, and so on, as the state attempted to build bridges into the countryside to bolster the *smychka* (worker-peasant alliance) of the 1920s. The state succeeded in establishing pockets of support in the village, which would serve not only as agents of change but also as new sources of cleavage and village disjunction as new political identities emerged and interacted, sometimes uncomfortably, within the peasant community.

Collectivization was to destroy most of these "cultural bridges," leaving what remained of the state's small contingent of supporters entrenched against a hostile community. Most of the natural cleavages and fault lines that criss-crossed the village in ordinary times receded into latency during collectivization as the community found itself united against a common, and, by this time, deadly foe. During collectivization, the peasantry acted as a class in much the way Teodor Shanin has defined class for peasantry: "that is, as a social entity with a community of economic interests, its identity shaped by conflict with other classes and expressed in typical patterns of cognition and political consciousness, however rudimentary, which made it capable of collective action reflecting its interests."[20] Whether it is described as a class or as a culture in Clifford Geertz's sense of a totality of experience and behavior, the "socially established structures of meaning" or "webs of significance" by which people act,[21] the peasantry clearly demonstrated the extent to which it was distinct and separate from much of the rest of Soviet society.

Implicit in this view of the peasantry as a class or culture is some echo of Robert Redfield's notion of peasant society and culture as "a type or class loosely defined" with "something generic about it."[22] In form and in content as well as in common cause and interest, a great deal about the peasantry's resistance to collectivization was "generic," demonstrating the durability and solidarity of the peasantry as a social and cultural category and its similarities to other peasants engaged in resistance at other times and in other places. The generic nature of the peasantry and its resistance, however, only goes so far in explicating peasant behavior in these years, for collectivization was largely unprecedented in intent, form, and scope, setting up at times a unique context to which peasant culture was forced to respond, challenge, and adapt. And, of course, the specifications of region, ethnicity, gender, class, and generation could also provide variations on a general theme while still showing loyalty to that theme. This work attempts to make general sense of regional differences in the content, forms, and dimensions of peasant resistance. It is, for example, clear what the general dynamics of various forms of protest were according to region in the Russian Republic and at times in other republics, and it is possible to make certain generalizations about resistance on the basis of a region's strength in grain production, but the possibility for more specific assessments awaits the further opening of archives in the former Soviet Union, especially those associated with the secret police. Likewise, only the most cursory assessments of the impact of ethnicity on peasant protest appears in this study, partly because the focus tends to be mainly Russian and partly because ethnicity likely played a significant, sometimes key, role in peasant resistance, therefore requiring and meriting a specialized study of the topic. And although I endeavor to draw the reader's attention to the very significant gender dimensions of peasant protest, I am unable to delve very far into issues of class and generation. I take the risk of generalization because I believe that there are certain common features to peasant resistance during collectivization that warrant a general study and that, by and large, the peasantry's experience of collectivization overrode regional and other differences if only for a historically short, but significant, period of time. Not all peasants resisted—indeed, as I will make clear, a determined minority sided with the state—but most peasants did, and they were unified by a shared politics, set of grievances, and course of action.

During collectivization, peasant resistance became a form of peasant politics—the only genuinely oppositional politics available to peasants then—that reflected a collective consciousness of intent, action, and hoped-for resolution, as well as a clear and sometimes even prophetic sense of national politics and goals. The peasant cohesion and solidarity of the collectivization era were direct manifestations of peasant agency and political consciousness. The base determinants of peasant resistance derived from reasoned concerns centered largely on issues of justice and subsistence, and supplemented by the primary elemental responses of anger, desperation, and rage. Peasant ideas of justice were integral to popular protest.[23] Collectivization was a violation—a direct assault on—customary norms of village authority and government, ideals of collectivism and neighborhood, and, often, simple standards of human decency. Support for collectivization *within* the community was equally a violation of the village ideals of collectivism, thereby making retribution a key derivative of justice in motivating acts of peasant resistance. Collectivization was also, as importantly, a threat to peasant household and community survival. Subsistence was a primary determinant of the shape of peasant politics and relations to the state.[24] It surely was a chief concern and responsibility of the peasant women, who dominated so much of the peasantry's responses to collectivization, as was common elsewhere when peasant survival was at stake. The contents and causes of peasant resistance to collectivization then were, to a great extent, "generic," while still manifesting specificity in derivation, context, and response.

The forms of peasant resistance constituted an additional component of the popular culture of resistance. Like content and causation, peasant forms of resistance were shaped by a set of customary concerns and ways of being and acting that, although frequently appearing irrational and chaotic to outsiders, had their own logic and, in most cases, a long-established history as approaches to challenging authority. Tradition itself became a resource for legitimacy and mobilization, as peasants sought justification for their interpretations of and responses to state policy.[25] Peasants made use of a customary array of resistance tactics: rumor, flight, dissimulation, and a variety of passive and active forms of resistance. Their choices were clearly and logically guided by the actions of the state and the issue of their resistance. Peasant forms of resistance were informed by pragmatism, flexibility, and adaptation, each a vital resource in opposing a powerful and repressive state. Peasants only turned to violence as a last resort, when desperation and retribution reached such a level as to provoke the peasantry into direct challenge. Often, violence came out of ordinarily nonviolent settings, such as meetings, demonstrations, and other interactions with Soviet power, when the violent actions of the authorities pushed peasants to answer with violence.[26] The forms of peasant resistance transpired, in large part, in ritualized, customary scenarios, acted out over and over again for their organizational merit and tactical utility in responding to power.

The antithetical nature of peasant culture and resistance most clearly expressed itself through metaphor and symbolic inversion, which constituted a form within a form or a vehicle for many specific types of protest. The discourse of peasant rebellion surfaced in the world of rumor, in which symbols of apocalypse and serfdom provided dominant motifs used to categorize the politics and behavior of the state and its agents. Apocalypse turned the Communist world on its head by associating the state with the Antichrist, while serfdom signified the ultimate Communist betrayal of revolutionary ideals. The massive destruction and sale of peasant property (*razbazarivanie*) served as another form of inversion, as the peasantry seemingly engaged in a wholesale attempt to overturn "class" in the village through social and economic leveling. Terror aimed at officials and activists and the chasing out of state authority was a literal inversion of political power. Dissimulation, another basic tool of resistance, constantly juggled power and weakness in attempts to hoodwink, disguise, and evade. Perhaps most important of all, the central role of women in peasant resistance demonstrated an inversion not only of power relations between the state and peasantry, but also a subversion of the traditional patriarchal order, indicating a complete denial of norms of obedience and submission. Reversals of power, inversions of image and role, and counter-ideology served up the justification, legitimation, and mobilization required to bolster peasant resistance in a stark symbolism of binary oppositions between state and peasantry, revealing once again a peasant culture of resistance.[27]

The peasant culture of resistance neither evolved nor functioned in a vacuum. Peasant resistance may be viewed as a reactive form of protest to the state-building and cultural domination of the collectivization era, as it was largely, although not exclusively, an attempt to preserve the status quo.[28] However, peasant politics did more than *react*. Peasant resistance was closely connected to national events and central policies. As a culture or class, the peasantry defined itself in opposition to and in conflict with other classes and, in this case, the state. Peasant resistance operated in concert with state repression. The study of peasant resistance is therefore as much a study of the peasant as it is a study of the state in its interactions with the peasantry. Peasant resistance alternately affected the radicalization or modification of state policy in the collectivization era. The dynamics of *razbazarivanie* and self-dekulakization, for example, were important features in the escalation of the tempos of collectivization and dekulakization as local authorities struggled to contain the mass destruction of livestock and to stem the tide of peasant flight by extending and increasing the levels of repression. Yet when peasant violence began to threaten both state stability and spring sowing in the early March of 1930, Stalin called a temporary retreat from the collectivization campaign. Passive resistance no doubt had the greatest, most sustained effect on state policy, forcing the state again and again to modify some of its more radical designs of transformation, especially after the 1932–33 famine. Throughout our period of study, peasant actions occurred not in isolation and not solely in reaction, but *in combination* with state policy, in a circularity of response and effect.[29] Peasant resistance, moreover, was a highly creative force, evolving and adapting its basic forms into ritualized scenarios and tactical tools in conjunction with day-to-day relations with authority.

The state is never absent from this study. The very nature of the sources, largely of official provenance, as well as the reality of Stalinism as a state-dominated sociopolitical structure, mean that the historian must view peasant politics through the filter of the state. However, as David Warren Sabean has pointed out in another context, "what is a fact about sources is not necessarily a weakness. Documents which perceive peasants through the eyes of rulers or their spokesmen begin with relationships of domination. . . . The issue is to examine the constitution of peasant notions within the dynamics of power and hierarchical relations."[30] The study of peasant resistance is therefore minutely concerned with official discourse, the language and mentality of Stalinism that transformed peasants into enemies and distorted the reality of peasant politics. Words like kulak, counterrevolution, sabotage, treason, *razbazarivanie*, self-dekulakization, incorrect excesses, mass disturbances, *bab'i bunty*, and myriad other terms—all, in due course, discussed—complicate our work by partly obscuring peasant voices and by sometimes opening the way for charges of attributing merit and actuality where neither may exist, or at least not in their most obvious form, when we have no choice but to adopt them ourselves. Yet a semiotic approach to the use of this terminology can yield valuable understandings of dominant voices and the state. If the state then casts an encompassing shadow over the peasantry in this study, that is because the peasant culture of resistance depended upon the state for its existence, evolving within and against the grain of Stalinism, and feeding on the dynamics of a civil war unleashed upon the peasantry by the state.

The degree and universality of peasant resistance—that is, the very existence of what I have chosen to call a peasant culture of resistance—demonstrates the relative autonomy of the peasantry within the "leviathan state" of Stalinism, revealing the endurance of defining characteristics of peasant culture, politics, and community during and even after the collectivization of Soviet agriculture. The tenacity and staying power of the peasantry, this view of collectivization as civil war, as a clash of cultures, challenges both the totalitarian model's stress on the atomization of society and the more recent school of thought, pioneered by Moshe Lewin, that posits the existence of a "quicksand society" incapable of generating cohesive classes able to defend their interests and resist the state.[31] This study does not intend to resurrect the old historiographical notion of a "we-they" split in Russian (and later Soviet) society by positing the existence of a peasant culture of resistance, but rather to suggest that the dichotomy of state and society (or at least of peasant society) was firmly fixed from below, representing a semantic weapon of resistance and a subaltern view of dominant powers rather than a sociopolitical reality. Soviet society therefore becomes something less of the aberration it is usually painted if the angle of vision is shifted to the peasantry's place in society, its relation to the state, and the content and forms of its resistance. At the same time, the specificity of the collective and individual experiences of collectivization remain on a grander historical scheme of things, and it becomes clear that the overall impact of the great peasant revolt and its bloody repression played directly into the dialectics and the savagery of Stalinism, forming a major part of the background of 1937.

1

The Last and Most Decisive Battle: Collectivization as Civil War

Never before had the breath of destruction hung so directly above the territory of the October revolution as in the years of complete collectivization. Discontent, distrust, bitterness, were corroding the country. The disturbance of the currency, the mounting up of stable, "conventional," and free market prices, the transition from a simulacrum of *trade* between the state and the peasants to a grain, meat and milk *levy*, the life-and-death struggle with mass plunderings of the collective property and mass concealment of these plunderings, the purely military mobilization of the party for the struggle against kulak sabotage (after the "liquidation" of the kulaks as a class) together with this a return to food cards and hunger rations, and finally a restoration of the passport system—all these measures revived throughout the country the atmosphere of the seemingly so long ended civil war.

—Leon Trotsky, *The Revolution Betrayed*

Like the Jews that Moses led out of Egyptian slavery, the half-savage, stupid, ponderous people of the Russian villages . . . will die out, and a new tribe will take their place—literate, sensible, hearty people.

—Maxim Gorky, "On the Russian Peasantry"

When the Communist party formally introduced the policy of wholesale collectivization, it claimed that the nation was on the eve of a great transformation. With the aid of urban Communists and workers, the state would "construct" socialism in the countryside. Through collectivization, "victory on the grain front" (and therefore "industrialization front") would be achieved. The "socialist transformation of the peasantry" would "eliminate differences between town and countryside" and rural illiteracy would be eradicated. The propaganda of the day told only half the story. It said nothing of the assault on peasant culture and autonomy or the brutal means by which the great transformation would be accomplished. Public traces of that side of the story could be discerned in the widespread calls "to overcome rural backwardness" and "to defeat peasant darkness" and in the less common but chilling refrain, "Bolsheviks are not vegetarians."[1] Much of what collectivization stood for and portended remained hidden from public discourse.

The official enunciations on collectivization represented what James Scott has labeled the "public transcript" of the dominant.[2] The public transcript on collectivization was a facade covering another, hidden transcript that revealed the great transformation to be a struggle over economic resources (chiefly grain) and culture. This is not to say that Communists necessarily distinguished between the two agendas, although some doubtless did. Nor is it to say that the Communist party did not often believe its own rhetoric: hypocrisy and delusion may be conveniently and mutually reinforcing. Stalinist official discourse (indeed, most state-enshrined ideologies) was in part a means of constructing logical and politically acceptable concepts for explaining and justifying often cruel realities. Ideology was handmaiden to the state. Disguised theoretical revisions, policy changes celebrated for their continuity, and a pseudo-dogma of excesses, mistakes, and deviations were brought in to maintain the balance between truth, belief (feigned or otherwise), and practice if reality clashed with ideology. When the curtain of the public transcript is opened to expose the party's hidden transcript, representing, according to Scott, "the practices and claims of their rule that cannot be openly avowed,"[3] a different side of collectivization is revealed.

Most peasants were neither convinced nor deceived by the state's public transcript. For them, collectivization was apocalypse, a war between the forces of evil and the forces of good. Soviet power, incarnate in the state, the town, and the urban cadres of collectivization, was Antichrist, with the collective farm as his lair. To peasants, collectivization was vastly more than a struggle for grain or the construction of that amorphous abstraction, socialism. They understood it as a battle over their culture and way of life, as pillage, injustice, and wrong. It was a struggle for power and control, an attempt to subjugate and colonize what through the course of Soviet history came increasingly to resemble an occupied people. Removed from the distorting lens of official propaganda, belief, and perception, collectivization was a clash of cultures, a civil war.

Primordial *muzhik* darkness

The history of state-peasant relations from the Russian Revolution of 1917 is the history of a continuing battle between two cultures. The Communists represented an urban, working-class (in the abstract),[4] atheistic, technological, deterministic, and, in their minds, modern culture, while the peasantry represented (to Communists) the antithesis of themselves, the negation of all that was considered modern. Before they were Communists, even before they were Bolsheviks, Russian Marxists were implicitly antipeasant. In glorifying a god of progress which, it was thought, doomed the peasantry to social and economic extinction, they rejected the very idea of the peasantry as a separate culture, as more than a spawning ground for workers.[5] The elements of determinism and will,[6] which featured so prominently in Russian Marxist and especially Bolshevik thinking and personality and that led to victory in October 1917, were projected onto the party, transforming it into a prime mover of history. History would be forged by the party, the self-proclaimed vanguard of politics, progress, and revolutionary truth. The brutalizing effects of years of war, revolution, and civil war, added to the starkly intolerant and utilitarian mentality characteristic of much of the prerevolutionary Russian intelligentsia which hatched the Bolsheviks, wrought a party prepared and determined to wage what Lenin called "the last and most decisive battle."[7] Narrowly, that battle concerned only the kulak—the capitalist farmer and official oppressor of poor and middle peasants, the allies of the working class. In reality, the battle was against all peasants and it would be waged in order to hurry history along its predetermined course, which would lead to the disappearance of this supposedly primitive, premodern social form.

Soviet power was based upon a "dictatorship of the proletariat and poor peasantry."[8] In 1917, when the Bolsheviks championed peasant revolutionary goals as their own, Lenin claimed that "there is *no* radical divergence of interests between the wage-workers and the working and exploited peasantry. Socialism is *fully* able to meet the interests of both."[9] In fact, the dictatorship, and the "alliance" it derived from, combined mutually irreconcilable aims and would quickly break apart in conflict. It could not have been otherwise given the contradictory nature of the October Revolution, a "working-class" revolution in an agrarian nation in which the industrial proletariat accounted for little more than 3% of the population, while the peasantry constituted no less than 85%. The Bolsheviks' revolution was a working-class affair, town business orchestrated by the most extreme of the radical intelligentsia. Lev Kritsman, a leading Marxist scholar of the peasantry in the postrevolutionary years, asserted that there were actually two revolutions in 1917—an urban, socialist revolution and a rural, bourgeois or antifeudal revolution.[10] The two revolutions represented different and ultimately antithetical goals. Following the forced expropriations and partitions of the nobility's lands, the peasantry desired no more than the right to be left alone: to prosper as farmers and to dispose of their produce as they saw fit.[11] Although some peasants may have shared the socialist aims of the towns, most were averse to principles of socialist collectivism. Communist class constructs could not easily be translated into terms that applied to the culture of peasants.

The validity of Kritsman's assessment was vividly apparent in the Russian Civil War, in which the town turned against the countryside, making violent forays into the villages to take grain and peasant sons for the Red army. The Communist party fought the war with the aid of the newly created revolutionary army and a powerful set of domestic policies sometimes subsumed under the heading of "war communism." The country had experienced a breakdown in the grain trade from the time of the First World War, as inflation skyrocketed and networks of supply and distribution disintegrated. By the time the Bolsheviks took power, the entire system of trade and supply was in shambles. The party would soon resort to the forced requisitioning of grain in order to feed the cities and the army.[12] In the initial phases of the civil war, the Communists sought to collect grain through the formation of committees of the village poor (*kombedy*). In theory, the *kombedy* were to unite the poor against the rich, to stir class war in the village. The poor peasants would aid the urban requisitioning detachments to find grain and, in return, receive a portion of the grain. In fact, the *kombedy* were a dismal failure. The peasantry resented the intervention of outsiders in their affairs. Most poor peasants saw the label of "poor" as an insult rather than as class enhancement. All peasants were united in their efforts to retain (at the very least) a fair share of the grain they had toiled to produce. As a consequence, most villages stubbornly defied the party's attempts at social division and resisted as a cohesive entity.[13]

Grain was the central and most divisive issue in the alliance of workers and poor peasants. Lenin recognized this fact as early as May 1918, when he declared that any "owners of grain who possess surplus grain" and do not turn it in, regardless of social status, "will be declared *enemies of the people*."[14] Here, there was no mention of the traditional Leninist breakdown of peasantry into poor, middle, and kulak. It was not simply the kulak, that theoretically determined class enemy and counterrevolutionary, who was at fault. Instead, actions determined political status. In consequence, Lenin declared a "ruthless and terrorist struggle and war against peasant or other bourgeois elements who retain surplus grain for themselves."[15] *All* peasants could be *enemies of the people* if they acted contrary to the policies of the party. Lenin was able to account for this seeming contradiction of class by reference to a "kulak mood [that] prevails among the peasants."[16] Kulaks were demonic, subhuman. Lenin referred to them as "avaricious, bloated, and bestial," "the most brutal, callous and savage exploiters," "spiders," "leeches," and "vampires"; he declared a "ruthless war on the kulaks," and called for "death to them!"[17]

The *kombedy* were abandoned before the end of 1918 in most parts of the country. The failure of this class-based policy forced Lenin, at least formally, to shift his emphasis from the poor to the middle peasant, while he continued to view the kulak as the party's basic foe and to endorse forced grain requisitioning. In a speech made in March 1919, Lenin said, "The kulak is our implacable enemy. And here we can hope for nothing unless we crush him. The middle peasant is a different case, he is not our enemy." At the same time as he drew social distinctions among the peasantry, Lenin continued to view peasant political activity that was contrary to Soviet interests as *kulak*. He denied, for instance, that there had been *peasant* revolts against grain requisitioning, insisting instead that these were *kulak* revolts.[18]

The middle peasant, the largest group among the peasantry after the revolution, was defined as a "wavering" stratum of the peasantry.[19] It was, as a social being, part petty producer, part laborer. Its socioeconomic interests therefore did not easily fit into Communist class analysis. This problem was resolved by grafting onto the middle peasant a dual political nature to fit its dual socioeconomic nature. The middle peasant, depending on circumstance and interest, could join forces with the kulak and counterrevolution or take the side of the poor peasantry and the revolution. It was the task, therefore, of the party to help the middle peasantry recognize its own best interests. Peasants, like workers who were also unable to arrive at consciousness unaided, must be "developed": "Any peasant who is a little bit developed and has emerged from his primordial muzhik darkness," said Lenin, "will agree that there is no other way [but to turn over his grain to the Soviet state]."[20] According to Lenin, "all class-conscious and sensible peasants . . . will agree that *all surplus grain without exception* must be turned over to the workers' state."[21] The implications of these statements were that the peasant who was not class-conscious might not hand over his grain. In that case, the peasant's political actions redounded to his socioeconomic status once again: consciousness determined being.

Through his subjective definition of class and the concept of the middle peasant as waverer, Lenin created a route by which Bolshevik class categories could in fact bridge culture. This sense of class was an abstraction, a party construction, but it allowed Communists to behave, on a theoretical level, in conformance with their ideas. This theoretical contortion was a seeping of the hidden into the public transcript. It enabled the party to attempt, at a public level and when possible, to win the middle peasant to its side, while providing it with a ready rationalization to treat the middle peasant—that is, the majority of the peasantry—as an enemy if it opposed the party's policies. Here was one of the theoretical underpinnings of Stalin's later war with the peasantry. In the meantime, for Lenin, the ultimate way out of these dilemmas, the final solution to the peasant problem, lay in the peasantry's extinction: "In order to abolish classes it is necessary . . . to abolish the difference between factory worker and peasant, to make *workers of them all.*" Unlike Stalin, however, even the Lenin of the civil war era was compelled to add that this remaking of the peasantry would take "a long time."[22]

The full implications of the cultural rift with the peasantry and the disastrous policies of the civil war became clear in late 1920 and early 1921, when the party found itself isolated from peasants *and* workers, and the Soviet state seemed to totter on the brink of destruction. In the cities, there was widespread working class unrest. In the countryside, peasant revolts were reaching ominous dimensions in Tambov, Siberia, and Ukraine. The final, symbolic blow to the regime came in early 1921, when the sailors of the Kronstadt naval base, long a stronghold of Bolshevik support, rose up against the Communists. Lenin was forced to call a retreat and abandon the policies of the civil war era.

At the Tenth Congress of the Communist party in March 1921, Lenin introduced the New Economic Policy (NEP). NEP was a retreat, and above all a concession to the peasantry. It eliminated the hated grain requisitions, replacing them first with a tax in kind and later a money tax; it legalized private trade and traders, and denationalized all but the most important industries, banks, and foreign trade. NEP eventually took the form of a kind of mixed economy, a market socialism. At the Tenth Congress, Lenin admitted that "the interests of these two classes [workers and peasants] differ." [23] He also warned that "so long as there is no revolution in other countries, only agreement with the peasantry can save the socialist revolution in Russia." [24] Lenin had learned an important lesson from the civil war. The party required the support of the peasantry—the majority of the population—to stay in power. The failure of "international revolution" to come to the aid of what even Lenin admitted to be "backward" Russia meant that some other theoretical prop was necessary to support the reality of a proletarian revolution in a peasant country. This prop was the *smychka*, or worker-peasant alliance. Soviet power would be able to hold out until the outbreak of international revolution, according to Lenin, only under the condition that the *smychka* be preserved while socialism was "constructed" in Russia, that is, while the country industrialized. To the end of his life, Lenin would insist that the maintenance of the *smychka* was imperative to the survival of the Soviet state.

In 1922, Lenin told the Eleventh Congress of the Comunist party that "we must prove that we can help him [the peasant], and that in this period, when the small peasant is in a state of appalling ruin, impoverishment, and starvation, the Communists are really helping him. Either we prove that, or he will send us to the devil. That is absolutely inevitable." [25] Lenin assumed a moderate stance on the peasantry after the civil war not for the sake of the peasantry, but in order to ensure the survival of Soviet power. He remained committed to socialism, in both town and countryside, and to the transformation of peasant Russia. He had become convinced, however, that the only way to change the peasant was gradually and through persuasion: "it will take generations to remold the small farmer and recast his mentality and habits." [26] In his last articles, Lenin argued that a cultural revolution—above all, universal literacy—was prerequisite to the peasants' transformation. Further, he maintained that the agricultural cooperative, which would cater to the material interests of the peasant while teaching collectivism, would provide a base for the development of socialism in the countryside. [27]

Lenin wrote in 1923 that NEP was intended to last for an entire historical epoch: one to two decades at best. [28] He left the party an ambiguous legacy. On the one hand, he advocated a gradual evolution toward socialism in the countryside. On the other hand, he maintained that the countryside, left to it own devices, would not spontaneously enter the path of socialism; that the conscious agents of history, in the form of the party and the working class, would have to take the initiative in building socialism in the countryside. Similarly to the ambiguities of Lenin's "What Is to Be Done?", Lenin's NEP legacy provided no answer to the problem of what to do if the peasant resisted change, resisted socialism. Further, there was a basic fault line in Lenin's class logic about the peasantry. In insisting that peasant activity contrary to Communist policies could be defined as kulak while at the same time maintaining that his approach to the peasantry was based on scientific Marxist class analysis, Lenin provided his successors with the conceptualizations that would be used in collectivization when Stalin launched a war against *all* peasants. This combination of the subjectivity of Bolshevik class categories and the iron determinism of theory, however willful in fact, created a potent and deadly mix that would allow the party to cast itself in the role of agent of historical destiny, empowered by a pseudo–science that could transform any opposition into the socioeconomically determined voice of class enemies, kulaks, and counterrevolutionaries slated for destruction by the "advanced forces" of history. Although Lenin's last writings urged the party to approach the peasantry with caution—and there is no reason not to take his words seriously—his legacy was fraught with contradictions and would provide the basic theoretical underpinnings for collectivization.

Planting socialism

Most Communists viewed NEP as a retreat. Although often portrayed as a "golden age" of the peasantry, NEP was destined to be no more than at most a retrospective golden age, visible only from the ramparts of the collective farms of the 1930s. During the 1920s, peasants continued to suffer the depredations of the centralizing, modernizing, and only temporarily and partially restrained state. Although peasants lived with relatively less interference from the state than ever before in their history, the state continued to exact tribute from peasants, making frequent and sometimes violent forays into the countryside to take taxes, grain, and, according to peasant complaints, the morals and faith of peasant youth. Rural officials, especially in the early 1920s, often maintained their civil war–style of hostile interaction with the peasantry despite the reigning spirit of class harmony. Lenin's cooperative plan was posthumously enshrined as the solution to the peasant problem. Little was done, however, to support peasants who became interested in forming cooperatives. Moreover, cooperative ventures faced the threat of the kulak label if they became too successful. The party's ally, the poor peasant, was also left with little more than ideological sustenance during these years. NEP was, most of all, according to Moshe Lewin, a policy of "drift."[29] The party was too consumed with factional fighting and the struggle for power after Lenin's death to pay serious practical attention to agriculture. The peasantry only entered the party's field of vision as each of the successive left oppositions raised the specter of the kulak bogey, claiming that rural capitalism was on the rise thanks to the overextension of NEP. Since rural social stratification was so slight in the 1920s, following the extensive social leveling of the revolution and civil war, it is safe to assume that the real issues were power and the continued existence of peasant Russia.

The party's chief economic priority during NEP was the industrialization of the nation, something that to many Communists was tantamount to the *construction* of socialism. In 1920, Lenin said that *"Communism is Soviet power plus the electrification of the whole country."* [30] Over the course of the 1920s, Communism would be equated with the rapid and large-scale industrialization of the country: the concept of building socialism would come to mean simply building, and the bigger and more modern the better. Industrialization, however, had to wait until the war-shattered economy was reconstructed. During NEP, the expansion of the grain trade was intended to provide the necessary revenues to finance the state's industrial development while at the same time granting a level of peasant prosperity requisite to the creation of an internal market of consumers of goods from the industrial sector. To ensure a net profit for industry, it was necessary to turn the terms of trade against the peasantry, charging higher prices for industrial goods and lower prices for agricultural produce. In 1923–24, this "scissors" in pricing led to a crisis of overproduction in industry and peasant unwillingness to sell grain. Consequently, the party was forced to lower industrial prices by inaugurating a series of reforms in industry. The consequent closing of the scissors was thought to hinder industrial growth, and, in fact, by 1927, the country entered into a manufactured goods shortage that would seriously impede trade between town and countryside.

The dilemma the party confronted was not new to Russian economic development. The alternatives appeared completely dichotomous: either the party could allow the peasantry to enrich itself, create a prosperous agriculture, and through balanced growth and social stability the needed revenues for industrialization would gradually accrue, or it could "squeeze" the peasantry through heavy taxation, maintain low agricultural prices and expand grain exports, and through a rapid accumulation of capital industrialization would be quickly achieved, after which revenues could be redirected to agriculture. In either case, the peasantry was perceived mainly as an economic resource, a troublesome one at that, and in effect, little more than an internal colony. In the mid-1920s, E. A. Preobrazhensky, a spokesman for the Left Opposition, urged that the terms of trade be turned against the peasantry, that a "tribute" be exacted in order to speed up capital accumulation and industrialization. With neither irony nor shame, he dubbed this process "primitive socialist accumulation," echoing and subverting Marx's detested "primitive capitalist accumulation" in the interest of Soviet power. Nikolai Bukharin, the party's leading theoretician and, in many ways, Lenin's heir to a moderate peasant policy, warned that primitive socialist accumulation would threaten the *smychka*, leading to massive peasant discontent and withdrawal from the market, as had occurred during the civil war. Bukharin worried that the very stability of the state would be at risk if the interests of the peasantry were so abused.[31]

The party's economic dilemmas were overshadowed and to a great extent determined by noneconomic factors. As in years past, it was war or the threat of war that decided the balance between the two approaches, and it was questions of politics and power that shaped decisions and policies. At the end of the 1920s, the brilliant theoretical contortionism of Preobrazhensky and Bukharin were eclipsed by the practical reality that NEP had entered into a dire crisis. In 1927, a war scare broke out, giving rise to popular fears of military intervention and elite manipulations of policy in the direction of an emergency order.[32] The nation came to resemble a siege state, a country at war with itself and the outside world. The mentality thus created represented the first of many layers of a political culture sometimes known as Stalinism. In the context of war scare, rapid industrialization became imperative: the nation's defenses had to be secured.

In spite of a good harvest, grain marketings dropped markedly in 1927. The reasons for this decline are complex. In part, peasants responded to the war scare in the same way town dwellers had: they hoarded. Hoarding, however, only compounded a problem that was much more fundamental. Consumption levels among peasants had risen during the 1920s, as peasants made the choice to eat more and sell less. They did this partly because they could, perhaps for the first time in their history; partly because they were taxed less than before the revolution; and partly because the sale of grain brought them little in return. By 1927, a "goods famine" had removed much of the incentive for peasants to market their grain. Further, following several years of good harvests after the scissors crisis, the party had lowered grain prices in 1926 to spur industrial development, therefore removing yet another incentive for peasants to sell their grain. The result was a disastrous shortfall in the state's grain procurement.

In the towns, food prices skyrocketed, lines formed everywhere, and rationing returned. Memories of the urban famine of the civil war haunted town dwellers and added to the panic of the war scare. The Stalinist contingent in the party interpreted the peasantry's actions as a "kulak grain strike," or a conscious and intentional sabotage of industrialization and, in consequence, the nation's defenses. Most Western analysts are confident that the immediate problem of grain marketings could have been resolved by a simple, administrative increase in grain prices.[33] By then, however, the problem was least of all an economic one. The grain procurement crisis, fueled by the combustible materials of the war scare, ignited a civil war–like mood and mentality among rank-and-file urban Communists and many industrial workers hell-bent on radical, maximalist solutions. Although there were a host of ancillary problems, threats, and enemies, the main issue, the chief obstacle to the party's sudden and all-out "great turn," became the peasantry.

In 1928, the party implemented what it euphemistically called "extraordinary measures" in grain procurement. Thousands of Communists and factory workers from the towns poured into the countryside to take grain and to override local officials, who by now were, if not in favor of NEP, at least used to it. They closed markets, set up roadblocks to ferret out private traders, and made widespread use of Article 107 of the criminal code against speculation and hoarding. Both "speculation" and "hoarding" were interpreted in the broadest terms possible as grain procurement brigades endeavored to seize any and all reserves of grain. Peasants viewed the extraordinary measures as a return to the forced grain requisitioning of the civil war. Repression and violence became everyday features of rural life as the grain procurement campaign shattered NEP's uneasy truce with the peasantry. Stalin assumed the role of chief advocate of extraordinary measures during his trip to Siberia in early 1928. There he lashed out against local Communists, who, he claimed, were not seriously worried about the hunger threatening the towns and Red army and were afraid to make use of Article 107.[34] This new hard line was vigorously opposed by the emerging Right Opposition led by Bukharin and Rykov. They argued that extraordinary measures were leading to the dreaded breakdown of the *smychka* and threatened the very survival of Soviet power. In what appears to have been a temporary compromise with the Right, Stalin backed down from the extraordinary measures after the April 1928 plenum of the party's Central Committee, but returned to them again in early 1929, when the flow of grain from the countryside once again stalled.

While the Right Opposition inveighed against the possibility of the loss of peasant support in the *smychka*, Stalin stubbornly maintained that the leading role of the working class in the *smychka* was paramount.[35] As early as 1926, he told a gathering of Leningrad Communists that "we do not defend just any kind of union of workers and peasants. We stand for that union, in which the leading role belongs to the working class."[36] To Stalin, *razmychka* (the break-up of the *smychka*) meant, above all, the disruption of the flow of grain to the towns. The consequent disorganization in food supply and grain exports threatened both industrialization and working-class support for the party, both of which in turn would jeopardize the nation's defenses.[37] Raising grain prices would harm the working class and lead to a *smychka* with the rich and a *razmychka* with the workers and rural poor.[38] Stalin defined the aims of the *smychka* as "strengthening the position of the working class," "guaranteeing the leading role of the working class within the union," and "the destruction of classes and class society."[39] Elsewhere, he claimed that the goal of the *smychka* was "to merge the peasantry with the working class," to remake the peasantry and its psychology, and "to prepare thereby the conditions for the destruction of classes."[40] In a later speech, he argued that the *smychka* was only useful when aimed against capitalist elements and exploited as a tool to strengthen the dictatorship of the proletariat.[41] For

Stalin, the peasantry played the role of ally only when and to the extent that it served the interests of the dictatorship of the *proletariat*. When the country entered the grain crisis of the late 1920s, it became clear to Stalin that the peasantry was no longer a suitable partner in the *smychka* and that a final solution to the accursed peasant problem was necessary.

Increasingly from 1927 and onward, Stalin proposed that the only solution to the grain problem was the creation of collective farms. He argued that a tribute (*dan'*) was required from the peasantry to pay for industrialization and to feed the towns and army, and that the best way to collect that tribute—and to ensure that it reached its maximum level—was through the collective farm. The tribute, however, would not come only from the kulak. At the April 1929 plenum of the Central Committee, as Stalin was discussing his notion of a tribute, a voice from the audience interjected that such a tribute should not be from the middle peasant. Stalin shot back, "Do you think that the middle peasant is closer to the party than the working class? Well, you are a sham [*lipovyi*] Marxist."[42] Stalin's Marxism pitted town against countryside and worker against peasant.

Stalin nevertheless continued to speak the Marxist-Leninist language of class when discussing the peasantry. He argued, for instance, that the kulak stratum was growing in size, that class struggle was worsening in the countryside, and that the peasantry was divided into poor peasants, middle peasants, and kulaks. And, officially, it was the kulak who was "wrecking" and "intriguing" against Soviet economic policy. Yet he insisted that it was a "mistake" to think that just any form of *smychka* would do. He supported only that *smychka* "which guaranteed the victory of socialism." Linking NEP and the *smychka*, Stalin said that "when it [NEP] ceases to serve the cause of socialism, we will throw it to the devil. Lenin said that NEP [was] introduced seriously and for a long time. But he never said that NEP [was] introduced forever."[43]

Stalin also claimed that it was wrong to assume that the countryside would follow the town "spontaneously" to socialism. He argued that the "socialist town must lead the petit-bourgeois peasant countryside . . . transforming the countryside to a new socialist foundation." The transformation, according to Stalin, would come about by *planting* [from the verb *nasazhdat'*] new, large-scale socialized farms in the countryside.[44] Later, he would speak of how the party had "turned [*povernuli*] the middle peasant onto the path of socialism."[45] And while the kulak would not be allowed into the new socialized farms—he would be "eliminated"—sociopolitical contradictions would remain in the collectives, including individualism and "kulak survivals [*perezhitki*]." "Elements of the class struggle"[46] would continue in the collective farm, *even without the kulak*.

Although he paid lip service to Marxist-Leninist notions of class and rural class struggle, Stalin clearly viewed the main elements in the struggle as workers and peasants, town and countryside. Like Lenin, he believed that kulak status could be determined by political behavior, and that the abolition of classes would occur ultimately only when the peasantry ceased to exist. For both leaders, the *smychka* was meant to ensure the ultimate destruction of classes. Unlike Lenin, Stalin's theoretical approach suffered less frequently from sophistries or ambiguities. The official and hidden transcripts of the party came together much more clearly in Stalin's writings and speeches. In a sense, Stalin was closer to reality than Lenin and the other party leaders. Where they faltered, he fully succeeded in bridging culture with class. He was able to do so because he saw the peasantry as one entity, *as a class*, indivisible by Marxist social categories. Stalin expanded Lenin's theory of the wavering middle peasant to encompass the entire peasantry, defining and treating the latter more simply as petty producer. This approach meant that the peasantry could side politically either with the revolution and the dictatorship of the proletariat or with the counterrevolution and the kulak. During collectivization, the peasantry would demonstrate a unity of interest and purpose in its resistance that would vastly enhance Stalin's rural revolution by allowing the state to reconstruct the social face of the peasantry, in effect to "kulakize" the countryside, through its association of opposition with kulak socioeconomic status. For Stalin, culture became class, and therefore assumed the role of chief adversary. None of Lenin's occasional caution would deter him. Rather, he would enter the war with the peasantry recalling only Lenin's teachings of the "last and most decisive battle" and his utterances about "primordial *muzhik* darkness," "leeches," "vampires," and a "ruthless war on the kulaks."

The great turn

On 7 November 1929, the twelfth anniversary of the Bolshevik Revolution, Stalin proclaimed in his article "Year of the Great Turn" that the middle peasant had begun to flock to the collective farms.[47] Collectivization had in fact increased dramatically by this time, surpassing the relatively modest rates projected for the socialized sector of agriculture after the Fifteenth Party Congress of December 1927 first placed collectivization on the immediate agenda.[48] At the Sixteenth Party Conference in April 1929, in its First Five-Year Plan on agriculture, the Central Committee had projected the collectivization of 9.6% of the peasant population in the 1932–33 economic year, and 13.6% (or approximately 3.7 million households) in 1933–34. These projections were revised upward in the late summer and fall of 1929, when first *Gosplan* (the state planning commission) called for the collectivization of 2.5 million peasant households in the course of 1929–30, and then *Kolkhoztsentr* (the central agency leading collective farm administration), with subsequent confirmation from *Sovnarkom* (Council of People's Commissars), resolved that 3.1 million peasant households would be incorporated into collective farms by the end of 1929–30.[49]

In actuality, by 1 June 1928, 1.7% of peasant households were in collective farms; and between 1 June and 1 October 1929 alone percentages rose from 3.9 to 7.5. The increase was especially marked in major grain-producing regions. The Lower Volga and North Caucasus surpassed all other regions, with percentages of collectivized peasant households reaching 18.1 and 19.1, respectively, in October.[50] The high rates achieved in the regional collectivization campaigns lay behind Stalin's statement that the middle peasantry was entering collective farms. By arguing that the middle peasant was turning voluntarily to socialized agriculture, Stalin was claiming that the *majority* of the peasantry was *ready* for collectivization. In reality, it was mainly poor peasants who were joining collectives. And, although there was apparently some genuine enthusiasm "from below," the regional campaigns had already begun to resort to coercion to achieve their high percentages.[51]

Even at this stage, collectivization was largely imposed "from above." Orchestrated and led by the regional party organizations, with implicit or explicit sanction from Moscow, *raion* (district level) officials and urban Communists and workers brought collectivization to the countryside. Grain requisitioning brigades, already obsessed with attaining high percentages, were transferred *en masse* to collectivization.[52] A volatile anti-peasant mood in the cities, especially among rank-and-file Communists and industrial workers and based on bread shortages, continuing news of "kulak sabotage," and long simmering urban-rural antipathies, infected these cadres and other, newer recruits from urban centers.[53] This combination of official endorsement, regional initiative and direction, and unrestrained action on the part of lower level cadres intertwined to create a radical momentum, an ever-accelerating collectivization tempo. The "success" of the regional campaigns then provided the necessary impetus for Moscow to push collectivization rates up even further, in what became a deadly and continual tug of war between center and periphery to keep pace with each other as reality exceeded plan and plans were continually revised to register and push forward collectivization tempos.

The November 1929 party plenum formally ratified wholesale collectivization, leaving the specifics of policy implementation to a Politburo commission that would meet the next month. The plenum was largely an affair of consensus and acclamation, resolving to push vigorously forward. Although some party leaders expressed their concern over the use of force and lack of preparation in the summer-fall campaign—most notably Siberian regional first party secretary S. I. Syrtsov; Lenin's widow, Nadezhda Krupskaia, who spoke of the disappearance of "persuasion" in the countryside; and Ukrainian delegation members S. V. Kosior and G. I. Petrovskii—most regional party secretaries expressed their enthusiasm for the policy, downplaying problems and promising collectivization within one to one-and-a-half years. G. N. Kaminskii, the head of *Kolkhoztsentr*, and V. M. Molotov, Stalin's right-hand man, along with a chorus of supporters repeatedly pushed the plenum to extremes, calling for the completion of collectivization in 1930 and, at one point, by the spring of 1930. Stalin responded to calls for more preparation and planning with, "Do you think everything can be organized ahead of time?" and discussion of "difficulties" was dismissed as "opportunism."[54]

While the pace of collectivization continued to accelerate, Agriculture Commissar I. A. Iakovlev led the December Politburo commission and its eight subcommittees in the preparation of plans and legislation on collective farm construction. The commission called for the completion of collectivization in major grain regions in one to two years; in other grain regions, in two to three years; and in the most important grain deficit regions, in three to four years. The commission also resolved that an intermediate form of collective farm, the artel, which featured the socialization of land, labor, draft animals, and basic inventory, would be the standard, and that private ownership of domestic livestock needed for consumption would be maintained. Any movement to extend socialization of peasant properties beyond the artel would depend on the peasantry's experience and "the growth of its confidence in the stability, benefits, and advantages" of collective farming. The kulak faced expropriation of his means of production (which would then be transferred to the collective farms) and resettlement or exile. The subcommittee on the kulak reported that "it would be hopeless to try to decide the 'kulak problem' by exiling the *entire* mass of the kulak population to remote territories." Instead, it recommended a differentiated approach to the "elimination of the kulak as a class." The most dangerous kulaks were to be arrested or exiled. A second group of less dangerous kulaks also were to be exiled, while a third category would serve as a disenfranchised labor force in the collective farms until they could prove themselves "worthy" of membership. Finally, the commission warned against any attempt either to restrain collectivization or to collectivize "by decree."[55]

The Politburo commission published its legislation on 5 January 1930. The legislation stipulated that the Lower Volga, Middle Volga, and North Caucasus were to complete collectivization by fall 1930, or spring 1931 at the latest; all remaining grain regions were to complete collectivization by fall 1931, or spring 1932 at the latest, thus accelerating yet again the pace of the campaign. No mention was made of remaining areas. The legislation also specified that the artel would be the main form of collective farm, leaving out any particulars from the commission's work. Stalin had personally intervened on this issue, ordering the editing out of "details" on the artel that should, he argued, more appropriately be left to the jurisdiction of the Commissariat of Agriculture. The kulak would be "eliminated as a class," as Stalin had already noted in his 27 December 1929 speech at the Conference of Marxist Agronomists, and excluded from entry into the collective farms. Stalin and other maximalists in the leadership were likely responsible for radicalizing further an already radical set of guidelines by revising the work of the December commission, keeping the legislation vague, and including only very weak warnings against violence.[56] Stalin, among others, apparently still believed in minimal planning, leaving the precise shape of collectivization to the "revolutionary initiative" of the masses, meaning in fact his lower level cadres in the field. And by the time this legislation was published, collectivization percentages in the USSR had leaped from 7.5 in October 1929 to 18.1 on 1 January 1930, with even higher rates in major grain regions (Lower Volga, 56–70%; Middle Volga, 41.7%; North Caucasus, 48.1%). Throughout the month of January 1930, reality continued to outpace planning. By 1 February 1930, 31.7% of all households in the USSR were in collective farms, with rates still higher in individual regions (Moscow, 37.1%; Central Black Earth Region, 51%; Urals, 52.1%; Middle Volga, 51.8%; Lower Volga, 61.1%; North Caucasus, 62.7%).[57]

The elimination of the kulak as a class, or dekulakization, had also spread far and wide through the country as regional party organizations enacted their own legislation and issued their own directives in advance and in anticipation of Moscow. A Politburo commission, chaired by Molotov, met from 15 to 26 January 1930 in an effort to draw up central legislation on dekulakization. Like collectivization, dekulakization had by now gone far beyond the initial plans of the December Politburo commission, in what had become a melee of violence and plunder. The Molotov commission not only had to respond to the increased pace of the campaign, but attempt to exert central control over it as a way to avoid complete anarchy while continuing to maintain the most radical momentum.[58] Following the policy recommendations of December, the commission divided kulaks into three categories. The most dangerous category, some 60,000 heads of households, faced execution or internment in concentration camps, while their families had their properties and all but the most essential items expropriated and were sent into exile in remote parts of the country. An additional 150,000 families, deemed to be somewhat less dangerous but still a threat, also faced expropriation and exile to remote regions. The main points of exile for these two categories were the Northern Region (scheduled to receive 70,000 families), Siberia (50,000 families), Urals (20–25,000 families), and Kazakhstan (20–25,000 families). The final category of well over a half million families were to be subjected to partial expropriation of properties and resettlement within their native districts. The term "kulak" was defined broadly and included not only kulaks (an ambiguous term to start with) but (using the parlance of the day) active white guards, former bandits, former white officers, repatriated peasants, active members of church councils and sects, priests, and anyone "currently manifesting c[ounter]-r[evolutionary] activities." Overall numbers of dekulakized peasants were not to exceed 3% to 5% of the population. The OGPU (Ob"edinennoe gosudarstvennoe politicheskoe upravlenie, or the political police) was charged with the implementation of arrests and deportations. The operation was to be completed in four months, and 50% by 15 April. *Raion* soviets, in combination with *sel'sovets* (rural soviets), poor peasants, and collective farmers, were responsible for drawing up lists of kulaks and carrying out expropriations. Warnings to avoid "substituting naked dekulakization for collectivization" and not to dekulakize peasants with relatives in industry or the military were included in the commission's directives and issued in late January and early February.[59]

Collectivization and dekulakization had long since jumped the rails of central control. Brigades of collectivizers with plenipotentiary powers toured the countryside, stopping briefly in villages where, often with gun in hand, they forced peasants, under threat of dekulakization, to sign up to join the collective farm. Intimidation, harassment, and even torture were used to exact signatures. Collectivization rates continued to rise through February, reaching 57.2% by 1 March, and the hideously unreal regional percentages of 74.2% in Moscow Region, 83.3% in the Central Black Earth Region, 75.6% in Urals, 60.3% in Middle Volga, 70.1% in Lower Volga, and 79.4% in North Caucasus.[60] The high percentages belied the fact that most collective farms at this time were "paper collectives," attained in the "race for percentages" held among regional and district party organizations. Collectivization often amounted to little more than a collective farm charter and chairman, the socialization of livestock (which might remain in former owners' possession until appropriate collective space was provided), and the terror of dekulakization.

Dekulakization was no fiction. Although deportations often did not begin until later, peasants labeled as kulaks found themselves evicted from their homes or forced to exchange homes with poor peasants; fleeced of their belongings, often including household items, trinkets, and clothes; and shamed, insulted, and injured before the community in what in one Pskov *raion* was labeled the "week of the trunk."[61] Dekulakization was sometimes carried out "conspiratorially," in the dead of night, as cadres banged on doors and windows, terrorizing families who were forced out onto the street, half-dressed.[62] Often, everything was taken from these families, including children's underwear and earrings from women's ears. In Sosnovskii *raion*, Kozlovskii *okrug*, Central Black Earth Region, an *okrug* level official told cadres to "dekulakize in such a way that only the ceiling beams and walls are left."[63]

The countryside was engulfed in what peasants called a Bartholomew's Night massacre.[64] As state repression increased, peasant violence increased, and as peasant violence increased, state violence increased, leading to a seemingly never-ending crescendo of arrests, pillage, beatings, and rage. The crescendo came to an abrupt halt, however, when, on 2 March 1930, Stalin published "Dizziness from Success," blaming the outrages on the lower level cadres who were indeed dizzy from success, but failing to admit any central responsibility.[65] Soon collectivization percentages began to tumble, as peasants appropriated Stalin's name in their struggle against the cadres of collectivization. Peasants quit the collective farms in droves, driving down percentages of collectivized households in the USSR from 57.2% in March to 38.6% in April, 28% in May, and further downward until hitting a low of 21.5% in September. The decline in regional rates was equally drastic. Between 1 March and 1 May, percentages of collectivized households fell in Moscow Region from 74.2% to 7.5%; in the Central Black Earth Region, from 83.3% to 18.2%; in the Urals, from 75.6% to 31.9%; in the Lower Volga, from 70.1% to 41.4%; in the Middle Volga, from 60.3% to 30.1%; and in the North Caucasus, from 79.4% to 63.2%.[66]

Collectivization resumed the following fall at a slightly less breakneck speed. The major grain-producing regions attained wholesale collectivization by the end of the First Five-Year Plan in 1932; other regions climbed more gradually toward that goal, generally reaching it by the end of the 1930s. In the meantime, more than one million peasant families (perhaps five to six million people) were subjected to some form of dekulakization during the years of wholesale collectivization. Of these, some 381,026 families (a total population of at least 1,803,392) were exiled outside their own regions in 1930 and 1931, the two key years of deportation.[67] The deportations were perhaps one of the most horrendous episodes in a decade marked by horror. Preparations for the deportation—transport, housing, food, clothes, medicine—appear to have been conducted *simultaneously* with the deportations. The results were catastrophic. Epidemics raged in the *spetsposelenie* ("special settlements"), striking down the very young and the old. According to a July 1931 report, more than 20,000 people had died by May 1931 in the Northern Region alone.[68] Statistics compiled by V. N. Zemskov indicate that 281,367 deportees would die in their places of exile between 1932 and 1934.[69] The "kulak" was to disappear from the Russian countryside forever, while the peasantry that remained was transformed into something akin to a subject population.

Stalinist metaphysics

Collectivization transformed the countryside into an internal colony from which tribute—in the form of grain, taxes, labor, and soldiers—could be extracted to finance the industrialization, modernization, and defense of the country. The Soviet peasant colony, like most colonies, had a "native culture" that was a repository of identity, independence, and resistance, and, as such, an impediment to full colonization. Collectivization was as much an onslaught on that culture as it was a struggle over resources. The cultural clash of collectivization began as a clash between town and countryside and developed into an effort to create a new *Soviet* culture in the village. The party's goal was to eliminate differences between town and countryside, worker and peasant—in effect, to destroy the peasantry as a culture. This war of occupation was reflected and waged in the discourse of collectivization and Stalinist cultural revolution.

The cultural chasm between town and countryside cut both ways; it was not purely an urban construct. For centuries, the countryside had served as a source of extraction for the Muscovite and later Russian governments; until as late as the first half of the nineteenth century, the state's relations with the peasantry were limited mainly to tax collection and army recruitment. The prerevolutionary Russian historian Kliuchevsky's oft-repeated phrase that "the state swelled and the people grew lean" rang true for much of the peasantry and was rooted in peasant political and historical consciousness. The 1917 Revolution did not alter this basic reality. On the contrary, the Russian Civil War expanded the cultural gulf. The brute destruction and violent depredations of both Red and White armies and the breakdown in urban-rural communications led to further cultural rift as well as economic regression in the countryside.[70]

The armistice of NEP did little to alleviate peasant enmity. During most of the 1920s, the town receded from the village, limiting its interventions in rural life to tax collections, soviet elections, and occasional and sometimes ill-begotten attempts at land reform (*zemleustroistvo*). The town was suspect and, for some villagers, glaringly alien. An ethnographer visiting the Novgorod area in the mid-1920s recalled that the peasants' initial reaction to the arrival of his research team was fear; the peasants took them for tax assessors. Suspicion was so intense that when some of the ethnographers began to draw sketches of the village, rumors flew that "foreign spies are coming, they are drawing maps." As the team traveled from village to village, the peasants of the region knew their every move.[71] Many peasants believed that the town—rather than the kulak—was the real exploiter. A Moscow-area investigator noted that he often heard peasants complain that the workers lived better while the peasants worked harder, paid more taxes, and suffered unfairly due to the price scissors.[72] The same sentiments were echoed repeatedly in the pages of the newspaper, *Krest'ianskaia gazeta* (*The Peasant Newspaper*), when peasants were invited to send letters to an "all-union peasant meeting" to mark the tenth anniversary of the revolution.[73] At the same time, during the war scare of 1927, official observers noted a widespread "antitown" mood in the countryside, with peasants expressing such sentiments as "We agree to support Sov[iet]power if it establishes identical rights for workers and peasants"; and "We peasants will not go to war, let the workers fight."[74] With the imposition of "extraordinary measures" in grain procurements in the late 1920s, peasant anger lent new force to these opinions. Throughout the countryside, peasants cried: "Throw out the Communists!" "Get rid of the workers coming from Moscow—don't interfere in our village affairs!" "Peasants live poorly because the workers and officials sit on them!" and "The city workers live on us; they take all we have."[75] Once collectivization began, peasants would treat the town and party in apocalyptic terms, declaring them to be tools of Antichrist, and hence offering up the ultimate expression of cultural schism.[76]

The town was generally less forthright, cloaking its sentiments in class language or paternalistic hues. There were exceptions. Maxim Gorky, later favored literary son of the revolution and Stalin, captured in 1922 the prejudices of the town and party in a frank, stark language free of sophistry or apology. Gorky viewed the drama and outcome of the Russian Revolution in terms of a conflict between town and countryside.

The town represented enlightenment and progress, while the village stood for "dark ignorance," savagery, and "a poisonous quality which devastates a man, and empties him of desire."[77] The peasantry was a parasite, able and willing to hold the town hostage. During the civil war, "the country-side clearly understood that the town depended on it, while until this moment it had only felt its own dependence on the town."[78] As a consequence, perhaps even in dumb revenge, "[i]n 1919 the nicest countryman quietly took the townsman's shoes, his clothes, and generally fleeced him, bartering grain and potatoes for anything necessary or unnecessary for the countryside."[79] Gorky believed that the countryside was triumphantly gloating: "he who has the grain in his hand holds authority and power."[80] He summed up his attitude to the peasantry by ascribing to it the cruelties of the revolution (just as another generation would blame the peasantry for the atrocities of Stalinism):

> I explain the cruel manifestations of the revolution in terms of the exceptional cruelty of the Russian people. . . . I cannot consider those who took on themselves the hard, Herculean labour of cleansing the Augean stables of Russian life as "tormentors of the people," to me they are rather its victims. I say this on the basis of the firmly-held conviction that the whole of the Russian intelligentsia, which for almost a whole century has manfully attempted to set on its feet the ponderous Russian people, lying lazily, negligently and lucklessly on its soil—the whole intelligentsia is a historical victim of a people vegetating on a fabulously rich land on which it managed to live astonishingly poorly. The Russian peasant, whose common sense has now been awakened by the revolution, might say of his intelligentsia: stupid as the sun, it, too, works for no reward.[81]

Gorky presented a mirror image of the peasantry's own hostilities to the towns, a transference of all the blame and guilt generated by the revolution away from the intelligentsia and onto the peasantry. His sentiments, many of which were shared widely in the party and in the town, were a projection onto the peasantry of culpability for all that the town detested: for Russian backwardness, for the failures and ineptitude of the Communist party's, indeed the entire radical intelligentsia's, dream of a radiant future. It was this point of view, this cast of mind, that formed the basis for a way of thinking in the Communist party that would allow and enable the party to declare war on the countryside and rob the peasantry of its humanity.

Few were as straightforward as Gorky in betraying the true nature of the contest between town and countryside. Although evidence of that contest would be everywhere once collectivization began, the language of class and paternalism obfuscated that reality even in Stalin's identification of class with culture. The essence of the conflict lay hidden in deeply held prejudices, perceptions, and stereotypes about the peasantry that, when added together, did much to determine the ultimate shape of collectivization.

In the eyes of many town dwellers and members of the intelligentsia, the peasantry was an abstraction. Long before the revolution, the peasantry was transformed into a generalization, a stereotype, a vehicle to carry the dreams or nightmares of educated Russians. The Communists continued this tradition after 1917, adding thick coats of ideology in the process. The civil war, however, depleted from the generalizations any of the positive, idealist, or more ambiguous assessments that the Populist thinkers of the nineteenth century had held so dear.[82] With the civil war, the peasantry became an enemy, an alien and adversary class. It was an obstacle, a hindrance to the town, the working class, socialism, and modernity. Hostility toward peasants was deeply embedded in the party's popular culture. In the years leading up to collectivization, and even more once collectivization began, the peasantry would be shorn of its humanity, reduced to a subhuman status that would enable and encourage the atrocities of the times.

The infantilization of the peasantry, a holdover from centuries past, began this process and served as the foundation of the Communist reconstruction of the peasantry. Before and after the revolution, peasant men were *muzhiki*, peasant women *baby*, terms which when used among peasants were familiar and friendly but when used by outsiders assumed a derogatory, pejorative aspect. *Muzhiki* and *baby* were most often dark, uncultured, ignorant, and ignoble; more seldom (after 1917) were they childlike innocents. In either case, the process of infantilization deprived them of agency and responsibility. They were in need of the civilizing guidance and leadership of the town. Stalin believed this when he argued that collective farms must be "planted" in the countryside by the more advanced forces of the town and party.[83] *Muzhiki* and *baby*, moreover, were classless. Devoid of political content, they lacked the necessary consciousness to form class according to Communist constructs—they were perhaps "aclass" or "preclass." As collectivization spread, these terms became increasingly elastic: the *muzhiki* contracted as the *baby* expanded. The party sought to hold male peasants responsible for political opposition: *muzhiki* often became kulaks. The *baby*, in the meantime, created such a stir in the countryside that it was in the interest of the party to remove political or class implications from *baby* protest or else face the risk of revealing publicly that the entire peasantry, not just the kulak, was up in arms and led, moreover, by women.[84] Finally, *muzhiki* and *baby* represented the face of Russian backwardness, an enemy of Soviet power. Initially, this association merely brought down upon the peasantry the missionary cultural imperialism of the towns. Once the collective farm system was established, peasant "backwardness," if revealed in the form of accidental breakage of machinery or other forms of negligence to collective farm property, became *counterrevolutionary*—which, in a Communist sense, it was—and a peasant could be fined, deported, or imprisoned for, unofficially, backwardness—officially, counterrevolution.[85]

Marxist-Leninist (and later -Stalinist) class categories were easily grafted onto infantile depictions of the peasantry, retaining—perhaps gaining—elasticity as political designations. Class stereotypes crystallized in the course of the 1920s, especially for urban Communists ignorant or simply disdainful of village life. Civil war hostility and Leninist theoretical gyrations held the stereotypes together. The poor peasant was the ally of the working class, partner in the dictatorship. The middle peasant "wavered," sometimes to the side of the revolution, sometimes to the side of counterrevolution. The kulak was the class enemy, "avaricious, bloated, and bestial."[86] In his novel *Brusski*, the Soviet writer Panferov captured the material face of social stereotypes in describing a NEP-style party official, a "city boy" come to the village:

> He always imagined a village as a large, dark lump divided into three sectors: the poor peasants, the middle peasants, and the rich peasants, the kulaks. The kulak had a large head and wore leather boots; the middle peasant had ordinary boots and wore a jacket; and the poor peasant ran about in bast shoes.[87]

Even the late Soviet General Petro Grigorenko, who became a dissident in the post-Stalin order before being forced into exile in the United States, recalled his conviction that "the world had seemed simple to me. The worker was the ideal, the repository of the highest morality. The kulak was a beast, an evil-doer, a criminal."[88] Grigorenko expressed well the Manichaean view of the world that animated much of Communist theorizing and brutalized the realization of its goals, enabling the party to demonize and therefore dehumanize social groups and entire classes deemed adversaries by its ideology.

Although class stereotypes became unalterable dogma in theory, they were the most malleable of concepts in practice, especially for poorly educated cadres in the field. Social determinism was utilized in reverse. Class stereotypes were subsumed by political stereotypes and the latter were then ascribed to class and the designation of social category. If a poor or middle peasant failed to behave according to the socially determined rules of class, he or she could easily lose standing. Already in the mid-1920s—as if echoing Lenin's civil war contradictions—urban *shefstvo* (patronage) workers new to the village often equated peasant hostility or opposition with kulak status.[89] Peasants who criticized officials, urban or otherwise, became kulaks.[90] During collectivization, poor and middle peasants were either for the collective farm or they were kulaks.[91]

Poor and middle peasants were not always "kulakized" for opposition. Class stereotypes, political and social, could be sidestepped for reasons of state. Too much opposition, too wide a stretching of the official class story, could not always be explained away by reference to kulaks and kulak politics. Instead, if need be and more often for women than for men, official diagnoses could revert to the infantilization of peasants. Peasants acted like kulaks, engaged in kulak politics, or took part in demonstrations of antisoviet behavior because they did not know any better. They were dark, ignorant, or simply hysterical, irrational *baby*, easily duped by the nefarious kulak. Infantilization could explain away sociopolitical failings or the inadequacy of doctrine by depriving poor and middle peasants of agency and responsibility.

The sometime inability of the middle peasant to act in politically correct terms was implicit in the social definition. The middle peasant need not be a kulak to misbehave. Fortunately, Lenin had provided a theoretical way out for this category of peasant: they wavered.[92] K. Ia. Bauman, first secretary of the Moscow regional committee of the party, was accused of elevating Lenin's theory on the wavering middle peasant into an enshrined dogma during collectivization. After the March 1930 retreat, the Moscow regional leadership supposedly refused to accept any blame for the atrocities of collectivization in the region, viewing the violence as inevitable due to the wavering nature of the middle peasant.[93] For Stalin, this theory stretched the official story and credibility too far, providing a rationalization for excesses as well as a rationalization for peasant oppositional behavior at a time when he was applying (temporarily) the brakes to collectivization. The theory detracted from the danger and culpability of the kulak and implied (correctly) that the majority of the peasantry was in open revolt. Nonetheless, the theory remained a convenient tool for explaining away pockets of peasant resistance.

The party was also able to rationalize the protest of poor and middle peasants through the creation of an entirely new political category not to be found in the canons of Marxism. This category of peasant was utterly devoid of socioeconomic content, and represented a political consciousness unrelated to being. Peasants in this category, especially once collectivization began, were *podkulachniki*, a word often translated as kulak hirelings or agents and meaning literally "under the kulak," or under the influence of the kulak. The *podkulachnik* might be the relative of a kulak, a former employee of a kulak loyal to his old master, a duped poor or middle peasant unaware of the promise of Communism, or an inexplicably antisoviet peasant defying social determinism.[94] The category *podkulachnik* represented a kind of transmigration of the kulak soul. Transmigration, moreover, could occur either between living peasants or from one generation to the next, for kulak ancestry was frequently grounds for identifying a peasant as a kulak during collectivization.[95] The antisoviet politics of a *podkulachnik* were "kulak," animated by a "kulak essence." The *podkulachnik* label was useful, for it enabled Soviet power to hold poor and middle peasants responsible for kulak actions when occasion demanded, thus providing peasants with a semiagency (for they still were literally "under the [influence of the] kulak") that they generally lacked. In the classification of *podkulachniki*, the party discovered the ultimate rationalization and disguise for a peasant resistance that in reality united all peasants as—in the broadest sense—a class against the state. By distilling a kulak essence into the socially amorphous *podkulachnik*, the party also furthered the cause of the social metaphysics of Stalinism, which depicted a world in which evil and demons relentlessly confronted the Communist party, the vanguard of the radiant future.

The kulak, ethereal or corporeal, loomed large in the Communist categorization of the peasantry. The figure of the kulak was the most perfectly formed of all of the class stereotypes of the peasantry. It slid into demonology, carrying the process of the dehumanization of the peasantry to its furthest reaches. The definition of the kulak was amorphous and slippery. The peasants' sense of a kulak generally had little to do with wealth or politics. Instead, a peasant became a kulak if he violated the moral economy of the village or its ideals of collectivism.[96] The party, meanwhile, attempted to define the kulak, at least officially, according to a wide variety of economic criteria, ranging from the hiring of labor to the ownership of different kinds of agricultural enterprises to the accrual of income not based on labor.[97] In practice, kulak status always remained in the eye of the beholder; kulaks were either seemingly too wealthy or antisoviet, broadly and arbitrarily defined. In the popular urban stereotype, the kulak was male, usually corpulent (like the stereotypes of capitalists and imperialists), and likely to be attired in a polka-dot shirt, well-made breeches, leather boots, and a vest.[98] His hut was spacious and covered with a metal roof. He made extensive use of hired labor, was wealthy, and exerted great influence in village affairs. On the more negative side, he was an exploiter, a manipulator, and a parasite. During collectivization, he was frequently likened to a beast (zver'). He was a terrorist, an arsonist. He hid behind corners, taking shots at Soviet officials with his sawed-off shotgun. He was the source of antisoviet rumors. He often worked through others, above all "backward" women and sometimes even "unconscious" poor peasants, to destabilize the new collective farms.[99] He "penetrated" the collective farm to wreak havoc from within. The kulak was held to be virtually incorrigible. These kinds of stereotypes entered into urban popular culture as accepted definitions of the kulak.

The ritualized definitions of the kulak were more in the realm of demonology than class analysis. It therefore became relatively easy for the kulak to lose his class moorings and become a kulak "by nature." A kulak remained a kulak even after dekulakization. Semantic contradictions aside, this caste-like constancy meant that the kulak's socioeconomic status was irrelevant. A peasant could also attain kulak status by virtue of ancestry: was his father, grandfather, or great-grandfather a kulak?[100] His immediate family, in the meantime, was by implication kulak as well, for the family too suffered the fate of expropriation and often deportation during the elimination of the kulak as a class. Kulaks who managed to join collective farms in the early phases of collectivization also remained kulak, despite the radical transformation in their socioeconomic status.

This perversion of social determinism meant that kulaks were, by nature, always dangerous and bound to be the enemy. The kulak, like the poor and middle peasant, was denied agency. His actions were counterrevolutionary by necessity. As such, he was less an informed political opponent than a terrorist or bandit, terms designed to reduce political activity to mere criminal behavior. The kulak was socially destined to be evil. This combination of false determinism and class stereotype akin to demonization made for a lethal compound, virtually ensuring that the kulak would not be viewed as human and hence enabling his tormentors to cast aside any possible doubts about his elimination.

The greater tragedy was that the kulak could be any peasant. Social determinism cut both ways. Although being may have determined consciousness for the kulak narrowly construed, consciousness—that is, antisoviet attitudes or behavior—determined being for all other peasants. One contemporary noted: "When we say 'kulak' we have in mind a carrier of a defined political tendency which is most often expressed by *podkulachniki.*" [101] The kulak was the "carrier" of this tendency; poor and middle peasants expressed and carried out the tendency. Here sophistries come full circle and class-bound definitions crumble into meaninglessness. Every peasant could be a kulak; every peasant could be the enemy; and all peasants could be the "most brutal, callous and savage exploiters," "leeches," and "vampires." [102] Stalinist social metaphysics come full circle back to the Leninist discourse of civil war.

The popular dehumanization of the kulak, of the peasant, enabled the cadres of collectivization, mostly urban, to behave without restraint in this last and most decisive battle with the enemy. Ukrainian-born American journalist Maurice Hindus captured well the spirit of the times when he described an activist's letter on collectivization:

> In Nadya's letter there was not a word on the subject [peasant reaction to collectivization]. There was no allusion to the peasant's inner turmoil, as though that were only an incidental trifle. Impassioned revolutionary that she was, she could not and would not be concerned with the hurt of the individual. Not that it had passed her unobserved, but it failed to stir her sympathy. She seemed no more concerned with the peasant's perplexity than is a surgeon with the pain of a patient over whose body he is wielding a scalpel. Her mind and heart were fixed on the glories of tomorrow as she visualized them, not on the sorrows of today. The agony of the process was lost to her in the triumph of achievement. [103]

The brutality of the encounter could not have occurred without the transformation of kulak into beast. Certainly there were other factors that contributed to the intensity of the conflict as well,[104] but reducing the enemy to a subhuman status has become a prerequisite of twentieth-century war. In *Virgin Soil Upturned,* the Soviet writer Mikhail Sholokhov caught the essence of this phenomenon in the bloodthirsty Communist official Nagulnov. In response to a local official's sympathy for the plight of the kulaks, Nagulnov raged:

> "Swine! . . . Is this how you serve the Revolution? Sorry for them? Why, I'd . . . give me thousands of old men, children, women. . . . And tell me

they've got to be done away with. . . . For the sake of the Revolution . . .
I'd do it with a machine-gun . . . every one of 'em!"[105]

A real-life Communist official, a member of a Moscow *okrug* party committee, proclaimed that in response to terror, "we will exile the kulak by
the thousands and when necessary—shoot the kulak breed [*otrod'e*]."[106]
Another official, responding to the question of what to do with the kulaks,
replied, "[we] will make soap out of kulaks," and a *sel'kor*, who had had
his throat cut by a peasant, stated, "Our class enemy must be wiped off
the face of the earth."[107] The forced deportations and expropriations of
hundreds of thousands of defenseless peasant families were chalked up as
revolutionary necessity. The terrible sufferings experienced by people
packed like cattle in box cars on their way into exile or sick and dying
from the disease that ran rampant in the special settlements were considered revolutionary necessity. The practice of collectivization fully demonstrated the unspoken premises and theoretical implications of the Stalinist
"public transcript," revealing the latter to be no more than the tip of an
iceberg of a Communist popular culture of antipeasant prejudice, suspicion, and hatred.

Even the language of the encounter was loaded with significance, revealing the contradictions between the official and unofficial faces of the
socialist transformation of the countryside. Collectivization would exact a
"tribute" from the peasantry, an exaction that had nothing in common
with socialism or the class struggle but could only be understood as a tax
levied on a subject population. The kulak was to be "eliminated" (from
the verb *likvidirovat'*), a term that officially meant the eradication of the
socioeconomic roots of the class but that during the civil war had implied
to shoot.[108] Terms such as "extraordinary measures" and "voluntary collectivization" were euphemisms designed to cloak reality. In the same
way, atrocities became mistakes, deviations, or excesses committed by cadres who were "dizzy from success" rather than by criminals or savages.
The term "excess" was often prefaced by the adjective "incorrect," thus
revealing clearly, and perhaps unintentionally, the official and unofficial
understandings of the tasks of collectivization. The concept of "revolutionary legality" supposedly underlined the whole process. Based on an
elaborate theory, revolutionary legality was most often little more than a
battering ram to be used against recalcitrant peasants. The Central Black
Earth regional first party secretary Vareikis, summed up revolutionary
legality by saying, "law?—it will come with time."[109] A Central Black
Earth regional party committee directive instructed local cadres that "it
would be criminal bureaucratism if we were to wait for the new laws [on
dekulakization]. The basic law for each of us—is the policy of our
party."[110] Official euphemisms of collectivization aimed at disguising the
reality of the encounter between state and peasantry that was so starkly
exposed in unofficial discourse. Euphemization cloaked, but also offered
legitimation of, Communist policies and practices. It provided a necessary

belief system for those who would participate in the new order, although it is not and never will be clear what the exact mix of belief, cynicism, and outright evil was among the cadres, high and low, of Stalin's revolution.

Based on fear and hate, Stalinist imagery and discourse dehumanized the peasantry. Deprived of agency as a result of an obscenely distorted social determinism or their infantilization, peasants had no control over their actions and were therefore reduced accordingly in their humanity, predestined to be eternal children, prosoviet automatons, or enemies. They were intrinsically robbed of choice and free will in official ideology and much of urban, popular discourse, and this, in a sense, made it easier to rob them of choice and free will in fact. Stalinist images of the peasantry were also vast projections of collective hatreds, a vital and requisite ingredient in the dehumanization of an enemy.[111] The peasant came to be regarded as alien in its own country. All that the town and state most detested was projected onto the peasantry. It was to blame for Russian backwardness, food shortages, and counterrevolution. The great divide of the Stalin revolution was not of class in a strictly Bolshevik sense, but of culture, not of workers and bourgeoisie, but of town and countryside. The divide certainly antedated the Communists, but was rent further apart by the consuming hatreds unleashed by the civil war, the cultural imperialism and modernizing ethos of the party's conception of building socialism, and the darkness and ignorance ascribed and transferred by town to countryside, by commissar to *muzhik*. This degradation of the peasantry spawned a political culture that cast peasants in the role of enemies, as subhuman, and cleared the way for the party's offensive on the peasantry.

The war on tradition

Collectivization was a clash of cultures acted out on the brutal battlefields of collectivization, yet it found its clearest and truest expression in the *underside* of the conflict, which took the form of a wholesale assault on the cultural traditions and institutions of the village. The assault had begun in the first days of the revolution, but only became a critical part of the more general strategy of subjugation when Stalin launched collectivization. Peasant culture—tradition, institutions, and ways of life—represented peasant autonomy. These islands of autonomy threatened the state's plan of domination, for they enabled the peasantry to maintain what Scott has described as "social space"

> in which offstage dissent to the official transcript of power relations may be voiced. The specific forms (for example, linguistic disguises, ritual codes, taverns, fairs, the "hush arbors" of slave religion) this social space takes or the specific content of its dissent (for example, hopes of a returning prophet, ritual aggression via witchcraft, celebration of bandit heroes and resistance martyrs) are as unique as the particular culture and history of the actors in question require.[112]

At some level, whether through conscious realization or blind antipathy to the peasantry and its ways, the state understood that peasant culture, intrinsically or potentially, contained within itself the elements of a culture of resistance. For Soviet power, peasant culture became yet another enemy to be eliminated.

The campaign against religion and the church is the best known and most obvious facet of the assault on peasant culture. Throughout the 1920s, Communist and especially Komsomol activists had taken part in efforts to eradicate religion in the countryside, largely through the activities of the League of the Militant Godless. During collectivization, these efforts assumed the dimensions of an all-out war on village religious institutions and symbols. From the second half of 1929, party cadres closed down churches, arrested priests, and removed church bells. On 30 January 1930, in its decree on dekulakization, the Politburo assumed leadership of this campaign, ordering the Orgburo to issue a directive on church closings and including priests among those to be dekulakized.[113] Religious holidays were forbidden, and many peasants were forced to give up their icons, sometimes for mass burnings.[114] In the Shelkovskii *sel'sovet* in Iukhnovskii *raion*, Sukhinchevskii *okrug*, in the Western Region, cadres lined up icons for execution by shooting, each with an inscription that the represented saint had been sentenced to death for "resisting collective farm construction."[115] In the Urals, several *okrug* level organs called on their counterparts in other *okrugs* to enter into a socialist competition to see who could close the most churches.[116]

These repressive activities aimed not only to instill atheism in the village, but to deprive peasants of key cultural institutions. Many contemporary reports from the 1920s concluded that Orthodox belief in the countryside had declined precipitously with the revolution, surviving mainly among women and elderly men.[117] The village church, however, remained a potent cultural symbol in the village. The church belonged to the community, serving as an icon of the village's history, traditions, and major life events from birth to marriage to death. The church bell also had great significance. Like the church, the bell was a thing of beauty, intrinsically important to the pride of the village. Yet it was more than that. The bell was a symbol of village solidarity. It was the tocsin that brought peasants together in the event of emergency. It was, as Yve-Marie Berce termed it, a kind of "emblem:"[118] in the case of collectivization revolts, its peals represented "political acts" designed to rouse and mobilize peasant opposition.

The profound importance of the village church and bell became strikingly apparent during collectivization. Entire villages rose up in rebellion over the closing of a church or the removal of a bell. The church also frequently served as the physical locus of revolt. Priests delivered sermons against collectivization in the church. The apocalyptic sentiment so widespread at this time emanated, if not directly from the church, then from the world it inhabited. And the actual physical site of the church could be a rallying point for peasant riots and demonstrations against Soviet power. For many peasants, the creation of the new collective farm order and the assault on belief were one and the same thing. As a peasant from the Western Region put it, "Look, Matrena, yesterday your husband joined the collective farm and today they took our icons, what is this communism, what is this collectivization?"[119] The closing of a church or the removal of a bell were acts designed to weaken peasant culture and resistance as well as to remind the village of its subject status.

The campaign against the church was eventually, at least formally, moderated in March 1930 by Stalin's temporary retreat. Troubled by international outcry[120] and peasant rebellion, Soviet power would, for a time, take a somewhat more restrained approach to the church. Peasant protest against church closures had served to unify and mobilize village communities against the state. A report from Tambov in spring 1930 made this point clear by noting that it was one thing to deal with the kulak, but another thing to deal with church and priest who are supported by all peasants. According to the report, the attack on the church was not helping collectivization.[121] In some areas, peasant protest actually led to the reopening of churches. In Sukhinicheskii *raion*, in the Western Region, for example, ten of sixteen closed churches were reopened after March 1930.[122] The church nevertheless remained a culturally antithetical symbol to the Communists. It was a repository of peasant culture and tradition, and hence of autonomy. The village church was the antipode of Communist atheism, of Communist culture, and as such it was slated for destruction. By the end of 1930, as many as 80% of village churches may have been closed.[123]

The church was not the only cultural institution targeted for destruction. As one of the 25,000 workers (the "25,000ers") sent to participate in collectivization put it, "We must ensure a war on old traditions."[124] Old traditions included "social spaces" intrinsic to peasant ways of life. The market was one such social space. The closure of agricultural markets began with the imposition of extraordinary measures in grain procurement. The closures served not only to facilitate the creation of a centralized command economy in agriculture and to deprive the peasantry of economic independence, but also to take away a major cultural thoroughfare for contacts with other peasants and urban society and the reproduction of peasant culture that took place at markets with the celebration of holidays and peasant arts, crafts, and popular entertainment. The abolition of the peasant land society (or commune) on 30 July 1930 in districts of wholesale collectivization and the transfer of many village responsibilities to the *sel'sovets* and new collective farm boards constituted yet another dimension in the subjugation of the peasantry.[125] With the end of the land society, and the consequent curtailment of the *skhod* (or peasant council), the state removed from peasants the right to even a limited self-government, depriving them of administrative and fiscal autonomy and even the right to independent political expression. The closing of mills and shops was also a part of the war on tradition. Not only did the closing of these peasant-run establishments increase village dependence on the state, it sealed off an important gathering place for sociability, discussion, and political expression, hence removing yet another site of peasant autonomy. The expropriation of the property of and the elimination of many village craftsmen and artisans as kulaks or "NEPmen" had a similar effect on the community, forcing peasants into greater dependence on the state and into becoming consumers of urban, machine-made products, while seriously harming the reproduction of peasant material culture.[126] All of these measures were intrinsic to the Stalinist socialization of the peasant economy. Yet they were equally vital to the Stalinist cultural revolution in the countryside and absolutely prerequisite to the establishment of Communist controls over the peasantry.

The removal of village elite and authority figures constituted a final dimension in the cultural destruction of the peasantry. The campaign to eliminate the kulak as a class went well beyond the repression of kulaks. Peasant leaders (kulak or otherwise)—responsible voices in the community, usually heads of households—were often arrested for giving voice to the protest against collective farms. In the nineteenth-century countryside, "if authorities found the behavior of a community to be seditious, it was the entrusted persons [mainly elders] who were first called to account."[127] In the collectivization era, the "entrusted persons" could be called to account in the event of a seditious act or as a preemptive measure. The OGPU directive of 2 February 1930 on dekulakization ordered the mass exile of "the richest kulaks, former landlords, semilandlords [polupomeshchiki], local kulak authorities [mestnye kulatskie avtoritety] and the whole kulak cadre," along with clergy and sectarians.[128] If the adjective "kulak," which in any case is largely ambiguous and hence meaningless, is deleted, only the designation "local authorities" remains. And there was a wholesale assault on local village authorities. Priests, members of the rural intelligentsia, former elders, and even descendants of once-powerful peasant families were all caught up in the repression. Also targeted were millers, traders, shop owners, and craftsmen—members of a village economic elite who maintained some autonomy from the village (sometimes even incurring its wrath) and were quite possibly able and willing to voice their objections to collectivization. Otkhodniki (seasonal, migrant workers) were frequently subjected to repression as well, perhaps because they, too, through their work outside the village, mistakenly believed that they had a freer hand and voice to dialogue with Soviet power.[129] Even midwives (babki) and local healers, often highly respected individuals in the community, could be prey to assault, although generally more through cultural opprobrium than repression.[130]

The generalized, repeated, and extended repression of local elites served to remove likely sources of traditional authority and outspoken opposition from the village. Not only, and perhaps not even most importantly, was the village robbed of its most successful and ambitious farmers; it was also deprived of its leadership, voices that could and often did represent the village against the state. These voices were soon silenced through arrest or fear. Soviet power replaced them with leaders from the towns, who would dominate collective farms and rural politics until the end of the First Five-Year Plan.

The creation of a new culture accompanied the attempt to destroy the old one. Soviet power sought to plant a Communist culture from the town in the village. New gods were to replace old gods. Stalin became the peasants' tsar-*batiushka* (little father tsar), and Mikhail Kalinin, designated the all-union peasant elder, became the peasants' secular representative in Moscow. Lenin completed the pantheon, and the images of all three occasionally adorned the corners of peasant huts left bare when the icons came down. In this new religion, concepts of good and evil became relative and were replaced by revolution and counterrevolution. The machine became an object of worship, the tractor a shrine to the new gods. In an irony lost on neither state nor peasant, church bells were melted down for the industrial drive in a kind of Communist alchemy, a transmutation of symbols of peasant culture into manifestations of the new, mechanized Soviet culture.[131] Churches were turned into socialist clubs and reading huts or, less decorously, warehouses or granaries. The new religion was Communism, and literacy, through the introduction of mandatory primary education and crash courses for adults, was the first step on the path to salvation. New holidays were created to celebrate the new religion. They were grafted onto Russian Orthodox holidays that in their turn had once upon a time been grafted onto peasant, "pagan" holidays. *Pokrov* (the festival of the Protection of the Virgin), celebrated on October 14, became the Day of Collectivization in 1929 and 1930.[132] Trinity was turned into Arbor Day, the Day of Elijah became the Day of Electrification, and Easter was to be celebrated as the Day of the First Furrow.[133] (How long these holidays were celebrated and by whom and how seriously remains an open question.)

Secular innovations heralding the new culture joined the more spiritual emblems of the new order. The collective farm replaced the land society, in some cases even coinciding with its former territory, while the collective farm assembly replaced the *skhod*. Tractors were supposed to supersede the horse, but production proved to fall short of need. In some parts of the countryside, factory workers who assumed the posts of the new collective farm chairmen attempted to introduce the eight-hour day, shift work, piecework, wages, labor discipline, and even factory whistles in an effort to "transfer the proletarian experience to the collective farms."[134] Carnival was filled with new cultural symbols largely alien to tradition. Komsomols used carnival to parody their enemies—the kulak, the priest, and the gendarme.[135] Teachers and students in one Siberian village used a truncated form of carnival to humiliate fellow villagers who had not fulfilled the grain requisition quota on the eve of collectivization.

They paraded through the village with banners, stopping at homes of delinquent peasants, where they chanted, "Here lives an enemy of Soviet power," and nailed signs to the gates exposing the inhabitants for all the village to see in what was likely an appropriated form of *charivari*.[136] New schools, new teaching, and a new religion to replace the old one were imposed on peasant youth. Peasant families were told that the *babki* and healers were old-fashioned and pernicious. They were instructed on proper hygiene and house cleaning. In the Ivanovo Industrial Region, the regional collective farm association (*kolkhozsoiuz*) Rules on General Order in the Collective Farm included a clause requiring collective farmers to maintain clean huts.[137] Elsewhere, local commissions were established to inspect sanitary conditions in collective farmers' homes.[138] Sometimes centrally imposed or encouraged, sometimes locally innovated, the new order sought to eliminate the differences between town and countryside and to rid *muzhik* Russia of backwardness, illiteracy, and filth.

The new culture was articulated in a new language, the language of Communism and the towns. An avalanche of acronyms and abbreviations came down upon the villages: *kolkhoz* (collective farm), *sovkhoz* (state farm), MTS (machine-tractor station), *trudoden'* (labor day payment), and other terms that would supplement the revolutionary vocabulary launched in 1917 and still not fully assimilated by most peasants.[139] The names of villages, although not lost, were overshadowed by the new names that Soviet power pinned on the collective farms like badges of cultural domination. A shift in this direction was already apparent before collectivization, as towns and villages across the nation assumed the names of Communist leaders or Soviet titles. A. M. Larina, widow of Bukharin and daughter of Yuri Larin, recalled her father suggesting to a *sel'sovet* chairman that surely a "prettier" name for a village called Mare's Puddle (*Kobyl'ia luzha*) could be found. The next time the Larins passed that way, they discovered the villagers had renamed their settlement Soviet Puddle (*Sovetskaia luzha*).[140] By the time of collectivization, new names rarely betrayed this kind of irony, although one wonders about a collective farm named "Six Years Without Lenin."[141] Most names used for collective farms were straightforward urban or Communist christenings. Collective farms were named after factories (Putilov, AMO, Serp i Molot) and leaders (Lenin, Stalin, and Marx being the most frequent), or received more lyrical designations, such as "Path to Socialism," "The Red Ploughman," or "Red Dawn."[142]

A new political art—poster art—reflected the ideals of the new culture. According to Victoria E. Bonnell, "Political art projected a rural world in which the *krest'ianka baba*, together with traditional peasant customs and attitudes, no longer had any place."[143] *Muzhiki* and *baby* practically disappeared from political representations in the first half of the 1930s. Instead, it was the "youthful and enthusiastic *kolkhoznitsa* [collective farm woman] building socialism" who epitomized the new order.[144] The "dawn of Communism" (to borrow a fairly typical collective farm name) in the countryside was trumpeted everywhere and along with it the death of the old peasant order.

Collectivization and the attempt to eliminate the differences between town and countryside, remaking *muzhiki* and *baby* into collective farmers and eradicating kulaks, led to the creation of a hollow culture imposed from above. Signs of sovietization and the new order were everywhere, but they remained superficial constructs grafted by force onto a culture that would not be so easily eliminated. The Communist acculturation of the countryside was economically barren, offering few of the rewards or privileges (admittedly scarce) that came with it in the towns. The new culture was an urban import, an imperialist tool forced upon a subject people whose native culture would survive, although truncated and forced underground, as a culture of inherent resistance.

Conclusion

The collectivization of Soviet agriculture was a campaign of domination that aimed at nothing less than the internal colonization of the peasantry. Domination was both economic and cultural. Collectivization would ensure a steady flow of grain—tribute—into the state's granaries and coffers. It would also enable Soviet power to subjugate the peasantry through the imposition of vast and coercive administrative and political controls and forced acculturation into the dominant culture. Although the Communist party publicly proclaimed collectivization to be the socialist transformation of the countryside, the "hidden transcript" and practices of collectivization revealed it to be a war of cultures.

The peasantry saw the conflict in similar terms. They too had a Manichaean view of the world, theirs draped in the language of apocalypse rather than class war, in which the town and Communism represented Antichrist on earth and it was the duty of all believing peasants to resist the collective farm, the tool of Antichrist. Collectivization posed a profound threat to the peasant way of life, to its entire culture. In response, peasants of every social strata united as a culture, as a class in a certain very real sense, in defense of their traditions, beliefs, and livelihood. Peasant resistance to collectivization would be rooted in their culture rather than specific social strata and would draw upon an arsenal of peasant tactics native to their culture. Peasant culture would live on in peasant resistance. For peasants, as for the state, collectivization was civil war.

2

The Mark of Antichrist: Rumors and the Ideology of Peasant Resistance

Like grass that in the rush of spring
Spreads fast from south to north,
A rumour through the countryside
From sea to sea spread forth.

That rumour grew both day and night,
To backwaters it rolled.
To a hundred thousand villages
With a hundred thousand souls,

No, never yet as in that year
In turmoil and in strife
Had people waited, pondered so
About themselves, their life.
—Alexander Tvardovsky, "Land of Muravia"

The collapse of all familiar notions is, after all, the end of the world.
—Nadezhda Mandelstam, *Hope Against Hope*

According to a Russian proverb, popular rumor is like a sea wave:[1] it rolls into a village, engulfing and upending everything in its midst. In the terrible years of collectivization, rumor held the Soviet countryside in a vise of fear and dread anticipation. Everywhere peasants listened to rumors about collectivization. Everywhere peasants discussed the meaning of the fate that lay in wait for them. Some said the Communists were bringing back serfdom. Some said the collective farm signaled the reign of Antichrist on earth. Others said collectivization was simply pillage and ruin. The rumors of collectivization provided peasants with an idiom of resistance and a Manichaean view of the world to match that of the Communists.

Rumors are omnipresent in peasant societies and tend to thrive in the especially propitious climate of fear and upheaval. Rumors become a form of underground news and dissident social expression in societies, communities, and groups that confront a censored and falsified press or that have difficulty accessing news. They take the place of formal news, drowning

45

out state propaganda, frequently through the total negation or inversion of the official line and the articulation of an opposing truth.[2] Yet during collectivization rumors functioned as more than simple news or alternative truths; they were a weapon in the arsenal of peasant resistance. Rumors spread fear, ensuring village cohesion in the face of danger from without.[3] By threatening peasants with serfdom, the mark of Antichrist, or the infamous common blanket (which implied communal sleeping arrangements and wife-sharing) if they signed themselves over to the collective farm, rumors guaranteed village unity and mobilized the community against the state.[4] The threat and reality of the times spawned an ideology based on this thick web of rumor that served to unite the peasantry, allowing it to overcome that regional peasant particularism so vaunted in the scholarly literature, as well as the less often noted social tensions and divisions within villages.

The nightmare of apocalypse pervaded the rumors of collectivization. Antichrist and the four horsemen of the apocalypse became figurative symbols in rumors portending the end of traditional ways of life. The Soviet state was the Antichrist, initiating his rule on earth through the collective farm. Collectivization was serfdom, a metaphor for evil, injustice, and the Communist betrayal of the Russian Revolution. Tales of wife-sharing and the common blanket were metaphorical allusions to the godless amorality of Communism-Antichrist that would reign supreme in the new order. Rumor served as political metaphor and parable, turning the world upside down through the creation of an alternative universe of symbolic inversion and thereby delegitimizing the existing order of things—the collective farms, the collectivizers, and Soviet power. Apocalyptic prophecies and belief were integral components of the peasant mind-set.[5] When activated in protest, they became intrinsically subversive, forcing peasants to choose between God and Antichrist, and functioning as a vernacular in the peasant culture of resistance.

Rumors are the symbolic imagery of a collective *mentalite*. Like prophesies, visions, and miracles, they are mental projections, in this case, projections of the political world of the peasantry.[6] They demonstrate "an indication of the level of political consciousness of the peasant, often suffused with religious or ritual beliefs, and [act] as the medium of its transmission among the subaltern masses in the countryside."[7] For the researcher, rumors thus serve as a "way into the peasantry," a map of the normally hidden and remote terrain of peasant attitudes and belief. During collectivization, rumors were the constituent elements of a peasant ideology of resistance.

Soviet power labeled the rumor mill the "kulak agitprop," the counterrevolutionary mirror of the party's own agitation and propaganda department. The state's derisive label belied the greater truth of the danger and political import of rumor as a mobilization device and counterideology. The rumors of collectivization recast the world into starkly Manichaean elements, subverting official dogmas of class struggle between rich and poor peasants and asserting in their place a battle between the forces of good and evil. The popular form of this counterideology represented a kind of offstage social space[8] *in the abstract*, derived from peasant cultural forms and therefore in its very essence antithetical to the Communist culture and politics of the towns. The world of rumor, like no other form of popular resistance, encapsulated and allegorized collectivization as civil war.

The world turned upside down

The peasant nightmare of apocalypse did not arise suddenly in the Soviet countryside with the advent of collectivization. An apocalyptic tradition existed among Russian peasants for centuries prior to the Russian Revolution. Long an undercurrent of popular protest, this tradition revived after 1917, becoming especially pronounced in the 1920s—a time of transition and uncertainty for much of the peasantry—and subsequently providing the dominant myth behind peasant protest against collectivization.

An eschatological frame of mind is neither an exclusively Russian trait nor a specific function of peasant society.[9] Apocalyptic thinking has been a feature of many different societies in many different time periods,[10] and the cast of mind associated with it is primarily a social phenomenon rather than a national attribute. This mode of thought thrives in times of transition, social dislocation, and crisis.[11] It becomes a metaphor of protest, and is often accompanied by prophesy, miracles, signs, and other paranormal phenomena. Apocalyptic forecasts accompanied the approach of the first Christian millennium, served as an inspiration in the crusades of the Middle Ages, and continued to play a role in early modern Europe during times of political and religious turmoil. In each case, apocalyptic passions were activated by dramatic social changes and were experienced by groups most seriously affected by such changes.[12]

Russia experienced a similar apocalyptic crisis in seventeenth-century Muscovy. The schism in the Russian Orthodox church was perhaps the major cultural watershed in a century of bloody conflagration and social upheaval spanning the decades from the Time of Troubles to the coronation of Peter the Great as emperor. The events of the seventeenth century unleashed a wave of apocalyptic foreboding which, in its most extreme forms, led to the identification of Peter as Antichrist and fiery self-immolation in the case of early Old Believers, who refused to see in the reformed ritual of the Orthodox church and in the Petrine reforms anything but the hand of Satan.[13] Apocalyptic passions inspired a subversive social protest movement against the state as well as providing Muscovites of the Old Belief with a traditional and familiar vocabulary with which to make sense of the profound social, political, and cultural changes engulfing old Russia.

Apocalyptic beliefs survived the passing of medieval and early modern times, only to reemerge in Europe in the nineteenth century and, in an explosion of intellectual and artistic brilliance, in fin de siècle Europe.[14] Expectations of an imminent end to history competed with more optimistic dreams of revolution in this time of change and uncertainty. Russia's fin de siècle was forged in a rapid and socially traumatic spurt of industrialization, a bloody and senseless war in the Far East, and the 1905 Revolution. A part of the intelligentsia emerged transfigured from these events. The ebulliently self-confident revolutionary tradition spawned a more pessimistic offshoot given to doubt and spiritual reawakening.[15] Apocalyptic themes informed a wide array of artistic and intellectual endeavors, ranging from the works of modernist painters Malevich and Kandinskii to the musical compositions of Scriabin, and from the philosophical writings of Solov'ev and Rozanov to the literary works of Russian symbolists like Belyi, Merezhkovskii, and Blok.[16] Some representatives of Russia's Silver Age, most notably the Scythians, welcomed the coming of the end, merging the revolutionary and apocalyptic traditions in a dream of a bloody social and spiritual renewal of Russia from the East, with the *narod*, the peasant masses, symbolizing the East and acting as agents of divine retribution and violent cleansing.[17]

The instability of early twentieth-century Russia created a climate favorable to the spread of an apocalyptic malaise among many social groups. Russia's calamitous turn-of-century eventually culminated in the outbreak of world war, revolution, and civil war. Three of the four horsemen of the apocalypse—war, famine, and disease—stalked the Russian land in an all too literal orgy of death and destruction. The First World War resulted in perhaps as many as five million casualties on the battlefields alone. The civil war exacted an even more terrible toll on the population, claiming some nine million lives, military and civilian, in battlefield deaths, starvation, and epidemic.[18] The apocalyptic fantasies of the Russian symbolists seemed to become a reality for vast numbers of Russians, and most especially for the Russian peasantry.

If the Russian Revolution was a partial fulfillment of the peasant dream of a black repartition of all the land,[19] then the chaos, destruction, and human losses of seven years of foreign and civil war were a veritable nightmare for the peasantry. Large parts of the countryside became battlegrounds and requisitioning zones for contending armies. In sheer numbers, the death toll of those years struck the peasantry hardest. The end of the civil war and the introduction of NEP was to allow the peasantry a brief interlude of peace before collectivization. This golden age of the peasantry, however, was always overshadowed by memories of recent violence and the survival of a civil war mentality among many local Communists. The peace between state and peasantry was deceptive, resembling more a temporary cease-fire than a permanent rapprochement.

The peasant mood of the 1920s could best be characterized as one of uncertainty and anxiety. Peasants remained suspicious of Soviet power, mindful of the recent Communist policy of forcible grain requisitions.[20] Tax and election campaigns often led to fear and conflict in villages. In most parts of the countryside, both the Communist party and the Soviet apparatus were so ineffectual and numerically weak that peasants' only interactions with officialdom came during these campaigns and tended therefore to be of a coercive nature, out of sync with the reigning spirit of NEP.[21] Communist attempts to divide the village along class lines through the disastrous civil war–era *kombedy* left peasants unsure of who was a kulak and of what precisely it meant to be a kulak, and, consequently, of what their and their neighbors' social and (by definition) political standing was.[22] Moreover, some parts of village society—notably its wealthier elements, clergy, Cossack veterans of the White armies, and so on—remained embittered toward the regime. For this sector of rural society, along with many other peasants, it was still not clear that the outcome of the revolution was final. This sense of instability was captured in the orders of a Urals peasant *sel'sovet* chairman, who decided that the weathervane on the soviet building should be a globe instead of a hammer and sickle: "In case the government changes, [we] would have to take away the hammer and sickle, but a globe will be suitable no matter what." This sentiment was expressed more ominously in the same region by "kulaks" who warned their local Communists that "soon we will throw you in the wells and not one [of you] will remain!"[23] For many, Soviet power was viewed quite simply as "not ours" (*ne nasha*).[24]

Communism represented an alien culture to many peasants. From the earliest days of the revolution, in popular consciousness the concept of the Bolshevik was mixed up with threats to morality, family, and religion, most often with good reason. Communist ideology in the sphere of morality and family could be liberating; Communist *practice* in these areas was frequently excessive, as Komsomol youth sought to transform sexual love into mere biological function and women into property. Regardless of ideology or practice, the enemies of the Soviet state exaggerated Communist ideas in these areas, going so far as to claim that the state had issued a decree on the "nationalization of women," thus inaugurating a myth that would resound through the countryside for years.[25] The Communist assault on religion and the church was both more serious and more sustained. During the civil war, the Soviet state had set out to undermine the Orthodox Church through expropriations, repression, and eventually the co-optation of a part of the Orthodox clergy into the new, reformed "Living Church." The attack on the church was so devastating that many peasants simply identified Communists with atheists. In his study of the language of the revolutionary era, A. Selishchev noted a peasant definition of "communist": "Kamunist, kamenist—[that is he] who does not believe in God."[26] During a research visit to Seredinskaia *volost'*, Volokolamskii *uezd* in the Moscow Region in the early 1920s, an investigator asked a peasant youth to tell him where the local Communists were. The youth replied that the village had no Communists, but did have an atheist, adding that he was a good person all the same.[27]

Memories of civil war violence and continued uncertainty about the stability of Soviet power served to alienate many peasants from the state and, frequently, from the city as well. This alienation was furthered by the economic devastation of the civil war years, which left agriculture depleted, and by the breakdown in communications between city and countryside which, according to some commentators, led to a regressive isolation of the countryside. Jeffrey Brooks has noted the deleterious impact of the breakdown in the distribution of newspapers and other print materials in the countryside in the 1920s.[28] Some contemporary observers pointed to an increase in superstition among peasants, and others noted the staying power of traditional healers, "white witches," and fortune tellers.[29] The cultural gulf that had traditionally separated peasants from urban Russia remained wide, growing even more in the years after the revolution.

As for every other social group in the Soviet Union, the 1920s were transitional years for the peasantry. However, the transition was slow, and left much of the peasantry caught midway between the values and mores of peasant society and those of the new order. The undermining of old ways frequently led to conflict and confusion rather than the creation of a new society. This breakdown was nowhere more glaring than among village youth. Many young people enthusiastically embraced the new order. The rural Komsomol was an active and, to many an older peasant, odious force in village politics, generally more vocal and visible than the rural Communist party. Village Komsomol groups, especially in the early 1920s, staged antireligious carnivals and plays, savagely satirizing the church and clergy.[30] This kind of Komsomol antireligious propaganda was often crude and insulting to older peasants, as was the less crude but equally offensive propaganda of young neophyte atheists who might seek to prove God's nonexistence by proclaiming, "There is no god. . . . And if there is may I be struck down instantly."[31] Antireligious *chastushki* (popular ditties) along the following lines doubly mocked tradition by filling popular form with subversive content:[32]

> All the pious are on a spree,
> They see god is not home,
> He got drunk on samogon [home-brew],
> And left to go abroad.[33]

Other *chastushki* parodied the fear and resentment of traditional-minded peasants while at the same time tossing a barb at the older generation:

> Grandpa Nikita is a pious one,
> He often prays in church,
> He's afraid
> Lest a komsomol his son become.[34]

These kinds of sentiments frightened and angered many peasants, who resented the Komsomol's and even the young Pioneer movement's hold on their children. In the Tver area, Pioneers were called spies, after one young Pioneer denounced his father for making *samogon* (moonshine); some peasants argued, "such spyoneer-pioneers we don't need."[35] Elsewhere, parents (primarily Old Believers and some Protestants) removed their children from Soviet schools in protest against discussions of Lenin in the classroom or student processions celebrating socialist holidays. One student was forced by his parents to sit in the church all day and read the Books of the Apostles after participating in the celebration of the seventh anniversary of the revolution.[36] A boy from the Kuban recalled his father's reactions to news that he was a Komsomol:

> I knew that he would not permit it. When I brought home my Komsomol rule book, father saw it and began to curse me and wanted to beat me. But I told him that I would complain to the party cell if he beat me. And father is afraid of the cell. That same day father ripped up the book and threw it in the stove.[37]

Some peasants blamed what they perceived to be a rise in "hooliganism" among youth to the new godless amorality of the Communists.[38] In fact, many commentators did note a decline in standards of morality among peasant youth, and pointed to an increase in sexual promiscuity, venereal disease, prostitution, and hooliganism in the villages.[39] For some peasants, all of this moral chaos revealed the hand of the devil in Soviet power ("commissars are devils"[40]); for others, judgments of godlessness or satanic inspiration substituted for good strong curses.

The transitional nature of the 1920s can also be discerned in what may be labeled a new kind of *dvoeverie* (or dual faith),[41] a syncretistic belief that combined peasant ways and new Communist practices in a tentative and uneasy assimilation. For example, there were reports of portraits of Lenin or Kalinin turning up in icon corners and of habit-ridden old peasants crossing themselves in front of these new holy images.[42] In a remote village in northwest Russia, one of the first young people to join the Komsomol in the early 1920s was Dmitrii Solov'ev, the grandson of a local witch (*koldun*). Dmitrii, himself a witch, had the reputation of a "Don Juan," in part because of his Komsomol status, in part because of the mysterious powers thought to belong to his family.[43] In Penza in the mid-1920s, a regional Communist party inspection commission reported a case of satanic possession in a Tatar village. The local mullah and wise woman had both failed in their attempts to exorcise the devil from a possessed village family. Local officials turned to the commission for help, but, according to the commission's tongue-in-cheek account, the devil refused to have anything to do with Communists and remained "stubbornly silent" when the commission members visited the hut in question.[44] Elsewhere, village priests were known to bless Soviet candidates before elections.[45] Some peasants moved tentatively away from old rituals like baptism and toward the newly created rite of "Octobering," but generally continued to maintain Orthodox funeral and burial rites. In one village, the death of an Octobered infant was interpreted as a bad omen and a signal to return to the old ways.[46] This fragile and contradictory *dvo-everie*, combining elements of an urban atheistic culture and a profoundly spiritual peasant culture, was but another expression of the uncertainties and ambiguities of a culture in flux.

The confusion and anxiety of the times were also reflected in other areas of peasant life and belief. Many contemporary Soviet observers noted an increase in certain forms of religiosity. According to A. Angarov, the number of religious associations in the countryside had increased two to three times in the course of the 1920s.[47] This growth was most notable among religious groups outside the mainstream of the Russian Orthodox church. Many commentators claimed a decline in belief among the Orthodox, noting that it was mostly women and elderly peasant men who attended Orthodox church services.[48] Russian sects like the Molokane and the Skoptsy experienced a growth in membership after the revolution.[49] However, it was the Protestant sects—in particular evangelical Protestantism—that appear to have increased most dramatically during and after the civil war.[50] In some areas, the popularity of evangelical Protestantism may have derived from its stress on literacy, sobriety, and fraternity, as opposed to the Communist stress on class war.[51] Elsewhere, the hellfire and brimstone dimension of evangelical and especially Baptist teachings prevailed, and appealed to many a peasant living through these crisis-ridden times. The popularity of Baptist preaching about the imminent end of the world and the second coming of Christ was an expression of the profoundly unsettled spiritual and physical world of much of the Russian peasantry.[52]

Some evangelical groups encouraged a total separation from the state, viewing Soviet power as godless and evil and refusing to send their children to Soviet schools.[53] However, the primary upholders of the view of the state as Antichrist were the Old Believers, many of whom had never recognized the state, be it Tsarist or Soviet. In 1917, Old Believer archbishop Melentii identified Soviet power as the Antichrist, and many Old Believers refused to recognize the state through the 1920s.[54] It is difficult to estimate precisely how widespread this opinion of the state was during the NEP years because it is difficult to determine how many peasants adhered to the Old Belief. Some Old Believers refused to carry official documents or in any way register with the state, and many an Old Believer family turned away the 1926 census takers in fear that they brought with them the mark of Antichrist.[55] The Old Believers' view of the state would find widespread appeal among peasants during collectivization.

Another expression of fear and uncertainty that tends to come to the fore during periods of instability is anti-Semitism.[56] Popular anti-Semitism was always a feature of village life, particularly in Ukraine. It is not clear whether anti-Semitism increased with the revolution and civil war, although some contemporary commentators thought so. According to one report, in the early 1920s, Old Believers called Communist supporters Jews, and said that the Communists served "Jewish interests."[57]

In Ukraine in the mid-1920s, it was reported that religious believers shouted "beat the *zhidy* [yids]" when Komsomols sang antireligious songs during a religious holiday.[58] By the late 1920s, it had apparently become common for priests to deliver hateful sermons on Jews and for some peasants to blame the Jews for current problems. It was even reported that readings of the anti-Semitic tract, the Protocols of the Elders of Zion, were taking place in some villages in the Novgorod area.[59] It must be stressed that the prevalence and dimensions of an articulated anti-Semitism are not at all clear and require further research. However, it would not be surprising if anti-Semitism were indeed on the increase in the 1920s and especially during the years of collectivization, since this type of hatred breeds in conditions of fear and instability. Moreover, like apocalyptic thinking, anti-Semitism provides a relatively simple view of a world in conflict to the death and split between the forces of good and evil, Christian and Jew that, when applied to contemporary Soviet politics, transformed Communists into Jews—a figurative variation on the theme of Antichrist—thus serving as another metaphorical negation of Soviet power.[60]

The most concrete expression of the tenor of the times made its appearance throughout the length and breadth of the countryside in the form of heavenly omens and signs. These otherworldly manifestations were less an expression of peasant superstition than additional testimony to the troubled spiritual world of the peasantry. Like apocalyptic beliefs, they helped peasants to make sense of rapidly changing times by injecting the hand of providence into their everyday life.[61] Throughout the countryside, there were reports of miracles, heavenly apparitions, and the renewal (*obnovlenie*) of icons. Cases of renewed icons (wherein old icons suddenly became clean and new) were reported in Voronezh, Kursk, Saratov, Samara, the Don, Kiev, and other areas in the 1920s. Peasants interpreted these phenomena as signs from God and often organized pilgrimages to the villages where the renewed icons were found.[62] In the Voronezh area in the early 1920s, there were reports of apple trees and maple trees being suddenly "renewed" (probably meaning sudden regeneration out of season); here, too, thousands of pilgrims gathered to pray.[63] In many cases, renewed icons and other miraculous apparitions were said to have healing powers. This was the case of a miraculous icon that reportedly cured a shepherd's paralyzed arm in the Urals region.[64] Rumors told of an apple tree that rose straight up more than 120 meters from the steep slope of a hill and supposedly had curative powers.[65] There were also rumors in many places of the sudden appearances of crosses, secret flames, and holy springs.[66] At a spring outside of a village in Barnaulskii *okrug* in 1924, an elderly peasant woman stopped for a drink and saw "holy figures." News of the sighting spread and peasants flocked to the area to pray and to seek healing from the spring. It was reported that people were still making pilgrimages to the spring as late as 1928.[67] Another miracle was reported in a village in Kuznetskii *okrug*. Here, three women went to a spring to pray for rain. On the first day of their prayers, they spotted a piece of paper the size of a matchbox. On the next day, they found a copper icon the size of a matchbox. Four days later, one of the women took the icon home, but the icon soon disappeared, reappearing at the spring. The villagers erected a cross and peasants soon began to make pilgrimages to this holy site. It was even rumored that a peasant who had laughed at the story fell off his horse and became ill.[68] Miraculous springs, crosses, and holy images appear in many cultures as "symbols of healing and regeneration."[69] In the Russian context, they served as a collective projection of the unease or dis-ease that held the countryside in its grip after the revolution and civil war.

Other miracles had more direct messages from the heavens about God and politics. On 5 December 1922, a meteorite fell somewhere in the countryside. Some people called it a "heavenly rock," some said it was made of gold, and still others claimed that it portended the end of the world. In Ranenburgskii *uezd*, a rumor (probably inspired by this meteorite) circulated that Jupiter was falling to earth, signaling the end of the world. This news led to a slaughter of livestock, based on the reasoning that the people might as well eat well as long as they were going to die anyway.[70] In the Vinnitsa area in the early 1920s, there were rumors of a renewed cross, the coming of the final judgment, and even the resurrection of corpses.[71] God himself was rumored to have come to Tyshtypskii *raion* in June 1926 and to have spoken to a local peasant. The peasant announced that on 19 June he would tell the world what God had said. Some three thousand people gathered to hear the message that the world would end in forty-seven years if people believed in God, but in twenty-seven if they did not. A cross was erected at the spot where God spoke to the man, and annual visits of some two thousand people were reported. In a village in Biiskii *okrug* in the summer of 1927, an elderly peasant woman reported having a vision of Christ telling her the location of a holy treasure. Local peasants and clergy dug at the site but found nothing. Nevertheless, the spot became a holy place with supposedly miraculous curative powers, and peasant pilgrims began to visit.[72]

The frequent manifestations and the appeal of supernatural occurrences among peasants were symptomatic of the times and testify to an undercurrent of apocalyptic foreboding among peasants in the 1920s. This apocalyptic undercurrent, however, should not be dismissed as mere peasant "darkness" or superstition. Apocalyptic themes in peasant imagery and discourse are intrinsically subversive in their dichotomous treatment of good and evil. An alternative symbolic universe is present in the apocalyptic and millennial themes that figure so prominently in many peasant societies undergoing periods of stress or upheaval, and represents a central aspect of the peasant culture of resistance.[73] According to Eric Wolf, "the disordered present is all too frequently experienced [by peasants] as world order reversed, and hence evil."[74] During NEP, some peasants viewed Soviet power as the Antichrist, while others insisted on reading eschatological meanings into natural and reported supernatural events. The hand of providence pervaded the everyday world of the peasantry, as well as the political relations between peasant and Communist. The alien culture of the state became the antithesis of peasant culture, the Communist Antichrist to the peasant Christ, through its association and, in the popular consciousness, merger with atheism, amorality, and force. Given the centrality of the Communist assault on peasant culture and religion, it is no wonder that peasants set up a symbolic universe that both provided a familiar set of standards by which to judge temporal power and expressed the profound sense of cultural malaise that characterized the peasant mood after the revolution.

NEP provided a breathing space, but it resembled the calm before the storm more than a golden age of the peasantry. Although NEP was a relative and most certainly a retrospective paradise for peasants, wedged in as it was between the civil war and collectivization, it remained a troubled time for much of the rural population. In the 1920s, the apocalyptic tradition remained only an undercurrent of protest and unease, and was but one among a diverse array of peasant languages of rebellion. In addition, it was usually more a state of mind reflecting the malaise and instability of the times than a vehicle of direct protest. Nevertheless, the apocalyptic undercurrents of the 1920s helped to condition the apocalyptic mind-set that would play such an important role in peasant protest during collectivization. These undercurrents also placed in high relief the contradictions between the urban world of Communism and the rural world of the peasant, setting the scene for the cultural collision that was collectivization.

The peasant nightmare

Collectivization led to an explosion of apocalyptic fears among the peasantry. Apocalyptic imagery and rumors were omnipresent. Collectivization rent apart the fabric of peasant life, destroying the natural routine of the village. In this context, the apocalypse provided peasants with a lexicon of current events and a vocabulary of rebellion. The apocalyptic vision symbolized the very real clash of two worlds at fatal variance with each other, and served to turn the existing Soviet order of things on its head. The apocalyptic tradition was used to delegitimize the collective farms and the state that backed them, thus becoming an idiom of peasant protest.

News of apocalyptic happenings was most often spread through rumors. Not all of the rumors of the collectivization era were apocalyptic in content. There were rumors that were more secular in nature, concerning economic and political issues. Economic rumors generally centered on taxes, grain prices, and requisitioning. Taxes and grain prices were traditionally the raw material for peasant rumor, as peasants debated whether to wait for grain prices to rise in the spring and what new taxes were pending.[75] Other rumors were connected to specific events, such as the publication of Stalin's "Dizziness from Success" article in early March 1930,[76] or told stories about political leaders. Several rumors from the collectivization era and earlier years suggested that Trotskii and Bukharin were the peasants' supporters in Moscow. In early 1930, rumors in the Ivanovo area claimed that "Bukharin and Trotskii are good . . . [while] Stalin wants to leave everyone starving."[77] In the Central Black Earth Region in early 1930, rumor claimed that Trotskii was in China, preparing an offensive against the Soviet Union.[78] Although the favorable view of Bukharin is understandable, Trotskii's inclusion here suggests a kind of inversion along the lines of "the enemy of my enemy is my friend." Other rumors of this type purported to view Stalin as the friend of the peasant, as, for example, in early 1930, when rumors that Stalin and Lenin's widow, Krupskaia, were coming to the countryside to arrest collective farm organizers floated through the villages of Kurganskii *okrug*.[79] Finally, there were many rumors whose content reflected regional issues or fears, such as rumors about "decossackization" in the Kuban and elsewhere or rumors about the coming of Romanian forces to slaughter collective farmers in Moldavia.[80] The most common type of collectivization-era rumor, however, was shaped by apocalyptic ideas and imagery, and generally included five basic themes: the reign of Antichrist, retribution, impending war and invasion, godless Communists and immorality, and the collective farm as serfdom.[81]

The first and most frequent type of collectivization rumor branded Soviet power and the collective farm with the mark of Antichrist. Throughout the countryside, it was rumored that the end was near and the reign of Antichrist had begun.[82] A widespread rumor in the Middle Volga Region in 1929 said that "Soviet power is not of God, but of Antichrist."[83] The nearest and most visible representative of Antichrist on earth was said to be the collective farm, although on occasion an agronomist, a workers' brigade, or even a tractor could be labeled "satanic forces" or the "servants of Antichrist."[84] Peasants were warned not to join the collective farm lest they be stamped (generally, quite literally, on the forehead) with the mark of Antichrist to identify them for damnation at the second coming or at the time of some unspecified uprising.[85] In Stalingradskii *okrug* in the Lower Volga, a cossack spoke of the imminent coming of Christ and warned that "the collective farm—this is the devil's branding, from which [you] need to save yourself in order to enter the kingdom of god."[86] In some places, it was reported that "unclean forces" resided in the homes of new collective farm members or that the collective farm was a punishment for the sins of the people.[87] According to an OGPU investigator, in the Lower Volga in 1930 "religious pretexts" were paramount in "kulak agitation" and rumors about the collective farms. Here, peasants claimed that "[t]he collective farm is incompatible with religion. There you will be forced to work on Sunday, [they] will close the church and not allow [you] to pray," and "Joining the collective farm you sign yourself on to Antichrist's list. Run from the collective farm, save your soul!" In Saratovskii *raion*, Atkarskii *okrug*, an Old Believer woman prophesied: "You will be forced to work on Sundays if you go into the collective farm, [they] will put the seal of Antichrist on your forehead and arms. Now already the kingdom of Antichrist is begun and to go into the collective farm is a big sin. About this it is written in the Bible."[88]

Many rumors included warnings of an impending day of retribution and judgment. Aimed at Communists and peasants who joined or might join the collective farm, these rumors prophesied doom for all those who had gone over to the side of Soviet power. In a cossack *stanitsa* (village) in the Kuban, a rumor circulated that 1 August 1929 would be a "black night," when cossack troops would massacre poor peasants and non-Cossack peasants. When the night of 1 August came, many of the peasants under threat fled to the steppes or gathered with weapons twenty to a hut.[89] In other areas, rumors foretold of a similar day of reckoning, labeling it, aptly enough, an impending Bartholomew's Night massacre. Rumors circulated in the villages of Chapaevskii *raion* in late summer 1929 warning of a Bartholomew's Night massacre of all who joined the collective farm.[90] Rumors of an imminent Bartholomew's Night massacre, warning of universal destruction according to the writ of God, circulated in Vladimirskii *okrug* in the Ivanovo Industrial Region in late January 1930.[91] Rumors of Bartholomew's Night massacres also accompanied collectivization campaigns in the Urals and Chuvash areas.[92] In the village of Bochkarko in the Khar'kov area, rumors told of a miraculous light issuing from the recently closed church. A sign on the church's cupola read: "Do not go into the collective farm and commune because I will smite you."[93] Elsewhere, threatening rumors were more secular in nature. Rumors in the Moscow Region, for instance, warned those who would join the collective farm that they would be expelled from their huts and that their huts would then be turned into firewood. In this same region, rumors maintained that peasants would have to eat rats in the collective farm and, more ominously, that in a neighboring village a woman's body was found hanging by the neck soon after she joined a collective farm.[94] In many parts of the countryside, peasants circulated rumors of an impending uprising. In spring 1930 in the village Sorochinskoe in Orenburgskii *raion*, Orenburgskii *okrug*, Middle Volga, the peasant Voronin told his neighbors that "now *muzhiki* everywhere are prepared and if there is an insurrection all as one will take part."[95] In the Central Black Earth Region in mid-1931, rumors of uprisings in other parts of the country and a miner's strike in the Donbas accompanied a new wave of collectivization. At the same time, in both the Central Black Earth Region and Western Siberia, there were rumors forecasting war and the imminent downfall of Soviet power.[96]

Rumors of war and invasion were natural outgrowths of rumors about Antichrist and divine retribution. Peasants had been skittish about war throughout the 1920s and especially during the 1927 war scare and grain requisitioning campaigns.[97] These fears continued into the collectiv-

ization era and spread throughout the countryside in the form of rumors
of impending invasion. The most frequent invaders named were the British, the Poles, the Chinese, and the Japanese, although at times the rumors spoke only of invading "bands" or "horsemen," thus directly calling
upon apocalyptic imagery. These rumors often included the news that
those who joined the collective farms would either be slaughtered by these
armies or be the first to be conscripted for military service.[98] The rumors
were partly inspired by Moscow's incessant war hysteria, thus demonstrating that peasants were cognizant of national politics. However, in this
instance, official propaganda fed directly into the apocalyptic mood of the
countryside, allowing peasants to put the war scare to their own use.
Rumors of war and invasion therefore hinted darkly at the coming of the
end and a terrible fate for those who, by joining the collective farm or
otherwise serving Soviet power, had signed themselves over to Antichrist.

Rumors concerning the godless nature of Communism and the moral
abominations of the new collective farm order made up another category
of rumor loosely related to the more overtly apocalyptic rumors. The
most common rumors of this type related to the family. Rumors about
wife-sharing and the common blanket for communal sleeping circulated
throughout the countryside.[99] According to an instructor from the Collective Farm Scientific Research Institute, these rumors "literally circulated
around the entire Union."[100] The common blanket rumors resurrected a
civil war myth that Communists were intent on nationalizing women.[101]
They were likely further inspired by one or two cases when local activists
actually did introduce practices dangerously close to the common blanket.
For instance, a *Rabkrin* (Workers' and Peasants' Inspection) plenipotentiary told women that they would all have to sleep, along with all of the
men, under one common blanket. And in the North Caucasus, local activists in one village actually confiscated all blankets, telling the peasants
that henceforth all would sleep on a seven-hundred-meter-long bed under
a seven-hundred-meter-long blanket.[102] Rumors of the export or cutting
of women's hair and the export or socialization of children often accompanied rumors of the common blanket.[103] At a women's meeting in Sha-
drinskii *okrug* in the Urals in May 1930, collectivization cadres actually
told women that they would have to cut their hair because the government needed hair for scrap materials.[104] In the North Caucasus in 1930,
there were reports that children would be exported to China to "improve
the race" (presumably of the Chinese).[105] In the Urals, rumors warned
that children would be sent to a special children's colony.[106] In the Leningrad Region, women and girls were frightened by rumors warning
that, with the coming of the collective farm, "they will take your children," "they will cut your hair," and there will be no trousseau.[107] In
other parts of the countryside, rumors spread that girls and women would
be exported to China to pay for the Far Eastern Railroad.[108] The women
of the village Starye Chleny in Starochelinskaia *volost'*, Chistopol'skii
kanton in Tatariia feared that in the collective farm their hair would be

cut like horses' tails, the children would be taken, they would all have to eat dog meat, and they would be given husbands that they "did not need."[109] In the Middle Volga village of Pokrovka in Chapaevskii *raion*, rumor had it that in the collective farm "all will be shared, both husbands and wives . . . [they] will cut off [your] hair. . . . They will take your children from you and you will not see them, they will raise them in a satanic spirit . . . [and] they will burn down the churches."[110] A rumor that circulated in Maikopskii *okrug*, North Caucasus, in late 1929 combined fears of moral decadence and apocalypse in a nightmarish vision of life in the collective farm:

> In the collective farm, there will be a special stamp, [they] will close all the churches, not allow prayer, dead people will be cremated, the christening of children will be forbidden, invalids and the elderly will be killed, there won't be any husbands or wives, [all] will sleep under a one-hundred-meter blanket. Beautiful men and women will be taken and brought to one place to produce beautiful people. Children will be taken from their parents, there will be wholesale incest: brothers will live with sisters, sons with mothers, fathers with daughters, etc. The collective farm—this is beasts in a single shed, people in a single barrack."[111]

Tales of moral abomination in the collective farms served as metaphors for the amorality, atheism, and evil of Communism. These tales fed into the apocalyptic mood by calling upon a belief system that implicitly linked the world of Communism-Antichrist to sexual immorality and other abominations.

Rumors comparing collectivization to serfdom also served as metaphor. In this case, serfdom became code for the Communist betrayal of the revolution, a code signifying the worst possible analogy for a peasantry in whose historical consciousness serfdom remained central. Throughout the countryside, peasants cursed the revolution and the Communist party. In the Central Black Earth Region in fall 1931, OGPU investigators recorded the following peasant remarks: "The Communists deceived us in the revolution, all land was given out to work for free and now they take the last cow"; "[They] don't give peasants any freedom, they persecute us and take [our] last cow"; and "Only bandits act this way, taking the last cow from a middle peasant."[112] In the Middle Volga, a middle peasant stated, "I worked as a worker for 30 years, [they] said to me 'revolution.' I didn't understand but now [I] understand that such a revolution means to take everything from the peasants and leave them hungry and naked."[113] In the same region, another peasant declared, "Here is your power [*vlast'*], they take the last cow from a poor peasant, this is not Soviet power, but the power of thieves and pillagers."[114] In the Leningrad Region, peasants compared the collective farm to the "old *barshchina*" (or corvee).[115] Similar analogies appeared in rumors in the Central Industrial Region, Western Region, Lower Volga, Middle Volga, Kuban, and elsewhere in the countryside.[116] In the village I'lino in Kuznetsovskii *raion,* Kimrskii *okrug,* in the Moscow Region in early 1930, peasants warned that "The collective farm is *barshchina,* a second serfdom."[117] An OGPU report on the Ukraine in early 1930 reported peasants saying, "They push us into the collective farm so we will be eternal slaves."[118] These rumors invariably warned peasants that collectivization meant disorder, hunger, famine, and the destruction of crops and livestock.[119] Some rumors warned further of the return of the *pomeshchiki* (landlords) or Whites, thus reinforcing the threat of enserfment while calling upon the imagery of invasion and the horsemen of the apocalypse.[120] The meaning of rumors comparing the collective farm with serfdom was clear to all peasants. It is unlikely that peasants actually believed the collective farm to be a return to serfdom per se.[121] Serfdom rather served as a metaphor for evil and injustice. Like themes of apocalypse, the collective farm as serfdom was a form of inversion, an inversion of Soviet power and the revolution.

Rumors from all these categories circulated throughout the collectivizing countryside. Each type of rumor was directly or indirectly derived from apocalyptic fears and beliefs. Rumors concerning the Antichrist were explicitly apocalyptic; those warning of retribution, war, and invasion called to mind the horsemen of apocalyptic tradition,[122] and rumors about moral abominations in the collective farm called forth the unholy triad of Communism-Antichrist-sexual depravity, the Communist component being the Russian contribution to a traditional linkage of the satanic and the depraved.[123] Rumors associating collectivization and enserfment, although not necessarily apocalyptic, used serfdom as a metaphor for evil, a secular, social apocalypse that, when tied to the Communist policy of collectivization, transformed Communists into present-day landlords and made a mockery of the 1917 Revolution. Each in its own way stressed the coming of the end. In the peasant image of apocalypse, there was no vision of the millennium to follow the second coming, no discussion of the kingdom of saints to follow the kingdom of Antichrist. The peasant apocalypse was essentially negative. Its stress on the end and the reign of Antichrist reflected the hopelessness and desperation that engulfed the peasant world in the years of wholesale collectivization. In the very act of negation, however, peasant rumors of apocalypse served to turn the Communist world on its head. The peasant reaction to collectivization was not simply reactionary; instead, its "crucial characteristic was to reverse the world . . . consciousness was expressed as a negation of the existing order rather than as a search for a new order."[124] Communism became Antichrist. All that was good and right and logical in the Communist worldview became its antithesis in the peasant world. It is in this sense that rumors of apocalypse served a seditious end and acted as an ideology of peasant resistance.[125]

The emphasis on the reign of Antichrist was indicative of the subversive nature of the collectivization-era apocalyptic mind-set. This emphasis ruled out the possibility of neutrality (on either side) in what had become a war between the forces of good and evil. The choice for all who cared about salvation was between God, on the one hand, and Soviet power, the collective farm, and Antichrist (all interchangeable), on the other. The political world and the spiritual world had become one, with the result that secular politics were filtered through the prism of apocalypse in the peasant idiom of protest. Apocalypse was therefore not simply a tool for understanding the cataclysm of the First Five-Year Plan, but was also a guide to action. If the choice was between salvation and damnation, the believer had no choice but to resist the policies and practices of the state. For this reason, apocalyptic warnings were aimed at those who joined or considered joining the collective farm. Apocalyptic rumors served to maintain peasant unity and became a call to arms in and around more active forms of peasant protest and resistance to collectivization.

"From the Lord God"

Fueled by fear and outrage, rumors spread like wildfire through the villages. Peasants shared the latest news from the rumor mill in small gatherings around the well or at the mill, market, or *posidelki* (young people's parties), or in conversations with neighbors.[126] The primary vehicles for the spread of rumors were said to be women and an assortment of marginal country people who, according to Soviet sources, were manipulated by kulaks, priests, and other "counterrevolutionaries." Women seemed the natural carriers for rumor, especially apocalyptic rumors, given their greater religiosity and the social and work activities that placed them in close contact with one another.[127] Similarly, marginal figures such as wandering pilgrims, beggars, and *iurodivye* (holy fools) appeared as logical transmitters of rumor, given their geographical mobility.[128] However, since rumors were so prevalent in the countryside, it is not clear whether these figures were indeed the actual agents of transmission or whether Soviet power simply labeled them so. By ascribing the world of rumor to the *baba*—and generally older ones at that—Soviet power may have, consciously or otherwise, sought to "feminize" rumor and thereby degrade its import through association with "women's business." In the same way, linking rumor to wanderers and other transients marginalized rumor and connected it to a largely archaic—and therefore politically irrelevant—rural stratum. In both cases, whether or not these elements were in fact the chief purveyors of rumor, Soviet power could *depoliticize* belief in rumor because it perceived peasant women, wanderers, beggars, and the like to be backward and politically illiterate. In this way, the state tried to politically defuse the explosive significance of rumor as counterideology.

Soviet power sought instead to localize the danger of rumor to the *source* of its transmission. Since the state considered women and other marginal characters to be little more than gullible primitives, the inspiration for rumors had to come from somewhere else. Predictably, it was the kulak and village priest who were held politically responsible for rumors. Whether kulaks initiated rumors or whether peasants were "kulakized" because they initiated or told rumors is an open question. According to Soviet sensibilities, though, *only* a kulak could hold such dangerous, counterrevolutionary political ideas, so a peasant spreading rumors ipso facto was a kulak. Several decades later, Solzhenitsyn reported that, as in a distant echo, camp rumors in the Gulag were invariably called "kulak rumors."[129] The kulak as rumor monger was joined by the village priest. And here it is completely logical to assume that the priest may have had some role in the dissemination of apocalyptic rumors, for collectivization spelled apocalypse for priests as surely as it did for peasants. Priests, moreover, were native speakers of the vernacular of apocalypse. An activist reported from the Penza area of the Middle Volga that

> everywhere priests are spreading the legend that in Penza at the Maiden's Convent a light issuing from the cross is burning day and night, and it is necessary to say that the people go there, the devil knows how many, to look at those miracles. Besides this, [the priests] say that soon the Roman pope will come, the government will fall, and all the communists and collective farmers will be crushed.[130]

In Rostov-on-the-Don, a deacon declared: "I pronounce onto you that the end of the world is coming. With the help of God, it is necessary to struggle against Antichrist and his sons."[131] Clergy in Gel'miazovskii *raion*, Shevchenkovskii *okrug*, in Ukraine, predicted that the simplest form of collective "would exist for 28 days, the *artel'* for 21 days and, beginning from 1 February, if a transition [occurs] to the *kommuna*, [we] will live for 42 days, and then the end of the world will arrive."[132] Elsewhere, priests warned their parishioners that the collective farm was a punishment for their sins.[133]

The counterrevolutionary import of rumor then was confined to official enemies. And with the responsibility for rumors safely localized, Soviet power could turn the full force of its repressive machinery against the rumor monger without fear of violating its own official line on who the enemy was. Rumor mongers whose rumors could be interpreted as propaganda or agitation subversive to the state were prosecuted under Aticle 58 (10) of the penal code—the infamous article concerning counterrevolutionary crimes—and received a prison sentence of not less than six months or, in cases in which individuals exploited religious or racial prejudices via rumors during mass disturbances, the death penalty. To the less-than-counterrevolutionary rumor monger, the state could apply Article 123 of the penal code, which invoked a sentence of one year of noncustodial forced labor (locally) and a fine for the commission of an act of deceit in order to arouse mass superstitions with the object of obtaining advantage.[134] In either case, Soviet power could choose when to make an object of those who sought to exploit the (supposedly) apolitical, gullible *baba* and her cronies, and one suspects that most rumor mongers escaped punishment in the absence of another offense. It is likely, moreover, that the *baba* and the wanderer took relief in and advantage of their own officially sanctioned lack of political agency and therefore responsibility.

That rumors were in fact not limited to kulak and priest or to *baba* and other marginals (even though they may have indeed been central actors) is made evident through the other forms rumors could assume in the cause of spreading news of the apocalypse. Rumors were frequently transmuted into more popular forms, such as *chastushki* or heavenly letters; at other times, the contents of apocalyptic rumors resurfaced in proclamations or at peasant meetings. *Chastushki*, a prerevolutionary staple of peasant popular culture, could be continually re-formed in reaction to current events. Many of the *chastushki* of this period told of hunger in the collective farm and warned peasants not to join. One such *chastushka* went as follows:

> The tractor ploughs deeply,
> The land dries up.
> Soon all the collective farmers
> Will die of starvation.[135]

Others warned that the penalty for joining the collective farm was the stamp of Antichrist. Passages from one such *chastushka* warned:

> Oh, brothers! Oh, sisters! Don't go into the collective farm . . .
> Antichrist will lay his mark upon you three times.
> Once on the hand,
> The second on the forehead for all to see,
> And the third on the breast.
> If you believe in god, don't join the collective farm . . .
> And if you are in the collective farm, oh sisters, leave . . . .[136]

Apocalyptic sentiments were echoed in heavenly letters written by the hand of God, the Virgin Mary, or Christ. In a village in Oirotiia, God wrote, "People no longer believe in me. If this [non-belief] continues, then in two years the world will come to an end. I can no longer be patient."[137] In a district in the Astrakhan area in early 1930, it was rumored that the Virgin Mary sent a letter, written in golden script, warning that sickness and punishment would descend upon the collective farms and that they would be destroyed by bands of horsemen.[138] In the North Caucasus in late 1929, a wandering pilgrim claiming to be Christ proclaimed the coming final judgment and displayed lists—"sent by the holy mother of God"— calling on all believers to quit the collective farms.[139] A heavenly letter circulated in Kamenskii *okrug* in Siberia had the stamp of a German business firm on its letterhead; the stamp reportedly gave the letter added authority in the eyes of the peasants.[140] Heavenly letters were a popular form for the spread of rumors in other peasant cultures beyond Russia.[141] The divine source of rumors served to legitimize their content—in this case, apocalyptic belief and protest—in much the same way pretenders to the throne had legitimized peasant protest in earlier, prerevolutionary Russian episodes of rural rebellion.[142] Although I know of no case of a charismatic prophet arriving with news of the coming end as so often happened in earlier, non-Russian bouts of apocalyptic fever, it appears that this was a time of many small and humble prophets spreading the word and, in light of the danger of such prophesy, moving on quickly.

Rumors were also spread at peasant meetings and through clandestinely distributed proclamations. In 1929, on the eve of wholesale collectivization, the entire countryside was abuzz with rumor and discussion about its impending fate. Peasant meetings to discuss collectivization were invariably classified as "kulak secret meetings" by the authorities and surely occurred in every village during these troubled times.[143] Anti-collective farm proclamations also appeared in the villages on the eve of and during wholesale collectivization.[144] Warnings that Communist party members and peasants who joined the collective farms would be massacred—usually at the time of some unspecified uprising—appeared in proclamations in regions as far apart as Western Siberia and the Leningrad Region.[145] In one part of Siberia, proclamations "from the Lord God" appeared forbidding peasants to enter the collective farm.[146] Elsewhere peasants received letters from fellow villagers who had left the countryside, warning that the end of the world was approaching and that the only salvation was to leave the collective farm.[147]

Although it is clear that apocalyptic rumors assumed many forms and were widespread in the countryside during the years of collectivization, it is not possible to determine precisely who believed in them at a literal level. The available sources do not permit an analysis of differentiated peasant responses according to gender or age. And the contemporary politicization of class definitions precludes any reliable form of social identification of believer. It is possible and indeed likely that different peasant groups responded differently to tales of the apocalypse. This analysis is not meant to suggest that all peasants believed literally in the apocalypse, nor should it be interpreted as an argument for a monolithic peasant community. The question of who believed necessarily raises the issue of whether some peasants may have simply exploited apocalyptic beliefs in order to mobilize resistance against the state. It is by no means unusual for peasants to make use of various kinds of stratagems in their protest. Daniel Field has suggested that Russian peasants in the 1860s manipulated official myths and assumptions about themselves for their own ends.[148] Peasant women routinely took shelter behind official images of themselves as backward and irrational in order to get away with what was in fact highly rational and political protest during collectivization.[149] It is probable that some peasants used the apocalyptic tradition as a device to mobilize peasant opposition against the state, because clearly the apocalyptic tradition served as a ready religious and moral sanction for peasant protest and illegal activity.[150] The important point, however, when considering the issues of belief and stratagem, is that, whether sincerely articulated or used as a mobilizing device, apocalyptic rumors *worked* in rallying peasants to resist collectivization, and they worked because the apocalypse provided peasants with a language of protest distilled through metaphor—"a fundamental procedure of folk discourse," according to Le Roy Ladurie[151]—which was both politically expedient and widely understood. The negations and inversions involved in apocalyptic forecasting served to raise the consciousness of the mass of the peasantry by providing an alternate truth, an alternate reality from which peasants could view and judge Soviet power. That many of the apocalyptic rumors contained implicit or explicit warnings to those peasants who might stray from the communal fold and go over to Soviet power and the collective farm further bolstered this consciousness, making rumors at times coercive instruments of persuasion used to reinforce community norms or ideals of cohesion and unity against the outside. From these perspectives, the issue of who believed becomes secondary, perhaps even irrelevant.

The world of rumor, whether reflected in oral transmission, traditional form, or in print, represented a kind of offstage social space for the articulation of peasant dissent. Rumor was a popular forum of social space *in the abstract*, in which peasants could create and maintain a political dialogue about Soviet power, Communism, and the collective farm. That rumor was a cultural form of discourse sustained in spite of the Communist onslaught against peasant culture made it as antithetical to the state as other social spaces such as the church and commune. The form, therefore, was intrinsically subversive, matching the evident danger of the content in its subversive potential. It granted peasants the necessary space in which to construct an ideology of protest that would unite and mobilize peasants against the state, while negating the legitimacy of Soviet power.

Conclusion

The apocalyptic undercurrents of the 1920s came to the fore in the course of wholesale collectivization, becoming a potent symbol of peasant opposition to the state. Peasants struggled to defend and preserve a way of life that was under attack politically and ideologically. For them, collectivization represented the culmination of that attack. It meant the victory of the October Revolution—or the Stalinist version of it, at the very least— and of the city over the countryside. As such, collectivization was more than simply an effort to take grain or to create collective farms: it symbolized a battle between two different worlds and two different cultures. This clash of cultures is clearly evident in the peasant vision of apocalypse that surfaced in the years after 1927 and especially in the years of collectivization. For much of the peasantry, the state was an alien force—"they," as opposed to the peasant "we." The dichotomy of state and society (or at least peasant society) was firmly fixed from below, and in the peasant mind it was also a dichotomy between the forces of evil and the forces of good. The apocalypse symbolized this clash of cultures and politics; the collectivization campaign became Armageddon.

Peasant popular protest was widespread and assumed many forms during the years of collectivization. Apocalyptic rumors were not its only expression, nor did peasants always filter their protest through the prism of the apocalypse. Many confronted the representatives of Soviet power directly, with a political language more clearly modern in form. Nevertheless, apocalyptic language appears to have been a dominant idiom of protest, in part perhaps because peasant protest in this period was largely self-generated. Unlike many earlier peasant revolts, urban social forces took no part in these protests, nor does it appear that outsiders (whether urban or rural) played much of a role in the peasant unrest of this era. The only possible exceptions were priests, who could only have reinforced the apocalyptic approach to politics. Lacking modern forms of political discourse and other, institutionalized outlets for protest, as well as the aid of sympathetic outsiders, peasants often fell back upon an older tradition of dissent in order to articulate their opposition.[152]

The widespread appeal of apocalyptic discourse during collectivization must also be explained by reference to the times. In the peasant mind, the apocalypse accurately described the current state of affairs. Given the dominant reality, it was neither irrational nor fanciful for peasants to conceive of their fate in apocalyptic terms. Violence and destruction dotted the terrain. The old world seemed to be coming to a frightening end, and peasants were victims of forces over which they had little control. Many therefore turned to older religious ideas and habits of thought, adapting and transforming them into a potent doctrine of revolt. The concept of the apocalypse restored a measure of control to the peasantry by serving as a tool for understanding what otherwise could only have been interpreted as a senseless and tragic war on the peasantry.

3

"We Have No Kulaks Here": Peasant Luddism, Evasion, and Self-Help

Thanks to Yakov Lukich's example, men began slaughtering their cattle every night in Gremyachy. As soon as it grew dusk, one could hear the short muffled bleating of sheep, the death squeal of a pig piercing the stillness, the whimper of a calf. Both the peasants who had joined the collective farm and the individual farmers killed off their stock. They slaughtered oxen, sheep, pigs, even cows; they even slaughtered their breed animals. In two nights the head of cattle in Gremyachy was halved. Dogs began to drag offal about the streets, the grocery stall sold nearly two hundred poods of salt that had been lying on the shelves for eighteen months. "Kill, it's not ours now!" "Kill, the state butchers will do it if we don't!" "Kill, they won't give you meat to eat in the collective farm!" the insidious rumours spread around. And the villagers killed. They ate until they could eat no more. Young and old had the belly-ache. At dinner-time the peasants' tables sagged under their loads of boiled and roasted meat. At dinner-time all mouths glistened with fat and there was belching enough for a funeral feast; and in every eye there was an owlish expression of drunken satiety.

—M. Sholokhov, *Virgin Soil Upturned*

The ideology of peasant resistance spread in the countryside through a dense web of rumor convincing some that the end was near and others that the world had been turned upside down and that it was time to topple the Soviet Antichrist. The peasant apocalyptic idiom, grafted onto the violent depredations of the state, forecast the imminent demise of peasant life and culture. Civil war between town and countryside was on the near horizon, and when it came peasants would rise up to meet their enemies in bloody conflagration. Ultimately, however, peasants turned to violence only as a last resort. Before entering into battle with the vastly superior forces of Soviet power, the peasantry attempted to shield itself against the blows of collectivization and dekulakization through collective and individual forms of self-defense. The apocalyptic discourse of peasant resistance would be reflected in practice as peasants struggled to invert and therefore subvert notions of class and authority in the collectivizing village through peasant Luddism, evasion, and self-help.

Peasant self-help assumed many different forms and no attempt is made here to present a complete catalogue. Instead, discussion is limited to those forms of self-help that were both widespread and indicative of a peasant culture of resistance. Peasant self-help may be viewed as a specific form of *implicit* resistance. Although often cloaked in *muzhik* vestments, peasant self-help was neither irrational nor the emanation of a backward peasantry. It was, rather, logical, political, and humane. Acts of self-help could be direct and clear protest, but were more likely to be expressed as part of the "weapons of the weak" [1]—in this case, the exploitation of official images of the irrational *muzhik* for peasant ends, through dissembling and adapting to the language of the oppressors, or through defensive acts of resistance such as masking or liquidating sources of wealth to alter socioeconomic status.

The most vivid and dangerous form of self-help was what Soviet power labeled *razbazarivanie*, or the "squandering" of livestock and sometimes farm implements, machinery, and even crops through destruction or sale. As protest, sabotage, or a way to liquefy assets, *razbazarivanie* enabled peasants to gird themselves against the economic perils of the new collective farm system. For some peasants, those labeled kulaks, *razbazarivanie* was one method among many of socioeconomic transfiguration or, to use the official term, *samoraskulachivanie* ("self-dekulakization"). Self-dekulakization embraced other stratagems, including, in the end, complete flight from the countryside so that self-dekulakization became self-depeasantization. Both *razbazarivanie* and self-dekulakization served as literal forms of inversion, as peasants endeavored to upturn Communist-imposed definitions of "class" in the village.

Peasants also attempted to protect or defend one another. Many villages banded together in support of their neighbors, friends, and relatives who were accused of being kulaks. The refrain "we have no kulaks here" was heard throughout the countryside, as every peasant learned that the kulak label, instead of dividing them, served as the great equalizer, once it was clear that it was *peasant* interests that were on the line and that almost *anyone* could be labeled a kulak. Support or defense of "kulaks," moreover, was an implicit form of resistance, dangerous and subject to interpretation by the state as a counterrevolutionary activity or the act of a *podkulachnik*. When all else failed, peasants turned to the most traditional of their defenses—writing letters and petitions to higher authorities. They wrote on behalf of themselves and others, individually and collectively. Their letter-writing was an exercise in protest, adaptation, and dissembling, but a hope and a plea for justice all the same.

The state was the ultimate victor in collectivization. Yet peasant actions of self-help were not without consequence. Peasant *razbazarivanie* of livestock was of such massive and destructive scale as to directly shape state policy in the short term and cripple the potential of socialized agriculture in the long term. At the cost of a kind of cultural extinction, self-dekulakization spared hundreds of thousands of peasants from expropriation, deportation, or worse. Yet, like *razbazarivanie*, it had a profound impact on the state's policies and the economy. Other forms of self-help may have helped individual peasants, but more importantly served, along with *razbazarivanie* in the villages, to demonstrate to the state the cohesion of the peasantry and its ability to act as a class in defense of its interests.

"Destroy the horse as a class"

The mad orgy of slaughter and gluttony in the fictional village of Gremyachy (described in this chapter's epigraph) has long served as the dominant image of peasant resistance to collectivization. Spurred on by rumor and example, peasants were said to have engaged in a nationwide bacchanalia, killing off their livestock and gorging themselves in an irrational and spontaneous display of massive panic and destruction. Their response to collectivization was supposedly an explosive demonstration of peasant *buntarstvo*, or elemental rebelliousness: They blindly destroyed, slaughtered, and massacred, all without the least thought of their own economic self-interest or preservation. The damage to domestic animal husbandry and livestock herds was catastrophic. The state placed the blame for the massacres on the kulak and on kulak agitation that stirred the "dark" and "volatile" *muzhiki* and *baby* into a destructive fury.

The late British Marxist historian Isaac Deutscher, always a discordant voice in a literature bound by consensus, offered a different view of the massive destruction of livestock, farm implements, and other peasant properties that occurred during the height of wholesale collectivization. In a brief discussion of collectivization, he referred to that destruction as "the *muzhik's* great Luddite-like rebellion."[2] Deutscher's choice of words is very much to the point, for there was in fact a kind of peasant Luddism at work on the eve of and during the collectivization of agriculture. *Razbazarivanie*, an act of massive sabotage of the new collective farm system, was a key component in peasant Luddism. Peasants protested the injustice of a "socialization" they viewed as plunder by selling or slaughtering their animals and other properties in an attempt to preserve something of their hard-earned work in the form of cash after sales, to store up a supply of food for the likely hungry times impending, or, if nothing else, to deny Soviet power the fruits of their labor. Peasant Luddism was a rational and economically, politically, and morally justifiable response, rather than the visceral and malicious reflex of childlike peasants engaging in an orgiastic and self-defeating explosion of peasant defiance.

The official concept of *razbazarivanie*, however, served as a useful political image for the state. The literal translation of *razbazarivanie* is "squandering," and that was an apt description for the way the state sought to portray peasant Luddism. "Squandering" removed the political edge from the peasant act, thereby muting the danger and denying the profoundly subversive political nature of this aspect of peasant resistance. In the state's description, peasants engaged in a collective insanity of self-destruction, under the influence, invariably, of kulaks and other counter-revolutionary agents. *Razbazarivanie,* then, was part of a Soviet political code that turned peasants into *muzhiki* and *baby* and peasant protest into a reckless, irrational, spontaneous, and dark force of nature.

The primary reason for this element of official denial resides in the political contradiction of almost an entire peasantry engaging in an act of "kulak politics" that presented the gravest threat to socialized agriculture, the state, and the nation. *Razbazarivanie* struck a near-fatal blow to the new collective farm system. Nowhere was the damage more evident than in the catastrophic decline in livestock (Table 3–1). The massive decline in livestock continued from the time of "extraordinary measures" in grain procurements in 1928 through the famine of 1933, with the two largest downward trends occurring in 1930 and 1932, the first of which is the topic of discussion here. At the Sixteenth Party Congress in 1930, Agriculture Commissar Iakovlev reported that, in the year from March 1929 to March 1930, the number of cattle (*krupnyi rogatyi skot*) declined by one-fifth, milk cows by one-eighth, sheep by one-third, and pigs by two-fifths.[3] At the same congress, S. M. Budennyi, civil war hero and Red army leader, claimed that, in the same period, horses had declined by 14% in the RSFSR (Russian Soviet Federative Socialist Republic) alone.[4]

Budennyi also reported on the drastic decline of horses regionally. The number of horses had declined in Siberia by 24.1%, in the North Caucasus by 9.6%, in the Middle Volga by 29.7%, in the Urals by 24.1%, in the Central Black Earth Region by 10%, and in the Western Region by 8.9%. In all, according to Budennyi, there had been a loss of some *four million* horses in 1929–30.[5] Although sometimes varying slightly, other sources present a similar picture regionally. In Siberia between March 1928 and March 1930, horses declined by 26%, cattle by 42%, sheep by 43%, and pigs by 72%.[6] In the Western Region between March 1929 and March 1930, the number of horses fell by 10.8%, cattle by 46.9%, and sheep by 23.9%.[7] In Belorussia, peasants disposed of 52,000 horses in the first quarter of the economic year 1929–30; of these,

Table 3–1. Livestock Decline in the USSR, 1928–35 (in Millions)

Livestock	1928	1929	1930	1931	1932	1933	1934	1935
Horses	–	34	30.2	26.2	19.6	16.6	–	–
Cattle	70.5	67.1	52.5	47.9	40.7	38.4	42.4	49.3
Pigs	26	20.4	13.6	14.4	11.6	12.1	17.4	22.6
Sheep & Goats	146.7	147	108.8	77.7	52.1	50.2	51.9	61.1

Source: Alec Nove, *An Economic History of the USSR* (New York, 1990), p. 176; and Stalin's report to the Seventeenth Party Congress in *XVII s"ezd VKP(b). Sten. otchet* (Moscow, 1934), p. 20.

35,000 were slaughtered or sold in December alone, along with 38,000 head of cattle.[8] Already by the late fall of 1929 in the Lower Volga, a region where collectivization began earlier than in most places, the number of horses and cattle had fallen by 783,000 and sheep and goats by 2,233,000 from the spring of 1929.[9] According to an OGPU report, so many livestock had been slaughtered in the Central Black Earth Region that peasants were feeding pigs with meat.[10] The losses of livestock nationwide were unprecedented. Self-dispossession had become a national obsession and villages were emptied of entire categories of farm animals. One peasant urged his neighbors "to slaughter more quickly, for they will take everything," while another peasant reasoned, "Today [I] am alive, but tomorrow [I] don't know what will be."[11]

Razbazarivanie was a direct response to grain requisitioning and collectivization, and accelerated in many parts of the country from the summer of 1929, almost simultaneously with the attempts of regional and local authorities to forcibly quicken the pace of collectivization. As peasants responded to collectivization with *razbazarivanie*, regional and local officials responded with the first wave, uncoordinated and regionally inspired, although certainly not opposed from above, of dekulakization. Making use of the Soviet penal code, local authorities had the power to arrest, imprison, expropriate the property of, and even exile individuals guilty of "willful" destruction of livestock or agricultural inventory (Article 79) and, further, could apply Article 58 (10) for counterrevolutionary crimes in cases when "kulaks" were found guilty of spreading rumors which then inspired acts of *razbazarivanie*.[12] This first wave of dekulakization was as yet, a de facto dekulakization but it was absolutely prerequisite to the official campaign that accompanied collectivization in the winter of 1929–30. *Razbazarivanie* also had the effect locally of accelerating the pace of collectivization and especially the socialization of livestock and other peasant properties as officials tried to head off further *razbazarivanie*. It was in the second half of 1929 that regional and local authorities "learned" how to deal with *razbazarivanie* by dekulakizing according to ambiguous, locally determined norms that extended the victims of this process far beyond actual kulaks.

The central response to *razbazarivanie* came somewhat later. *Kolkhoztsentr* issued a decree on 10 December 1929 suggesting that local organs in districts of wholesale collectivization socialize 100% of the draft animals, 80% of the pigs, and 60% of the sheep.[13] The decree, which was never directly endorsed by the Politburo, was a wildly radical response to *razbazarivanie*. Interestingly enough, this decree was issued *before* the December 1929 Politburo commission on collectivization completed its work. The decree, however, appears to have been taken seriously by some regional authorities, who in many cases had been making use of extensive socialization to deal with *razbazarivanie* since the summer of 1929. The *Kolkhoztsentr* decree was repeated in a Western regional party committee resolution of 7 January 1930 and may have been seconded by other re-

gional authorities as well.[14] Stalin had removed warnings about the degree
of socialization within the collective farms from the draft decree on collectivization submitted to him by the December Politburo commission.[15] The
5 January 1930 decree on collectivization ("On the Tempos of Collectivization and Measures of State Aid to Collective Farm Construction")[16]
then left local authorities on their own to work out the degree of socialization and, by implication, the problem of *razbazarivanie.*

As collectivization and dekulakization accelerated further in late 1929
and early 1930, so too did *razbazarivanie.* State policy and peasant response proved to be mutually reinforcing. From (at least) January, the
collectivization campaign had gone beyond the control of Moscow. Initially, this process was not at all unsatisfactory to the center, but the
consequences of the resulting mayhem became more apparent with increasing news of *razbazarivanie* and other peasant disorders. From mid-
January, the center initiated a process wherein it attempted to regain control of collectivization and dekulakization without yet slowing tempos. It
would admit failure only in early March 1930, when Stalin issued the call
for a temporary retreat.[17] In the meantime, on 15 January 1930, a new
commission was established, under the supervision of Molotov, to draw
up legislation on dekulakization.[18] From this commission was issued in
late January and early February the *only* central decrees and instructions
explicitly enacting dekulakization into law. That is, for the first time, the
center issued orders on procedures for the implementation of dekulakization, as well as articulating formally and in detail the campaign as *policy.*[19] At about the same time that the Molotov commission was appointed
to put together legislation, several key laws were published on *razbazarivanie.* The timing could hardly have been coincidental. The central government issued a decree on 16 January 1930 titled "On Measures to
Struggle with the Destructive Squandering of Livestock," and the Russian
republican government issued a similar decree of the same date, extending
the law to the *razbazarivanie* of agricultural inventory as well as livestock. Both decrees placed the blame for *razbazarivanie* on the kulak and
his agitation, which, many lamented, was far superior to Soviet agitation
at this point. The decrees included stiff penalties for "kulaks" guilty of
razbazarivanie, penalties ranging from deprivation of the right to use land
to confiscation of property to exile for up to two years. According to the
central decree, farms that squandered livestock before entering the collective farm could not be admitted or, if already in the farms, were to be
expelled. The Russian decree was somewhat more lenient, offering such
farms the chance to remain within the collectives if they could come up
with the cash value of their squandered properties. Finally, a general order
forbidding the destruction of all young animals was included.[20] That last
point was generalized in Siberia on 27 January 1930, when a temporary
ban was imposed by regional authorities on the slaughter of *all* livestock
in rural areas, a ban that reinforced a 1929 decree designed to prevent the

export of livestock products from the region.[21] The central government issued a decree on 21 February 1930 forbidding such arbitrary restrictions on interregional trade, but by 1 November 1930 had widened its own ban on the slaughter of young animals to include a ban on the slaughter of a number of different kinds of adult livestock.[22]

The local response to *razbazarivanie* was to increase the tempos of collectivization, socialization, and dekulakization. That had always been the case, but the clear articulation of central policies on collectivization and dekulakization in January raised the stakes. Many regional party authorities appear to have reacted negatively to the center's decrees on collectivization and especially dekulakization, arguing that *too much* time was allowed for the implementation of the campaigns. The elapsed time between the announcement and the implementation of policy would simply open the way for further *razbazarivanie*, self-dekulakization, and even flight, according to these regional authorities. Ever since mid-December, before the central decrees had been issued, Vareikis, Central Black Earth regional party committee first secretary, had been calling for a shortening of the "transition period" to lessen the damage to livestock and property.[23] In a speech on 9 January 1930, A. A. Andreev, first secretary of the North Caucasus regional party committee, also called for accelerating the socialization of livestock to offset *razbazarivanie*, although he did caution that it was "not correct at the given stage" to socialize homes, gardens, and poultry.[24] At a meeting of the Lower Volga regional party committee in late January, local party representatives again argued against what they saw as "a rather lengthy period" for the implementation of dekulakization, claiming that this amount of time would present "kulaks" with the opportunity to squander their property and leave.[25] A *Pravda* correspondent captured the mood of officials in Ialtinskii *raion* in the Crimea in early 1930 in the following paraphrase: "Why do we need to wait for the decrees from meetings of *batraks*, poor and middle peasants—[we] need to hurry, otherwise [we] will be late. It's better to take property by means of the 'mauser'."[26] And, according to a Central Committee report from early January, the local "method" of guarding livestock from *razbazarivanie* followed "mainly along lines of socializing it."[27]

The continuous acceleration of tempos, however, failed to stem the tide of *razbazarivanie* and other acts of peasant resistance. Instead, the campaign flew off the tracks, as state repression and peasant resistance continued to feed off each other, escalating the conflict into what Moscow saw as a dangerous confrontation. By early March 1930, Stalin was forced to call a retreat to the campaign, a retreat in which the center would abnegate its own responsibility for atrocities and blame them all on regional and local officials. The dynamic of collectivization and dekulakization in the second half of 1929 and first two months of 1930 was based on the interplay between peasant resistance, local and regional responses, and central initiatives and reactions. *Razbazarivanie* played a central, but unintended, role in pushing collectivization forward, although it must not be forgotten that the entire process grew out of the wider context of the generalized barbarism of Stalin's revolution.

Peasant Luddism had its own context. It arose as a response to the state's agricultural policies and originated in the grain procurement crisis of the late 1920s. Stalin had characterized that crisis as "sabotage" and, in a sense, he was correct.[28] Peasants cut back on the amount of grain they marketed and eventually even their sown acreage as a rational economic response to grossly disadvantageous state pricing policies and market forces. Some peasants adapted to changed economic conditions by transforming their grain into *samogon* (home-brew) or turning their attention to livestock products, both of which were more profitable endeavors for peasant families at that time.[29] The state's response was to return to civil war styles and practices with the imposition of forced grain requisitioning. As the state implemented these "extraordinary measures," the conflict escalated, eventually driving the market out of Soviet agriculture altogether and replacing it with a centralized and coercive administrative-command system of economics.

The main object of *razbazarivanie* was livestock, the most easily liquefied asset in many peasant farms. Throughout the countryside, crop failure, harsh grain requisitioning, and the consequent damage to fodder stocks had already led to a decline in livestock by the time collectivization began, as peasants found that they could no longer feed their livestock and attempted to preserve what they could of their grain reserves for the economic preservation of their farms and their families' subsistence.[30] According to Iakovlev, in 1929 the main areas so affected were Crimea, Urals, and parts of the North Caucasus and Volga regions.[31] Although grain and, of consequence, fodder shortages continued to play a role in *razbazarivanie* through the collectivization era and especially from 1931 on, when signs of famine became more prevalent, the primary impetus to the widespread *razbazarivanie* of 1929–30 was collectivization.[32] Peasants resisted collectivization and all it brought by slaughtering or selling their livestock and sometimes other properties before entering the collective farm.[33] In some cases, they attempted to justify their actions by reference to the oft-repeated official promises of the coming "tractorization" of the countryside. Whether in earnest or dissembling as *muzhiki*, peasants claimed horses and other draft animals would no longer be necessary with the advent of the tractor. A Rostov peasant wrote Budennyi that he believed that if his collective farm had horses they would get no tractors, but "if there are no horses, [the government] will give tractors."[34] According to the OGPU, some local cadres indirectly encouraged *razbazarivanie* by making false promises about the advent of tractors, which led peasants to reason, "What do I need with a horse, [we] will receive a tractor and all the same there is not enough hay."[35] Ukrainian peasants summed up the matter more directly: "In the collective, livestock are not necessary. There Sovvlast' [Soviet power] will work the land with tractors. If [you] don't sell the livestock now, it will be confiscated in the collective." [36] In fact, in areas of the North Caucasus serviced by the state machine-tractor stations (MTS), the decline in livestock herds was especially acute; here approximately 50% of livestock was "squandered." [37] Perhaps in reaction to this purported misunderstanding, the state took special care to keep secret plans for providing 20,000 tractors to districts of wholesale collectivization. In minutes of the Politburo commission on collectivization, which treated any number of highly sensitive issues, the discussion on tractors was set off from the rest of the proceedings in a separate section labeled "top secret." [38] Budennyi, for one, gave the appearance of accepting the *muzhik* rationale for *razbazarivanie*. At the Sixteenth Party Congress, he said, "Unfortunately, our farmers reckon in the following way: if he receives, say, 120 horse power in a tractor, then it is necessary to eliminate 120 horses from the face of the earth." At this point, there was an interjection from the audience: "As a class." Amid laughter in the hall, Budennyi responded, "Yes, destroy the horse as a class." [39] The episode is revealing as an example of Communist humor, Sixteenth Party Congress style, and as a demonstration of the (at least) official image of the dumb *muzhiki* killing off livestock in hope of tractors. Whether this response was in paternalistic earnest or was simply representative of a public face hiding a politically unacceptable antipeasant hatred is debatable and perhaps beside the point. What is clear is that whether or not state and peasant believed in this rationale, both tacitly seized upon it as one of several politically convenient explanations for the mass rebellion that was *razbazarivanie*.

The fact of the matter is that peasants would sooner kill or sell their livestock than turn it over to the collective farm. As one old peasant put it in the summer of 1930, "One thing at least we have now learned . . . and that is not to keep more than one cow or horse and at most only two pigs and a few sheep." [40] This sentiment was echoed by another peasant who said, "It's all the same—soon everything we own will be socialized. It's better now to slaughter and sell the livestock than to let it remain." [41] The more precise motivations of peasants can only be surmised. Surely some saw the issue as one of ownership, pride, and justice: what's mine is mine. As one peasant put it: "[We] must hurry to sell the livestock, because all the same the livestock will go to the collective and will not be ours." [42] Ukrainian peasants from Khar'kovskii *okrug* declared: "We will not enter the collective because [we] know our property will be used by the poor. Better that we, in an organized way, destroy our horses, burn our property, than give it to those sluggards." [43] Some feared a fate worse than socialization: arbitrary dekulakization stemming from the possession of what some urban official might consider a kulak quantity of livestock. Others knew or anticipated, correctly in the event, that the new collective farm would not be able to properly care for their livestock. In the Central Black Earth, regional authorities wisely, although belatedly, anticipated this concern and in a 14 February 1930 decree ruled that "socialized" livestock should remain in the care of former owners in cases when the collective farm could not provide adequate care.[44] This response, incidentally, was just one of many instances of regional and local authorities adapting to peasant needs, or learning to play the game. In some cases, peasant concern for the upkeep of their animals was not only based on rational economic calculation and foresight, but also, and especially in cases concerning the family horse or cow, love for a cherished animal. In his memoirs, wartime defector Peter Pirogov captured this sentiment. "Zorka" was the family's favorite horse. Peter's uncle had raised and trained the horse with special care. The family doted on it and treated Zorka as a pet—according to Pirogov, as a member of the family. When Zorka was socialized, she was neglected and, in fact, brutally mistreated by collective farm officials who, according to Pirogov, did so intentionally, realizing the pain these actions caused the family. The horse soon died, and when it did, the family repossessed Zorka over the objections of the collective farm administration. The family insisted on burying the horse. Their friends joined with them to prevent the collective farm officials from re-expropriating Zorka, and even attended the burial, which turned out to be as much a demonstration of love for Zorka as of the family's dignity.[45]

Peasants also engaged in *razbazarivanie* as a matter of economic calculation. Livestock was an asset that could be liquefied, and many peasants reasoned that if they were going to lose everything anyway, they might as well enter the collective farm with cash in hand. This response served as an insurance policy and a way to keep what was rightfully theirs.[46] Further, according to several official reports in late 1930, some peasants sold their livestock, especially draft animals, as a way to avoid cartage obligations imposed upon them by the state.[47] The dominant image of peasants slaughtering and eating their livestock obscures the equally widespread phenomenon of livestock sale. The Soviet countryside became one huge peasant market in livestock, meat, and hides in 1929–30. Following a tour of the provinces, Tataev, a member of a Politburo commission on the sale of peasant horses, claimed, "In all the districts where I was, at the communal dining halls they sell all meat dishes; moreover the portions are large."[48] Livestock prices plummeted as the market became glutted. In the Kuban, where horses normally sold for 80 to 100 rubles, the going price fell to 20 rubles by early January 1930.[49] In Kuban and the Stavropol area, the prices for cows fell on average five times.[50] In Terskii *okrug* in the North Caucasus, according to the OGPU, the bazaars were "bursting" with livestock in late December 1929; here a work horse cost 10 to 15 rubles and a cow 10 to 20 rubles.[51] At the Voskresenskii bazaar in the Moscow region, cows cost 200 to 250 rubles and horses 175 to 200 rubles in October 1929; by early January, the price for cows was 125 to 150 rubles and for horses, 25 to 30 rubles.[52] In the Kimry bazaar, also in the Moscow region, by early 1930, 400 to 500 cattle were going on sale, compared to the usual 40 to 50.[53] By early 1931, in parts of Nizhegorodskii *krai* market prices for livestock had plummeted to pre-World War One levels, notwithstanding the decline in the value of the ruble.[54] The fall in prices made repressive state fines and levies almost worthless. The *piatikratka*, a fine worth five times the market price of some designated piece of property, was levied against households that were tardy in tax payments, guilty of "squandering" property, or accused of hiding grain. It was a routine punishment for peasant households charged with violating Article 61 of the penal code for refusing to fulfill state requirements (such as requisitioning). In Siberia in mid-January 1930, authorities claimed that the *piatikratka* had lost its effectiveness due to the fall in market prices. It therefore became necessary for the Siberian authorities to apply stronger measures, such as forced labor and deportation.[55] *Razbazarivanie*, once again, fed directly into the escalation of state repression.

Peasants were also harmed by falling prices. Some, in fact, chose subterfuge over sale in their engagement with *razbazarivanie*. Reports from several parts of the country pointed out that peasants were allowing livestock to starve to death and then attempting to collect insurance premiums. Since the premiums had not been fully adjusted to reflect the current and wildly fluctuating market prices, peasants stood to gain. In Chapaevskii *raion*, in the Middle Volga, there were 360 cases of peasants attempting to collect insurance at four to five times the market price.[56] Similar reports of insurance fraud came out of the North Caucasus.[57] Here was a classic example of peasants working the system to maximum benefit as they attempted to resist their fate in the collective farm.

Livestock was not the only peasant property to be "squandered." Cases of machine-breaking were reported throughout the country. In a village in Kramatorskii *raion*, Artemovskii *okrug*, Ukraine, "kulaks" reportedly broke up machinery they had recently acquired for use in what the authorities labeled a "false collective farm" (*lzhekolkhoz*) and that was designated for expropriation.[58] There were also reports of machine-breaking in Siberia, Middle Volga, Kuban, and North Caucasus in 1929 and 1930.[59] A *Sovkhoztsentr* (the agency in charge of state farms) report of February 1930 claimed that there were cases of "kulaks" throwing stones and metal into machinery in the state farms.[60] Officials described these cases as conscious "wrecking" and "sabotage" rather than the result of mistakes, neglect, or ignorance about technology. It is possible and indeed probable that much machine-breaking during collectivization was the result of the latter. Officials, after all, were blinded by a mentality of sabotage and omnipresent enemies and defined problems accordingly. However, some part of the machine-breaking of the First Five-Year Plan period must surely have derived from intentional vandalism. This was likely the case when peasants destroyed their own machinery rather than allow it to be expropriated by the state for use in the collective farms. Although motivations are seldom clear-cut in the peasant world of politics, the results of peasant Luddism speak too loudly to dismiss a certain

amount of politically inspired sabotage of machinery. Machinery, moreover, was the ultimate symbol of the new order and, as such, a blow
against a machine was a blow against Soviet power.

Razbazarivanie involved other property in addition to livestock and
agricultural machinery. In a Urals village that surely reflected the experience of many other villages, peasants sold their grain, clothes, and even
cooking utensils before entering the collective farm.[61] In Kuznetskii *okrug*
in Siberia in late 1929, peasants destroyed some 148,000 beehives rather
than allow the collective farms to take them over. Peasants in the Kuban
destroyed fruit orchards.[62] Other peasants cut back on their sown acreage.
This response began in 1928 with the imposition of extraordinary measures. In the Lower Volga, for instance, by the fall of 1929, "kulaks" had
cut their sown acreage by 10% to 20% on average, with some households
cutting back by as much as 30% to 35%.[63] In mid-January 1930, *Traktor-
otsentr* (the agency in charge of the machine-tractor station network) sent
an urgent memorandum to the Commissariat of Agriculture and other
agricultural agencies notifying them that in many districts of wholesale
collectivization peasant households were destroying (through sale or consumption) seed reserves designated for spring sowing before joining the
collective farm, supposedly in the hope of receiving seed from the government. The memorandum labeled this phenomenon "alarming."[64] In some
places, grain was diverted to the production of *samogon*. Already in February 1928, no less than 16,000 Siberian producers of *samogon* faced stiff
state fines.[65] Although the practice was illegal, peasants continued to produce *samogon* well into the collectivization period. Maurice Hindus que-
ried peasants about the prevalence of *samogon* in the summer of 1930:
"In reply to my question as to how they dared make it in the face of the
existing ban, they laughed and assured me that as long as fields and
swamps were endless, the Soviets could not see everything."[66]

And indeed the Soviets could not see everything, or they could choose
not to see everything. The very use of the word *razbazarivanie* implied a
blindness, at least officially, to the politics of the confrontation. And as
much as the state tried to pin the blame for *razbazarivanie* on the kulak,
it was clear that *razbazarivanie* was an all-peasant national rebellion. *Razbazarivanie* was the most basic and widespread peasant response to collectivization, but it did not end in 1929–30. In 1931, 7.4% of all collective
farms experienced some incident of *razbazarivanie*, whether by intention
or neglect, and 35.1% of all collective farms had one or more episodes of
machine-breaking, again, whether by intention or not.[67] In 1932, a second
massive wave of *razbazarivanie* swept through the countryside in response to famine, a new campaign to socialize livestock, and a temporary
central thaw in politics that led to the opening of limited collective farm
markets.[68] The 1929–30 episode in *razbazarivanie*, though, was distinctive: peasants entered the collective farm, but they did so at the costs of
its ruin.

The nationwide scale and gravity of *razbazarivanie* testify to its political implications and impact. Its short- and long-term influence on the further evolution of socialized agriculture was more profound than any other act of peasant resistance in the immediate years of wholesale collectivization. In the short term, *razbazarivanie* pushed the state into a dangerous and ultimately self-defeating escalation of collectivization and dekulakization tempos. In the long term, the state succeeded in accomplishing its goals of mass collectivization and dekulakization, at an enormous price. The massive destruction of livestock in 1929–30 drastically impeded the development of socialized agriculture and livestock. Both state and peasantry would suffer the tremendous consequences of such destruction. Despite the cost, however, the peasantry had acted as a class, defending its interests in this contest of cultures. The profound political implications of this solidarity and this level of destruction explain why the state chose to characterize peasant Luddism in the manner of Sholokhov's orgiastic peasants.

"Now the kulak will have to be careful to liquidate his farm in time"

Samoraskulachivanie, or self-dekulakization, was a state label applied to peasants who sought by way of socioeconomic self-transformation to escape the repression aimed at the kulak. Most often, this transformation involved *razbazarivanie* and flight from the countryside. The official use of the word "self-dekulakization" reflected a sadistic irony regarding the desperate plight of entire categories of rural inhabitants who faced cultural extinction. The state chose to portray self-dekulakization as a form of voluntary dekulakization rather than the extreme act of resistance it was. Further, the term implied a typically senseless and wild *muzhik* response shaped by "squandering," deceit, and subterfuge. Self-dekulakization, however, occurred on such a massive scale that it was anything but wild or spontaneous. Instead, self-dekulakization was a calculated economic, social, and political response that manifested itself from as early as 1927–28, when the state first began to apply pressure on the kulak and to exact a tribute from the peasantry. Peasant families facing the excessive tax demands of the state self-dekulakized in an effort to pay off their taxes with the proceeds of sales or to change their socioeconomic status and consequently their tax status. As state pressure intensified and economic repression was replaced by political repression, peasant families with the kulak stigma found themselves confronting a choice between suffering the state's repression or self-dekulakizing to save themselves. Since self-dekulakization often meant, in essence, "self-depeasantization," these families made the ultimate statement of resistance.

The dynamics of self-dekulakization were dramatic and clear. Self-dekulakization impacted heavily on the number of state-defined kulak households in the country. According to official statistics, in the RSFSR, the number of kulak farms declined from 3.9% of the peasant population in 1927 to 2.2% in 1929; in Ukraine, the decline was from 3.8% to 1.4%.[69] According to Lewin, kulaks reduced their sown acreage by at least 40% between 1927 and 1929.[70] In the RSFSR in these years, there was a decline of some 30% to 40% in kulak ownership of the "means of production" (e.g., agricultural tools and machinery).[71] By late 1929 and early 1930, kulak farms had sold 60% to 70% of their livestock and up to 50% of their agricultural machinery in many parts of the country.[72] The weight of the gross output of kulak farms in grain-producing regions declined from 10.2% in 1927 to 5.8% in 1929.[73] Regional data further illuminates these dangerous trends. In the Middle Volga, for example, the percentage of kulak households among the peasantry fell from 5.9% in 1927 to 4.8% in 1929.[74] In Siberia, kulak farms cut back on sown acreage by 12.2% between 1927 and 1929. The percentage of draft animals and cattle in Siberian kulak households declined in these same years by 24.2% and 27.9%, respectively.[75] These statistics are particularly revealing when one considers that these drastic measures occurred *before* the winter collectivization and dekulakization campaigns of 1929–30. Peasants labeled kulaks self-dekulakized in response to the oppressive burdens of taxation (which aimed at a de facto dekulakization), grain levies, and fines and penalties for failure to pay taxes or fulfill grain levies.

The self-dekulakization that occurred prior to wholesale collectivization left relatively few bona fide kulak farms in the countryside by 1929–30. This fact, if no other, makes it abundantly clear that dekulakization struck far beyond the kulak. As a consequence, it is likely that not only kulaks self-dekulakized. Peasant self-dekulakization continued at dramatic rates during collectivization, revealing its true face as self-depeasantization. According to Russian estimates, some 200,000 to 250,000 families self-dekulakized during these years. In other words, some one million people altered their status as peasants in order to free themselves from state repression. Most of them fled to cities and industrial centers, leaving agriculture forever.[76] In addition to this quarter million self-dekulakized, countless others who were actually dekulakized by the state but not deported eventually melted away into the cities. In Siberia, according to data on twelve *okrugs*, no less than 4,000 farms self-dekulakized in 1929–30.[77] Although self-dekulakization probably occurred most often by family or clusters of families, it could be as radical as the near depopulation of a village. That is what happened, for instance, in the village of Bugria in Novosibirskii *okrug*, Siberia, where 300 of the village's 400 households liquidated their farms and fled in January 1930.[78] Peasants everywhere lived in fear of dekulakization, and it is likely that the sentiment expressed by an Odessa area peasant resonated throughout the villages: "First the kulaks were those with 4–5 horses and 5–6 cows, but now kulaks are those with 2 horses and 2 cows. Now the kulak will have to be careful to liquidate his farm in time."[79]

Various kinds of *razbazarivanie* were common methods of self-dekulakization. Threatened with the kulak label, peasants destroyed or sold off their properties. Sown acreage was reduced and agricultural inventory sold. In Astrakhan, the *okrug* commission on dekulakization reported that kulaks were even using the post office to self-dekulakize, through mass mailings of cash and other goods to friends and relatives in other parts of the country.[80] In some cases, kulaks attempted to sell their farms even though land sales were illegal, a direct violation of the law on the nationalization of land. Therefore, the usual subterfuge was to sell (legally) the house and other buildings on the land as a ruse for the actual sale of the farm. In other cases, land sales could be disguised as long-term rentals.[81] Despite the reality that buyers were a scarce resource at this time, there is still some evidence from Soviet legal journals to indicate that illegal land sales may have been increasing at the end of the 1920s.[82] In a study of 633 cases of illegal land sales, rentals, and exchanges in 1929, it was reported that 12.5% of these transactions were directly linked to attempts to lessen the burden of the tax on kulak farms.[83] In late 1929, in Rzhaksinskii *raion*, Tambovskii *okrug*, Central Black Earth Region, several kulaks reportedly sold their homes with the permission of the *raion* soviet executive committee; one family sold its house for 7,500 rubles and another for 4,500 rubles, 1,000 rubles of which reverted to the executive committee as a "fine." In B. Inisol'skii *raion*, Stalinskii *okrug*, Lower Volga, the *raion* soviet executive committee itself paid a kulak family 4,500 rubles for its home. Elsewhere, official sources reported cases of collective farms buying homes and other buildings from kulaks.[84] The exact number of land sales is probably impossible to gauge given the usual practice of disguising such transactions through the sale of buildings on the property and the generally illegal nature of these sales. Doubtless there were many peasants who tried to leave the countryside through this route while it was still possible to leave without total economic ruin.

Another form of self-dekulakization, or perhaps semi-self-dekulakization, was to split the family farm. *Razdely*, or household partitions, were a stratagem employed to decrease the economic might of a farm or, at the very least, to save some portion of the farm or family by dividing the farm among sons. Cases of kulak *razdely* were already reported in 1928–29 during the tax campaigns; many of the *razdely* were purely formal, remaining paper fabrications for tax purposes.[85] Information on *razdely* is difficult to come by and one suspects that many families may have attempted *razdely* but were refused permission by local officials. At the end of January 1930, for instance, the Central Black Earth Regional court ordered the immediate cessation of registrations of peasant *razdely*.[86] Cases of *razdely* were, however, reported in the Leningrad Region and North Caucasus at this time.[87] The case of the Anukhin family *razdel* illustrates, to some extent, the use of *razdel* as stratagem. In 1930, this family was dekulakized and deported. Before that, however, they had managed to split up the household and spin off a small farm for one of the sons and his family. For the time being, the son was spared the fate of his parents and even managed to join the collective farm by 1931 as a bursar. The son never ceased in his efforts to secure his family's return. His selfless efforts on their behalf doubtless contributed in some way to his being charged in 1934 with wrecking and consequently receiving a twenty-year prison term.[88] The OGPU reported in early 1931 that the practice of fictive *razdely* continued in many parts of the country, as "kulaks" divided up their property among relatives and friends "for the time being."[89]

By far the most prevalent method of self-dekulakization was flight, an age-old stratagem of peasantries faced with oppression. Peasants labeled as kulaks fled before, during, and after the state's dekulakization campaign. Most fled in the dead of night.[90] Some fled after expropriation but before the state managed to deport them or, in the case of kulaks not subject to deportation, in the months following expropriation, as a way to escape from the economic dekulakization of exorbitant taxation. Some one million strong, the self-dekulakized generally joined and became indistinguishable from the great First Five-Year Plan period peasant migration to the cities. In the years of wholesale collectivization alone, some 9.5 million peasants moved permanently to the cities, most of them (83%) young males of working age.[91] In the Middle Volga, approximately one-fifth (or almost 6,000) of all kulaks fled during dekulakization.[92] In the Western Region, kulaks were reportedly fleeing east (to Moscow, Urals, and Siberia) after selling off their properties, leaving what belongings they could with friends and relatives, or simply abandoning them. In Velikie Lukii *okrug*, 50 kulaks scheduled for dekulakization by the OGPU fled.[93] According to data on 17 *okrugs* in Siberia, 3,600 kulak families and 4,600 kulaks without families fled in late 1929 and early 1930. In Omskii *okrug* alone, 1,000 kulaks fled without their families in the first quarter of 1930. According to data on 13 Siberian *okrugs*, 4,900 kulaks arrived in the *okrug's* cities in the first three months of 1930.[94] The OGPU reported a continuous flow of kulaks out of the countryside in the North Caucasus, especially from the Kuban,[95] and a Commissariat of Agriculture report on Zatabol'skii *raion*, Kustanaiskii *okrug*, Kazakhstan in April 1930, spoke of mass flight, noting that in some villages as many as 40% of the population had fled.[96] On a more human scale, Solonovka village in Volchikhinskii *raion*, Slavgorodskii *okrug*, Siberia, lost 127 of its 548 families between May 1929 and February 1930 due to the fears and realities of state repression.[97] An early 1930 report on Moscow Region noted in alarm that kulak heads of households had "disappeared." The report's author went on to say that family members of the departed peasants responded simply and uncooperatively to queries about a household head's fate with, "[He] went off somewhere."[98]

These Moscow area kulaks reportedly fled to relatives in other villages or went off on *otkhod* in search of work in the cities. According to the aforementioned report, there were "enormous family connections among Moscow area kulaks."[99] Most peasants left the village during collectivization by way of traditional *otkhod* routes rather than in some unorganized and spontaneous flight.[100] From as early as 1927, kulaks had begun entering *otkhod* in far larger numbers than previously.[101] *Otkhod* became a method of self-dekulakization by which peasants could divert part of their income into cash as well as partially self-depeasantize. In the Voronezh area, the kulaks of Mokhovatka left on *otkhod* shortly after hearing news of deportations of peasants in neighboring villages.[102] In Irkutsk *okrug*, in Siberia, kulaks reportedly fled to the gold mines, a place where many of their kind would eventually end up working involuntarily.[103] In the Central Black Earth Region, the Ivanovo Region, and the North Caucasus, peasant *otkhodniki* began giving up their land holdings in large numbers. The OGPU claimed that this practice had assumed a massive scale in the Ivanovo Region, an important area of out-migration, while Vareikis labeled the practice a "mass phenomenon" in the Central Black Earth Region.[104]

Many peasants attempted to migrate within or beyond the borders of the Soviet Union. Kulaks from Borisovskii *raion*, Omsk *okrug*, in the Far East, migrated to Kazakhstan.[105] Among what OGPU sources label antisoviet elements, in a series of *raions* in Samarskii, Ul'ianovskii, Orenburgskii, Syzranskii, and Buguruslanskii *okrugs* in the Middle Volga Region in early 1930, there was a "tendency" toward mass departures to Siberia, Central Asia, and industrial areas. In Ilenskii *raion*, Orenburgskii *okrug* alone, as many as two hundred kulak families left, selling their property for a trifle. Here kulaks reportedly persuaded many middle peasants to leave with them, telling them that "life is good there, the grass is green."[106] Peasants who fled their native regions most frequently departed for Siberia or Central Asia.[107] Others attempted to leave the country. Kulaks in Zakavkaz'ia tried to flee by crossing over the border into Persia, while Tatar peasants from Sudakskii and Karasubazarskii *raions* in the Crimea petitioned Kalinin for permission to emigrate to Turkey.[108] German, Czech, and Polish peasants were arrested in large numbers attempting to cross the border into the West, and countless numbers of German peasants and peasants of other non-Slavic ethnic backgrounds sought permission to emigrate.[109] Elsewhere, peasants labeled kulaks simply ran away and hid in the forest or hills waiting for the time when they could go home.[110] Pirogov recalled a dekulakized neighbor who lived in hiding, coming into the village for visits only at night.[111] Documents from the North Caucasus also note cases of kulaks going into hiding locally.[112] Doubtless, in these cases, there must have been some amount of village collaboration in aiding and supporting runaways and maintaining secrecy in the face of Soviet power.

The flight of kulaks was part of a larger peasant response to collectivization. Millions of peasants fled the villages during the years of collectivization, most in search of industrial work, most in fear or in opposition. Flight was one of the oldest and most natural, if perhaps most painful, responses of the Russian peasantry to the coercive incursions of state power. Peasants voted against collectivization and the regime with their feet, in the millions. The overwhelming majority of those who left were young and male.[113] The age and gender dynamics of peasant flight impacted on peasant resistance not so much by "diminishing the likelihood of active resistance"[114] as by altering its nature, resulting at times in a reversion to older, sometimes archaic, forms of protest and rebellion, as in the case of apocalyptic rumors. And the prevalence of peasant women in almost all forms of protest during and after collectivization also may have derived in part from the flight of young peasant men. Peasant flight from the village was implicitly, if not explicitly, an act of resistance that assumed massive dimensions.

Not all officially labeled kulaks opted for the drastic decision to leave the countryside forever. Some attempted to remain in place by disguising their status, or perhaps leaving on a temporary basis. In several parts of the Central Black Earth Region, kulaks reportedly were buying trade union cards from peasant union members for prices up to 2,000 rubles. With union card in hand, they then went off in search of work in neighboring *okrugs*.[115] Other peasants attempted to obtain falsified certificates attesting to their middle or poor peasant status. In Gzhatskii *raion*, Viazemskii *okrug*, in the Western Region, some village soviets provided kulaks with fictitious documents.[116] The same practice occurred in Berezovskii *raion*, Khoperskii *okrug*, in the Lower Volga, where a number of peasants in possession of false documents were found out and arrested at the *raion* railroad station.[117] It is likely that, with the right connections and the necessary fee, peasants could obtain the documentation they needed to alter their socioeconomic status.[118] Ivan Tvardovskii, brother of the poet and later editor of *Novyi mir*, Aleksander Tvardovskii, was a member of a peasant family that was expropriated and deported. Ivan not only managed to escape (several times) from exile, but was also able to forge papers and later to obtain false documents and even a genuine Soviet passport.[119]

Other peasants facing the kulak brand chose a more drastic way out that could be labeled the emigration of the soul. In the early 1990s, St. Petersburg journalist Bella Ulanovskaia visited an elderly woman—"Baba Niusha"—in the deep and remote woods of the central Russian countryside. Baba Niusha and her family lost their land in the 1930s. Her response to a life of hardship and state repression was to seek solitude and separation in the life of a hermit: "And the sadness befell me to get away from people," she explained.[120] Baba Niusha lived for many long decades in isolation and, despite her solitude, maintained keenly her hatred for the Soviet state.[121] In *The Gulag Archipelago*, Aleksandr Solzhenitsyn cited a case similar to that of Baba Niusha's solitary fortitude. He wrote that in 1950 the government came across, by chance, an entire village of Old Believers hidden away in the deep woods. The Old Believers had fled there during collectivization.[122] It is impossible to know how many peasants simply disappeared, into themselves or into the woods, during these years. However, an even more drastic kind of emigration of the soul was possible, and that was suicide. It is not clear how many peasant suicides there were in these years, but there were occasional reports of them. In a village in the Tagil'skii *okrug* in the Urals, on the eve of his dekulakization, a peasant man killed his wife and children before burning himself to death. Another kulak in the same area drowned himself in the river.[123] In Leninskii *raion*, Kimrskii *okrug*, in the Moscow Region, a middle peasant took his own life after a local Communist with whom he had quarreled forced the village's poor peasants (under threat of their own exile) to disenfranchise him. Following the search of his house, he committed suicide.[124] Merle Fainsod reported that a wave of suicides among wealthy peasant households swept the Western Region.[125] Suicide was the ultimate tragic protest against the state, a state bent on destroying entire categories of peasants and, in the process, their culture and way of life.

Self-dekulakization not only impacted fatefully upon individual peasants and their families; it was also a major economic blow to the state. Like *razbazarivanie*, self-dekulakization threatened the economic viability of the young collective farm system, which depended upon the acquisition of dispossessed kulak properties. The act of self-dekulakization also challenged the control of the center and served as a symbol of peasant defiance. The state's response to self-dekulakization was similar to its response to *razbazarivanie*: force and further dekulakization. Already by December 1929, N. Antselovich, a member of the Politburo commission on collectivization, recommended the formulation of plans for dekulakization in those areas that had not yet undergone wholesale collectivization— a recommendation contrary to the official rationale for dekulakization, which maintained that dekulakization was a necessary corollary of wholesale collectivization—noting, "It is necessary to take into account that the kulak is already reacting in all regions to our policy with *razbazarivanie* of inventory, property, and cutbacks of sown acreage."[126] By mid-January 1930, the Molotov commission's work on the kulak was informed in no small part by the need to centralize and coordinate the campaign on dekulakization in order to prevent further economic damage caused by *razbazarivanie* and self-dekulakization. On 1 February 1930, the government issued a second decree against *razbazarivanie* and flight, this time specifically aimed at kulak households.[127] The government also issued on 4 February 1930 a decree that instructed the Finance Commissariat to order all banks to immediately halt any cash transactions with kulaks in order to avoid a run on the banks.[128] In many parts of the country, regional authorities made the decision to hasten the tempos of dekulakization in order to attempt to stem the tide of self-dekulakization. In Gzhatskii *raion*, Viazemskii *okrug*, in the Western Region, local authorities concluded that self-dekulakization occurred because the implementation of dekulakization was *too slow*; here, only 83 of 156 designated kulaks remained by the time the state moved in with arrests.[129] In the Lower Volga, *raion* authorities argued that the central decrees on dekulakization provided too long a period for implementation and that this time lag allowed kulaks to sell their property and flee.[130] R. I. Eikhe, the first secretary of the Siberian party organization, made the same argument, also at the end of January 1930, calling for more rapid tempos in collectivization and dekulakization.[131] The 5 February 1930 Northern regional decree on dekulakization specifically called for a speedy implementation to avoid *razbazarivanie* and flight.[132] The 4 February 1930 Astrakhan *okrug* party committee decree on dekulakization ordered *raion* authorities to carry out dekulakization *simultaneously* in all *raion*s in a minimal amount of time to avoid self-dekulakization.[133] And in Mikushkinskii *raion*, Buguruslanskii *okrug*, in the Middle Volga, deportations began everywhere in the district precisely at 4:00 A.M.[134] By 1931 and the second round of dekulakization, the lesson was clear, as is evident in a 10 March 1931 Western regional party committee decree on dekulakization ordering expropriations and deportations to be carried out in *one day* throughout the region in order to avoid the *razbazarivanie* and self-dekulakization of the previous year.[135]

If self-dekulakization fed into the escalating madness and destruction of the state, it was nothing short of a disaster for the peasantry. Self-dekulakization led to the economic destruction of hundreds of thousands of the most vital farmers in the country. One can only imagine the pain of the decision to liquidate a farm by a family whose life had been devoted to agriculture and who had prided themselves on their successes. Some of these families eventually made lives for themselves elsewhere and even prospered in later generations, removed to the comparatively better conditions of the city. How many were psychologically destroyed we will never know, although it is likely that their fate was still far better than that of those who faced forced dekulakization by the state. Self-dekulakization represented, in a sense, a process of cultural self-destruction or self-extinction and, in that light, may be seen as a retrospective metaphor for the entirety of the state's disastrous revolution from above in the countryside.

"We have no kulaks here"

Not all kulaks managed to escape or self-dekulakize in time; most did not. More than one million peasant families—five million people, at least— were dekulakized during collectivization. Of these, a moderate estimate places the number of families deported beyond their native regions in 1930 and 1931 at 381,026.[136] The plunder and forced deportation of these households left a deep mark on the village. Peasants labeled kulaks tried desperately to be allowed to remain and even join the local collective farm. Their relatives, neighbors, and sometimes even local officials attempted to deny the existence of kulaks in their villages. When all else failed, many peasants demonstrated what was perhaps the most dignified of all measures of resistance—simple human kindness and support for their doomed neighbors—revealing through their actions the central importance of community in peasant culture.[137]

Expropriation meant ruin, and deportation was a fate worse than death to many villagers who had hardly traveled beyond the nearest market town. Hindus described an elderly peasant couple who were deported during dekulakization but subsequently "rehabilitated" thanks to the intervention of their son, a trade union member. They never fully recovered from their experience. The elderly man, Ivan Bulatov, told Hindus:

> I had never been away from this village, not any farther than the town of P——, where I would go to the fairs. I had never lived among any other people but my own . . . and of a sudden I was to part from everything and everybody I knew. With my bare hands so to speak, with only five poods of rye and a few poods of other foods, I was to journey to that cursed Kotlas way up North. O, dearest, you should have been there.

At that, both Bulatov and his wife broke down in tears remembering their ordeal.[138] Peasants tried desperately to avoid the fate of the Bulatovs.

When it became clear that dekulakization was the policy of the day, some peasants who faced the kulak's fate sought to demonstrate their loyalty to the Soviet order. Already in the summer and fall of 1929, when an experimental wholesale collectivization was underway in the Chapaevskii *raion* in the Middle Volga, official sources were reporting cases of kulaks promising to turn over all their inventory in return for the right of admission to the collective farm.[139] Another summer 1929 report, this one from Kuban, also depicted kulaks trying to join the collective farm, with one peasant promising to turn over his mill, his house, and a pair of horses.[140] Peasants who would later be classified as kulaks had already been admitted to collective farms in many parts of the country. Their collective farms were subjected to purges after November 1929. In Kungurskii *okrug* in the Urals, for example, the authorities purged collective farms of all who were considered to be kulaks. In this *okrug*, one so-called kulak, who reportedly once worked with the Whites and initially opposed collective farming, eventually took the lead in organizing his local collective. According to the report, "he left and broke down crying" when later he was expelled from the collective farm he had helped to create.[141] A peasant scheduled for dekulakization in the Crimea was quoted as saying, "I am a Soviet kulak [sic] and so I read the laws and know about dekulakization and sympathise with this business—take all my property, all my goods, but let me stay in my village."[142] In early 1930, a dekulakization brigade called on a kulak *khutor* (an independent homestead outside the village) in the Middle Volga. The brigade discovered what they described as a house built in an urban style (*po-gorodskomu*) with individual rooms, a hallway, a separate kitchen, and a dining room. In a voice of sad resignation, the owner told the brigade that he had not expected them so soon. He had hoped to prevent his ruin by giving everything to the collective farm and helping it with his own extensive knowledge of agronomy.

According to the report, he had led his farm *"po zhurnalam"* (by the book). This farmer subsequently lost everything; he was expropriated.[143] Short of bribery or self-dekulakization, officially designated kulaks soon learned that there was no way to deal with Soviet power. Negotiation and compromise were not possibilities.

Peasants, both officially designated kulaks and others, attempted to blunt the force of dekulakization by arguing that there were no kulaks in their villages. This claim was a virtual refrain through the late 1920s and the collectivization era when peasants fiercely resisted the imposition of class-based policies.[144] During collectivization, the refrain became a shield to ward off antikulak actions. The refrain was sometimes echoed by rural officials in the *sel'sovets* and even in the local party cells, who would also claim, "We have no kulaks."[145] A July 1929 report claimed that kulaks all say "we are all laborers." Villagers denied social stratification of any kind by saying, "we have neither poor peasants nor kulaks."[146] In the village of Ekaterinovka in the Don in late March 1930, peasants held a "mass meeting"—perhaps emboldened by Stalin's "Dizziness from Success"—at which six peasants (labeled *podkulachniki* in the source) called for an end to the artificial division of peasants into classes.[147] Denials of stratification and arguments for equality examplified peasant opinion on the issue of urban imposition of social categorizations. These responses were by no means spontaneous. They surely derived from a long and arduous debate among peasants, conducted around tables, at the well, and in the fields on the injustice of outsiders labeling them poor peasants or kulaks.

Denial of the kulak's existence was an implicit form of resistance, an implicit act of defense on behalf of the whole village. The defense of an individual neighbor (or neighbors) branded as a kulak was a more dramatic step, requiring an amazing degree of bravery and selflessness. Unlike forms of resistance that could be cloaked in the *muzhik* image or acts of terror that could be conducted surreptitiously, the nonviolent defense of a kulak required a peasant to step out, identify himself or herself, and speak directly to the point while risking categorization as a *podkulachnik* or worse. The point that peasants spoke to was justice, and peasant justice in the context of collectivization had become antisoviet and therefore always potentially counterrevolutionary. That danger, however, did not stop peasants from acting. For example, on one collective farm in Opochetskii *raion* in the Leningrad Region, the peasants actually voted against expelling kulaks from their collective farm.[148] Similar cases were reported in other parts of the country in these years.[149] In February 1930, the OGPU recorded that four village *skhods* in Georgia refused to support the exile of kulaks.[150] In Bulaevo and Novo-Nikitino villages in Kashirinskii *raion*, Orenburgskii *okrug*, Middle Volga, a meeting of poor peasants "point blank" refused to exile the third category of kulaks, saying "we dekulakized them, now let them stay and work with us."[151] After kulak homes were searched in the village of Karadzhi in Evpatoriiskii *raion* in

the Crimea, a meeting of poor peasants declared, "If you carry out dekulakization and exile the kulaks, then we will go together with them."[152]
At a collective farm meeting in the Kuban, one woman mustered the courage to speak on behalf of kulak children, arguing that they could be
brought up as good children and that mercy must be extended to them
when the deportations begin.[153] Following the dekulakization of their
neighbors in Stezhinskii village, Sosnovskii *raion*, Kozlovskii *okrug*, Central Black Earth Region, four thousand peasants took sacred communion
at church and some three thousand of them put on black mourning arm-
bands.[154] On the morning of 3 March 1930, in the town of Zapniarka in
Tul'chinskii *okrug* in Ukraine, the weeping relatives of arrested kulaks
about to be exiled gathered in front of the prison to bring their relatives
food, water, and money. As they were being transported to the train station for the deportation, the heads of households begged that their families be spared. In response, the authorities allowed some elderly peasants
to remain, throwing everyone else into the train cars.[155] In other cases,
peasants petitioned higher authorities on behalf of neighbors. For example, in the village Krasnoiarsk in Omskii *raion*, Western Siberia, the collective farm woman Sidorova organized a petition for what the OGPU
claimed was her relative, the kulak Paletskii whose wife was a *batrak*.
Sidorova managed to obtain twenty-five signatures.[156]

Peasants also responded with violence to the dekulakization of friends
and especially relatives. After the kulaks were torn from their homes and
replaced with poor families in Slobodskie Dubrovki in Krasno-Slobodskii
raion, Mordovskaia *oblast'*, a crowd of two hundred peasants gathered to
demand the removal of the poor peasants from the kulak homes.[157] In the
village Pavlovka in Kuchko-Elanskii *raion* in the Penza area, seventy peasants armed with rakes and pitchforks installed the dekulakized peasants in
their own homes while demanding the liquidation of the collective
farm.[158] Countless riots and acts of terror derived directly from the issue
of dekulakization and other forms of repression aimed at officially designated kulaks.[159]

Most peasants were powerless to offer any kind of overt defense to
their ill-fated neighbors as they watched in horror the nightmarish activities of the marauders. Ivan Tvardovskii remembered well the scene of his
family's expropriation. He recalled that a neighbor was forced to serve as
witness. In what must have been pained desperation of unfathomable
depths, the neighbor sat wringing his hands and quietly told the family
that he had no part of his choosing in all of this. Other neighbors provided the family with food for their forced journey.[160] When kulaks were
thrown out of their homes in Atkarskii *raion* in the Lower Volga, their
neighbors took them in.[161] In Ugodsko-Zavodskii *raion* in Moscow Region, a place where even official sources reported that the "excesses" had
been *awful*, peasants and, in some cases, collective farms provided food
and shelter for expropriated peasants. In one village in this *raion*, the
repression was apparently so unspeakably horrid that the collective farm

refused to accept property taken from kulaks.[162] The postwar émigré Fedor Belov recalled peasants boycotting the sale of expropriated property in a demonstration of quiet solidarity against the injustices.[163] Later, in the summer of 1932, peasant Tolstoyans ordered to destroy the house of an expropriated kulak simply walked away. Boris Mazurin described what happened:

> In the taiga our brigade was ordered to tear down two houses in the Shorian Tatar village of Abashevo. We got there and found out that one was the home of a dispossessed kulak. His whole family was living in the house and would not come out.
> "How can we tear it down?" we asked.
> "Just tear it down, that's all."
> "But people are living there!"
> "Tear it down!"
> Our people looked at it, stood there a while, turned around and left. They were not about to tear it down.[164]

Throughout the country, there were reports of peasants aiding dekulakized families who had suddenly found themselves without a roof over their heads, although official reports labeled such aid "pity" and consistently claimed that the kulak was politically isolated.[165]

Soviet power had, by necessity and the rules of its own perverse logic, no choice but to minimize the existence of solidarity in the villages. Admission of the truth could only negate the Communist dogma on class struggle and expose collectivization for what it was, a virtual civil war between the state and the peasantry. Those occasional reports that admitted the cohesion of villages in resistance to the state remained classified and publicly unacknowledged.[166] Official reports instead often emphasized extensive family connections within villages to explain away support for kulaks.[167] They further claimed that relatives of deported kulaks carried on extensive correspondence with the exiles, exploiting their descriptions of the horror of exile in order to gain sympathy and support.[168] There is no doubt that "family connections" were indeed important in the villages of Soviet Russia, but this fact does not consequently diminish the significance of village cohesion; on the contrary, it enhances it. Official sources also tended to describe support for kulaks as the result of "backwardness," coming especially from peasant women who were by definition perceived to be backward and apolitical. With this explanation, Soviet power simply depoliticized all such support, allowing gender (or, more accurately, female gender) to supersede class, or, from another perspective, demonstrating the classless nature of the Soviet-constructed *baba*. Finally, in the most ironic twist of all, support for kulaks could be blamed on the kulaks themselves, particularly in cases when kulaks were expropriated but not deported. According to Justice Commissar N. M. Ianson, leaving kulaks in the village allowed them to become antisoviet agitators.[169] Ianson's argument, no doubt, figured in the revised logic of the second round of dekulakization in late 1930 and early 1931, when in many regions the earlier three-scale hierarchy of kulaks was abandoned and *all* kulaks were subjected to deportation.[170]

Peasant support for neighbors who were labeled kulaks did not signify an absence of social stratification or conflict in the precollective farm village; it did not mean that all peasants were in fact equal, that there were no kulaks in the village, that there were no social or political tensions, or that some minority of peasants did not side with Soviet power. Supporting neighbors and arguing that "we are all equal" were instead a part of the public face that the peasant community presented to the outside world. During collectivization, most peasants united in solidarity against Soviet power, outsiders, and what had become an aggressively alien culture. They recognized that collectivization and dekulakization were not about class war or a *smychka* with the poor, but rather represented key elements in the state's war against the peasantry and its culture *as a whole*. A frequent rumor in the village at this time was that the repression against the kulak was just the beginning. First, they would take away the kulaks, then they would come for the middle peasants, and finally the poor would suffer the same fate.[171] At a peasant assembly in a Ukrainian village in early 1930, collectivization was said to be "the *final solution* to peasant farming." Here a peasant warned his neighbors: "You think that they, having destroyed two or three kulak farms, will stop at that—you are mistaken. All peasants are petty capitalists. Get in line and your farm will be destroyed."[172] Few peasants appear to have shared the illusions of intellectuals, who never saw themselves reflected in the face of the enemy until it was too late. Most peasants realized that all kulaks were peasants and all peasants could be considered kulaks. In the countryside, the image of the enemy never became an abstraction, and however violent and brooding the peasantry may have been, it had not succumbed to the kind of atomization bred by dogma, hatred, fear, and guilt that led some Soviet intellectuals to turn on each other and shut their doors on their neighbors in 1937. In this respect, the "kulak" was in fact a major force with which to contend.

"If we are kulaks, then all Siberia is kulak"

The tradition of complaint in the form of letters and petitions addressed to higher authorities remained strong during collectivization. Peasants wrote letters to Stalin and Kalinin, newspapers, and party and government agencies in their efforts to gain redress. They wrote their letters individually and collectively. They protested bravely, they begged humbly, and they asserted the rights of Soviet citizenship. In doing so, they drew—whether knowingly or not—on a long tradition of petition. When all else failed, and when peasants stopped short of violence, they complained. They addressed their complaints beyond the locality, to the center or, at the least, to a newspaper or regional authority. In this way, peasants attempted to use the center against a criminal or derelict local officialdom. The tradition of complaint, moreover, was ingrained not only in peasants and other Soviet citizens, but in the government as well. By the late Stalin period, the right of complaint was so thoroughly a part of this political culture, in which civil law and litigation were frequently meaningless, that there were special mailboxes in the concentration camps of the *Gulag* labeled, "To the Supreme Soviet," "To the Council of Ministers," "To the Minister of Internal Affairs," and "To the Procurator General."[173]

Even in relatively peaceful years, peasants wrote volumes of complaints. The newspaper *Krest'ianskaia gazeta*, for example, claimed to receive 35,000 letters a month in the mid-1920s. At that time, most letters concerned complaints about taxes, land reform, local officials, and problems of everyday life.[174] With the advent of collectivization, peasant letters became pleas for help against lawlessness and injustice. From late 1929 through the spring of 1930, Stalin received some 50,000 peasant letters of complaint. Kalinin, the official "all-union peasant elder" and head of the Central Executive Committee of the Soviet government, received some 85,000 letters in the same period.[175] Peasants also complained to the legal consultation offices of various "Houses of the Peasantry" (*Dom krest'ianstva*), which they may have assumed had an interest in their affairs. From 2 February to 3 March 1930, the Moscow House of the Peasantry received 2,113 complaints; from 16 February to 22 February, it received an additional 1,838; and from 11 March to 17 March, it received 1,535 complaints. In addition to the mail-in complaints, every day more than 200 peasants, about one-half of whom sought aid for matters relating to dekulakization, came in person.[176] The RSFSR Procurator was also besieged. In February 1930, he received 2,862 complaints and, in March, an additional 5,827. The Procurator said that most complaints concerned what were labeled "incorrect excesses," an oxymoron in any other context. He went on to complain that "it is difficult to consider normal those cases when peasants travel many thousands of kilometers to Moscow with complaints that could and should be resolved locally with no less success." The thrust of the Procurator's argument was that many local courts refused to handle these cases, refused to struggle against "incorrect excesses."[177]

Peasants also sought the intervention of regional authorities against the abuses of local officialdom. In Siberia, for example, peasants sent 35,400 complaint letters on "unfair dekulakization" to the party regional committee in the first half of 1930. (Of the 28,700 letters examined, 13,100 were said to be "satisfactory.")[178] In the Ivanovo Region, between January and June 1930, an average of seventy petitioners per day visited the regional procurator and an additional seventy to eighty written complaints arrived daily by post.[179] There is no doubt that other regions and regional offices were similarly besieged. There is also no doubt that many regional offices, like their local counterparts, either refused to address problems or were paralyzed into inaction by the center's radical policy vacillations in the spring of 1930. As a result, on 5 April 1930, Justice Commissar Ianson ordered the formation of "special groups of procurators and members of the court [to go] into the most unfavorable" regions with plenipotentiary powers to adjudicate complaints concerning dekulakization.[180] In the end, some petitioners were lucky enough to have their cases reviewed and dismissed. Of 46,261 families deported to the North, 35,000 submitted petitions to the review commission; 10% of the 23,000 families whose cases were actually reviewed were deemed to have been "dekulakized incorrectly" and 12.3% were categorized as "doubtful." These fortunate few returned, sometimes broken beyond repair, like Ivan Bulatov, who was quoted earlier, and generally unable to secure the return of their expropriated possessions. Many would not survive the next round of dekulakization.[181]

Complaining was a dangerous act of subversion in the eyes of some local authorities and, when it was not "in season," in the eyes of higher authorities as well. In Irkutskii *okrug* in Siberia, peasant *lishentsy* (disenfranchised people) were arrested under Article 58(11), a very serious charge of counterrevolution, for gathering signatures for a petition to send to Kalinin. Higher judicial authorities subsequently reviewed the verdict, concluding that "the kulak essence [*sic*] of these peasants is doubtful."[182] A peasant who wrote to Kalinin and gathered hundreds of peasant signatures for a petition was faced with expulsion from the collective farm. This peasant was attempting to save his father, who had been arrested by the OGPU for counterrevolutionary crimes that he supposedly committed in *1918 or 1919*.[183] In a letter written in the summer of 1929, Soviet writer Mikhail Sholokhov complained that Khoperskii *okrug* authorities in the Lower Volga were denying travel documents to peasants who wanted to go to the regional center to complain. He also wrote that the post office was forbidden to accept any peasant telegram addressed to the Central Executive Committee, over which the all-union peasant elder presided.[184] Given these obstacles, the very decision to complain constituted an act of resistance. And by the time Stalin had called for a retreat in early March 1930, local officials had reason to fear. The center, in an effort to pacify the peasantry, cynically blamed local authorities for the "mistakes" and "excesses" of the winter collectivization campaign. Peasants recognized the opportunity the retreat granted, and some took advantage of the situation by playing the part of loyal subjects petitioning the good tsar in Moscow against the corrupt acts of local officials.

Peasant letters took many forms. The majority expressed straightforward and defiant protest. Most letters concerned the use of force in collectivization, threats and intimidation from officials, and the panicked reaction of peasants. The peasants of an Eletskii *okrug* village in the Central Black Earth Region, for example, penned a collective letter to Kalinin informing him that they had joined the collective farm under compulsion. The local authorities threatened them with exile to Solovki, the dread prison islands of the North, and allowed no criticism. One peasant wrote to Kalinin that "with us, they carried out collectivization not by explanation, but by intimidation. They told the peasants who were not entering [the collective farm] that whoever did not go into the collective would be sent with the kulaks to the banks of the Amur, deprived of land . . . and also arrested."[185] In April 1930, the peasants of the village Kisel in Ostrovskii *raion*, Leningrad Region, wrote Kalinin the following letter:

> Our rural soviet chairman carried out collectivization by force. He yelled at anyone who did not agree to enter the collective farm, just like the old gendarmes. Whoever did not sign was led to the table by the arm and forced to sign. And whoever did not want to sign was told that his teeth would be knocked out and his hide pulled off.[186]

Another peasant complained that he had been arrested for publicly reading Stalin's "Dizziness from Success" to fellow peasants.[187] A group of peasants wrote a collective letter to Kalinin, telling him that they had been threatened with deportation to Solovki if they did not join the collective farm. They said that if they made any attempt to protest, they were called counterrevolutionaries. They ended their letter by asking Kalinin if it was legal to deport middle peasants.[188] Some of the most touching letters came from youngsters. One peasant boy wrote the following (unpublished) letter to the central Communist party newspaper, *Pravda*:

> We have 7 people in our family. [We] had a house, with an iron roof, one horse and a foal of one and one-half years, a two-year-old calf, five sheep, and 3 desiatinas of land.
> [We] paid 7 rubles in agricultural taxes. [They] came and took everything: the foal, calf, samovar, separator, three sheep, potatoes, beets, hay for fodder, and [they] wanted to throw us out of our home. . . .
> Five of us remain living in our village, me, 15 years old, my seven-year-old brother, 2 sisters: one, five years, the second nine months, and my mother who is 48 years old. [Another] sister lives with [other] people so as not to starve, and [another] brother ran away somewhere where [they] will feed him.
> [I] ask soviet power to defend [us].
> [They] gave our cow to one activist for 15 rubles, and after a week he sold her back to us for 75 rubles.[189]

Another fifteen-year-old peasant boy began his letter to Kalinin with "Hello Mikhail Ivanovich, how are you and how is your health?" He went on to explain that he had been expelled from school as the son of a former elder: "Mikhail Ivanovich, my father was the elder for only 3 months." Moreover, he had served as elder twenty-five years previously and had died in 1924. Both of the boy's parents were dead, and he lived with his two older brothers. Their family was refused entry into the collective farm. The boy asked: "How are we guilty, we are young, inexperienced farmers." He wrote further that they had always fulfilled their requisition quota and were middle peasants.[190]

Some peasants camouflaged their letters with traditional language and obeisances to the powers that be. Interestingly enough, letters that evoked a *muzhik* image were few in number. However, the very act of writing to Kalinin could be construed as a pro forma prostration before the "all-union peasant elder," especially if the possibility is considered that peasants may not have taken Kalinin's role as seriously as he did. His image as elder, though, was of great comfort to the leadership, which manipulated, when useful, the image of Kalinin the elder in attempts to mediate peasant anger. Mark Aleksandrov, a brave old man from a village in the Pskov area, addressed his letter to the "all-Russian *starosta* (elder)." After humbling himself sufficiently, he went on to say that the rural soviet chairman acted like a Tsarist gendarme, and ended with the following personal note: "I am an old man of 73, a poor middle peasant. . . . I have lived 13 years under Soviet power and I have not once seen such violence." [191] A group of 252 peasants from L'gov village in Brianskii *okrug* also wrote to Kalinin. Their letter was framed in very humble language and involved a discussion of the vast difficulty of arriving at conclusions, especially in regard to the issue of whether entrance to the collective farm was voluntary. They "petitioned" Kalinin about putting an end to local officials' coercion and cursing. They added, just in case Kalinin had doubts, that "we know and fully confirm the First Five-Year Plan," thus indicating a wise or wily political sensibility. They wrote further that they did "not categorically refuse the collective farm." The problem, though, was that "as we are backward [*temnye*], we need a model for [us] dark masses, what kind of rights [do we] have in the collective farm." They asked again whether entry to the collective farm was voluntary and also whether the authorities had the right to take away "our wives' home-spun cloth, looms, sackcloth, coats, etc." [192] One can almost hear the "wives" in the background demanding that the letter writer ask this and that. Alternately, one can imagine peasant men deflecting attention from themselves to their wives in an attempt to evoke sympathy or to maintain an apolitical style by accentuating the (by definition) apolitical *baba*'s complaints.

No less than those to Kalinin, peasant letters to Stalin also betrayed a naive monarchism, whether genuine or manipulated. There was always the hope that justice had survived somewhere; although, for peasants who could see, it was clearly Stalin who was responsible for collectivization. Nonetheless, letters framed in traditional and humble language served a purpose. They may have been little more than a kind of *muzhik* form letter with all sorts of stylized and ritualistic code for dealing with power, a form that peasants had been using from time immemorial to petition grandees. However, even if this was the case, peasants surely recognized not only the usefulness of the form, but the fact that this form represented a relatively safe and ostensibly apolitical way to approach Soviet power. What appears to be servility should also be viewed as a defensive shield, based on traditional peasant dissembling before the powers that be.

Many more peasants wrote their complaints in a new style, one that could be dubbed the Soviet poor peasant style. The Soviet style "form letter" for peasant complaints was, in large part, biographical, and the biographies generally followed certain sociopolitical conventions. (This is not necessarily to deny the accuracy of these biographies—for many, in fact, represented lives typical of those times—but to underscore the peasant use and manipulation of a correct class and biographical approach.) In these letters, the peasant complainants were inevitably born into poverty, frequently worked as *batraks* (migrant agricultural laborers) in their youth, usually went on to serve in the Red army during the civil war, and *always* maintained a staunch loyalty to Soviet power. Peasants understood the importance of a socially pure past, given the tendency of local officials to delve into the recent and sometimes not-so-recent past in search of suspect roots. They also were most likely aware of the fact that families with records of service in the Red army or in industry were exempt from dekulakization. So, for example, after he was officially labeled a kulak, the peasant I. M. Vaniukov wrote to *Krest'ianskaia gazeta* from his village in Siberia. He carefully listed all his property, noted clearly that his family was poor before 1917, and said that he had served in the Red army. He argued that "if we are kulaks, then all Siberia is kulak."[193] Vaniukov's conclusion was likely correct in exposing the reality behind official rhetoric. The peasant M. I. Nefedov from Khoperskii *okrug* in the Lower Volga wrote to *Krest'ianskaia gazeta* complaining that he too had been labeled a kulak. Like Vaniukov and countless others who so claimed, truthfully or not, Nefedov said he was born a poor peasant and had worked as a *batrak* between the ages of nine and twenty-two. In 1915, he was disabled in an accident. During the civil war, he and his son, he was careful to reveal, did *not* serve in the Red army (he was disabled), but both were active in Soviet governmental roles in the village. During NEP, "thanks to Soviet power," he finally managed to achieve some economic success—another common theme in these form letters. Given his past and his continued status as an invalid, Nefedov felt that he was now being punished for his achievements.[194] Another peasant wrote to Kalinin petitioning to have his tax status as a kulak reviewed. His daughter-in-law penned the letter because of his illiteracy. He, too, told of how he grew up in poverty, pulled himself up by the bootstraps, and finally achieved some success in the 1920s. Then calamity befell him when all three of his horses died and he had to hire labor to help bring in his harvest. It was, presumably, this issue which earned him the kulak status. It should be noted, though, that the death of his draft animals was indeed a calamity and that a peasant in this situation would have no choice but to hire outside help or face the loss of an entire year's work. This peasant concluded his letter by indicating that he had never failed to pay his taxes, had always fulfilled his duties to Soviet power, and—in a common variation of theme—that his *son*, Ivan, had served three years in the Red army.[195] Finally, thirty-one "poor peasants" from Balashovskii *okrug* in the Lower Volga wrote Kalinin about the refusal of local authorities to admit a fellow poor peasant to the collective farm. They described him as "an honorable laborer, from a poor family" who had worked for (and, by implication, been exploited by) a merchant before the revolution and had participated in the 1905 Revolution.[196]

Other letter writers appealed to perhaps disingenuously ascribed Soviet sensibilities concerning justice as well as class. Anna Semenova Strel'nikova wrote to Kalinin from her village in Kozlovskii *okrug* in the Central Black Earth Region. Local authorities had refused permission for her and her young children to enter the collective farm because her husband had been charged with hooliganism for his part in a drunken brawl in 1926. Strel'nikova argued that this fight was neither counterrevolutionary nor antisoviet. She hoped that Kalinin would help her family because Soviet power "is not vengeful to laborers because of an individual personality in the family but functions in the interests of the laboring peasants of the USSR."[197] Another peasant from the Leningrad Region refused to join the collective farm and consequently faced expropriation and arrest. He wrote Kalinin twice. In his first letter, he began with the obligatory "I am a poor peasant" and said he had served in the Red army, but he then went on to say, "I don't want to go into the collective farm because I want to be free [*vol'nyi*] as they say and said when we fought against the Whites [and] Petliura bands. But it's interesting what happened to the slogans of our party of the *vozhd'* [leader] Lenin." In his second letter, written about one week later, he bravely argued that "intimidation of peasants by party and soviet officials should not happen. This is the land of the soviets, and not the land of the old, dying order."[198] Both authors' letters are examples of peasants calling upon the promise and rhetoric of the established order to justify their complaints, although, especially in the second case, they may have had little real belief in the efficacy of Soviet justice.

There was one additional way in which peasant letter writers could appeal to Soviet sensibilities. They could write denunciations, a form that would be perfected in the course of the 1930s. Peasants wrote denunciations aimed mostly, although not exclusively, at local officials and collective farm leaders. They claimed frequently that the collective farm was in the hands of "aliens," a broad but useful category that usually included kulaks, traders, elders, clergy, and any variety of "counterrevolutionary."[199] Although these types of letters would appear more frequently after 1931,[200] they were already surfacing during collectivization. Peasants, like officials, understood the subjectivity of words like alien and kulak and counterrevolutionary, and could easily appropriate the terms for their own purposes. Moreover, who was to say that a collectivizer was *not* an alien?

Peasant letter writers also came in different "forms." Some letters were penned by individuals. Among these individuals, it is interesting to note the fair number of women letter writers. Given the relatively low literacy rates among peasant women, this fact is at first glance surprising.

However, given that the state perceived peasant women to be ignorant and apolitical *babas*, capable of occasional hysteria but not genuine political activity, there may be a certain logic to women putting their signatures to letters. The *baba* may have been able to speak out in ways that would have been too dangerous for her husband, father, or son. Alternately, it may simply be that women were often left behind after the "kulak" head of household was taken away and therefore of necessity and out of desperation donned the mantle of petitioner. A sizable proportion of letters were collective compositions, thereby continuing a tradition in peasant letter writing that predated the Soviets and is generally characteristic of communal peasantries. The very idea of the collective letter may simply have been "traditional"—that is, another kind of peasant "form letter." However, here too, there was an internal logic to the collective letter. Peasants must have realized the wisdom of raising their voices together, not so much in an effort to exert more power—for power was not theirs—but in an attempt to share a collective responsibility for the letter. A collective letter meant that no one person could be designated the ringleader or instigator, and there was a sense that the entire village would not be punished. It would be interesting to see if the tradition of collective letter writing continued into the famine years, for in those years entire villages were subject to wholesale repression, including deportations of entire villages.[201] Whether or not collective letter writing continued, peasants continued to write letters of protest and entreaty, attestations of Soviet citizenship, and denunciations throughout the rest of the decade.[202]

The tradition of peasant letter writing remained strong into the Soviet period for a number of reasons. As an oppressed, subordinate people, Russian peasants had long had little access to what was, to begin with, a less-than-perfect legal system. Moreover, tsars and commissars alike had propagated the myth of a direct link between the people and the leader, be it tsar-*batiushka* or *vozhd'*. Whether or not at any time in their history peasants entirely believed in this myth, it was all they had—short of turning to violent means—as a first line of self-defense against the encroachments of the very authorities to whom they appealed. Many peasants must have hoped against hope that they would receive help from above. And help from above did come just often enough to sustain the myth. Yet regardless of whether they believed, at another level, peasants wrote letters not simply as an act of desperation but as a form of *protest*, a way to speak out. Some protested directly. Others adopted a humble *muzhik* tone thought to be suitable for the lords in Moscow. And still others appropriated Soviet discourse and sensibilities for their own ends. Peasant letter writing during collectivization became an exercise in protest, adaptation, and dissembling. Peasants wrote letters to have their voice heard in a political system in which—short of the all-union elder—they had no representation. Litigation by letter was the only recourse for hundreds of thousand of peasants during collectivization, and remained throughout the Soviet period a customary and standard form of self-help.

Conclusion

Peasant Luddism, self-dekulakization, letter writing, and other self-help measures served as a first line of defense against the blows of collectivization and dekulakization. Millions of peasants attempted to alter or mask their socioeconomic status through *razbazarivanie* and self-dekulakization. In doing so, they developed to a radical extreme traditional peasant tactics of avoidance, concealment, and survival, similar in bare essentials to the age-old peasant response to census takers, tax collectors, and hardship, while at the same time transforming and adapting such tactics to meet the unprecedented challenge of collectivization. Millions of other peasants chose flight as their only means of defense, following in the tracks of generations of their forebears who had also sought to escape the centralizing powers of the state through migration or flight to the steppes. When all else failed, peasants petitioned the state for redress, protesting, making use of the myth of a benevolent central authority, or appropriating the language of their oppressors in a bid for justice.

Peasant self-help was an implicit, and sometimes explicit, protest. *Razbazarivanie*, self-dekulakization, support for kulaks, and letter writing were all forms of political expression. Each act carried with it, to a greater or lesser degree, the potential of state reprisal. When they could, peasants tried to mute the political import of their actions by playing the parts of *muzhiki* and *baby*, dissembling, or appropriating dominant modes of discourse. In this way, the *form* as well as the *content* of peasant protest derived from a culture of resistance common to Russian peasants—and, indeed, to peasants of many nations—from time immemorial.

Peasant self-help tactics often assumed a collective character. *Razbazarivanie*, self-dekulakization (at times), and letter writing could take the form of collective endeavors, uniting the village against the state and its officials. The sympathy and support shown to peasants labeled kulaks was also an expression of village cohesion, demonstrating that "peasants" and "kulaks" lived, or believed they lived, or claimed to live, in a political and cultural symbiosis in which the fate of all depended on the fate of one and the fate of one decided the fate of all. This demonstrative cohesion exposed the true nature of the state's intentions. Peasant unity of purpose both undermined and enhanced the Stalin revolution in the countryside. It undermined it by vast destruction and entrenched opposition as well as by the accelerating dynamics of the interplay between *razbazarivanie* and self-dekulakization and the ever-increasing chaos of the tempos of collectivization and dekulakization. It enhanced the Stalin revolution by allowing the state to reconstruct the social face of the peasantry according to its own perverse political logic, associating protest and kulak. In this way, the state "kulakized" the countryside and could therefore wage war on the *entire* peasantry according to the "iron laws" of history. This tendency would be further accentuated by peasant active resistance.

4

Sawed-Off Shotguns and the Red Rooster: Peasant Terror and Civil War

"Whoever enters the collective farm will be killed."
                                        —from a placard in the village Dubrovich

"A fire was bound to break out here!"

                                                                —peasant women

"Throw the Communists in the fire!"

                                                        —a peasant crowd's threat

A civil war culture was integral to the First Five-Year Plan revolution. It established the mobilization atmosphere and siege mentality so essential to Bolshevik fortress storming. It dehumanized the enemy and granted people permission to engage in acts that under normal circumstances would be defined as criminal or immoral. The policies of the Stalin revolution further enhanced this culture by pushing the enemy into a corner from which violence was frequently the only outlet. Violence fed on violence, state terror provoked and reacted to antistate terror, and a civil war mentality dominated the times.[1]

Peasant terror reflected, described, and reinforced the culture of civil war. The word "terror" was a state label and cloaked a broad, unofficial spectrum of peasant politics. Terror usually denoted murder, attempted murder, and assault and battery, but could also include arson and threats. Generally, terror consisted of acts of individual and anonymous violence most often committed by male peasants and aimed at peasant activists and local officials. It was an act of last resort, to be engaged in only when all else had failed. For urban residents, especially Communists, it brought to mind images of kulaks with sawed-off shotguns, thus amplifying the nation's siege mentality. The state diminished peasant acts of violent protest aimed at officials and activists by prefixing "terror" with "kulak," demonizing the perpetrators, and beatifying the victims. And, like other useful revolutionary buzzwords, the term "terror" was politically elastic. It could at times—and especially after 1930, when individual acts of violence were less common—mean anything the authorities deemed antisoviet or counterrevolutionary. After 1930, the label (along with sabotage, wrecking, and counterrevolution) became more useful to the regime than kulak, although the latter always retained its adjectival value.

In spite of the source and connotations of the label, "terror" is a meaningful category in the peasant politics of collectivization. Peasant terror was part of a popular culture of resistance. Like peasant apocalyptic discourse and the practices of Luddism and evasion, terror was used to overturn the existing order of things, to invert and therefore subvert power in the village by taking aim at officials and activists who served Soviet power. Some of the forms of terror and most of its content were customary. Murder and assault are generic examples of man's inhumanity; *samosud* (summary justice), arson, and threats were often specific peasant incarnations. Peasant terror was animated by justice and solidarity.[2] Although an understanding of peasant moral economy and the degree to which it was violated is apt here, the phrase seems to wilt in the context of the times. Threat and retribution are perhaps more pertinent descriptive terms for the internal logic of peasant terror. Terror was, first, a threat to any member of the community who had broken or meant to break ranks with the village collective and to any official who believed violence or injustice against the community could occur without cost. Terror was, second, a form of retribution levied against those who had helped to carry out repressive government policies against the community. As such, peasant terror served an important purpose as a form of active resistance and an instrument of village politics.

Peasant terror—or "kulak terror," as it was most often labeled in official rhetoric—was both a myth and a reality. There is no question that what qualified as terror according to official labels existed in reality. In anger or despair, peasants lashed out at their enemies to ward off further blows or to seek revenge. Neither side had a monopoly on fear. The concept of kulak terror, however, also served to support the regime myth that revolution, class war, and the onset of socialism justified repression, inhumanity, and a pervasive martial order. That it was said to exist was as important as its existence in reality. Peasant terror was a central prop in the culture of civil war of the Stalin revolution.

The scale of terror

Describing the Smolensk countryside of late 1929, Merle Fainsod wrote, "A pall of terror enveloped the villages. As reports of killings and arson multiplied, Party members were warned 'to stay away from the windows' while working in Soviet institutions and not to walk the village streets after dark."[3] The warning was reflected in the anxiety of urban plenipotentiaries like the 25,000er Sablin, who wrote from the North Caucasus that he could not go out at night because "one could expect bullets from around the corner."[4] Fear was palpable in the village of Aleksandrovka (in the Lower Volga) in late 1929, when a workers' brigade arrived to find a nearly deserted settlement; the adults had gone into hiding, leaving behind the children and a few *batraks* (agricultural laborers).[5] The threat of violence, of a sudden ambush or "bullet from around the corner," was pervasive in the countryside during collectivization.

This atmosphere of fear and violence—of terror—derived its force from multiple sources. The newspapers of the epoch howled with reports of kulak terror and martyred Communists; party and factory meetings regularly featured speakers with news from the grain front—always with the potential to become triumphantly funereal, in the event that a comrade had fallen in battle for the sake of the revolution; and the cadres of Soviet power launched a campaign of state terror in the countryside. The party leadership encouraged and maintained the atmosphere as a cover for antipeasant operations and a mobilization device designed to divert systemic grievances to contrived "enemies" and to inspire the shock troops of collectivization.

It was also in the interest of peasants to maintain an atmosphere of terror. In the best of times, it might ward off further blows from the state. In the worst of times—which were most times—it increased the potential for violence and, in the aftermath of peasant terror, brought about swift and brutal retaliation. It was a combination of rage, justice, and retribution that inspired peasants to maintain the atmosphere of terror, an atmosphere built upon a traditional web of peasant practices in threat and intimidation.

Aggregate, national statistics on terror are available from 1928 to 1930. Terrorist incidents increased dramatically from a total of 1,027 in 1928 to 9,903 in 1929 to 13,794 in 1930. Table 4–1 depicts the seasonal dynamics of terror, demonstrating the correlation between state terror and peasant terror.[6] In 1928 and 1929, the fall grain requisitioning campaigns provided the main backdrop to peasant terror; in 1930, peasant terror increased dramatically in response to both grain requisitioning in the fall and, most importantly, to collectivization. According to OGPU compilations, in 1929, 43.9% of terrorists acts were directly connected to grain requisitioning. In 1930, this percentage dropped to 10.2%, while terrorist incidents related to collectivization and dekulakization rose to 57.2% of all cases.[7] Table 4–2 presents a breakdown of the official causes of terror in 1930. Although collectivization officially accounted for the primary cause of peasant terror in 1930, it is, in fact, extremely difficult to differentiate causes of terror in this year. It is likely that terror arising from dekulakization, church closures, and other issues were most easily subsumed under the catch-all of collectivization. Further, the category "acts of activists," which ostensibly refers to "excesses" and criminal behavior, is most certainly directly or indirectly related to one or more of the state's campaigns. Even so, within each category, the seasonal dynamics of peasant terror and its relation to state terror is immediately appar-

Table 4–1. Aggregate National Statistics on Terror,
1928–30

Month	1928	1929	1930
January	21	642	808
February	48	329	1,368
March	23	351	1,895
April	31	247	2,013
May	51	546	1,219
June	43	851	796
July	77	474	762
August	76	757	928
September	103	1,167	946
October	135	1,864	1,440
November	216	1,295	954
December	203	570	665
Total	1,027	9,093	13,794

Source: Sekretno-politicheskii otdel OGPU, "Dokladnaia
zapiska o formakh i dinamike klassovoi bor'by v derevne v
1930 godu," p. 40 From *The Tragedy of the Soviet Countryside.* 5 vols. V.P. Danilov, R.T. Manning, and L. Viola,
eds. (Forthcoming).

ent, with the number of terrorist incidents arising from collectivization
and dekulakization peaking in the first third of the year, and the number
of terrorist incidents concerning requisitions rising in the months of the
fall requisitioning campaign.

The aggregate data on terror can be further broken down into its
composite elements. In 1928, there were 212 murders, and for the first ten
months of 1929 there were 353 murders.[8] Table 4–3 shows the monthly
breakdowns of different types of terror and the huge increase from earlier
years in the number of murders in 1930. As terror increased from the
late 1920s into 1930, so too did its severity. The murders of over 1,100
mainly village level officials and activists, along with over 5,000 assaults
on officials, represented an emergency of crisis proportions, sufficient to
alarm and terrorize any government, particularly one that perceived of
itself, and perhaps defined itself, as under siege and engaged in a life
or death struggle with enemies within and without.

Regional statistics further illuminate the widespread dimensions of terror. Table 4–4 depicts the OGPU's calculations of regional incidents of terror in 1930. The highest incidence of terror occurred in grain-producing
regions, regions such as Moscow and Central Black Earth where collectivization was particularly violent, and in regions with strong traditions

Table 4–2. Causes of Terror in 1930

Month	Requisitions	Tax	Collect.	Land Reform	Elections	Dekulak.	Religion	Sowing	Hunger	Acts of Activists
Jan.	86	18	384	1	2	51	13	11	–	232
Feb.	25	14	768	1	3	222	5	49	–	272
Mar.	5	6	1,234	4	1	154	12	52	–	420
Apr.	6	4	1,243	18	1	168	4	28	–	531
May	3	–	667	8	–	107	1	10	1	420
June	3	8	442	9	1	99	1	6	1	225
July	15	8	362	4	–	63	2	1	3	291
Aug.	124	6	420	7	–	52	–	–	–	309
Sept.	248	15	341	6	–	61	–	–	2	272
Oct.	422	22	450	4	1	60	–	–	1	480
Nov.	301	13	296	1	12	48	–	–	–	283
Dec.	164	10	175	3	86	19	–	–	–	208
Total	1,402	124	6,782	66	107	1,104	38	157	8	3,943

Source: "Dokladnaia zapiska o formakh i dinamike klassovoi bor'by," p. 71. Two columns from the original table (including 63 cases of terror) have been omitted: 10 cases connected to *kontraktatsiia* and 53 cases related to "*bytovoi* terror" in the East.

Table 4–3. Monthly Breakdowns of Types of Terror in 1930

Month	Total	Murder	Attempted Murder and Assault	Arson	Misc.
Jan.	808	95	439	251	23
Feb.	1,368	112	740	462	54
March	1,895	131	869	841	54
April	2,013	127	773	1,055	58
May	1,219	105	369	705	40
June	796	87	322	370	17
July	762	80	275	362	45
Aug.	928	113	282	471	62
Sept.	946	85	349	444	68
Oct.	1,440	114	540	709	77
Nov.	954	90	445	384	35
Dec.	665	59	317	271	19
Total	13,794	1,198	5,720	6,324	552

Source: "Dokladnaia zapiska o formakh i dinamike klassovoi bor'by," p. 71.

Table 4–4. Statistics on Terror per Region in 1930

Region	Incidents	Region	Incidents
Ukraine	2,779	Belorussia	533
Central Black Earth	1,088	Transcaucasus	508
Urals	977	Tatariia	421
Siberia	904	Far East	343
North Caucasus	842	Kazakhstan	332
Lower Volga	711	Central Asia	302
Moscow Region	707	Bashkiriia	291
Western Region	679	Ivanovo	285
Nizhkrai	643	Northern Region	119
Middle Volga	636	Crimea	85
Leningrad Region	609	Total	13,794

Source: "Dokladnaia zapiska o formakh i dinamike klassovoi bor'by," p. 67.

of peasant dissent, thus demonstrating a regional as well as seasonal logic to peasant terror. These regions also experienced the most widespread peasant rioting during collectivization.

Most terrorist attacks were directly linked to collectivization and de-kulakization, irrespective of region (see Table 4–5). As in the case of national statistics, the causes of large numbers of regional terrorist incidents fell under the heading of "acts of activists." This category, again, only makes sense within the context of the state's repressive campaigns, when the "acts of activists" working for the state provoked peasant violence. Finally, Table 4–6 provides a breakdown of regional terror according to type.

The statistics on terror must be approached with skepticism given the repressive context in which they were gathered and reported and, most important, the general state of chaos, fanaticism, and revolutionary obduracy characteristic of the times. The term "terror," moreover, was highly elastic, and could include different categories depending upon the observer. The most complete and detailed data was compiled by the OGPU, which presents its own set of problems. The OGPU naturally had vested interests in terror. Terror, after all, was the OGPU's specialty and presented opportunities for the "organs" to enhance their power and prestige as well as their personnel and operating capital.[9] For these reasons, even the seemingly careful and precise compilations of the OGPU should be viewed with caution.

The statistics presented here represent at best an estimate of the number of violent incidents that could be categorized as terror. Terrorist cases, it should be reemphasized, were those cases of violence aimed at local officials and village activists. The very nature of the target of the crime ensured that the state would not consider these ordinary criminal acts. An argument could be made, however, as to whether the *motives* for all terrorist crimes against the representatives of Soviet power were actually—to use Soviet terminology—terroristic, counterrevolutionary, or class based, and, if not, whether the statistics are as elastic as the labels. The Communist party regional committee in Kareliia, for example, specifically mandated that "cases of kulak incidents which are classified as criminal must be eliminated and [re]classified as political,"[10] and one suspects that other regional organizations may have passed similar resolutions. Soviet central legal authorities occasionally decried the wide and arbitrary interpretation of counterrevolutionary crimes. Too often, according to *Sovetskaia iustitsiia*, journal of the Justice Commissariat, an ordinary drinking bout turned violent was labeled counterrevolutionary in cases when an official or activist was involved. *Sovetskaia iustitsiia* further reported that violence frequently occurred during religious holidays or other events when alcohol was consumed liberally. And, in some areas, as many as 50% of terrorist cases were eventually overturned by higher courts.[11] This kind of evidence casts doubt on a certain percentage

of even those cases that were not overturned upon leaving the local jurisdiction, and is certainly a reminder of the need for caution when dealing
with Soviet statistics. On the other hand, it is important to note that
official concern for miscategorization of violent peasant crimes tended to
come only in the aftermath of major campaigns when the judicial and
penal systems were bursting with peasants and the carrot had been
brought out temporarily to replace the stick. Too many terrorist cases and
too many peasant terrorists stretched the official Marxist-Leninist line of
the Stalinist leadership well beyond the class war of rich and poor peasants, and risked allowing "kulak terror" to spread into a more political
and less counterrevolutionary "peasant resistance." It was far easier to
retreat temporarily from repression and to blame lower level officials for
stretching the counterrevolutionary label.

From the peasant perspective, it was *always* beneficial, as well as customary in dealing with officials, to attempt to disguise a crime, making it
appear as an accident, the result of drinking, or some other peasant version of "dizziness." And luring an official or detested activist into a lethal
drinking bout that resulted in a brawl or act of violence may have provided the perfect cover for a very politically inspired revenge and retribution. The OGPU recorded what it thought was just such a case in the
village of Moskovskoe in Talitskii *raion*, Tiumenskii *okrug*, Siberia, in
July 1930. According to the report, the former trader, Glazkov, with his
cronies lured the poor peasant activist, Poskotin, to his home under the
pretext of a drinking party. Once there, Glazkov provoked a fight that
ended with a knife in Poskotin's heart. The next day, Poskotin's brother
was beaten up, and activists were warned that "not one of [them would]
remain alive."[12] Whether this case represents terror disguised in peasant
dress or an OGPU obsession with counterrevolution and inability to dis-
tinguish counterrevolutionary activities from routine village feuds and
conflicts, it demonstrates well the two faces of peasant violence. The fact
remains, moreover, that drinking customarily represented some combination of peasant sociability and peasant politics, in the latter case serving
as a traditional "negotiating" lubricant for deals, conflict resolution, and
other village business and thereby making even less certain the political
essence of a drinking bout turned violent.[13] That religious holidays provided the backdrop for many acts of terror should also not surprise us.
On religious holidays, peasants reclaimed the village and placed tradition
at center stage. In this setting, state injustice and repression appeared all
the more glaring. The illusion of peasant unity and strength a holiday
(and/or the right blend of homebrew) generated may well have prompted
radical choices by desperate peasants or, at the very least, provided a traditional cover for violence.

The reality of the resistance behind what are clearly less than perfect
statistics and official categorizations is sustained by several other important factors. First, the timing of terror is crucial. Peasant terrorist inci-

Table 4–5. Causes of Terror per Region in 1930

Region	Requisitions	Tax	Collect.	Land Reform	Elections	Dekulak.	Religion	Sowing	Hunger	Acts of Activists
Ukraine	167	14	1,695	–	4	265	12	36	–	579
North Caucasus	95	1	285	2	9	57	1	15	–	148
Cen. Bl. Earth	225	2	577	1	3	66	3	5	–	206
Middle Volga	102	1	192	2	2	68	3	7	–	259
Lower Volga	69	1	261	–	1	120	–	7	1	251
Siberia	3	–	125	2	–	78	1	7	–	226
W. Sib.	53	2	1	1	8	5	–	–	–	235
E. Sib.	27	1	2	–	2	4	–	–	–	121
Urals	88	6	426	–	1	145	1	20	1	289
Moscow	97	5	445	3	23	3	4	–	1	126
Leningrad	44	21	419	–	10	28	–	–	2	82
Western	63	14	379	12	9	43	–	2	–	157

Ivanovo	24	7	132	3	2	16	1	–	–	100
Belorussia	10	–	391	3	–	29	3	–	–	97
Nizhkrai	67	14	326	9	12	35	1	1	–	178
Far East	44	2	209	3	–	23	8	–	2	52
North	9	1	60	1	–	2	–	1	1	44
Bashkir.	25	5	132	–	–	29	–	4	–	96
Tatariia	57	4	209	1	1	31	–	–	–	118
Kazakh.	65	3	113	–	3	27	–	27	–	94
Crimea	14	–	31	–	2	16	–	5	–	17
C. Asia	25	8	70	5	–	–	–	10	–	131
Transcaucasus	2	4	227	13	3	7	–	5	–	247
North Cauc. nat'l areas	27	8	75	5	12	7	–	5	–	90
Total	1,402	124	6,782	66	107	1,104	38	157	8	3,943

Source: "Dokladnaia zapiska o formakh i dinamike klassovoi bor'by," p. 73. Siberia was divided into western and eastern sectors in June 1930. This division is reflected in this table and in the tables that follow.

Table 4–6. Types of Terror per Region in 1930

Region	Total	Murder	Attempted Murder and Assault	Arson	Misc.
Ukraine	2,779	176	708	1,884	11
North Caucasus	613	50	329	223	11
Cen. Bl. Earth	1,088	93	287	700	8
Middle Volga	636	32	265	305	33
Lower Volga	711	30	288	383	10
Siberia	442	43	223	138	38
W. Sib.	305	21	147	109	28
E. Sib.	157	12	43	92	10
Urals	977	58	488	343	88
Moscow	707	26	315	311	55
Leningrad	609	29	404	141	35
Western	679	53	280	325	21
Ivanovo	285	13	144	120	8
Belorussia	533	29	140	358	6
Nizhkrai	643	54	266	317	6
Far East	343	18	166	97	62
North	119	20	57	37	5
Bashkiriia	291	44	157	80	10
Tatariia	421	32	231	113	45
Kazakhstan	332	45	217	46	24
Crimea	85	2	61	18	4
C. Asia	302	155	125	18	4
Transcaucasus	508	134	231	126	17
North Caucasus nat'l areas	229	28	148	40	13
Total	13,794	1,197	5,720	6,325	552

Source: "Dokladnaia zapiska o formakh i dinamike klassovoi bor'by," p. 73.

dents occurred in conjunction with state campaigns, rising and falling in correlation with the state's degree of involvement in the countryside and reaching a high point in the crucial year of 1930.[14] Second, the amount of terror varied regionally, with the highest number of cases occurring in key grain-producing areas, areas with strong traditions of peasant resistance, and/or areas targeted centrally or regionally for intensive socialist shock treatment. This information suggests that what was officially labeled terror and, by implication, an arbitrary, socially determined phenomenon connected to kulaks, was in fact logical in place and timing and therefore likely to be a rational, if brutal, side of the peasant politics of collectivization.

The civil war within the civil war

In November 1929, the Soviet government called attention to the "very strong resistance of kulakdom" in a decree promising aid to the victims of "kulak violence."[15] Soviet people—mainly local officials and activists— were suffering at the hands of the class enemy. Those who suffered were routinely (or ritualistically) described in the press as loyal soldiers of the revolution and Soviet power, as conscious and developed, always of humble origin, and generally with a long history of service to the state. Here was supposed proof positive for Communists that the rural class struggle was a reality.

Whether or not the rural class struggle was a reality, there is evidence to support a certain logic in the pattern of victimization wherein the main sights of the enemy were indeed trained on local officials and activists, and, in some cases, even their families.[16] That these victims came exclusively or primarily from one side of the class barricades cannot be conclusively determined. It is clear, though, that these social actors—mainly peasants—supported Soviet power and collectivization policies, and paid for their support within their own communities. They were part of what was likely a small minority of peasants who supported collectivization and who constituted the opposing side in a peasant civil war within the civil war.

Regional data provides evidence to support the conclusion that victims were primarily local officials, mainly *sel'sovet* officials, and activists. Merle Fainsod found evidence of 47 acts of terror in the Western Region in October 1929. Among the victims were 10 *sel'sovet* chairmen, 8 *sel'sovet* secretaries, 8 grain delivery officials, and 21 activists.[17] Additional data on the Western Region from the Procurator's office for all of 1929 indicated that 63% of terrorist acts were aimed against officials in the lower soviet apparatus and 37% against activists (50% of whom were collective farmers).[18] This pattern of victimization was also evident in the Central Black Earth Region in the months between August and December 1928, when some 80% of victims of terror were village activists (including *sel'sovet* members).[19] Central Black Earth data for the period of 1 May to 10 June 1929 show the following breakdown of victims: 55 lower soviet officials, 2 policemen, 1 state farm employee, 12 collective farm members, 1 *sel'kor*, 21 poor peasant activists, 8 Communists or Komsomols, and 8 cultural organization officials.[20] Although national data is scanty before 1930, a press count of murder victims in the period from 15 August to 15 October 1928 included 24 *sel'sovet* officials, 15 Communists, 6 Komsomols, and 14 *sel'kors*.[21]

Data for 1930 demonstrate further that the targets of peasant terror came primarily from the ranks of lower level officials and village activists. Table 4–7 depicts the pattern of victimization per region. This set of OGPU statistics, which adds up to the 13,794 cases noted earlier, also includes *objects* of terror. Consequently, collective farms (2,836 incidents,

Table 4–7. Victims of Terror per Region in 1930

Region	Lower Soviet Officials	Collective Farmers	Activists
Ukraine	313 (11%)	599 (22%)	952 (34%)
N. Caucasus	57 (9%)	152 (25%)	268 (44%)
Cen. Bl. Earth	226 (21%)	233 (21%)	273 (25%)
M. Volga	163 (26%)	111 (17%)	196 (31%)
L. Volga	109 (15%)	125 (18%)	262 (37%)
Siberia	91 (21%)	113 (26%)	101 (23%)
W. Siberia	57 (19%)	34 (11%)	145 (48%)
E. Siberia	14 (9%)	9 (6%)	66 (42%)
Urals	154 (16%)	235 (24%)	314 (32%)
Moscow	102 (14%)	192 (27%)	242 (34%)
Leningrad	160 (26%)	253 (42%)	121 (20%)
Western	137 (20%)	214 (32%)	162 (24%)
Ivanovo	57 (20%)	81 (28%)	89 (31%)
Belorussia	37 (7%)	200 (38%)	129 (24%)
Nizhkrai	100 (16%)	229 (36%)	198 (31%)
Far East	46 (13%)	106 (31%)	59 (17%)
North	20 (17%)	30 (25%)	38 (32%)
Bashkiriia	52 (18%)	78 (27%)	108 (37%)
Tatariia	88 (21%)	113 (27%)	136 (32%)
Kazakhstan	52 (16%)	75 (23%)	160 (48%)
Crimea	13 (15%)	16 (19%)	39 (46%)
C. Asia	36 (12%)	45 (15%)	210 (70%)
Transcaucasus	82 (16%)	123 (24%)	217 (43%)
N. Caucasus nat'l areas	48 (21%)	22 (10%)	118 (52%)
Total	2,114 (15%)	3,388 (25%)	4,603 (33%)

Source: "Dokladnaia zapiska o formakh i dinamike klassovoi bor'by," p. 72. (Percentages are rounded to the nearest whole number. Miscellaneous "victims" have been omitted; therefore, regional percentage totals are less than 100%.)

or 21% of the total) and government buildings (753 incidents, or 6% of the total) were the objects of terror in roughly one-quarter of all incidents, in these cases mostly arson and vandalism. Although there were fewer political murders after 1930, there is evidence to suggest that most victims of any type of terror in those years continued to be rural activists on the collective farm level. According to the RSFSR Supreme Court, collective farm officials (who increasingly were peasants after 1930) and collective farm activists made up the majority of victims from this time.[22] This claim is logical, if not at this point empirically verifiable, given the relatively lower profile of the *sel'sovet* with the development of strong collective farm boards.

The main targets of peasant wrath, then, tended to be people closely associated with Soviet power who resided locally. Most of these people— whether activists or *sel'sovet* officials—were peasant in social origin. Outsiders who were victims tended to be either resident plenipotentiaries, such as the 25,000ers, or resident outsiders, such as those who were part of the soviet apparatus and teaching staffs.[23] These individuals were far easier targets than the plenipotentiaries and higher level officials, who made only occasional and generally brief forays into the village and moved too quickly to be caught in a set-up other than a riot or *babii bunt*, both of which seem to have claimed lives less frequently. The early-1930s ambush murders of the Ingush regional party secretary, a North Caucasus regional party instructor, and two members of the Kabardino-Balkari regional party committee (in two separate incidents) by so-called peasant brigands in the dangerous, mountainous regions of the area were the exception rather than the rule.[24] Although the murders of these high officials fueled the fires of civil war culture, the main front was within the village and primarily pitted the peasant community against the activist peasant minority that had thrown in its lot with Soviet power.

Peasant terrorists, who represented a far broader constituency than their victims, were always described in official documents and literature as kulak terrorists whether or not they were in fact kulaks. The adjective "kulak" was much more inclusive than the noun, modifying kulaks, *podkulachniki*, traders, shop owners, all manner of *byvshie liudi*, and any temporary or permanent aberrant behavior. The kulak (almost always male) hunted down his honorable victim with sawed-off shotgun, spying from around corners and aiming sniper fire into soviet institutions or hearths. If he dressed the way political cartoons portrayed him, he was clad in a polka-dot shirt and high leather boots and was corpulent and often mustachioed.[25] His nature was "dark" (as opposed to conscious) and he had a history or family background (because class was often in practice treated as a genetic trait in the 1920s and 1930s) of exploitation of the poor. The kulak terrorist was, in short, a projection of all the evil that Communists claimed to be purging in the creation of the radiant future.

"Scientific" class analysis aside, who in fact the agents of terror were is another question entirely. Although the kulak naturally and inevitably was, at one level or another, held to be the primary culprit, his socially pernicious matter clearly leaked into other social strata, even according to Soviet sources. According to official statistics, in Siberia, kulaks constituted the lion's share of terrorists in the second half of the 1920s—between 60% and 70%, depending on the year—while middle peasants made up about one-third, and poor peasants just under one-tenth, of terrorists.[26] Contemporary legal data on the Western Region in fall 1929 indicated that about one-half of terrorists were middle peasants, peasant officials, and the well-to-do strata of the village, leaving a politically unsatisfactory (from the Soviet point of view) impression of social voluntarism that failed to conform to official ideology.[27] A similar breakdown appeared in the OGPU's 1930 data on the class composition of terrorists, which indicated that kulaks were responsible for most, but not all, of the incidents—some 54%. Middle peasants ranked second, accounting for approximately 20% of all incidents, while poor peasants, "*byvshie liudi* and antisoviet elements," criminal elements, and the socially mutable "miscellaneous" made up the roughly one-quarter remaining.[28] A regional breakdown of this data reveals that the social composition of terrorists was highly uneven, depending upon region. In certain regions, like Ukraine, North Caucasus, Moscow Region, Western Region, and Belorussia, the percentages of poor and middle peasant terrorists came close to half or more than half of the kulak terrorists (see Table 4–8). Data on social composition should be viewed with caution, given its provenance and the highly political definitions of class. The OGPU data, in particular, may well have been doctored for the benefit of its audience. Furthermore, OGPU data for 1930 pertains to only about half of all terrorist incidents, the other half remaining unsolved.[29] Despite these caveats, it is of interest that relatively high percentages of nonkulak terrorists appeared in the data. This seeming social anomaly was often qualified by noting strong family ties between terrorists and kulaks, thereby bringing forth what can only be described as a genetic notion of the basis of class.[30] Other times, the large proportion of nonkulak terrorism was explained away with the claim that the kulak organized and inspired terrorist activities, swaying the inevitably "wavering" middle peasant and duping the poor. Whatever the case, it is likely that the percentages of nonkulak participants in terror were underrepresented in the official data, given a state ideology that sought socioeconomic motivation behind all acts of opposition.

Although statistically hazy, the social composition of the agents of terror offers scant proof of rural class struggle. Although kulaks (officially) made up some 50% of all terrorists, peasants of other social categories accounted for the rest. The terrorists were, in all likelihood, peasants from all walks of life, albeit—if the official data is to be trusted at all—skewed toward the stronger peasants in the village. They were the insulted and the injured (or their friends and relatives), but only by the most arbitrary and migratory political implication were they *class* enemies. They represented the peasant's side in a civil war in which the front was the village and the shock troops an embattled and unpopular minority of local officials and peasant activists who had gone over to the other side. The contest was aptly reflected in the Soviet stock phrase "*kto-kogo*" (or, colloquially, who will beat whom), but the parties in *kto-kogo* were, on the one hand, the state, town, and rural enclaves of Soviet power and, on the other, the peasant community in the countryside, rather than socialists and capitalists, or proletarians and kulaks. Finally, the issue of who was who in this battle of victims and agents remained in the eye of the beholder.

The gender makeup of terrorists is much clearer. Most peasant terror-

Table 4–8. Agents of Terror per Region in 1930

Region	Kulaks	Middle Peasants	Poor Peasants	*Byvshie Liudi* and Antisoviet Elements	Criminal Elements	Misc.
Ukraine	1,833	636	251	42	190	557
N. Caucasus	224	112	20	18	29	86
Cen. Bl. Earth	733	156	43	26	56	63
M. Volga	361	92	27	7	9	51
L. Volga	241	53	27	9	7	73
Siberia	215	67	22	2	8	37
W. Siberia	73	50	9	10	11	32
E. Siberia	46	15	3	–	1	4
Urals	460	160	72	20	32	68
Moscow	142	100	15	4	10	135
Leningrad	446	159	48	14	26	104
Western	387	226	45	41	23	24
Ivanovo	110	35	16	27	13	33
Belorussia	299	291	45	15	27	13
Nizhkrai	316	102	20	16	12	6
Far East	198	88	14	1	–	13
North	43	39	7	3	6	16
Bashkiriia	239	45	30	14	10	17
Tatariia	182	134	34	18	21	23
Kazakhstan	273	36	23	12	43	48
Crimea	47	21	7	–	–	1
C. Asia	184	48	21	43	70	87
Transcaucasus	186	34	14	12	138	5
N. Caucasus nat'l areas	132	35	4	6	20	5
Total	7,370	2,734	817	360	762	1,501

Source: "Dokladnaia zapiska o formakh i dinamike klassovoi bor'by," p. 72.

ists were male. Unlike female peasants, who were less vulnerable owing to official images of the apolitical *baba*, male peasants were at greater risk in carrying out acts of resistance. While women tended to dominate open, collective forms of protest, males were more likely to choose the relatively anonymous avenue of terror. Additionally, terror may very well have represented a specifically male culture of violence that was easily transformed into a tool of politics. The instruments of terror—whether shotguns or threats written by men who had a higher incidence of literacy— were generally in the male domain. Given their dominant position in village power structures, the *muzhiki* became the main caretakers of village conformity, unity, and revenge.

"Remember, you sons of bitches, we'll get even with you"

Threats in the form of anonymous letters (*anonimki*) and proclamations (*listovki*) were the most basic form of intimidation practiced by peasants in their struggles to defend their self-interest and maintain village cohesion during collectivization. Threats were made against individuals, property, specific institutions, and even the Communist party. Customary forms of protest in popular confrontations with authority, anonymous letters and proclamations were "crimes of anonymity," a relatively more feasible resistance option for people, especially male peasants, who could not risk direct confrontation, lacked alternate mean of defense and redress, and hesitated at the brink of violent action.[31]

In 1930, the OGPU claimed to have uncovered 3,512 proclamations and 1,644 anonymous letters. Doubtless, the figures are far from complete and, moreover, take into account only written threats. According to the OGPU, approximately 20% of these documents could be classified as "insurrectionary," meaning that they included explicit threats against the central government. About one-fourth were directly concerned with collectivization and dekulakization. The remainder dealt with a variety of problems, including the persecution of believers, grain requisitioning, and "general dissatisfaction." The high point for the appearance of proclamations and anonymous letters in 1930 was the key period of January to April, after which there was a steady decline until the resumption of grain requisitioning in the fall.[32]

Threats were sometimes catalogued directly under the heading of terror in Soviet official documents. However, threats were so widespread— especially verbal threats—that the authorities could never be certain which threats were likely to be realized (precisely the desired effect). When, for instance, the Urals Regional court sentenced peasants who uttered threats under the draconian Article 58 (8) of the penal code, an article on counterrevolutionary crimes, the Supreme Court overruled the practice, ordering threats to be treated under the ostensibly apolitical and much less severe Article 73 (1), which concerned threats against activists and officials.[33] According to the OGPU, only 3% to 10% of persons issuing threats were caught in the first place, a predictable outcome given their aims and anonymity.[34] Threats were an everyday occurrence in the countryside. Officials knew that, and peasants knew that. Whether issued seriously or as a reflexive gesture to injustice, as a display of opposition that could later be retracted and excused or could be kept secret, threats kept activists and officials on guard and under siege.[35]

Peasant threats were normally private affairs, made anonymously and in writing. Exceptions occurred when peasants tried to "persuade" other peasants against collective farming. For example, in Viatskaia *guberniia* in the spring of 1929, "kulaks" threatened a group of Komsomols about to formally register a collective farm that, if they continued their activities, they would find themselves banished beyond the fields, without pastureland or access to the village, and facing sure starvation.[36] And in Ostrogozhskii *okrug* in the Central Black Earth Region, "kulaks" threatened to shoot anyone who joined the collective farm.[37] More often, threats were written and slipped under doors or posted on trees. Activists, local officials, and resident plenipotentiaries such as the 25,000ers and workers' brigades routinely received threats. In early 1930, peasants in Ukraine issued the following threats to activists and collective farmers: "[We] will slaughter all you collective farmers in one night"; "We will burn your huts and grain"; and "Who[ever] is for the organization of the collective farm, [we] will kill like a dog."[38] In Dubrovich village in the Leningrad area, signs were posted that read, "Whoever enters the collective farm will be killed."[39] A 25,000er was handed a note that read: "If you want to live, watch yourself, or we'll throw you into the river."[40] An activist in the Crimea was slipped a death threat during a question-and-answer session at a dekulakization meeting.[41] Members of a workers' brigade in the North Caucasus received the following note:

> Remember, you sons of bitches, we'll get even with you. . . . Comrades—
> you think that we don't know who raises his hand to ruin the kulak. . . .
> Death to Sharafan Mikhail, Trush Stepan, Denisenko, Ul'ian. You have
> forced us to the point comrades that it is impossible to be patient any longer.
> . . . Don't think this is just a trifle, [your names] are entered into a death
> deed. Already comrades you have earned no mercy. Comrade Babenko from
> [the factory] "Krasnyi aksai" a rumor has reached our neighborhood that
> [you] will be killed.[42]

A local activist in the Gor'kii region who "unmasked" his collective farm as a kulak farm in disguise in 1932 and, fortuitously, was subsequently elected to chair the purged and reorganized farm was warned that he would be killed "like a cockroach" for his deeds.[43]

These kinds of personal threats, like other forms of terror, were an attempt to keep local people in line and to chase away dangerous outsiders. Threats were mostly of murder and arson, and were usually extravagent in the eloquence of their bloody or incendiary intent for the consequences of betrayal and treacherous action on the part of peasant activists and local officials. They were essentially a warning and, to fellow peasants, a coercive tool to maintain the face of village unity. They sometimes worked when supernatural threats involving the Antichrist and his apocalyptic horsemen failed to move more scientific-minded activists. They had the advantage of holding out the threat of a cockroach's death, while in most cases stopping short of real action. Personal threats were a beginner's exercise in opposition, an attempt to scare away enemies without *generally* incurring the more serious consequences of active forms of resistance.

Proclamations were more ambitious instruments of intimidation. Their purposes were twofold. First, they were aimed at the peasant population in an effort to mobilize opposition among friends and spread fear among waverers. Second, they were directed at the agents of Soviet power, within and beyond the village, as a warning—whether purely fanciful or not—that their fate and that of the state was in serious peril. Many proclamations openly called on peasants to overthrow the government. A proclamation uncovered in July 1930 in the Belgorodskii *okrug* village of Moshchenoe in the Central Black Earth Region called for open rebellion:

> Dear brothers and sisters. In the present moment inevitable ruin is being prepared for us by the hands of the hangmen Communists and Komsomols. You will die of starvation. In order to prevent this ruinous end, it is essential and necessary for us to unite into one front against the hangmen and betrayers of the laboring peasants' and workers' world. Dear brothers and sisters, let us say forever: "down with the reign of communism and the hangmen commissars," for they are leading us to inevitable death. Long live the social-democratic party, which gives us the possibility to live freely on the land, for God has created people to be free on the land, but the brutality of communism has put on all laborers a yoke from which the entire *mir* is groaning. In order to escape this, we need to destroy the party of communists, cooperation, coops, and collective farms. Down with atheism, long live freedom of religion. Down with cooperation, long live free trade. Dear brothers and sisters, help us, when we make [our] raid on the Communist Party, in order to destroy Soviet power. It is time for us to wake up. We have had enough of paying 15 rub[les] for a *pud* of grain or 100 rub[les] for shoes. We must all defend ourselves and say to the atheist communists "the end of your reign is come, let the peasantry and orthodoxy prevail." [44]

Another proclamation, signed "Detachment of the Green Partisans" and uncovered by the OGPU on 9 June 1930 in the Kanskii *okrug* village of Ivanovka in Siberia, called for peasants to rise up and murder their oppressors, as well as the activists who had betrayed the village ethos of collectivism:

> Citizens, for 12 years the Russian people have stood in a vise of violence and arbitrary rule [*proizvol*]. For 12 years a government of thieves and murderers [have] oppressed the laboring people and wished to make it into slaves. For 12 years the people have been patient, but any patience is now at an end. The end has come for the people's patience. For now, further patience is impossible. The time for retribution has come. In Siberia, the peasantry, deprived of its share and crushed, goes into the *taiga* in the thousands. This hunted and oppressed people will form a mighty partisan green army which will sweep its oppressors from the face of the earth. And we are already here. Act accordingly, massacre all your "activists," who suck the blood of the people. At the first call, all peasants must rise up against their oppressors.
> Long live the green partisan army. [45]

Proclamations were often noteworthy for their literary flair and bloodthirsty extravagance. Like the "Green Partisans'" threat, a proclamation written on a piece of torn notebook paper, signed "Union of Liberation," and discovered on 26 June 1930 in the Belgorodskii *okrug* village of Borisovka in the Central Black Earth Region, promised a violent end for the agents of Soviet power, including the local poor peasants whose "yoke" was supposedly stifling the community, while making use of an interesting combination of traditional language ("*miroedy*," or mir eater, traditionally used for exploitative elements in the village and now turned against Communists) and revolutionary rhetoric ("arise all people . . . "):

> Citizens. Wake up, prepare a punishment for the bloodsuckers [*miroedy*]. We are starving and cold, [we] are gradually perishing. . . . We expect nothing good, for us it remains only to rise up, to slaughter all the villains, then things will improve for us. . . . Go and demand—give [us] work, bread, we are hungry. Arise all people, demand truth, all people are equal where there is freedom. No, this is the yoke, the noose of the poor peasant. Rise up, destroy, beat, [have] no mercy, no fear, all as one explode like the blizzard that was [19]17. Citizens, don't wait for better times, rise up and punish untruth.[46]

Many of these proclamations augmented their violent rhetoric by calling for the formation of peasant combat detachments (*otriady* or *druzhiny*), and warning ominously that "we are not one or two," that peasants were going into the *taiga* "in the thousands," or that an underground opposition was in place. The following proclamation, which surfaced in the Achinskii *okrug* village of B. Iar in Siberia on 11 June 1930, was a typical example:

> Peasants, workers, employees [*sluzhashchie*], and Red army soldiers. The predatory policies of our government have led the people to open rebellion. We are forced to take up arms to save our farms from complete destruction.
> Already the hour is approaching when we will go out with weapons in hand and destroy the power of the aggressors.
> Our battle task now is to organize strong, fighting peasant detachments. We will arrive at victory then when we are united in steel, armed detachments.
> In each hamlet, village, and settlement, organize armed detachments.
> Be ready at the first call to rise to the defense of your rights of free labor and of [your] ravaged farms.
> Red army soldiers, workers, employees, don't listen to the beautiful lies of your leaders.
> Listen to the masses, your brothers, wives, and children, led into poverty and a half-starved existence. Down with violence, long live free labor, long live the truthfully elected order.[47]

Some of these proclamations also made reference to presoviet or civil war–era political parties and organizations, such as the "Social Democratic party," the "People's Democratic party," the "Green Partisan army," and the "Union of Liberation," thus calling upon earlier traditions of political resistance. These proclamations and others demonstrate knowledge of politics and national developments. References to "freedom of speech, press, conscience, [and] religion," the "rights of free labor," "free peasant farming," and so on were frequent. A July 1930 proclamation from Stalingradskii *okrug* in the Lower Volga is a good example:

> Citizens of great Russia. The People's Democratic party calls on you to throw off the yoke of the unprecedented red terror. Citizens remember the slogans of the years of revolution—freedom of speech, press, conscience, religion; factories to the workers, land to the peasants, etc. And what have the people gotten from these slogans. A dictatorship of the ruinous communist party gave instead of the promises of the slogans a robbery of all the laboring population unprecedented in the history of humanity. Instead of freedom of conscience and religion, the mass closing of churches against the wishes of the people. Instead of freedom of speech and the press—the brutal suppression of the thought and speech of people—terror for the workers, and instead of bread—hunger; instead of land, the peasantry gets taxes and in the final analysis the country is being led to an unprecedented impoverishment.
>
> The People's Democratic party calls on you, the great people, to throw off the yoke of the red terror which crushes all the morale and freedom of the life of people. Down with the thieving dictatorship of the party, the Communists, down with the red terror. Down with arbitrary rule over people, down with perpetual ownership of the land, down with collectivization which is a hidden form of slave labor.
>
> Long live the free people, the free people's democratic republic, free labor, free life, freedom of speech and the press, freedom of conscience and religion; all mills and factories under the control of the government, all land to the people.
>
> [Signed:] People's Democratic party[48]

References to collectivization policy, grain requisitioning and exports, Communist involvement abroad, and other developments indicate that peasants clearly were in tune with politics on the national level, as well as conscious of their rights.[49]

Proclamations from Ukraine differ from the Russian ones in their displays of national awareness, calling at times for a "free Ukraine," an "independent Ukraine," or simply a battle with Communist *zhidy* (a pejorative for Jews).[50] The following proclamation was discovered in the Krutianskii *raion* village of Strimbakh in Ukraine in July 1930:

> Citizens, down with the bandit gangs, down with the villainous communars. Long live free Ukraine.
>
> The destruction of communism is the responsibility of each [person]. Dear citizens address yourselves to the request to distribute these proclamations in the village. Villagers, be prepared for the struggle with bolshevism. The Ukraine is defecting from Russia. The time is come and we from the underground will go out and show ourselves in the villages in order to smash the enemy with you.
>
> The destruction of communism is the responsibility of each [person]. The Bolsheviks know that the Ukrainian people does not like the government and fears that Ukrainians are not connected to the Ukrainian democratic par-

ties. Don't forget this slogan: "The destruction of communism is the responsibility of each [person]." It is necessary to remember this and be prepared at any time to destroy it. All forward toward a better future.[51]

A proclamation from the Ukrainian village of Rogachakh in Bordicheskii *okrug* demonstrates a similar national consciousness:

> Brother peasants, we are all suffering under the oppression of the *pany* [landlords]-communists. They rob us. We are naked. [They] give us neither holidays nor Sundays, nor freedom of religion, such as no where else in the world. Arise brothers and sisters, fight with knives, scythes, stakes. Save yourselves. Strength will be with us. Battle the communist zhids. Throw him [*sic*] out of power, don't believe him, he sits on your back, he drives you, [he] eats your bread. Gather everyone [in preparation] for the uprising. Write this proclamation in other villages. Each who received the proclamation must write it three [times] and secretly pass it on to his brother. We have big forces. Organize to save yourselves, your freedom, and Christian faith. Rise up, wake up from [your] slumber. Long live independent Ukraine.[52]

The provenance of these proclamations will probably never be absolutely certain. Some proclamations were machine-printed, and may have come from outside of the village or from groups with some rudimentary form of organization. Further, extant proclamations tend to display varying levels of education; some seem clearly peasant in origin; others, perhaps, betray the hand of an intellectual. What they shared in common, however, was a consciousness that collectivization was a war on the peasantry, on its rights and freedom, having nothing in common with the Revolution of 1917.[53] In this sense, regardless of derivation, proclamations sought to speak for the peasantry as a whole, calling for justice and retribution and further augmenting the atmosphere of terror in the Soviet countryside.

"Fire!"

Arson, another prop in the atmosphere of threat and intimidation, was a key feature of peasant terror. Literally and figuratively, arson was a bright display of resistance, visible far beyond the village in which it began. It was an integral part of the peasant popular culture of protest, in Russia and elsewhere, serving as a traditional and generally anonymous means of settling accounts and grievances.[54] Arson was known throughout the land as the "Red Rooster," and its meaning was recognized with a threatening, sardonic grin by peasants and fear by the authorities. When the Red Rooster flew, the tocsin of peasant wrath rang out and all knew that it heralded revolt.

Arson was a sometimes clever tool of protest, because a fire's designation as arson could reside in the eye of the beholder. When an accidental fire raged through the homes of peasant Tolstoyans about to be evicted by the state from their agricultural commune, the authorities immediately branded the fire arson, while neighboring peasant women knowingly concluded, "A fire was bound to break out here!"[55] In the life of any village, most of which were made up of wooden huts and had only the most primitive fire-fighting capabilities, fire was a natural, frequent, and tragic occurrence. Given this reality, arson could always be a fire, or a fire, arson. For peasants, arson was a fire, or at least could be made out to be an ordinary fire and thereby provide a cover for subversion. For the authorities who needed a scapegoat, an excuse for intervention, or who were simply accustomed to reflexively branding any development that ran counter to state interests as kulak sabotage, any fire could be arson. This was what happened in the case of the peasant Belov, who was accused of setting a collective farm bathhouse on fire and was almost executed for this act. The key witnesses in the case turned out to be children who had been playing with matches and apparently were as capable as adults of manipulating political labels and accusations in their own defense.[56] As ruse or pretext, arson was a useful tactic. Whether ruse or pretext, arson and fire in the midst of political conflagration instilled terror in the hearts of collectivization supporters and contributed to the spread of state terror.

In light of arson's elastic definition, statistics on arson must be viewed with caution. In addition, arson statistics are scattered and incomplete. Government data on arson cases related to grain requisitioning and the heated soviet election campaign in the period from November 1928 to January 1929 indicate that the highest incidence of arson occurred in the Central Black Earth Region (42 cases), Middle Volga (23 cases), Tver *guberniia* (12 cases), Moscow *guberniia* (11 cases), and Lower Volga (11 cases).[57] In 1930, the incidence of arson increased dramatically. According to OGPU records, there were 6,324 cases of arson in 1930, of which 1,884 were in Ukraine, 700 in the Central Black Earth Region, 383 in the Lower Volga, 343 in the Urals, and 358 in Belorussia.[58] In the final quarter of 1930, reports out of Elanskii *raion* in Siberia claimed that "the collective farm hayricks burned day and night," while two additional sources stated that there were 347 acts of arson committed in all Siberia in 1930, which amounts to almost one act per day.[59] According to *Kolkhoztsentr*, 15% of the nation's collective farms experienced some form of terror in 1931. Of the 15% of collective farms—numerically, about 30,000 farms—one in five—or about 6,000—experienced arson. The regions with the highest rates of arson were, predictably, the Central Black Earth, Middle Volga, and Lower Volga.[60]

Arson was aimed primarily at activists and local officials. Arson served as a warning to peasants who would go against community interests and as retribution for disloyalty or participation in antipeasant policies. In 1928–29, arson was often employed against peasants who tried to organize or actually joined collective farms.[61] In Kaluzhskii *okrug*, Central Industrial Region, in late 1929, rumors spread that all activists' homes would be burned to the ground.[62] In Irbitskii *okrug*, Urals, home of the famous "Gigant" collective farm, arson raged through the countryside in the second half of 1929 as peasants were coerced into the megafarm. The Gigant village of Larina, for example, was torched at a cost of 33 homes. After an antireligious carnival celebration of International Youth Day in the village Ignat'evo that parodied priests and kulaks, arsonists destroyed 20 homes.[63] Elsewhere, peasants torched the property of newly organized collective farms or combined arson with the lynching of unpopular activists or officials.[64]

Revenge for breaking village ranks was clearly the motive in the arson of Komsomol Fedor Zhitkov's house in Bronnitskii *uezd*, Moscow *guberniia*. On 20 August 1928, at 7:00 P.M., the village assembled for an election meeting. Suddenly, the sky filled with smoke and the tocsin rang out. Zhitkov's house was in flames. The culprits, later executed, were described as "kulak types"—one was a trader, another had engaged in counterrevolutionary crimes during the Russian Civil War. Through the efforts of the "honorable, conscious, and energetic" Zhitkov, the kulak types had earlier been disenfranchised. Before torching Zhitkov's house, they engaged in antisoviet (antizhitkov) propaganda, arguing that some green kid (*mal'chishka*) had taken over village affairs and was disenfranchising economically solid farmers. The burning of Zhitkov's house was revenge loud enough for other would-be turncoats to hear.[65]

Revenge was also the motive in the arson-murder of a village official in the Middle Volga in summer 1929. This case involved the relatives of Ivan Meshcherinov, a former landowner who had been exiled in 1927. His relatives became active foes of the local collective farm, charging that its members were branded with the mark of Antichrist, and were consequently expropriated. Several days after the expropriation, the relatives set fire to the *krestkom* chair's house. The chair, his wife and child, and four others were burned to death in a conflagration that engulfed twenty homes. The arsonists were sentenced to death.[66]

As wholesale collectivization came to the village, arson was turned against collective farm property and the property of local people who participated in collectivization and dekulakization.[67] In many parts of the country, the arson of activists' property was preceded by anonymous threats to the activists promising retribution.[68] In some areas, arson was used as a diversion. Collectivization meetings were broken up with cries of "Fire!" and in some cases actual fires were started during meetings.[69] A cry of fire was a foolproof way to end any village meeting. Panic was the reflexive response to any such cry, and afterward peasants had a ready-made excuse for the diversion.

During and after wholesale collectivization, arson continued to play its traditional role of village mediator extraordinaire. Wronged peasants, especially those who had been dekulakized or, later, purged from the collective farm but left to live in the area, were generally the prime suspects in cases of collective farm arson. Simple revenge was the main motivation. In August 1930 in the Buguruslanskii *okrug* village of Aleshkino in the Middle Volga, dekulakized peasants (most of whom were escapees from exile) and "criminal elements" set fire to collective farm property and twelve peasant huts. Five of these huts were the former homes of kulaks now inhabited by poor peasants. During the fire, the arsonists prevented the collective farmers from extinguishing the fire, and beat up the *sel'sovet* chair and several activists in the confusion.[70] Fifty-year-old Foma Lederkin was dekulakized in 1930 and forced to move in with an aunt. He retaliated by torching the collective farm club and ended up working on Belomor canal as a slave laborer.[71] In 1932, the 23-year-old peasant Martynov was assessed a taxation rate normally reserved for kulaks. When he could not pay the tax, the authorities expropriated him, forcing him to leave for work in Moscow. On a visit home, he discovered that the local collective farm had converted his former home into a collective farm building. According to the published account of the case, during a drinking spree with an old neighbor, Martynov convinced his neighbor to torch his old house. These cases were typical of the arson of the times.[72]

Although reported cases of arson decreased with the completion of wholesale collectivization, arson continued to be a popular form of terror and intimidation. Whether a fire was a revenge-motivated act of arson, or labeled an arson as an exercise in scapegoating remaining kulaks or peasant dissidents for collective farm negligence, is a question that cannot be definitively answered. What is clear is that fire, represented as arson, invoked fear and punished peasant turncoats, while serving as the peasant flag of resistance throughout the land.

"We will stand up to our knees in blood before we'll give up our land"

Threat, intimidation, and arson were peasant tactics designed to influence village politics and frighten the opposition.[73] Violent assault—whether murder or beating—against the state's agents served as the court of last appeal. Violence was the real stuff of terror. It was what Soviet authorities feared and it was what made the culture of civil war in the First Five-Year Plan a reality. Violence became a central mechanism of peasant justice in this era of official lawlessness and, to use the Soviet catchword, excesses (*peregiby*). It was aimed mainly at local officials, resident outsiders, and peasant activists, and served as revenge and retribution for misdeeds against individuals and the collective. It also—like threat and arson—continued to serve as a warning, *as terror*, to others who might contemplate either, in the case of officials, trampling further on the will of the community or, in the case of peasants, breaking ranks and crossing over to Soviet power.

Violence came in many forms. Sometimes it occurred immediately after a grain requisitioning or collectivization meeting, as in the case of the North Caucasus officials who were ambushed on the road out of the village.[74] Other times it was a delayed action that occurred only after sufficient planning and preparation. Outside plenipotentiaries, resident plenipotentiaries, local officials, and activists alike could face ambush on the road or in the woods, sniper fire in or out of the village, or a sudden confrontation by an angry crowd.[75] Generally, such violence occurred under the cover of darkness to maintain anonymity and to terrorize. And terrorize it did. The sawed-off shotgun and the bullet from around the corner became the stuff of First Five-Year Plan legend, as newspapers alternately titillated and incited readers with tales of gunfights with kulaks and revolutionary class war in the dark and wild villages of peasant Russia. The reality of violence was less exciting and more brutal, and, instead of dark and wild, it was often reasoned, measured, and deeply rooted in the peasant politics of collectivization.

The soviet election campaign of 1928–29, surrounded as it was by extraordinary measures, provided an early focal point for peasant dissatisfaction with the state's leftward shift in grain policy. Throughout the countryside, there were calls for soviets without Communists, secret ballots, election boycotts, and the organization of peasant unions.[76] The extent of peasant alarm and antagonism was revealed in a Smolensk village in which peasants believed, "Better Lenin than Leninism. The best Communists were killed or died. Scoundrels remain."[77] In some places, peasants gathered clandestinely to prepare alternate lists of soviet candidates and campaigned against Communists. Official preelection meetings were frequently broken up by the time-honored practices of creating such a din that nothing could be heard, coming to the meeting drunk, or threatening candidates.[78] In the Urals, two poor peasants were shot after their election to the *sel'sovet*, and elsewhere in the Urals six Komsomols were beaten up for their participation in the election campaign.[79] According to a government report, between the third and fourth quarters of 1928, cases of terrorist attacks in Siberia rose from 127 to 371. Beatings, along with threats and arson, accounted for most of the terror nationwide, and among the hardest hit regions were the Central Black Earth Region, Middle Volga, and Lower Volga.[80]

Violence continued at a lesser rate through the spring and summer of 1929, but it was in the fall of 1929 that terrorist murders and assaults began to increase dramatically, in correspondence with renewed grain requisitions and the beginnings of wholesale collectivization. In October 1929 the Politburo, alarmed by these developments, authorized the OGPU and the Commissariat of Justice to make use of "quick and decisive measures," including execution, against kulaks responsible for acts of terror.[81] Murders and assaults were reported in all regions of the country. Although riots and especially *bab'i bunty* (women's riots) were the hallmark of peasant protest in the initial wave of wholesale collectivization, terrorist attacks also reached their peak in the first half of 1930.[82]

Collectivization provided the main forum for terrorist attacks. The price for participation in collectivization could be a bullet or a beating. A key issue around which many terrorist assaults revolved was the campaign against the kulaks. "Unmasking" a peasant as a kulak or taking part willingly in a peasant family's dekulakization was the ultimate violation of the village ethic of collectivism. Vera Karaseva of Belaia Glina in the North Caucasus was murdered in late 1929 following her performance in a Komsomol play featuring *chastushki* that unmasked the local kulaks.[83] Another Komsomol, in the Middle Volga, faced a similar fate for identifying kulaks with hidden grain reserves.[84] In the village of Zori, Lioznenskii *raion*, Vitebskii *okrug*, Belorussia, peasants actually wore masks, in a simple attempt at disguise or in a symbolic gesture to the unmaskers, as they beat a poor peasant activist.[85] In the Apsheronskii *raion* village of Apsheronskaia in the North Caucasus, peasants brutally beat two women activists for participation in grain requisitioning campaigns, another violation of village norms of unity that perhaps assumed especially serious dimensions because of the gender transgressions involved in a peasant woman's activism. On 15 August 1930, peasants attacked one of the women, cutting off her hair and stuffing it into her mouth, burning her, and beating her into unconsciousness. Several days later, another woman was beaten, left with her scarf stuffed into her mouth and her stomach badly burned.[86] In these cases, peasant anger was turned against other peasants who had broken with the community and sided with the enemy. The extent to which this kind of behavior was a violation of village norms becomes explicit in an OGPU report of a secret "kulak-SR" meeting in a village in the Lower Volga, at which peasants issued a decree ordering the "physical destruction of turncoats."[87]

Terror was also aimed at resident outsiders and officials in an effort to silence them and warn others of the dangers of working for Soviet power. Elizaveta Pavlovna Rasguliaeva of Siberia was one of many prosoviet teachers to face peasant execution. Rasguliaeva had been active in the state's grain requisitioning and soviet election campaigns and reportedly helped to unmask kulaks. Before being shot by a bullet that came through the window of her hut, she was the subject of frequent threats and had found herself completely ostracized by the village community.[88] In the Urals, *sel'sovet* member M. P. Rogachev was murdered by kulaks scheduled for exile; his fate was shared by a collective farm official in the same region, who was murdered by dekulakized peasants seeking revenge.[89] In the village of Anfaliva in the Moscow region, a peasant identified in the sources as a *podkulachnik* went on a shooting spree, taking aim at the *sel'sovet* chair, a Komsomol, and three workers, until he himself was finally gunned down in the street.[90]

Retribution was not always as neat as a bullet in the head. *Samosud*, or peasant summary justice, sometimes occurred during collectivization and was usually aimed at peasant activists.[91] An early case of *samosud* occurred in the village of Appak-Dzhankoi in the Crimea in 1928. Here the village was split into two hostile camps. According to the report on the case, the "kulaks" decided to celebrate New Year's Eve "in the old way" (*po-staromu*)—that is, a crowd of some thirty male peasants walked around the village drinking and singing. Surely not coincidentally, the crowd ended up in front of the *sel'sovet* building, where an antireligious youth meeting was going on. When the organizer came out, the crowd jumped him, chased him down after he got loose, and beat him. The crowd then broke into the *sel'sovet*, beating everyone they could find, including the *sel'sovet* chair.[92] In Tiumenskii *okrug*, Siberia, in early 1930, villagers armed with pitchforks and stakes broke into the hut of the poor peasant Postupinskii, a member of the local tax and grain requisitioning commissions. The villagers trampled Postupinskii, dragged him from his hut, and drowned him by throwing him through an icehole.[93] In Novo-Pokrovka (Bystroistokskii *raion*, Siberia), peasants set fire to the hut of the party cell secretary, who was also a grain requisitioning plenipotentiary. When he tried to run from his burning home, his attackers caught him, beat him, and threw him back into the fire to be burned alive.[94] In a village in Rubtsovskii *okrug*, Siberia, a peasant who was active in promoting collectivization was hunted down and shot, after which his murderers broke into his home, killed his wife and children, and burned down the hut.[95] In the Gor'kii region, a collective farm chair narrowly escaped being tossed into a fire by an angry crowd during the arson of the collective farm.[96] Other cases of *samosud* were reported in the Briansk, Leningrad, Perm, Middle Volga, and Moscow countryside.[97]

Samosud was a customary, however exceptional and brutal, method of dealing with crimes against the community in peasant Russia.[98] From the outside looking in, *samosud*—when it took the form of a crowd lynching—appeared to be a spontaneous outburst of irrational, cruel violence. In fact, *samosud* was never aimless, but clearly focused on specific targets. Victims were neither hapless nor sinless and had probably been warned and threatened prior to the attack. Lynchings appear to have been organized in advance to some extent rather than exploding irrationally, given that specific people were targeted and hunted down. And collective participation in a murder or assault provided a cover of anonymity for the individuals involved as well as bonding participants in mutual responsibility and culpability for the crime. Finally, the outward and official images of *samosud* could be manipulated after the fact by peasants who could claim that a kind of madness had overtaken the mob. *Samosud* was a part of an older popular culture of protest in Russia and served as an "enabling mode of protest"[99] rather than some dark, visceral response by primitive *muzhiks*.

Samosud likely accounted for no more than a small minority of the terrorist acts of the collectivization era. However customary, collectively insured, and individually anonymous *samosud* may have been, the preferred form of terror remained the sniper's bullet or assault in the wood. Under cover of distance or darkness, the most deadly form of peasant opposition wisely maintained a disguise of anonymity as individual peasants sought justice, when all else had failed, with the only means at their disposal.

After 1930, when the state's campaigns and interventions began to ebb, terror continued, but at a lower rate, and was targeted almost exclusively at collective farm officials and activists. For example, according to *Kolkhoztsentr* data, more than one out of every three collective farms— or more than 10,000 farms (out of a total of some 30,000 farms experiencing "class struggle" in 1931)—were subject to some kind of physical attack on its cadre of officials and activists. Not surprisingly, the highest rates of terror had shifted away from the major grain-producing regions to grain-consuming areas and ethnic minority regions, which were now feeling the brunt of collectivization.[100] The overwhelming majority of terrorist attacks involved peasants or their relatives seeking vengeance against an established local activist responsible in some way for their repression. The few exceptions to this generalization were the attacks on shock workers, normbreakers, and Stakhanovites (especially women) who, although not necessarily engaged in repressive operations, were still clearly breaking ranks with what was left of the village community.[101] Retribution murders and assaults occurred throughout the 1930s and could be linked to an activist's participation in grain collections, exposing grain theft, or collective farm purges, all of which concerned life-or-death issues for collective farm families.[102] Most frequently, however, peasants sought retribution for a local official's or activist's work going back to 1930–31 and the repression of the kulaks. Peasants bided their time while antagonisms simmered. As conditions deteriorated in the village and a new desperation set in, peasants lashed out at old enemies who had violated communal solidarity and generally continued to wield authority. Terror became an instrument of village politics and the new village history.

The murder of the civil war hero Strigunov in Prokhorovskii *raion*, Central Black Earth Region, in April 1933 is a good example. Strigunov was an activist par excellence: he was a Red army veteran and a *sel'kor*, he had served in the *sel'sovet* and *raion* soviet, and he had been a collective farm chairman. During dekulakization, Strigunov was responsible for the deportation of several kulaks, some of whose relatives remained in the collective farm and, according to the report, even joined the party. From 1930, Strigunov was in continuous conflict with these relatives. They accused him of slandering them with the kulak label and sued successfully in a *raion* court in 1931, as a consequence of which Strigunov received a six month prison sentence that was soon overturned by the regional court. The same charges were repeated twice more in the *raion* court and twice more overturned at the regional level. At some point, Strigunov began to write denunciations to Moscow, calling for the liberation of the village and collective farm from counterrevolutionaries. With all legal avenues exhausted and Strigunov escalating hostilities in a most dangerous fashion, the relatives took matters into their own hands and downed Strigunov with a bullet through the window.[103] It is not clear—but should not be ignored—to what extent this case became entangled in more than a war between accusers and accused and entered into a power struggle among local Communists, given the relatives' party membership. What is clear is that the kulak label readily became a tool of village politics, and that peasants of every social and political complexion adapted the new political demagoguery to their own needs, appropriating the language of their oppressors.

The *sel'kor* Saprykin was murdered in Voronezh in 1935 for his denunciations. He reportedly had exposed class aliens and corruption in his collective farm. For this, he was expelled and fined, supposedly illegally. He was eventually reinstated and saw to it that the collective farm leaders were fired. Soon after, Saprykin was murdered by his enemies.[104] The activist Sonin was murdered in 1932. He had participated in the village's dekulakization process. Sonin continued his vigilance after collectivization, reporting on kulak infiltration and theft. He was beaten to death by some of his former victims, one of whom reportedly taunted him with each blow: "This is for you activist, for dekulakization."[105]

Another case that demonstrates the extent to which terror became entangled in peasant politics in later years occurred in the Lower Volga in 1934. Mainina, the *sel'korka* of the district newspaper, *Krasnyi khoper*, was sitting at her table with neighbors when a bullet—which missed any target—came crashing through the window. The previous summer Mainina had unmasked several local officials as "kulak-oriented." So to the authorities the case was cut and dried: the kulak-oriented officials were immediately arrested. Within a short time, however, the story began to unravel. Mainina, it happened, had a lover, one Peresedov, who was the son of a runaway kulak. Peresedov, himself, had returned to his village when his civil rights were restored but came home to find that he could not retrieve his property. The kulak-oriented officials exposed by Mainina were the same officials who were responsible for Peresedov's plight. Moreover—and here the story becomes very thick, in the best Soviet rhetorical style—it turned out that Mainina's own father and brother had been expelled from the collective farm for theft, that her father had fought alongside the Whites, and that an uncle lived abroad. As the original story came apart, the new version of events placed the lovers squarely at the center of the action: they had forged the threat letters to Mainina and planned the shooting to set the officials up. Witnesses were found to testify that Peresedov had been loitering near Mainina's hut just before the shooting. In the end, the kulak-oriented officials were redubbed collective farm activists and the *sel'korka* and her lover became kulak-oriented class aliens. If any or all of this report is true, then what Mainina attempted was to turn the table on the officials, using their weapons, their politics, and their sensibilities. Mainina's ploy, despite its failure, was a truly inspired diversion, a part of a long tradition of peasant dissimulation artfully adapted for play in the Soviet period.[106]

Conclusion

Peasant terror derived from and was conditioned by state terror. Its dynamics were closely correlated to those of the state's campaigns in the countryside. Incidents of violent resistance were most widespread in grain-producing regions and areas that experienced unusually brutal repression. These dynamics were clearly apparent, for example, in the Central Black Earth Region, an area in which peasant terror assumed alarming rates and in which state terror was so out of control that the Central Black Earth Region was dubbed "region of excesses" at the Sixteenth Party Congress in June 1930.[107] As a form of peasant politics, terror generally arose only in the most desperate of circumstances and after all recourse to state and judicial authorities had been exhausted.

As peasants were forced to resolve their own conflicts, they turned to earlier forms of peasant justice. Peasant violence in the collectivization era derived much from traditional community practices in maintaining order and establishing justice. Although politicized and sovietized by events, peasant terror was animated by customary norms of justice, retribution, and community cohesion, demonstrating the flexibility and adaptability of peasant resistance. Arson, threat, *samosud*, and other forms of violence were a part of a popular culture of resistance. The tactics of peasant terror were masked by disguise, dissimulation, anonymity, and an escape route of double meanings. Peasants manipulated official images of *muzhik* psychology, dissembling before power and sovietizing their actions to fit the crime. The "hidden transcript"[108] of peasant resistance erupted to the surface, but carried with it many of its disguises from the underground of the peasant popular culture of resistance.

Peasant terror was about intimidation and justice. It was neither arbitrary nor irrational. Its use and targets illuminate the central fissures of the Soviet countryside during collectivization. First, it is clear that the terror was animated less by class war than civil war against all Soviet power. Second, and perhaps most important, the fact that peasants aimed much of the violence against fellow villagers—activists—suggests a degree of intravillage strife, a civil war within the civil war, that has gone unexplored in the Western literature. It appears that this strife was not necessarily an issue of class or social status, but rather conflict arising from the violation of traditional community norms or ideals of cohesion. The extreme coercive pressure of the outside authorities appears to have reinforced a new and repressive attempt by peasants to maintain village unity and insularity in the face of all odds.[109]

From the state's point of view, peasant terror was both dangerous and useful. The danger was clear from the consequences. The usefulness of terror derived from the ways in which it could be manipulated to sustain the violent momentum of the state's campaigns and to rationalize the repression of the peasantry. At one point, the state had even planned a great show trial to highlight the perfidy of the kulak and his allies in the government. The trial of the "Laboring Peasant Party" would have featured noted agrarian specialists Chaianov, Kondrat'ev, Makarov, and others, had it not mysteriously failed to be staged. The key charges in the trial were to have been accusations of fomenting "systematic acts against village communists" and responsibility for the violence.[110] Like the peasantry, the state had its own "hidden transcript" undergirding the public one.

In the end, terror served state interests more than peasant interests. As a tool of resistance, terror was ineffective from the peasant point of view. Its benefits were short-lived and it could only serve to escalate violence as long as the state held in its hands the machinery of repression. Unlike passive resistance, which would be effective over time, terror reinforced and intensified the repressive and centralizing nature of the state. Still, terror served as an effective, offstage symbol of peasant resolve, playing in the wings to the peasant rebellion that would take center stage in 1930.

5

March Fever: Peasant Rebels and Kulak Insurrection

Comrades! [I] call on you to defend your property and the property of the people. Be prepared for the first and the last call. The rivers and seas will dry up and water will flow on to the high Kurgan and blood will flow in the streams and the land will rise up high in black whirlwinds. . . . You will see . . . that soon flames will burst out. I call on you to defend each other, don't go into the collective farm, don't believe the chatterboxes [*boltuny*]. . . . Comrades, remember the past, when you lived freely, everyone [lived] well, poor and rich, now all [live] poorly. . . . [T]here is deception everywhere. . . . [B]e prepared for the first call.

—anonymous proclamation

An epidemic of March fever swept through the Soviet countryside in the early stages of wholesale collectivization. The designation "March fever" (*martovskaia likhoradka*) comes from a Communist official who used the phrase to characterize the unrest that erupted in the village at that time.[1] "March" referred to March 1930, the high point of a peasant rebellion against the state that began during the grain requisitioning campaigns of the late 1920s and, in many cases, continued beyond March 1930. The "fever" was the wave of mass disturbances that rolled over the countryside and threatened to engulf the nation in peasant war. The foundation of March fever was peasant solidarity, and it was precisely this solidarity that became in the eyes of the state a contagion as it spread from village to village.[2] March fever captured much of the Communist perception of and contempt for peasant opposition, casting it in a pathological light, depoliticizing and delegitimizing it. In Communist terms, it was an aberration, a disease caused by kulak and *podkulachnik* incubus, or by the culture of dizziness borne by fanatical cadres intoxicated by the supposed successes of collectivization.

March fever, however, was no fever at all. What the state labeled a fever was in fact a massive peasant rebellion, reasoned in cause and content. In village after village, peasants rose up in collective acts of revolt— first in angry demonstrations, protest, and subterfuge at the myriad offi-

cial meetings convened at this time to convince, cajole, or coerce peasants
to sign on "voluntarily" for "socialist transformation," and then in a con-
vulsion of local riots that came as a direct, if desperate, response to forced
collectivization, grain seizures, dekulakization, and atheization. Brigandage, driven by the newly marginalized, mostly young male peasants, was
less practiced, but continued when open rebellion no longer was a possibility. Like terror, collective acts of rebellion came as a last resort, arising in
conditions of extreme duress at the height of state repression. Unlike terror, most collective acts of rebellion drew upon the strength and cohesion
of the community, requiring its collective will and public participation.

March fever was the most effective, short-term peasant political response to collectivization. It brought the state to its knees and had a mul-
tifaceted and contradictory impact on rural policy decisions during the
Stalin revolution. In response, state ideology, rhetoric, and paranoia
transformed the peasant rebellions of this period into a peasant fever in-
duced by "kulak insurrection" and all manner of "dizziness," but having
nothing formally to do with peasant politics and the civil war that was
collectivization.

The scale of rebellion

Peasant rebellions assumed threatening proportions in the fall of 1929.
When peasants responded to negative terms of trade between industry
and agriculture by withholding grain from the market, the state responded
not by raising grain prices, but by employing massive force to seize grain.
Grain seizures transformed the peasant response from economic sabotage
and boycott to active resistance, as peasants attempted to hold onto the
fruits of their labor and to ensure their own survival in an economy close
to the subsistence level. Peasant unrest reached such disturbing levels that
in September 1929 a Central Committee report warned that "the class
struggle [in districts of wholesale collectivization] is so exacerbated that in
the literal sense of the word [the situation] is reminiscent of the front,"[3]
while a Politburo directive of 3 October 1929 called for "quick and decisive
measures," including execution, against kulaks involved in counterrevolutionary disturbances.[4] According to Olga Narkiewicz, it was precisely the
threatening dimensions of peasant unrest brought about by forced requisitioning that pushed the state into collectivization.[5]

Far from stemming the tide of peasant unrest, the wild excesses of the
collectivization campaign of winter 1929–30 touched off a major peasant
conflagration. Isolated voices in and out of the leadership had attempted
to warn of the likely consequences of forced collectivization at and preceding the November plenum of the Communist party.[6] Once collectivization
was well underway by late 1929, warnings and reports of violence on both
sides poured into government offices on all regional levels.[7] In many parts
of the country, regional party organizations followed the example of a
Lower Volga *raion* party committee which warned subordinates of the

likelihood of peasant violence in the course of collectivization.[8] Even the Red army experienced unrest as peasant soldiers received news from their families back in the village of impending and present disaster.[9]

Just as peasant violence pushed the state toward forced collectivization, it would also prompt the decision in March 1930 to call a temporary retreat in the face of mass peasant unrest. The Central Committee revealed its motives in a secret memorandum of 2 April 1930, which read in part:

> Information about mass disturbances of peasants in the Central Black Earth Region, Ukraine, Kazakhstan, Siberia, [and] the Moscow Region coming into the C.C. [Central Committee] in February cannot be characterized as anything but threatening. . . . If we had not immediately taken measures against the violations of the party line, we would have had a wide wave of insurrectionary peasant uprisings, a good part of our lower officials would have been slaughtered by the peasants, [and] the sowing would have been broken.[10]

The signal for retreat had come in early March, with Stalin's publication of "Dizziness from Success."[11] Instead of calming peasant unrest, however, the article had the unintended effect of placing Stalin's name temporarily at the head of the peasant movement and unleashing further unrest as local officials panicked or refused to allow peasants to disband collective farms. In the Central Black Earth Region, for example, there were eleven mass revolts in just two days following the appearance of Stalin's article in the region. These disturbances included as many as one thousand peasants and made their way as close as twelve kilometers from Voronezh, the provincial capital. News of similar disturbances poured into Moscow, eventually once again forcing the hand of the center. It was at this point that the Central Committee issued the 2 April memorandum with a frank assessment of the degree of the danger and more concrete instructions for the now demoralized cadres in the field on how to continue. According to Russian historians, by the time this memorandum was issued, the situation had become so threatening as to present the possibility of a general peasant uprising.[12]

March fever manifested itself through many different symptoms, although the underlying cause remained state policy and the intimidation and atrocities practiced by Soviet officials. The diversity of the symptoms and the necessity always to rely on state diagnosis make it difficult to quantify the exact dimensions of the rebellion. In categorizing peasant disturbances, the state and its agents used a series of terms, some with distinct meanings, others without, and almost all heavily laden with official perceptions, obfuscation, and condescension. The most frequently used word was *vystuplenie*, which could mean any act of public defiance unless prefixed by "mass" (*massovoe*), in which case it was an angry demonstration or riot. *Vystuplenie*, on its own, however, comes from the verb *vstupit'*, which literally means to step out. A *vystuplenie*, then, is a stepping out of line, an outbreak of some kind. In a sense, *vystuplenie* became a generic code for peasant unrest; it was an "incident" or a "disturbance," code words used by many politically repressive regimes to describe and depoliticize popular acts of protest. The phrase *massovye vystupleniia* (translated below as "mass disturbances") appears most frequently in documents, especially those of OGPU provenance, and, like *vystuplenie*, generally served as a generic term for mass disturbances of all kinds. The word *volnenie* was another frequently used term for the categorization of unrest. Literally translated, *volnenie* means a disturbance or agitated state, and is therefore again a slightly sanitized term for revolt, containing more than a hint of elite condescension and capturing the official view of "dark masses" rising up in senseless mayhem. Like *vystuplenie*, *volnenie*—without the "mass" prefix—could be used generically to refer to any manifestation of collective unrest. *Bunty* (riots), *volynki* (riots in the diminutive), and *svalki* (melees) were much clearer terms for riots, each signifying a traditional and spontaneous *muzhik* outburst carried out by irrational and backward primitives. These terms joined *vosstaniia* and *miatezhi*, meaning uprisings and mutinies, which were much clearer, less sanitized descriptions of collective acts of peasant rebellion. They were sometimes modified by the adjective *povstancheskii*, signifying a large and serious insurrection with organized and well-armed participants, spanning several districts and explicitly treasonous in intent.[13] Despite the clarity of the terms, *bunty, svalki,* or *volynki* might be forgiven by the authorities, while *miatezhi, vosstaniia,* and *povstancheskie vystupleniia* were most certainly considered counterrevolutionary acts with an implicit kulak adjective and the attributes of subversion and conspiracy. We depend on local cadres' reporting and higher officials' interpretations for the choice of descriptive term. Labels may have corresponded to the size, dynamics, and danger of a disturbance, or they may simply have reflected the effect the official observer or interpreter intended to have on his audience of superiors. Some combination, contradictory to be sure, of official denial, rationalization of political opposition, and paranoid exaggeration also filters into the reporting as well as the reception. It is important to keep these points in mind when surveying the statistics, which should be approached with caution.

Aggregate, national statistics on mass disturbances are available from 1928 to 1930. Mass disturbances—*massovye vystupleniia*—increased dramatically in these years, rising from a total of 709 in 1928 to 1,307 in 1929 to 13,754 in 1930. Table 5–1 depicts monthly dynamics, demonstrating the seasonal correlation between state terror and peasant rebellion. While in 1928 and 1929, spring and fall grain requisitioning campaigns served as the primary causal factor in mass disturbances, in 1930, collectivization became the spark to revolt. In 1929, approximately 30% of mass disturbances occurred in conjunction with requisitioning; 23.5% on "religious grounds" (meaning mostly the harassment of believers and clergy, but also in some regions church closings); and only 6.5% were

Table 5–1. National Statistics on Mass
Disturbances, 1928–30

Month	1928	1929	1930
January	10	42	402
February	10	22	1,048
March	11	55	6,528
April	36	159	1,992
May	185	179	1,375
June	225	242	886
July	93	95	618
August	31	69	256
September	25	72	159
October	25	139	270
November	33	108	129
December	25	125	91
Total	709	1,307	13,754

Source: "Dokladnaia zapiska o formakh i dinamike klassovoi bor'by," p. 40.

due to collectivization. In 1930, 70.6% of the total were brought about
by collectivization and dekulakization; 10.8% by religious persecution
(generally, church closings, removals of bells, and arrests of clergy); 8.9%
by food difficulties; and only 3.3% by requisitioning.[14]

Table 5–2 outlines the full range of official causes of mass disturbances by month. The year 1930 marked the high point for mass disturbances.[15] The first half of the year was dominated by rebellions sparked
by the state's collectivization and dekulakization campaigns and the assault on the church. The climax of the revolt came in March, when peasant rebels took full advantage of the official confusion and demoralization
caused by the state's temporary retreat. In the spring and early summer
months, hunger riots and mass disturbances over the return of property
to rehabilitated "kulaks" and peasants who quit collective farms in March
assumed precedence. In the final five months of the year, disturbances
caused by forced grain requisitioning were most prevalent.[16] After 1930,
mass disturbances became rare, as peasants found other avenues of safer,
quieter, generally passive resistance, or suffered and complied in a silent
and fearful resignation.[17]

Regional data provide further insight into the dynamics of mass disturbances in 1930. Grain-producing and black soil regions—areas designated for wholesale collectivization and especially those that were densely
populated—experienced the largest number of disturbances. Most of these
regions were traditional areas of peasant rebellion and regions hit hard by
the excesses of the times. Table 5–3 depicts monthly regional break-

Table 5–2. Official Causes of Mass Disturbances in 1930

Month	Collect.	Dekulak.*	Church Closings†	Sowing /Harvest	Requisitions	Taxes	Food Problems	Goods Shortages	Misc.‡
Jan.	158	68	159	7	2	–	4	–	4
Feb.	723	178	103	19	2	1	9	–	13
Mar	5,010	749	514	160	2	5	65	–	23
Apr.	789	457	391	147	–	2	172	–	34
May	284	338	126	154	3	1	433	–	36
June	175	214	69	37	4	1	348	3	35
July	170	177	38	9	29	2	141	5	47
Aug.	50	61	25	7	73	1	17	3	19
Sept.	12	40	10	2	65	3	9	7	11
Oct.	6	33	23	1	173	11	9	2	12
Nov.	3	17	12	1	67	3	10	6	10
Dec.	2	7	17	–	36	11	3	1	14
Tot.	7,382	2,339	1,487	544	456	41	1,220	27	258

Source: "Dokladnaia zapiska o formakh i dinamike klassovoi bor'by," p. 68.

* Literally, "Iz'iatie i ushchemlenie ASE."

† This column combines church closings and removals of church bells.

‡ This column combines four columns from the original: (1) other economic and political campaigns, (2) reelections of soviets, (3) cotton requisitions, and (4) misc.

137

Table 5-3. Statistics on Mass Disturbances per Region in 1930

Region	Month												Total
	Jan.	Feb.	Mar.	Apr.	May	June	July	Aug.	Sept.	Oct.	Nov.	Dec.	
Ukraine	45	200	2,945	169	208	186	83	55	46	129	23	9	4,098
N. Caucasus	36	56	335	159	133	99	137	42	22	21	17	4	1,061
Central Black Earth	57	130	737	181	99	54	40	18	13	13	11	20	1,373
M. Volga	38	54	263	135	70	71	52	31	14	21	14	14	777
L. Volga	27	37	203	208	254	157	70	9	4	13	15	6	1,003
Siberia	8	18	127	128	169	63	30	4	1	7	5	5	565
Urals	2	12	111	114	79	29	10	6	2	1	1	–	367
Moscow	10	114	284	136	30	18	35	14	8	14	7	6	676
Leningrad	4	12	56	38	6	4	–	2	–	1	1	1	125
Western	53	60	95	139	32	30	13	3	5	4	3	1	438
Ivanovo	12	13	83	30	19	11	6	1	2	6	3	4	190

Belorussia	4	77	208	150	16	22	22	3	2	1	1	2	508
Nizhkrai	17	24	83	86	50	26	15	5	4	5	7	4	326
Far East	–	2	10	14	9	8	7	–	–	1	–	–	50
Northern	1	–	2	7	6	1	5	–	–	–	–	–	22
Bashkiriia	13	12	109	36	10	3	5	3	–	1	4	–	196
Tatariia	28	33	254	97	39	31	44	11	2	3	1	5	548
Kazakhstan	3	20	43	64	61	26	16	20	7	6	–	–	266
Crimea	7	11	46	10	16	10	3	4	–	–	3	1	111
C. Asia	1	29	219	16	28	13	–	4	8	10	3	5	336
Transcaucasus	19	95	139	20	15	5	5	1	4	4	5	1	313
Nat'l Areas of North Caucasus	15	39	176	55	29	19	20	20	15	10	5	8	406
Total	402*	1,048	6,528	1,992	1,375*	886	618	256	159	270*	129	91	13,754*

Source: "Dokladnaia zapiska o formakh i dinamike klassovoi bor'by," p. 69.

*The correct sums are 400, 1,378, 271, and 13,755. The compiler appears to have made several, very slight mistakes in the figures in the columns because the given totals, which are not the correct sums, are cited elsewhere in the document.

downs. In almost all regions, the peak of rebellion came in March or, somewhat less frequently, in April. Thereafter, the incidence of mass disturbances declined precipitously in most grain-consuming regions and somewhat more slowly in grain-producing regions, with the exceptions of Siberia and Lower Volga, where mass disturbances declined only after May.

Information is also available on the number of peasants participating in mass disturbances. In 1929, 244,000 peasants took part in disturbances. According to data on only 10,071 incidents, their number rose to 2,468,625 in 1930.[18] The number of peasants involved in mass disturbances grew in proportion to the number of overall disturbances, increasing from 109,486 participants in January 1930 to 214,196 in February to 1,434,588 in March.[19] Table 5-4 provides information on the size of

Table 5-4. Statistics on the Size of Mass Disturbances per Region in 1930

Region	Disturbances	Disturbances In Which Number of Participants Is Known	Participants	Mean Average
Ukraine	4,098	3,208	956,587	298
North Caucasus	1,061	926	227,000	245
Central Black Earth	1,373	998	315,035	316
Lower Volga	1,003	732	119,175	163
Middle Volga	777	661	140,383	212
Moscow Region	676	516	117,502	228
Siberia	565	340	49,995	147
Tatariia	548	224	55,290	247
Belorussia	508	230	35,985	157
Western Region	438	381	64,047	168
Urals	367	288	34,777	121
Central Asia	336	290	115,950	400
Nizhkrai	326	181	44,373	245
Transcaucasus	313	163	48,620	298
Kazakhstan	266	162	19,455	120
Bashkiriia	195	72	17,225	239
Ivanovo	190	137	21,797	159
Leningrad Region	125	87	10,655	123
Crimea	111	101	12,420	123
Far East	50	39	3,474	89
North Region	22	16	3,230	202
Nat'l Areas of North Caucasus	406	319	55,650	175
Total	13,754	10,071	2,468,625	245

Source: "Dokladnaia zapiska o formakh i dinamike klassovoi bor'by," pp. 67, 69.

disturbances and the number of participants according to region. Disturbances in grain-producing and black soil regions tended to involve the greatest number of participants overall. It is more difficult to provide a precise assessment of the size of individual incidents. According to mean averages, disturbances appear to have been relatively large within the context of most villages.[20] National republics and Russian regions with large ethnic minorities tended to have some of the largest rebellions, followed closely by the grain-producing and black soil regions.

The majority of disturbances nationwide were local, either confined to a single village or encompassing a cluster of neighboring villages, and, although not spontaneous in the strict sense of the word, took place according to a more or less familiar and functional scenario requiring little or no planning or organization. Soviet sources, however, long claimed the existence of "groups" and "organizations," modified by "kulak" or "counterrevolutionary," that were behind peasant disturbances. According to the OGPU, 176 of the 13,754 mass disturbances that took place in 1930 had an insurrectionary (*povstancheskii*) character, meaning they were very large and well-organized uprisings going beyond the boundaries of individual villages and sometimes even *raions* and involving a temporary seizure of local power.[21] The OGPU also claimed that counterrevolutionary groups in Ukraine, Middle Volga, Siberia, North Caucasus, and elsewhere had endeavored to make contact with like-minded elements in the cities and the Red army (which may have meant little more than a critical letter to a peasant son in the factory or army).[22]

Most data on counterrevolutionary groups and organizations derives from OGPU sources based on repressive operations against these entities. In 1929, in the Middle Volga, for instance, 65 kulak underground groups were said to exist; in Mordovskaia Autonomous Region in the Middle Volga, over 300 counterrevolutionary groups were liquidated in 1929 and 1930.[23] In early fall 1930, the OGPU claimed to have liquidated a counterrevolutionary group active in 23 villages in Iletskii, Pokrovskii, and Sorochinskii *raions* in the Middle Volga. The group consisted of 59 people who had planned an uprising with the goals of rehabilitating kulaks, ending collectivization, and returning to the tax policies of 1926–27.[24] In the Moscow region over 200 groups were liquidated in 1930, and in Moscow's Egor'evskii *uezd* an attempt was reportedly made to organize a conference of peasant protesters linking up four *volosts*.[25] In the North Caucasus, some 4,000 kulak organizations were repressed in 1929 along with in 1930 the repression of—depending upon the source—anywhere from 283 to 441 groups and 78 counterrevolutionary organizations, with well over 6,000 participants.[26] A cossack organization called "Save the Khoper and Don" was said to exist and allegedly had branches in 180 villages in seven *raions*, mostly in the Lower Volga. Also in the Lower Volga, the OGPU claimed to have liquidated 32 counterrevolutionary groups and 191 kulak groups with more than 3,000 members in February 1930 alone.[27] In the Urals, 350 groups were liquidated in 1930.[28]

In Siberia in the second half of 1929, 15 kulak organizations with 145 members and 140 counterrevolutionary groups with 1,089 members were liquidated. Between 1 February and 10 March 1930, the authorities repressed an additional 19 insurgent counterrevolutionary organizations and 465 kulak groups, with over 4,000 "kulak" participants.[29] Here, in mid-February 1930, a "counterrevolutionary insurrectionary organization" was liquidated in the Irkutskii *okrug* village of Umygan. The organization had supposedly planned an uprising for 17 February, but the arrest of 26 peasants (including 22 kulaks and 4 middle peasants) prevented its realization. When the organization's participants were arrested, a group of 150 women, "raising a hysterical cry," surrounded the *sel'sovet* in an attempt to liberate friends and relatives.[30]

An archival report based on the unpublished notes of a *Pravda* correspondent provides interesting details on one so-called counterrevolutionary organization's preparations for an insurrection in the Crimea. In the Muslim Tatar villages of Sudakskii and Karasubazarskii *raions*, a "mass movement" in favor of emigration to Turkey in protest against collectivization had arisen, supposedly under the strong influence of mullahs, kulaks, and criminals. The center of activities was in the village Uskiut where in 1928 there had already been several serious disturbances. The organizational leadership of the movement reportedly collected arms, held regular "conspiratorial meetings," organized a cavalry, and made contacts among nearby boatmen for an escape to Turkey if the need arose. The leadership maintained ties with neighboring villages and even had supporters in Simferopol, where two NEPmen supposedly donated 200 rifles to the cause. In late 1929 and early 1930, *skhod* meetings were held to decide whether individuals would give their support to the uprising. Simultaneously, at the mosques, signatures were collected for a letter to Kalinin requesting the right to leave for Turkey, and money was gathered to send someone to Moscow with the letter. Whether the real insurrection consisted of the collection of signatures at the mosques around the movement for emigration or actual plans for an uprising by a conspiratorial organization, potential troubles were headed off by the timely intervention of the regional authorities, who sent in a detachment of Red army soldiers and made mass arrests (of some 200 people). Although the correspondent was silent on the final pacification of the region, he did note that the local peasants insulted and even stoned the soldiers. More suggestive was the suicide of one soldier who, according to the correspondent, made his "social position . . . clear" with this act; viewed from a different perspective, his suicide probably signified that he was morally sickened by the actions he witnessed and incapable of continuing his duties.[31]

The difference in meaning between groups and organizations, kulak or counterrevolutionary, is far from clear, although there was doubtless some distinction in the minds or fancies of Communist bureaucrats working in the apparatus of repression. That these groups actually existed as organized entities is also not clear. What passed in police reports as liquidated counterrevolutionary or kulak organizations may simply have been rebellious or troublesome peasants scapegoated as a warning to others and as an accomplishment to be served up to paranoid superiors prone to see conspiracies everywhere.

Typically, mass disturbances were purely village affairs, involving the entire community. Women often took the lead in demonstrations at meetings and village-level riots, sometimes with children in tow, while men tended to be most active in larger disturbances that went beyond the boundaries of a single village. Data on the social composition of participants is rare, and generally unreliable, given the politically subjective definition of class in the village and the inevitable tendency to blame kulaks and *podkulachniki* for unrest. The probability is that the village as a whole, irrespective of social status, formed the backbone of collective resistance. This is most likely to have been the case in villages with minimal socioeconomic differentiation in which the average size of disturbances appears to have approximated village size as in the Moscow and Central Black Earth regions. One of the very few instances of social reporting on participants in disturbances comes from Luzhskii *okrug* in the Leningrad Region from late 1929-early 1930. Of 274 "anti-collective farm *vystupleniia*," the participants included 29.2% kulaks, 51.1% middle and poor peasants, 7% clergy, and 5.1% local soviet officials.[32] The high percentage of middle and poor peasants, along with the probability of an inflated kulak percentage, given the politics of social analysis, indicates that villages as collective entities participated in mass disturbances. Even the OGPU was forced to admit that because of widespread atrocities, the kulak had support "from the side of a more or less significant mass of poor and middle peasants."[33]

There were occasional reports of Populist or Socialist Revolutionary (SR) leadership and involvement in peasant disturbances, although it is generally unclear whether these participants were outsiders or local peasants. The OGPU reported the liquidation of a counterrevolutionary-insurrectionary group led by SRs in the villages Lopatino and Kozlovka in Lopatinskii *raion*, Lower Volga. The organization purportedly encompassed 6 villages and included 6 SRs and 47 kulaks among its active membership.[34] According to another official source, an uprising in a village in Turkovskii *raion*, Lower Volga, transpired under SR leadership.[35] In Siberia, a counterrevolutionary group calling itself *"Chernye"* (the dark ones) was liquidated in August 1930. The OGPU claimed that it was active in 50 villages in more than 4 *okrugs* and had among its members former SRs.[36] At the same time, reports coming from Russia and published in the émigré Populist periodical, *Vestnik krest'ianskoi Rossii*, claimed that members of its party took part in collectivization disturbances and were subject to frequent arrest. The *Vestnik* proclaimed that there were more than 200 places in Russia where political work was being led under its flag.[37] Even allowing for the occasional participation of a Populist outsider in raising calls for a peasant union[38] and soviets without Communists[39] or in fomenting rebellions, peasants themselves were certainly sufficiently politicized by the experience and realities of the post-1917 order not to have required prompting. One suspects that outside participation was limited, in any case, for Communist interpretations of peasant unrest relied heavily on shifting official responsibility away from peasants, and therefore exaggeration rather than underreporting on this issue is likely.

Clergy, mainly Orthodox priests, and lay members of church councils are also sometimes cited as leading protest against collectivization and, in particular, inspiring agitation that labeled Soviet power the Antichrist.[40] The Tver *okrug* committee of the Communist party called the church council "the counterrevolutionary headquarters [*shtab*] . . . around which all counterrevolutionaries against collectivization are grouped."[41] In the Middle Volga in February 1930, the OGPU reported that illegal meetings were often held "under the guise of a church council meeting," which likely meant that the church council had assumed a position of leadership in the struggle against collectivization.[42] Church councils, in fact, appear to have played an important role in resistance.[43] In early 1930, in the village Slavkino in Atkarskii *okrug*, Lower Volga, the head of the church council mobilized the village women, urging them to liberate the priest who had just been arrested. Three hundred women gathered at the *sel'sovet*, demanding, "Give us back *batiushka* [the little father]."[44] In the villages of Ostrovka, Sysa, and Teliatnika in Riazanskii *okrug*, in the Moscow region, the church councils occupied the *sel'sovet* buildings during demonstrations against collectivization.[45] A report from the Moscow region claimed that women were being pushed into church lay leadership roles, probably because of the vocal stance women took against Soviet power at this time, and in Posledovskii *sel'sovet* in Pronskii *raion*, Riazanskii *okrug*, a woman was elected church elder.[46] Members of church councils were likely to have had the necessary stature to assume leadership roles in village politics as well as to be politically vulnerable enough to be highly motivated participants in revolt.

Priests also played a role in peasant protest. They were said especially to target women in their attempts to raise protest, a claim which is difficult to substantiate because official sources generally denied women agency in political protest, instead assigning the responsibility for women's rebellion to any available "counterrevolutionary" force in the village.[47] In many villages, however, priests made common cause with peasants. When Father Pokrovskii, who served several villages in Romashkovskii *raion*, Tverskii *okrug*, Moscow Region, told a crowd of one thousand women that he would no longer be permitted to hold services, the women headed for the *sel'sovet*, crying "down with Soviet power and communists, long live the priest and the church. . . . [We] will not go into the collective farm."[48] A priest in the North Caucasus told his congregation that "the collective farm is our ruin. Go to the general meeting and declare there openly that the collective farm is the ruin of all people."[49] In Kimrskii *okrug* in the Moscow Region, a priest sermonized that "the end of the world is approaching, Antichrist has come to earth. Come to the church. Tomorrow I will give my last sermon." The next day, a large crowd of people showed up only to witness, amid noise and protest, the arrest of the priest.[50] Whether through church sermons, counsel, or direct action, priests had their own reasons to participate in peasant protest. The widespread apocalyptic imagery in the ideology of peasant protest may certainly have been an atavistic peasant response, but it was surely influenced by Orthodox priests desperate for understanding and on the edge of a terrifying precipice foretelling their own end. Collectivization, a shared enemy, and the defense of common cultural symbols surely brought peasants and priests closer together than ever before in their checkered history of mutual distrust and dependence.

Peasant disturbances during collectivization assumed massive and threatening dimensions, rivaling earlier episodes of peasant unrest in modern Russian history.[51] Mass protests at meetings and local riots, the most common forms of disturbances, were largely peasant affairs in composition and in the traditional forms they assumed. Planning and organization were likely of a minimal nature and it is doubtful that a vast network of kulak and counterrevolutionary conspirators or outside agitators (beyond, perhaps, the local priest) existed anywhere but in the political rhetoric of Soviet power. This is not to rule out the likelihood of certain categories of village inhabitants—disgruntled ex-Communists, veterans, *otkhodniki*, prosperous peasants, and widows, as well as the occasional SR, priests, and church council members[52]—exercising leadership in rebellions, but rather to emphasize that riots and other forms of collective protest were a part of *peasant* politics, located firmly in the tradition of a peasant culture of resistance.

"Down with Antichrist"

March fever, before and after March 1930, began in rumor, flight, destruction of property, and, most directly, in meetings. Meetings on collectivization, dekulakization, and every conceivable Communist topic descended upon the villages of Soviet Russia as at no other time since the Revolution of 1917. Most meetings were organized and led by outsiders—*raion* plenipotentiaries, Communist officials, women's organizers, 25,000ers—and frequently were an effort to dissect the village, according to Communist perceptions of peasant political opinion and behavior, into groups of poor peasants, women, youth, Komsomol, party, and so on. When peasants were not being herded into meetings or cajoled in hut-to-hut agitation sessions, they themselves assembled—in their homes, at the well, mill, or marketplace—to debate collectivization. *Peasant* meetings, though, were redefined as kulak and therefore ceased to be regarded as anything but subversive, which in a sense they were, for they accorded peasants some small bit of autonomy and social space to consider peasant needs and issues, all implicitly and, increasingly, explicitly antithetical to Soviet power.

Official meetings presented an interesting conjuncture of peasant and Communist sensibilities. They were a forum for policy articulation, but they were conducted on peasant "turf."[53] In many cases, Soviet power was too intimidating for peasants to engage in protest, in particular direct protest, especially when organizers laid their guns on the table or threatened villagers with deportation to Solovki or the "bogs" (a recurrent threat and fear).[54] At other times, and more often than is generally assumed, peasants managed to find a path of resistance or at least to articulate their feelings of injustice and outrage at what they viewed as the theft, pillage, and destruction of their way of life. Protest could be direct or it could be expressed in subtler forms, making use of the traditional and frequently veiled weapons of the weak.

In any form, peasant protest at meetings was dangerous. Protest, angry and direct, or mild and taking the form of questions and doubts, was an affront to Soviet power. Communist plenipotentiaries and officials of all kinds framed resolutions to be voted on by the simple, recurrent, and leading question, "Who is against Soviet power?" To be against collectivization, dekulakization, the closing of a church, the opening of a nursery, the designation of a peasant as poor, or even the very person of a meeting organizer was to be or could be construed as "against Soviet power." The concept of Soviet power served as a kind of Communist totem to state and party cadres building socialism in the name of new gods, on faith and often with a blinding hatred or disregard for peasants. The totem, moreover, was empowering, for Soviet power, in the hands of any official, was personal power, a kind of charm. It became a mask of legitimation behind which officials led their struggles with opponents when politics and debate no longer mattered. Solzhenitsyn witnessed this personification of Soviet power in the Gulag after the war. He quoted a camp guard who, in response to some kind of minor protest, barked out, who "spoke out against the Soviet government?" In his usual sardonic tone, Solzhenitsyn explained, "People will protest that this is a universal approach, that even out in freedom every little chief declares himself to be the Soviet government, and just try to argue with him about it."[55] Every "little chief," though, *was* Soviet power in a contest that set up a line of barricades through the heart of the nation. During collectivization, peasants confronted this absurdity backed by force and could find themselves silenced and figuratively disarmed by the threat that opposition to Soviet power carried, for opposition to Soviet power and its physical incarnations was, quite simply, treason.

The personification of Soviet power was a useful tool in the arsenal of the Stalinist order, high and low. It was not, however, the only resource available to cadres seeking to force votes out of peasants. Forbidding discussion and amendments to resolutions, some organizers simply posed the question as "who is for" and "who is against" (whatever the resolution concerned).[56] Others had their own, more original approaches to handling peasants. With a sadistic, schoolmasterly bent, backed by more than the rod, a plenipotentiary in the Central Black Earth Region would yell, "Who is that? Name!" and then ostentatiously write a few lines in his notebook in response to any objections at meetings.[57] In a *khutor* in Uriupinskii *raion*, Lower Volga, a RIK (*raion*-level soviet executive committee) plenipotentiary had peasants vote on closing the church by holding two votes: one for a temporary, and one for a permanent, closure. In each case, 26 voted "for" and 48 "against." The plenipotentiary's mathematical ingenuity allowed him to add the "for" votes and arrive at a total of 52 "for" and 48 "against," and consequently closed the church according to his idea of revolutionary legality.[58] And throughout the countryside, officials could avail themselves of brute force, threatening peasants with deportation and displaying sidearms.

In reality and in spite of the enormous force that backed it, Soviet power feared confrontations with peasants, for the potential for violence or, at the very least, disruption was ever-present, as relatively small contingents of cadres, backed by local officials of sometimes dubious loyalty, were confronted and outnumbered by entire villages. This in fact was the conclusion of a Commissariat of Agriculture plenipotentiary who visited the village Stezhka in the volatile Kozlovskii *okrug* in Central Black Earth Region. There had already been two mass disturbances there and the situation was tense. On his arrival, the plenipotentiary called a meeting that lasted for eight hours—not an unusual occurrence in those days—and was attended by 2,000 people. At the meeting, the peasants demanded the return of the kulaks and the division of land without the application of class principles. The plenipotentiary, in his own words, was forced to "listen patiently to the cries and unhappiness" of the villagers and to recognize that mistakes had been committed. According to him, the local authorities "fear[ed] the masses" and had even advised him against holding meetings with peasants. The plenipotentiary, however, believed that a reasonable and unconceited approach was all that was necessary: "When I asked forgiveness from the peasants for the mistakes and violations of our party line by the local officials . . . then the peasants in their turn also recognized their mistakes."[59] This case speaks both to the fear of officials and the ability of peasants to behave reasonably if treated in a civilized manner. Civilized manners, however, were a rarity in those times, and most officials, whether out of fear or disgust, approached peasants brutishly, with untrammeled force.

The potential for and reality of state violence at meetings could be overwhelming. Peasants were frequently arrested and labeled kulaks just for criticism (*za kritiku*, as they termed it). The omnipotence of Soviet power often led peasants to challenge the regime from the side rather than head on, applying more artful and cautious tactics to attempt to halt a meeting's end goal. Noise and silence were two of the most frequent and seemingly apolitical tactics. In response to the Central Black Earth organizer who demanded the names of protesters, peasants refused to speak, in a sense boycotting the meeting, which continued on in total audience silence. Here, incidentally, the village women, realizing the futility of such meetings, had stayed away to begin with.[60] At a meeting in a Ukrainian village, officials met with silence from the outset. The organizers of this meeting subsequently forbade anyone to leave the room before agreeing—and therefore breaking silence—to enter the collective farm. Everyone sat in silence until one peasant asked permission to leave to relieve himself, which he did under guard. After that, all the peasants felt a similar call from nature and demanded release. The meeting ended, for the time being, in stalemate.[61] Later, during the famine years, a March 1933 report from the North Caucasus spoke of "kulaks" using "food difficulties" (a code for starvation) to create a "conspiracy of silence" at meetings in which there were no questions, no discussion, no responses to reports.[62] Although the 1933 report made a conspiracy out of silence, generally the tactic succeeded at least in stalling and temporarily frustrating the little Soviet powers, as well as providing a cover for dissent. And even allowing for peasant intimidation, who is to say that silence was not a conspiracy, traditionally and almost instinctively agreed upon as a dignified response to unbridled power?

Noise served a similar purpose, and was often even less obvious as a tactic of protest. Cadres frequently spoke of disorderly meetings. Some 25,000ers prided themselves on taming the *muzhik* and transforming meetings that earlier had been full of racket, with all speaking at once, into orderly, proletarian-like assemblies.[63] What these cadres failed to see was how useful it was for peasants to create disorder in the collectivization-era context and play upon prejudices of irrational *muzhiki* incapable of reasonable and orderly discourse. In the Kuban, noise was used frequently to block speakers.[64] In the Central Black Earth Region, peasants created a din at collectivization meetings when the time came to vote.[65] At a meeting in the village Cheremyshevo in Mordovskaia *oblast'*, peasant women would not allow the speaker to say a word, crying out "hurrah" [*ura*] repeatedly until the meeting was broken up.[66] In the village of Khan'kovets in Mogilev-Podol'skii *okrug* in Ukraine, officials attempted four times to conduct a meeting on collectivization; each time, peasant women broke up the meeting with shouts of "Down with collectivization!" and "Down with the brigades!"[67]

Drunkenness was another frequent disruption at meetings. Whether to steel nerves, to laugh in the face of Communist sobriety, or simply because they were alcoholics, male peasants sometimes came to meetings drunk, creating such pandemonium that the meeting would have to be stopped.[68] Drunkenness could serve as cover for protest, for certainly Communists understood the poor *muzhiki*'s supposed weakness for drink: alcohol remained apolitical to Communist sensibilities. Although apolitical, alcohol was still a danger to collective farm organizers and was recog-

nized as such by at least some officials. A plenipotentiary working on
dekulakization in Mikushkinskii *raion*, Buguruslanskii *okrug*, Middle
Volga, for instance, banned the sale of alcohol after he discovered that the
peasants slated for deportation were drinking heavily. He was angered to
discover later that they shared their penchant for drink with the RIK
chairman, who had almost immediately ordered the reopening of the local
liquor store.[69]

In *Red Bread*, Maurice Hindus offers a detailed description of a
women's meeting that illustrates well the noise-silence routine. In summer 1929, officials came to the village to tell women of the coming good
life of communal kitchens, nurseries, electricity, clubs, equality, and so
on, that awaited them in the collective farm. After the lecture,

> a party man called for questions and discussion. Not a word came in reply.
> Nobody seemed to have anything to say. Again the party man prompted the
> chairman into calling for expressions of opinion; again no response. . . . At
> last one woman summoned courage to speak, and there followed of a sudden
> an explosion of voices, a babel of shouts. The party man called for order. He
> insisted that only one person at a time should speak . . . again there was
> silence. Then once more someone spoke up, only to be instantly over-
> whelmed by a fresh burst of shouts. The party man became wroth. With a
> violent flourish of his arms he restored silence, and with stern earnestness
> he pleaded for orderly behavior. But . . . try as hard as they might, those
> impassioned women could not speak one at a time. No sooner would one of
> them begin saying something than all the others would follow suit until the
> air shook with their booming voices. After a few minutes of this disorder a
> humped old woman with a dusty kerchief on her head spat violently at the
> whole gathering in the manner of *muzhiks* when they are displeased with
> something, and exclaimed, "Only pigs have come here; I might as well go
> home."

At this point, a local peasant official took over the meeting with a rousing
oratory, the refrain of which was "Are we pigs or are we not?" According
to Hindus, "the meeting continued, but not without confusion."[70] It
should be noted that these same women, individually or in groups, had no
problem dispassionately telling Hindus their stories and grievances when
officials were not present.[71]

These silent and noisy rituals of hidden resistance were joined by
other forms of masked protest. Peasants in the village Istomina in the
Moscow Region resolved that they "welcomed collectivization, but would
not join the collective farm," thus providing direct evidence of the supposed wavering nature of the middle peasantry to confused urban cadres.[72] At a women's meeting in the Kuban in 1930, only 76 of 300 women
in attendance responded to the roll call. When pressed for an explanation,
organizers were told that this silence was a reaction to signing up for the
collective farm earlier. The women claimed that they had not known the
meaning of their signatures then and were now skeptical about giving
their names for anything. An activist later responded, more in duped frus-

tration than anger, that he had explained the meaning of their signatures "tens of times."[73] Following the publication of Stalin's "Dizziness from Success," peasants in one village made the collective farm chairman, in the course of a five-hour meeting, read the resolution on "Dizziness" six times before agreeing to vote.[74] In other cases, peasants obstructed state business by holding religious rituals or other kinds of celebrations during meetings in order to draw off attendance.[75]

In all of these cases, peasants were able to frustrate or halt meetings by playing the role of dark and ignorant *muzhiki* and *baby,* incapable of understanding or following the agenda of Soviet power. The ruse was successful in the very short term, and it was difficult to hold anyone responsible, for peasants will be peasants. And whether or not noisy and drunken disorders or "conspiracies of silence" were simply routine attributes of peasant meetings or responses wrought by fear and desperation, it is still the fact that in the collectivization era the practice, or tactic, *worked,* and it worked to the benefit of peasants against Soviet power, demonstrating Eric Hobsbawm's dictum that "[t]he refusal to understand is a form of class struggle."[76]

Peasants could also assume an aggressive stance at meetings, confronting Soviet power directly. During the first phase of collectivization in late 1929 and early 1930, peasants frequently stood up to officials at meetings, attempting to use the forum to defeat official motions or disrupt proceedings. In some villages, peasants simply voted against all measures proposed by Soviet power and refused outright to organize a collective farm.[77] The OGPU reported a North Caucasus village meeting resolving: "[We] will not go into your collective and [we] do not wish to think about it."[78] At a Crimean village meeting dedicated to closing the local church, peasants voted down the state's resolution in a resounding defeat of 218 to 8.[79] At an Odessa village meeting, the peasants, with only a few exceptions, refused to include a group of middle peasants on the list of peasants to be dekulakized. When they refused to vote for or against the list, the meeting chair announced that they too would be dekulakized.[80] In early 1930 in the village Nosterovo, Iur'evskii *raion,* Aleksandrovskii *okrug* in the Ivanovo area, a general meeting of peasants overturned the decision to close the church and turn it into a warehouse.[81] Elsewhere, peasants took over meetings on collectivization and passed their own decrees, generally to abstain from the organization of a collective farm.[82] Examples of decrees from the Middle Volga give some sense of the peasantry's political consciousness. In the village Mukmenovo in Asikeevskii *raion,* Buguruslanskii *okrug,* peasants decreed "To consider incorrect the line of the Communist party and authorities [*vlast'*] in relation to peasant farming with wholesale collectivization and tractorization." In N. Piatino village in Chembarovskii *raion,* Penzenskii *okrug,* peasants decreed "To resolve that the measures being carried out by Sovpower [*Sovvlast'*] are not in the interests of the peasantry and in particular of our village and therefore to vote down wholesale collectivization." The village Isakla in Buguruslanskii *okrug* decreed "To put off going into the collective farm until 1931," while a Petrovskii *raion*, Orenburgskii *okrug* village decreed "To abstain from wholesale collectivization in view of the fact that in many collective farms there is no equality or order, and personal deprivations are worse than in the individual farms."[83]

Literally everywhere there were reports of peasants breaking up official meetings.[84] In the Western Region, a March 1930 meeting was broken up with cries of "Down with Soviet power."[85] At a meeting in a village in Buguruslanskii *raion*, Middle Volga, in early 1930, peasants cried, "Down with the Muscovites. . . . Down with the workers. . . . We can make do without you."[86] In the village N. Nikulino, also in Buguruslanskii *okrug*, a former participant of the civil war era Chapany uprisings[87] demanded official documents from the collective farm organizers to prove their right to hold a meeting; when they failed to produce papers, the meeting was broken up, thus demonstrating the utility of legal form as a tool of resistance. In January 1930, in the village Arkhangel'skoe in Kuznetskii *okrug*, Middle Volga, a meeting was shut down when a poor peasant named Surkov stood up and declared: "You are pillaging the peasantry and have pillaged all the kulaks. . . . Under the tsar we lived better, the collective farm is a noose. Down with slavery, long live freedom." Shouts of "hurrah" and "that's our Surkov" (*vot tak nash Surkov*) followed his speech. The peasants then forced the officials presiding to give Surkov a certificate testifying that "he spoke correctly," after which they left the meeting with cries of "Down with the collective farm."[88] In the village Aleksandro-Bogdenovka in Vol'skii *okrug*, Lower Volga, middle peasants broke up several meetings. At one, a woman banged her fist on the organizer's desk and yelled, "To hell with your collective farm."[89] In a village in Tagaiskii *raion*, Ul'ianovskii *okrug*, Middle Volga, women broke up a meeting, shouting that they did not need a collective farm; elsewhere in this area, villagers resorted in a time-honored practice to sounding the tocsin—the church bell—to break up a meeting and create the general pandemonium that came with the sounding of the tocsin.[90] Shouts of "Fire," "Beat the plenipotentiaries," and "Down with Antichrist" put a halt to collectivization meetings in many parts of the country.[91] In the *stanitsa* Kanevskii in the Kuban, peasant anger and intransigence led the collective farm organizer simply to give up. He told the meeting (using the informal "*ty*"): "You don't want to be in the collective farm, then [you] don't have to." The peasants responded with cries of "Citizens, leave the meeting, we don't want collectivization. [D]own with [it], [we] don't need [it]," and walked out.[92] In most cases, though, neither peasants nor organizers were so willing to come to "agreement."

Many meetings ended in violence or with a riot. In June 1929, a *sel'sovet* plenipotentiary was flogged at a meeting in the Northwestern Region.[93] In Kramatorskii *raion*, Artemovskii *okrug*, Ukraine, a mobilized worker was beaten during a general meeting on collectivization.[94] In the village Krotkova in Syzranskii *okrug*, Middle Volga, a crowd of "drunken

podkulachniki" arrived with their wives at a *raion* meeting on collectivization, yelling "Down with communists, we don't need the collective farm."
They physically attacked the presiding officials, forcing them to flee for
their lives.[95] In a Buguruslanskii *okrug* village, the peasant women created
a din at a meeting, harassing the meeting's secretary and ripping up his
protocols. They succeeded in shutting down the meeting, after which they
headed for the school, breaking all its windows and attempting to pull
down the red flag, and in the process threatening the local activists.[96] At
a meeting in a Penzenskii *okrug*, Middle Volga village, in early January
1930, the 600 peasants (mostly women) attending began to shout, "Down
with the poor." They then broke up the meeting and assaulted the presiding officials, including the teacher. The teacher and his wife fled to the
sel'sovet, but were pursued by the crowd. The *sel'sovet* chair fired off
warning shots to stop the impending lynching. The shots ended the encounter, leaving peasants demanding elections for a new *sel'sovet* chair.[97]

Whether peasant protest at meetings was masked and indirect or
clearly oppositional and violent, it derived from a set of reasoned political
concerns about the fate of family, belief, and community. Although
largely hidden from the historian, intense debate, thought, and passion
surely lay behind peasant activity at meetings. Some sense of the politics
and reasoning of the village appears in the transcript of a 16 February
1930 meeting of the peasants of the collective farm *Oktiabr'* (in Talovskii
raion, Borisoglebskii *okrug*, Central Black Earth Region) with Kalinin.
Kalinin, who, interestingly enough, comes through as the paternal leader
he was portrayed as in official propaganda, sought to understand the disproportionately large number of expulsions from the collective farm. He
soon found himself caught between the excuses of the farm's leaders and
the grievances of a rank-and-file concerned that some of their neighbors
had been treated unjustly. When Kalinin asked how the expulsions occurred, one official replied that the poor peasants discussed each case and
"we think we didn't hurt anyone." At that, a voice from the audience
interrupted: "Mikhail Ivanovich, in my opinion some people were hurt.
Among the expelled were some with many children, they themselves led
and organized the collective farm and they were purged out of malice,
they are not guilty." An official later explained that one member was
purged because he was a *lishenets* (or a person deprived of civil rights)
and had served in the police force, to which a voice from the audience
yelled out, "He served only 6 months in the police in 1902." Other peasants complained of being forced to vote for lists without discussion: "Mikhail Ivanovich, the comrades say to us: you believe in the Com[munist]
party? We say, yes, [we] believe. Then if [you believe] you must vote for
the list." Kalinin responded: "But you must answer this way: we believe
in the Com[munist] party, but all the same we wish to discuss the list."
The peasants were able to offer reasoned defenses in support of each of
the expelled members. Although the conversation has the appearance of a
spontaneous encounter, the criticism in fact was not wholly extemporane-

ous, for it was derived from a shared sense of justice and ethical norms that were firmly entrenched in peasant consciousness and politics long before Kalinin arrived on the scene.[98]

Peasant consciousness and politics were at least partially formed and articulated in gatherings of an entirely different nature: meetings clandestinely called by peasants for peasants. Surely many of the "kulak and counterrevolutionary organizations" noted above were in reality a label for peasant meetings. These meetings were often simply gatherings in peasant homes, the bathhouse, the church, or some other central and safe location to discuss the fate of the community.[99] During the 1928–29 soviet election campaign, secret meetings to discuss candidates and tactics were reported throughout the country.[100] Meetings in late 1929 and in 1930 to discuss collectivization and especially Stalin's "Dizziness from Success" article were also recorded in many parts of the countryside.[101] In the *khutor* Rybuska in Rudnianskii *raion*, Kamyshinskii *okrug*, Lower Volga, a peasant woman described as the daughter of a kulak trader held a clandestine meeting for women in her home, where she reportedly called the collective farm "bondage." After the meeting, she led the women to the *sel'sovet* where they presented declarations to quit the farm.[102] In 1930 in the cossack village of Ekaterinogradskaia in the Tersk area, a secret meeting of peasants still outside the collective farm was held at which, reportedly, the collective farm's board of shame (*chernaia doska* [black board], or listing of collective farmers whose work performance was poor during a defined period of time) was burnt. A few days later, the local party cell decided to arrest what the sources labeled "these agitators and bandits." The party members surrounded the home where the meetings were held, but before they managed to make their arrests, shots rang out from within, killing and wounding several of the activists. When the smoke had cleared, twenty-three "white bandits" were arrested.[103] Chance, an informant, or a forced interrogation after the fact were likely the source of information on these meetings. It is probable, although our evidence is necessarily scant, that these meetings were a frequent occurrence, an opportunity—formal or informal—for peasants to discuss their fate and plans for action, whether or not peasants categorized them as meetings and whether or not they were as clearly subversive as these two cases. When Soviet power classified them as meetings and prefixed them with the dangerous kulak or counterrevolutionary label, it aimed not only to silence opposition but more significantly to remove offstage social space,[104] where the peasant culture of resistance—far from the eyes of historians and officials—is shaped, and thereby to disable it.

Whether disguised by artful dissimulation or openly and daringly practiced, peasant protest at meetings was an important form of collective action. Throughout the country, the state's agents had to work much harder than generally believed to control meetings and to secure the seemingly pointless but necessary signatures for collective farm organization in what can only be described as a charade of "revolution from below." Peasant protest at meetings often took the form of a kind of ritual of resistance, a customary chorus of verbal, or nonverbal, protest that peasants had acted out in the presence of their masters time and again. It was part of a culture of resistance, learned or perhaps intuited, as safe protest by peasants facing imminent danger and overwhelming power. Despite the ruse and the safety it accorded, such protest remained an act of amazing courage, a profound political statement from a culture under siege. Most of the time, it was contained within meetings. But at other times, protest was direct and violent and served as the preamble to a larger scenario of popular resistance—the peasant riot, "meaningless and merciless," to use the descriptive phrase made famous by Russia's great writer, Alexander Pushkin.[105]

"Meaningless and merciless"

Or so Pushkin claimed. Peasant riots were in fact anything but "meaningless." Like popular riots elsewhere, peasant riots in the collectivization era displayed similar patterns as they echoed through the land. Unplanned, generally leaderless, and seldom initiated by a single prompt, riots all the same bespoke a rebel consciousness founded upon peasant political, economic, and cultural interests. The objectives of riots—disbanding a collective farm or preventing its organization, taking back grain and socialized livestock, liberating kulaks, defending the church—as well as the targets of violence—officials, peasant activists, government and collective farm buildings—were indicative of the political nature of the disturbances and the political consciousness of peasant rebels. The unity of peasant interests cut across regional differences, and riots transpired as repeat performances with stylized behavior, set roles, and similar goals. The ritualistic aspects of riots and the underlying peasant consciousness do not negate the very real rage and explosive nature of the disturbances. Riots were rooted in frustration, desperation, and outrage. They were a last resort of the powerless confronted by unending injustice.

Ritualized displays of rage, riots constituted a specific genre in the peasant culture of resistance, with defined roles for participants and fairly routinized procedures for the accomplishment of goals. Women often assumed leading parts in riots, especially in the early phases. The men, meanwhile, initially stood to the side, observing, intimidating, sometimes armed with stakes, scythes, and pitchforks, advancing only when violence erupted and sometimes taking charge when disturbances snowballed into insurrection. Most disturbances began with nonviolent approaches to Soviet power, at meetings or on the streets, as peasants (often women) attempted verbally to defend their farms, neighbors, or church. Such encounters could turn ugly quickly if officials insolently rebuffed peasants or disregarded their demands, treating them as dark *muzhiki* and *baby*, as beasts of burden. If pushing and jostling ensued, the sounding of the tocsin—the church bell—was sure to follow, disrupting meetings and calling all the village out. The "noise protest" of meetings continued with shouts of all kinds, demands, and cries for an end to injustice as peasants assembled, perhaps near the *sel'sovet*, symbol of authority, perhaps near the collective farm office or granary, symbols of the new order. If the crowd's demands were still not met, or, worse, if the official response was aggressive or provocative, the crowd could easily become violent, calling for a *samosud* or *rasprava* (retribution, generally bloody) over the authorities, who were always outnumbered at this stage. Wise officials hid; otherwise they could find themselves under attack or chased into the nearest safe refuge. Most riots were more about intimidation than physical violence, and were an attempt to clear the way of officials and activists in order to accomplish the goals of revolt.[106] Even the OGPU admitted that physical force was used against officials in only 1,616 riots (or approximately 12% of the total) in 1930, resulting in 147 deaths, 212 injuries, and 2,796 assaults.[107] Once the official presence was disposed of, the crowd took control and set policy accordingly—liberating arrested kulaks, taking back property, disbanding the collective farm, or reopening the church. Some riots were accompanied by political vandalism and assaults on the symbols of power—the destruction of portraits of leaders, the ransacking of offices.[108] In extreme cases, the crowd formally took over the reins of local government, sometimes reelecting the *sel'sovet*, other times going so far as to reinstate the institution of *starosta* (village elder).[109] Most riots came to an end of their own accord, as their objectives were met and Soviet power appeared to vanish. The OGPU claimed that only 993 riots (or about 7% of the total) were suppressed through the use of army, militia, or OGPU forces, or irregular armed party detachments, and mostly in the months of February through April.[110]

The state attempted to explain away peasant riots by diverting blame from objectionable policies to kulaks, counterrevolutionaries, dark masses, and local officials who abused their power. The last factor in particular had a major bearing on peasant disturbances, but the causal origins of riots resided in the reckless and repressive policies of Moscow that local officials had to implement. Collectivization, in all its aspects, undermined the integrity of the village, threatening the economic survival of families, the cohesion of the community, and the cultural traditions of the village. The collective farm and the forced taking of grain were direct threats to peasant subsistence. The expropriation and deportation of peasants as kulaks violated peasant ideals of collectivism, amounting to an assault on peasant community and autonomy. Finally, church closures and bell removals literally and, perhaps equally importantly, symbolically struck at the heart of village traditions, at major symbols of the cultural institutions that held the community together as no other, at the primary significations of local pride and beauty. Although the direct cause of collectivization was, at least in its ideological dimensions, uniquely Communist, the perils that collectivization represented were, in a sense, "generic" causes of peasant rebellion, timeless and cross-cultural.

Riots dotted the rural terrain from the late 1920s, when the state began forced grain requisitioning. In Siberia in 1928, 13 peasant riots, each with from 15 to 300 participants, occurred. Most stemmed from food difficulties and resistance to requisitioning; in several places peasants took back their grain by force and torched grain warehouses.[111] Biiskii *okrug* in Western Siberia, a particularly turbulent area in 1930, experienced 43 mass disturbances against requisitioning in spring 1929, some 16 of which were categorized as "large and serious," with more than 7,000 participants.[112] In the village Mikhailovskoe in Mikhailovskii *raion*, a peasant riot broke out in mid-April 1929 over forced requisitioning. Here, "for two days, the crowd ruled in the village," ordering the release of arrested peasants, beating the chairman of the requisitioning commission, and forcing a guarantee from officials that no one would be punished for the uprising. The revolt concluded with a large meeting of some 900 people (700 of them women) who presented a "platform" demanding the end of requisitioning and the return of expropriated property. In the nearby village of Sliud'ianka, a crowd of 200 people (mainly women), supposedly led by a kulak named Rubanovich, surrounded the *sel'sovet*, demanding an end to requisitioning and threatening to burn down the building. The crowd dispersed only with the arrival of the militia. At the same time, in the village Abash in Bashelakskii *raion*, up to 100 women gathered at the *sel'sovet*, shouting for an end to grain requisitions because, they said, "we have no bread, there is nothing to eat." They began to beat the *sel'sovet* chairman until their attention was diverted by the arrival of an *okrug* soviet executive committee plenipotentiary whom they dragged from his cart and attempted to beat, but who eventually succeeded in calming the crowd.[113]

In the Ukrainian villages of Novo-Lazarevka and Novo-Skelevatka in Kazankovskii *raion*, Krivorozhskii *okrug*, mass disturbances occurred in late November 1929 over atrocities committed by *raion* authorities. In Novo-Lazarevka, *raion* officials arrested 10 people for resisting requisitions, locked them in an abandoned house, and boarded up the doors and windows so that no one would be able to pass them food or drink. The mother of one arrested peasant threatened suicide if they took her last grain. The *raion* party secretary told her, "Go ahead and hang yourself, give her a rope . . . the revolution won't suffer over this." He then ordered that a light burn in all homes through the night, and for three nights no one in the village slept. In Novo-Skelevatka, the same officials arrested local members of the requisitioning commission who refused to use force against their neighbors. They then made the entire village spend the night in the frost, beating peasants and taking all their grain. Some peasants were forced to dance naked in a cellar to the accompaniment of an accordion, while others who did not hand over their grain had to wear slanderous placards on their chests, in what seems like a reverse appropriation by officials of certain peasant customs of rough justice. The revolts that erupted in response to these actions were suppressed by OGPU and militia troops.[114]

The riots in Novo-Lazarevka and Novo-Skelevatka sparked a series of disturbances in neighboring villages as word of the violence of the requisitioning commission spread. In a number of villages, peasants succeeded in chasing out requisitioning officials. In Novo-Osinovka, villagers beat up requisitioners, forcing them to hide out in the *sel'sovet* where they sat locked up until evening, while, in the meantime, the crowd outside grew to 500 people. In Glushkova, peasants forced requisitioners to flee. Several days later, OGPU troops arrived in the district to carry out mass arrests. In Glushkova and Novo-Osinovka, large crowds of peasants attacked the prisoner convoys, armed with rocks and stakes, in an attempt to liberate their neighbors. In Glushkova, the peasants disarmed and arrested four police officials. Some hours later, OGPU reinforcements arrived, only to confront a crowd now swelled to 1,000 people armed with pitchforks, stakes, scythes, and rocks, heading for the village where the arrested peasants were being held. There, the crowd was met and dispersed by OGPU and militia contingents firing a volley of warning shots.[115]

The riots against "extraordinary measures" were motivated by the threat to subsistence that requisitioning posed. Although forced grain extractions were the basis of most pre-1930 mass disturbances, especially in grain-producing regions, they were not the only causes of riots at this time. Of the 94 mass disturbances in the Central Black Earth Region in 1929, 28 were over requisitioning; 51, church closures; 8, land reform (*zemleustroistvo*); and 4, collectivization.[116] In the Middle Volga, a series of riots erupted over collectivization and the closing of churches as early as the spring of 1929. In the village Delezerka in Chelnovershinskii *raion*, Buguruslanskii *okrug*, a crowd of more than 100 people, supposedly led by kulaks and the priest, rose up in revolt, assaulting local party members and destroying the *sel'sovet* in response to the closing of the church and attempts to organize a collective farm. Although the *raion* authorities reportedly panicked and attempted to call in the army, the disturbances came to an end when "responsible" *raion* officials arrived.[117] In the village Lebiazh'e, Melkesskii *raion*, Ul'ianovskii *okrug*, peasants broke up a collectivization meeting, again supposedly under the leadership of kulaks and members of the church council. The riotous crowd, soon grown to several thousand, yelled, "[We] should beat the communists, the *sel'sovet* chairman, and the [party] cell secretary. There are [too] few people, beat the tocsin." In the Muslim village Enganaevo in Cherdaklinskii *raion* in the same *okrug*, the authorities had made plans to carry out land reform in preparation for the organization of a collective farm. Several hundred wealthy (*zazhitochnye*) peasants were to be removed to distant fields. When the *sel'sovet* plenum on land reform opened on 9 April 1929, the tocsin immediately began to toll, bringing together a crowd of 500 peasants, shouting: "[We] will not let them exile the wealthy and the mullahs, don't let them disunite us, poor from rich." The crowd roughed up several officials, and the disturbance continued into the next day, when the crowd swelled to 1,500 strong in its attempt to resist the arrest of the mullah. An armed detachment of 100 troops finally came in to suppress the uprising, at which time 13 people were arrested.[118]

Several Tatar villages also rose up at this time in response to religious persecution. On 27 April 1929, in the village Sr. Tigona, Spasskii canton, Tatar Republic, a group of 200 peasants, holding a white flag, broke the lock which had earlier (21 April) closed the church. They then beat up the local activists and threw into the mud portraits of Communist leaders, including Lenin. In the end, the militia somehow restored order. An analogous disturbance occurred in the village Egoldaevo in the Riazan area in May when a workers' brigade arrived to close the church. A crowd of 500 people (mainly women) gathered, threatening the workers with knives and stakes and hurling rocks at them.[119]

Elsewhere, riots broke out in the course of the 1928 and 1929 soviet election and tax campaigns.[120] In the Siberian village of Mamantova in Barnaul'skii *okrug*, a pitchfork riot ensued when officials attempted to sell off kulak property for nonpayment of taxes. A similar riot occurred in the Siberian village of Korchino; here a militia officer was killed and a *sel'sovet* chair wounded.[121] Although the entire countryside experienced turmoil in these years, the key Russian areas affected appear to have been North Caucasus, Siberia, Urals, and Leningrad Region, where, according to a Russian scholar, over one-half of all pre-1930 mass disturbances occurred.[122]

Rioting peaked in the first half of 1930, with its most dangerous impact in March. In these months, the state's campaign of rural repression was at its most intense and roused the peasantry into a vast rebellion. Riots against the collective farm were the most basic and widespread type of riot, accounting for the majority of all mass disturbances in the countryside in 1930.[123] Such riots could aim to prevent the organization of a collective farm or to disband one. They could also be preoccupied with more selective issues of collective farm organization, such as the socialization of livestock and seed grain or the land reform that frequently preceded collectivization. The organization of collective farms, however, did not occur in isolation from the other campaigns of repression launched upon the village. Riots against collective farms were inextricably tied in with protest against dekulakization and church closures. The size and gravity of peasant disturbances as well as the intra- and, at times, inter-village unity displayed sent a shock wave through the party that ultimately would register only in early March. Although most revolts were small and localized, many assumed alarming dimensions and evolved dangerously from anti–collective farm protest into insurrection against the state.

Ukraine led the nation in revolt, accounting for some 2,945 incidents in March 1930 alone. Here revolts tended to be large in size, and the overall number of participants in the 1930 rebellion came close to one million.[124] Already in the first three months of 1929, the OGPU registered 144 mass disturbances in Ukraine. As grain requisitioning intensified, their number increased to 116 in August 1929, 195 in September, and 336 in October. The high point of revolt came in the first half of 1930. By 10 March, peasant rioting had spread to eighteen *okrugs* (and over 110 *raions*) of the republic. In Tul'chinskii *okrug*, 189 villages rioted in a situation the sources describe as "complete anarchy." Peasants closed or destroyed *sel'sovets* throughout the *okrug*. In Dzhulinskii *raion*, an armed detachment of peasants seized power, proclaiming themselves dictators of the *raion* and placing peasant elders in charge of communities. The rebels were arrested after entering into what they supposed to be negotiations with the OGPU. A crowd of 600 to 700 people then merged on the *raion* center of Sobolevka to demand the rebels' release. The crowd failed in its attempt: the authorities fired on the peasants and arrested twenty people. In the village of Goriachevka in Miastkovskii *raion*, a crowd of up to 1,000 people, led by women and children, forced an OGPU cavalry brigade to retreat. The crowd demanded the liberation of the kulaks and the return of their property.[125]

In Ukraine, collectivization and grain requisitioning were especially violent. Resistance was accentuated by national tensions, which likely increased the solidarity of peasant rebels, especially when they were faced with collectivizers of different nationalities (most often Russian or Jewish).[126] According to historian Valerii Vasil'ev, in several *raions* of Tul'chinskii *okrug*, peasants rebelled under the slogan, "Down with Soviet power, long live independent Ukraine."[127] Rebel proclamations that surfaced in Bordicheskii and Donetskii *okrug*s also called for an independent Ukraine.[128] Throughout Ukraine, peasants rose up in defense of their property, neighbors, and culture, displaying a sense of political and national outrage and purpose unparalleled in the union.[129]

Tatariia, Bashkiriia, Transcaucasus, and Russian regions with concentrations of ethnic minorities also experienced large disturbances, but only Central Asia came second to Ukraine in the size and gravity of its disturbances.[130] Here, in the months from January to March 1930, 249 mass disturbances were recorded. The mean average of the number of participants in individual disturbances was 400, larger than anywhere else in the Soviet Union and reflective of the very large and often well-organized rebellions that took place in the region.[131] Mass revolt in Central Asia continued into 1931 in Uzbekistan, where 164 mass disturbances were recorded with 13,980 participants, and in Turkmenistan, where in the period from March to August 1931 the Basmachi uprising engulfed the entire region until the Red army managed to suppress the insurrection.[132] The resistance in much of Central Asia demonstrated a scale and degree of organization unlike that in most of the rest of the nation, perhaps, in part, due to the continuing persistence and strength of *basmachi* resistance to Soviet power from the 1920s. Here peasants organized themselves into armies to battle the Red army, and many *raion* centers were placed on full military alert.[133] The state frequently labeled Central Asian revolt "*basmachi,*" "*bai*-inspired counterrevolution," and banditry, in an effort to delegitimize what was truly a civil war within a civil war, inspired by ethnic hatred fueled by collectivization.[134]

The strength of peasant rebellion was often in direct correlation to the proximity to the border.[135] In Belorussia, for example, the overall number of mass disturbances was relatively low, but their concentration and intensity along the border more than offset low numbers. Here, officials claimed peasant rebels had ties to foreign counterrevolutionaries, most likely relatives in nearby border areas.[136] Mass *volynki* swept through Belorussia. In the village Liaskovich (35 to 40 *versts* from the border) in Petrikovskii *raion*, Mozyrskii *okrug*, peasants rose up in revolt on 7 March, beating and chasing out plenipotentiaries and local officials and putting a halt to the deportation of kulaks. Peasants here even succeeded in repulsing a squadron of fifteen militia. Two days later, a squadron of border guards arrived with two light machine guns. Crowds of peasants continued to try to block the removal of the kulaks, letting loose a volley of sticks and stones in response to warning shots from the guard. Only after a second round of shooting, which this time resulted in the wounding of three peasants, did the crowd disperse. In the aftermath of the revolt, twelve were arrested, one killed, and another seriously wounded "attempting to escape."[137]

The largest and most serious episode of rebellion in Belorussia occurred in Mogilev-Podol'skii *okrug*, where, from 10 to 22 March, a wave of "kulak *vosstaniia,*" called *volynki* locally and consisting mainly of women, rolled across the region. *Sel'sovets* were closed, and Soviet power effectively disappeared in many places. Collectivization here had reached 56% of peasant households by early March and, in individual *raions*, up to 90%. The rebellion began in Shargorodskii *raion*, where crowds of thousands of peasants attacked and destroyed the RIK building. From here, peasant emissaries set out to other villages, calling on peasants to take back their property and quit the collective farm. Each village was told that the neighboring village had already joined the revolt. According to the official report on the uprising, some villages in this land-hungry *raion* refused to join the rebellion and, in fear of being burned out, organized self-defense brigades. At an official meeting in the village Kotiuzhany, a peasant man named Lipa took the lead in calling on villagers to rise up. The next day, officials attempted to arrest him, but the village women came to his rescue and chased the police out of the village. All of the *raion* centers of Mogilev-Podol'skii *okrug* were rocked by disturbances; several even fell under the control of the rebels. In the end, the OGPU restored order, the precise details of which are not specified in the sources.[138]

The Russian republic, the primary focus of this study, accounted for the greatest number of disturbances in the country, a perhaps predictable outcome, given that Russia was the country's largest republic. The major grain-producing regions (North Caucasus, Lower and Middle Volga) experienced widespread and serious revolt. First in line to complete wholesale collectivization (by the fall of 1930, or spring 1931 at the latest), these regions felt the full impact of the state's coercive campaigns.

The Volga regions were traditional areas of peasant unrest from the times of Bolotnikov, Razin, and Pugachev, through the 1905 and 1917 revolutions and into the collectivization era. More than 100 disturbances occurred in Lower Volga as early as fall 1929, already a key period for wholesale collectivization in this important grain-producing region where percentages of collectivized households increased from 5.9% in June to 18% in October, with significantly higher percentages in areas officially targeted for wholesale collectivization.[139] Mass disturbances here escalated in early 1930 and continued beyond the March 1930 retreat, in fact increasing somewhat from 203 mass disturbances in March to 208 in April and 254 in May.[140] In the Middle Volga, more than 140,383 peasants took part in some 662 of the region's 777 mass disturbances.[141]

In the village Cherepakha in Serdobskii *raion* in the vicinity of Penza in the Middle Volga, the attempt to remove the village's kulaks from their homes led to what the sources describe as a melee (*svalka*) in which eight officials were killed.[142] On the night of 13 January, in the village Russkie in Samarskii *raion*, Samarskii *okrug*, the peasants called a meeting in order to dismantle the collective farm. When they were told by officials to go home, the villagers refused, roused the entire village, and gathered in a crowd, yelling, "Let's do a *samosud*, let's have an uprising."[143] A mass disturbance with as many as 1,500 participants occurred on 24 March in the village N. Vyselka in Achadovskii *raion*. The disturbance began with the beating of the tocsin. Once the crowd assembled, it issued a demand to the *sel'sovet* that all socialized property be returned to the peasants and that all expropriated properties be returned to the kulaks. The crowd also demanded that the *sel'sovet* turn over to them two particularly detested activists who had "sown discord among the peasants." Failing that, the crowd went to the building which housed the School of Collective Farm Youth, and a part of the crowd—the women—broke in and ransacked the place. Next, the peasants unceremoniously threw the poor out of the expropriated kulaks' homes and returned the homes to their former owners. The sources indicate that the disturbance ended with the removal of the ringleaders and "explanatory work" (a euphemism of uncertain but portentous content).[144] In the village Shakino in Khoperskii *okrug* in the Lower Volga, the peasants refused to allow the deportation of the kulaks. The village's women surrounded the cart holding the kulaks, and the kulaks themselves refused to leave. In the confusion, several kulaks fled, and the authorities were forced to send in reinforcements.[145]

One of the most serious uprisings in the Lower Volga occurred in the village of Nachalova in the Astrakhan area on 22 February 1930. At 6:00 P.M. of that day, the Nachalova tocsin sounded the alarm. A crowd approached the *sel'sovet* from two directions. The crowd was arranged in typical peasant formation—children in front, women next, and the men bringing up the rear—probably in hopes and demonstration of a peaceful protest. Approximately 700 people—from a village with 980 households—participated. According to one of the reports on the disturbance, the telephone wires had been cut and many people in the crowd were drunk. Some of the men were armed—two "kulaks" had hunting guns, and the rest various kinds of blunt instruments. As the crowd, children in front, approached the *sel'sovet* building, shots were fired from within the building. The local officials had barricaded themselves there as soon as they heard the tocsin. The shooting provoked what may have been a peaceful crowd into violence. The peasants stormed the building and chased down the officials as they attempted to flee. (The latter had quickly run out of ammunition, according to the sources.) Some part of the 6, or possibly 8, party members and collective farm activists who were killed in Nachalova during the unrest were murdered at this time, lynched and killed with blunt instruments. The first to hear of the disturbance was the neighboring collective farm which quickly dispatched 12 people armed with rifles; Astrakhan sent an additional detachment of 8 party members and police. Although it is not clear from the sources, the uprising probably collapsed with the lynchings and before the outside forces came in. In any case, on the 22nd, 127 people were arrested, all but 13 of whom were sent on to Astrakhan. On the next day, an additional 113 people were arrested (consisting of 105 men and 8 women, divided into 78 kulaks, 11 middle peasants, 21 poor peasants, one *batrak*, and one collective farmer). Another 20 participants fled into the woods. The scale of the arrests was so large that the *okrug* special commission on dekulakization requested the emptying out of a military barracks to hold the Nachalova peasants. Once the riot was quelled and the arrested dispatched, the church bell was removed, and the dead hurriedly buried; by mid-March plans were made to organize a special home for children orphaned by the events in Nachalova.

The Nachalova uprising was of sufficient magnitude for Sheboldaev, the Lower Volga regional party secretary, to become involved and report directly on the matter to Stalin. Sheboldaev ordered that no information on the uprising be released to the press and that the dead be buried quickly and without ceremony to avoid further unrest. The causes of the uprising were attributed, as was most often the case, to excesses on the part of local officials. In Nachalova, the church had been closed without discussion and the priest arbitrarily arrested. Further—and central in importance—the identification and expropriation of the kulaks had roused village ire to a fever pitch. The local officials had dekulakized 26 families and removed them from their homes into reading huts and other available buildings to await deportation. The delay between expropriation and deportation, frequently a cause or avenue for unrest, provided an opportunity for the peasants of Nachalova to attempt to save their neighbors. According to interrogations, the uprising had in fact been planned, on the night of February 21–22, and was well organized. This claim is not unlikely, but it does not necessarily square with the reports of drunkenness and it should also be placed against the backdrop of Soviet power's proclivity to see conspiracy everywhere. In all, from six to eight people were murdered (depending on report) and an additional eight wounded—mostly on the government side, according to the official reports. The deportation of the kulaks—the main cause of the uprising—was still not carried out as of early April 1930, either in spite of or because of the rebellion.[146]

Following in the footsteps of Nachalova, several outbreaks of serious unrest occurred in the Astrakhan area in mid-March 1930 in Krasnoiarskii and Enotaevskii *raions*. In the village of Baranovka in Krasnoiarskii *raion*, threats to massacre Communists and poor peasants were in the air. Street gatherings to discuss rehabilitating kulaks and organizing a *samosud* of poor peasants were also reported. One of the organizers of a planned uprising here (that seems not to have taken place) was said to be, naturally, a freed kulak. An armed detachment came to the village and made preemptive arrests to prevent the unrest from escalating and from finding common cause with the more serious disturbances in Enotaevskii *raion*.[147] In Enotaevskii *raion*, mass disturbances broke out in mid-March in a series of villages in response to the deportation of kulaks. In the village of Vladimirovka, on 14 March, a crowd of 3,000 peasants took over the village, calling a meeting at which it was decreed to return all expropriated properties to kulaks, to rehabilitate kulaks, to dekulakize and banish the brigade members who had carried out the state's policies, and to divide the seed grain. After the meeting, the peasants carried out a search of the brigade's headquarters, banishing all party members and brigadiers from the village to the accompaniment of a volley of stones. In neighboring Enotaevka on the morning of 20 March, the tocsin sounded the alarm over the removal of eight kulaks during the previous night. A crowd armed with rifles and revolvers gathered, demanding their liberation and refusing to disperse until a salvo was fired into the air. Meanwhile, back in Vladimirovka, an armed detachment had entered with the purpose of removing "antisoviet elements." The villagers opened fire on the detachment, forcing it to retreat to Enotaevka. There, the peasants refused to allow the detachment to send out couriers for reinforcements, while bands of rebels from the village of Nikolaevka made their way to Enotaevka in support of the peasants. Telegraph and telephone lines into Astrakhan were cut and the arrival of official reinforcements was made difficult by bad roads and the need to cross over the Volga. The roads to Vladimirovka and Nikolaevka were taken over by rebels, while the troops in Enotaevka found themselves cut off and under siege. In Vladimirovka, the peasants surrounded their village with trenches. On the next day, the rebels, reportedly armed with guns and large quantities of ammunition, approached the besieged Enotaevka, halting two kilometers outside the village in the expectation of reinforcements from the Kalmyk steppe. Soon, however, a battle broke out between the rebels and OGPU troops, and with the arrival of reinforcements, the rebels were destroyed. According to OGPU sources, the disturbance was led by a "counterrevolutionary-insurrectionary group" with a "significant" number of middle and poor peasant participants.[148]

The Volga German Republic was also rocked by mass disturbances. From the end of December through the first half of January, riots erupted in more than twenty villages, with the number of participants in each ranging from 200 to 250. In seven villages in Frankskii and Kamenskii cantons, uprisings lasted from seven to ten days. The Lower Volga regional party committee concluded that the coincidence of these mass disturbances clearly indicated that there was a "united center" leading the "movement." Collectivization was ferocious in ethnic minority regions where nationality issues doubtlessly accentuated tensions, and especially in the well-groomed and often prosperous German settlements where, to many Communists, particularly Russians, German farmers looked like kulaks. In these villages, church closings and bell removals were carried out as a form of "socialist competition," according to official sources. As a result, mass disturbances, mainly by women, occurred throughout the region and demanded the rehabilitation of kulaks, the reopening of churches, an end to the socialization of domestic livestock, and reelections of *sel'sovets*. Mass exits from the collective farms also occurred. The Lower Volga regional party committee blamed the unrest on a combination of local officials' excesses and peasant solidarity based on a common religion and beliefs, and the strong authority of the prosperous peasants in the community.[149]

The North Caucasus, which was Cossack territory and home to a multitude of restive ethnic minorities, was another key center of peasant rebellion. Here, more than 227,000 peasants rose up in revolt.[150] Many of the mass disturbances were large and well-organized. In mid-January 1930, a serious riot broke out in the North Caucasus *stanitsa* of Temirgoevskaia in Kurganskii *raion*, Armavirskii *okrug*. Approximately 76% of the village's households were in the collective farm by this time. On 10 January, peasants, mostly women upset about the socialization of dairy cows, broke up a meeting on collectivization. For the next two days, unofficial peasant meetings continued in all parts of this large village. The local party and Komsomol members were denied the right to vote and decrees were passed against the collective farm and the socialization of the means of production. On 13 January, top-level *raion* officials came to the village to carry out a meeting on the upcoming sowing campaign. The meeting was disrupted and there were even attempts to beat the *sel'sovet* chairman. On the same day, proclamations appeared on the street calling for the people to seize power. The next day, the population assembled near the *sel'sovet* in an effort to continue with their daily "meeting." Local party members tried to block the meeting with the argument that they had already voted against the collective farm, but the peasants continued to demand a meeting. Having been "categorically" refused, the peasants surrounded the local activists, trying to beat them. At precisely that time, the tocsin rang out, and within minutes 5,000 to 6,000 people had gathered in the village square. A cavalry brigade of 23 troops soon arrived, but found itself surrounded by the crowd. This impasse finally led to the opening of negotiations between officials and a group of former partisans and poor peasants from among the rebels. An official meeting followed, at which time, according to the official report, the rebels admitted their mistakes. Afterwards, rumors flew of insurrections elsewhere, stray shots were heard long into the night, and the rebels sent runners to neighboring villages to share the news of the week's events.[151]

The Sal'sk rebellion, which began in the village of Ekaterinovka in Vorontsovo-Nikolaevskii *raion*, Sal'skii *okrug*, in early February, was one of the North Caucasus' largest and most dangerous uprisings. The rebellion erupted over the issue of dekulakization and socialization of property. Anywhere from several hundred to several thousand people, depending upon the source consulted, assembled in Ekaterinovka to demand the release of the arrested kulaks and the return of property. When its demands were not met, the crowd stormed and ransacked the *sel'sovet*, where the confiscated property was held. Several party and Komsomol members joined the crowd. On the second day of the revolt, neighboring villages rose up in support as the news of the Ekaterinovka revolt reached them and set off a chain reaction of disturbances. In the *khutor* V. Khanzhenkovo, 450 peasants resisted the deportation of the kulaks, attacking local officials and rescuing their neighbors. At the same time, a group of women attempted to liberate four other kulaks who had been arrested earlier. Their actions led officials to flee in terror into the *sel'sovet*, and, within a short time, groups of women from the neighboring villages of Pavlovka, Pudovyi, and Petropavlovka arrived to reinforce the rebellious women. According to Soviet sources, the revolt quickly transformed itself from an anticollectivization protest to an antisoviet rebellion. Demands were made for "Soviet power without Communists and without collective farms," and in several places peasants elected commissions to dissolve party cells and return confiscated property, thereby demonstrating a sense of order and political process. The uprising continued for six days and was so threatening that the town of Sal'sk was placed on military alert, weapons were issued to party and Komsomol members, and plans were drawn up for the defense of the town. In the end, the uprising was suppressed with the aid of party cadres and Red army soldiers. The postmortem on the uprising blamed kulaks and local excesses for the troubles, in a far from original diagnosis but one that appealed to Moscow and a certain center-based Communist logic. Here, as elsewhere, most of the expropriated kulaks had been left in place awaiting deportation or resettlement. Consequently, according to official sources, they were free to "agitate" against Soviet power. In addition, local Soviet power was blamed for excesses, violations of the class line (in reference to theoretically illegal repressions of poor and middle peasants), and "administrative tendencies";

as a result, six *sel'sovet* chairmen were arrested and a series of *sel'sovets* dissolved. The real issue, of course, was central policy, the usual brutalit-ies of the cadres on the scene notwithstanding, although it should be re-membered that some among them, most probably local people, had joined the revolt. Sal'skii *okrug*, moreover, had experienced serious unrest from at least fall 1929 when from 30% to 60% of livestock and as many as 70% of draft animals were slaughtered or sold in parts of the *okrug* as a response to forced grain seizures and collectivization.[152]

The Don was an especially troublesome part of the North Caucasus, with its large and fiercely independent Cossack population. Here, official sources noted that former partisans from the civil war played an im-portant role in disturbances.[153] In the Slavianskii *raion stanitsa* of Ivanov-skaia in the Don, a riot broke out on 9 March. A crowd of 200 women from one sector of this large *stanitsa* took back their recently socialized livestock, beating up the stableman in the process. The crowd soon grew to 1,000 people as it approached the center of the *stanitsa*. A "platoon" of collective farmers attempted to stop the crowd, but was met by gunfire, which it returned. A melee then broke out with shooting, resulting in deaths on both sides and at least 50 people wounded. Soon the peasants began to disperse, while the collective farm "platoon" shot at them as they fled and pursued them to their homes. That evening, the *sel'sovet* held a meeting to discuss the upcoming plowing of collective farm fields. The next day, in response to this meeting, a group of women in another sector of the *stanitsa* took back their horses. The disturbances in Ivanov-skaia ended with the "removal of counterrevolutionary elements" and "explanatory work."[154]

On 25 March in the Novo-Cherkasskii *raion stanitsa* of Aleksandrov-skaia in the North Caucasus, a crowd of 500 women, supposedly led by kulaks and "white guard elements," demanded the return of their seed grain. The local officials attempted to dissuade them, but only further incited the crowd, which began to call for the *samosud* of the *sel'sovet* chairman. As the chairman fled into hiding, the crowd turned its anger on other officials and activists, who received beatings. Several of the officials managed to get out of the *stanitsa*, while the remaining went into hiding. The crowd calmed down only with the arrival of a cavalry division of the militia. On the next day, more than 600 people gathered at the *sel'sovet* with new demands and a mood described by the OGPU as "pogrom-like." The crowd stoned the militia and armed itself with stakes from a nearby fence. An OGPU platoon soon arrived, which succeeded only in further exciting the crowd which dragged several soldiers from their horses. In order to try to localize the rebellion, workers and Communists from nearby factories and towns were mobilized. It took the arrival of a second OGPU platoon to disperse the crowd. The next day, the OGPU removed the leaders of the revolt.[155]

In Siberia, where land was plentiful and peasants had a much greater stake in the existing status quo, riots, uprisings and brigandage were widespread in the open and untamed expanses of the territory. From January through March 1930, 65 mutinies (*miatezha*), 153 mass disturbances according to the OGPU, were registered in Siberia, some of them massive in scope.[156] As in the Lower Volga, mass disturbances in Siberia continued with some increase after March 1930; the numbers rose slightly, from 121 in March to 124 in April and 254 in May.[157]

A series of mass *volynki* over the expropriation of kulaks erupted in Inderskii *raion*, Novosibirskii *okrug*, Siberia, in late January. In the village Komar'e on 27 January, a crowd of 500 people gathered during the operation to inventory and expropriate kulaks. The peasants demanded a meeting, shouting "Away with the *raion* and *okrug* workers." The plenipotentiaries called a meeting and read their official reports to the peasants. The peasants listened and then cried, "You are finished, now we will speak. Down with communists, down with the tractor." They demanded a return of all expropriated property, repeating their demands the next day at the *sel'sovet*. Similar *volynki*, mainly composed of women, occurred in the villages Ozerki and Inder. A *volynka* in Sogornoe lasted for three days (28 to 30 January) and forced all local institutions, including the school and consumer shop, to close. *Raion* officials came to the village to attempt to pacify the population and called a meeting, to which 600 peasants, mostly women, came. At the meeting, the peasants demanded the rehabilitation of the kulaks and the return of their property as well as the exile of poor peasants and activists. As the mood heated up and several poor peasant activists came under attack, the authorities suggested the creation of a commission—to include participants in the *volynki*—to investigate the village's complaints. This action succeeded in splitting the opposition, leading to the return of peace, some seven arrests, and the flight of three local kulaks.[158]

Serious disturbances were reported throughout Ust'-Kariiskii *raion* in the thinly populated Eastern Siberia; in this *raion*, 19 officials were murdered during peasant uprisings. Large-scale uprisings also occurred in Muramtsevskii *raion*, Barabinskii *okrug* in Western Siberia.[159] Here, in response to the deportation of kulaks, 1,000 people, partially armed, mostly with pitchforks, some with hunting rifles, rose up in the villages of Kondrat'evskoe, Tarmakla, Lisino, and Kokshenevo on 2 March. Rioters surrounded the convoy that was escorting the local kulaks out of the *raion*. They also dismantled a collective farm and beat up local activists. Villagers capped off their revolt by holding a procession with icons. According to the OGPU report on the rebellion, the organizational center of the revolt was in the village Kondrat'evskoe and at some point the *raion* center of Muromtsevo was even occupied by the rebels. The Kondrat'evskoe peasants apparently sent emissaries through the *raion*, who attempted to drum up support and arms. The rebellion was liquidated only on 6 March.[160] According to a poor peasant who wrote to Stalin about the rebellion on 26 March, refusing to sign his name in fear for his life, the rebellion was caused by the extreme force used by outside plenipotentiaries and local officials in collective farm organization. This peasant wrote that anyone who refused to join, including poor and middle peasants, was exiled as a kulak, and for that reason, all the villages of the *raion* "rose up as one." The peasant claimed that 6 people were killed in Kondrat'evskoe and 50 in another village called Razin. He ended his letter with a request for the immediate detachment of "people from the center, dedicated to Lenin" to investigate the affair, and added a plaintive "please [look] into this matter" to the request.[161]

Uch-Pristanskii *raion*, Biiskii *okrug*, in the Altai region of Siberia was especially hard hit by peasant insurrection. Biiskii *okrug* had been a trouble spot from 1929, when it experienced repeated unrest over grain requisitioning.[162] On 9 March 1930, an armed insurrection, which covered one quarter of the entire *raion*, broke out in the territory. The sources quite naturally labeled it a "kulak mutiny," although statistical data on participants indicate that 38% of the "kulaks" were middle peasants and 24% poor peasants. According to the sources, the rebels had plans to seize all the *raion* centers of Siberia and had compiled lists of those to be shot. Reportedly, a large part of the *raion's* party and Komsomol contingent was arrested, and nine or ten Communists shot. The rebels successfully entered the *raion* center, seized the arsenal (warehoused at a school) and the police station, and emptied the Uch-Pristanskii prison. According to recently published archival documents, one of the main organizers of the rebellion was a *raion* OGPU plenipotentiary named Dobytin, who, along with a band of followers, shot the police guard in Uch-Pristan and released all the arrested kulaks from their jail cells. At the same time, eight activists were disarmed and locked up, nine people who resisted were shot, and as many as 140 rifles were taken from the arsenal. Dobytin then organized a "band" of approximately 400 "kulaks and antisoviet elements" and headed in the direction of Oirotskaia *oblast'*. The situation was serious enough for the *raion* center to go on full alert, posting guards at all the most important points in town. Published sources remain silent on the further development of the insurrection, only indicating, too simply for comfort, that troops were dispatched and the uprising was quickly put down.[163] Siberian rebellion, particularly in the east, appears to have been especially violent, often involving organization and communication above the village level.

Hardest hit in the Russian Republic was the volatile Central Black Earth Region. Although not scheduled to complete wholesale collectivization until fall 1931, spring 1932 at the latest, this region endured some of the worst atrocities committed during the campaign and experienced dizzying rates of collectivization between January and March 1930.[164] Here disturbances tended to be large, with a mean average of more than 300 participants per incident.[165] Already in 1929, there were 94 mass disturbances with 33,221 participants.[166] In 1930, the number skyrocketed to 1,373 mass disturbances.[167] In restive Ostrogozhskii *okrug* alone, 16 mass disturbances with 17,000 participants were registered between 12 January and 14 February 1930. In Kozlovskii *okrug*, another dangerous area, peasant insurrection (*vosstanie*) seized some 54 villages by the end of March 1930, with 20,000 peasants participating. According to OGPU reports, in parts of the Central Black Earth Region, the crowds in mass disturbances included as many as 2,000 participants.[168] Here villages were large and fairly socially homogeneous, with very low rates of social differentiation, making it likely that entire villages participated in disturbances. Population density, moreover, was relatively high in the region, allowing for close communication between rebellious villages.[169]

Many riots here assumed "a semi-insurrectionary character," according to Vareikis, who believed that riots were prepared in advance with something like a general staff directing the action and arming participants with pitchforks, axes, stakes, and, in some cases, sawed-off shotguns and hunting rifles.[170] In the village Lipovka in Losevskii *raion*, Rossoshanskiii *okrug*, a riot, characterized as an insurrection and supposedly led by the village's "counterrevolutionary elements," broke out on 30 March 1930. Here, the villagers banished the local authorities and elected a *starosta*. Emissaries were sent to neighboring villages, guards were posted around the village, and a lookout was established on the church's bell tower. When a detachment of OGPU troops arrived, they were met by a crowd of 1,000 peasants, who, according to the report, quickly "deployed" and began shooting at the troops. The shooting continued for an hour, resulting in the deaths of 18 peasants, and eventually forcing the villagers into retreat.[171] In the village of Pravaia Khava, on 31 March, several hundred rioters took back their seed grain and destroyed the office of the collective farm administration. On the next day, a detachment of 45 OGPU troops arrived to attempt to pacify the village. They were met by an angry crowd, which now included peasants from neighboring villages. When a squadron of Red army troops arrived, peasants surrounded the soldiers, threatening to kill and disarm them. The crowd only dispersed when the solders fired a volley into it, killing five and wounding three.[172]

In late March 1930, a particularly dangerous uprising eventually encompassing four villages began in the village of Gridasovaia in Kurskii *okrug* when peasants came out in defense of a kulak scheduled for deportation. As an armed detachment attempted to lead the kulak out of the village, the peasants surrounded it and blocked the deportation. At this point, 30 "communards" from a local collective farm intervened on the side of Soviet power, escalating the conflict. The tocsin then rang out and villagers arrived on the scene from all directions, armed with pitchforks, stakes, and shotguns. The peasants forced the communards to retreat. As they retreated, several of their number fired into the air in an attempt to force the villagers to back off from their pursuit. By this time, peasants from three neighboring villages had come to the aid of Gridasovaia. The crowd stormed the *sel'sovet*, lynched a plenipotentiary, and wounded an activist. The town of Kursk, upon hearing of the disturbance, sent out a detachment of 120 people to pacify the village. With the arrival of these forces, the size of the insurgency quadrupled, and what the sources label "a real battle" ensued. The uprising was soon crushed. Three peasants were killed in the fighting and many more were likely wounded and hidden away. Sixty people were arrested before the dust settled on Gridasovaia.[173]

The Moscow Region, a grain-consuming area, also suffered a disproportionate amount of state violence while enduring extremely rapid collectivization in early 1930.[174] In the Moscow Region, 2,198 "rural disturbances" were already reported in the first nine months of 1929, while more than 500 "group and mass anti-collective farm disturbances" were recorded in January through April 1930, with most occurring in Riazanskii and Bezhetskii *okrugs*.[175] As in the Central Black Earth Region, social differentiation in most Moscow Region villages was minimal, perhaps accounting for the relatively large size of individual disturbances (a mean of 228 participants in villages averaging about that in population size).[176] According to a recent Russian source, the "peasant movement" in Moscow Region seized five districts and required the intervention of the Red army before it could be quelled.[177]

Several large disturbances took place in the Riazan area in February and March 1930. On 22 February, a rebellion broke out in the village Veriaevo in Pitelinskii *raion* in connection with the socialization of livestock, forced searches of homes, and other excesses. Here, the peasants chased out the plenipotentiaries, some of the villagers pursuing them to the neighboring village of Gridino. The remainder of the Veriaevo peasants reclaimed their socialized possessions, and then proceeded to ransack the *sel'sovet* building and chase down village activists. The disturbance ebbed by the early evening, at which time the peasants established their own sentries around the village. Meanwhile, in Gridino, the plenipotentiaries faced the wrath not only of the pursuing Veriaevo peasants, but also of the Gridino peasants, who turned out into the streets in response to the pealing of the church bell. Runners from Veriaevo then headed for all of the neighboring villages to recruit other forces; by the end of the day, several villages had joined in, the village of Andreevka sending a peasant detachment that came streaming into Gridino with a black flag. The next day, a detachment of urban forces arrived in the area to attempt to quell the disorders. When they arrived in Veriaevo, they first met a deadly calm. Soon, however, the village women began to assemble and try to block the detachment from proceeding further. When individuals in the detachment shot into the air to scare the women, the church bell began to toll, bringing the entire village out into the streets. The people demanded that the forces either stop shooting or leave. Urban detachments met with the same sort of reaction in the other villages. In the next few days, outward calm was restored as villagers pledged not to use the church bell, but beneath the surface passions continued to boil.[178] Later, in early March, the area again exploded into revolt. Like many similar uprisings, this one began locally and then set off a chain reaction of similar revolts in other villages as news arrived of the initial mutiny and hope of relief lingered against all odds. The rebels severed telegraph and telephone lines, cutting off all communication with Riazan. The short-term outcome of the rebellion was the temporary collapse of the area's collective farms, which toppled one after another as peasants took advantage of a moment's opportunity.[179]

The peasant revolt of 1929–30 played a key role in shaping the dynamics of state policy and policy implementation, in the end, profoundly shaking the confidence of the central leadership while leaving local cadres in fear and disarray. This wave of revolt, as it manifested itself before and after March 1930, was March fever, and March fever, broadly defined, was cause and consequence of the temporary retreat heralded by Stalin's "Dizziness from Success." The Central Committee explicitly stated that the retreat was precipitated by *the threat of peasant revolt.*[180] The revolt, however, not only was not quelled by the state's volte-face, but in fact was propelled forward with frightening velocity, reaching its peak in most areas in March. The retreat represented a temporary withdrawal of authority, leading to vast confusion and demoralization among lower level officials, which facilitated peasant revolt.[181] The retreat and its reception by Soviet officialdom sent a signal to peasants of confusion and demoralization in the center, in the provincial capitals, and locally among officials and activists. A Urals correspondent for the newspaper *Bednota* put it this way: "And suddenly like a bomb exploding over head [there appeared] Stalin's article . . . the second round [was] the C[entral] C[ommittee] decree." He wrote further that the article was viewed in the countryside as "a kind of manifesto . . . people gathered in the woods for anticipated readings, secretly in the barns, [and everywhere they] uttered exclamations [akhnuli]."[182] Peasants seized the opportunity to protest openly, take back their property, and quit the detested collective farms. Stalin's article, a copy of which could cost as much as 15 rubles and was the subject of group readings and even *skhod* meetings in many villages,[183] was both pretext and opportunity. Peasants interpreted "Dizziness" as they saw fit, turning it into a weapon of peasant politics.

Stalin was pushed into the vanguard of peasant protest. As they quit their collective farm, peasants in a village in Kamyziakskii *raion*, Astrakhan, declared that "Comrade Stalin said in [his] article that we are free to do what we want and therefore we consider it better not to be in the collective farm."[184] A peasant in Tatariia, who said he had joined the collective farm only out of fear, read Stalin's article four times and claimed to know it "by heart."[185] One peasant called Stalin "little father [batiushka] Stalin," while many used Stalin's name and authority as a cudgel against local authorities.[186] In B. Ianisol'skii *raion* in Ukraine, peasants said, "The government is good, but the local officials are very bad," in a Soviet-style version of naive monarchism, while a Khoperskii *okrug*, Lower Volga peasant said, "We have two governments—one in the center which writes [for us] to take back all [our property] and the other local one which doesn't want this."[187] At an early April meeting in a Novosibirskii *okrug* village, peasants applauded when they heard of the 2 April Central Committee decree on collective farm privileges—a follow-up, forced, of "Dizziness"—and shouts of "hurrah," "we won," "the party supports us," and "power is on our side" were heard.[188] "Dizziness" legitimized protest after March 2 and accompanied peasants into open revolt when local authorities failed to move quickly enough to appease peasants after the winter maelstrom.

The naive monarchism displayed by peasants, their reverence for "*batiushka* Stalin," need not be taken at face value. It may very well have served as a convenient and artful club with which to pound local officials who no longer had the absolute support of the center. Peasants could play upon images of the *muzhiki* as Orthodox *narod* (folk) in need of a tsar figure. Or they could simply rise up in revolt legitimized by nothing more than their own dignity. They saw the opportunity that policy disarray presented them and acted accordingly, manipulating the newest party line, dismantling collective farms, halting kulak deportations, and throwing out Communists. Most local officials were entirely discredited. At a meeting in Bezmenovo in Cherepanovskii *raion*, Novosibirskii *okrug*, Siberia, on 28 April, for example, peasants simply took over the meeting, ordering officials to rehabilitate kulaks and to read all the secret RIK directives on the kulaks. In the same *raion* at this time, peasants broke up another meeting, threatening the RIK plenipotentiary with retribution, while cries of "what the general *skhod* decides is law" were heard. The meeting was broken up and attempts made to beat the "*likvidatory*" (i.e., those who had participated in dekulakization). In the village Petropavlovka in Maslia-ninskii *raion*, local kulaks broke up a meeting, demanding retribution from the *sel'sovet* chairman and beating up two activists. After the official presence was disposed of, the peasants opened a new meeting that resolved to secure the return of deported peasants, liquidate the collective farm, and, in two hours, evict all collective farmers from the homes of expropriated kulaks. After the meeting, the kulaks took back their property and homes.[189]

By far, the primary act of resistance was the enormous exodus from the collective farms that began in the second half of March.[190] The percentage of collectivized households in the RSFSR fell from a high point of 58.6% on 1 March 1930, to 38.4% on 1 April, to 25.3% on 1 May, and downward to a low point of 21.8% on 1 October.[191] The largest decline in collectivization in the RSFSR occurred in the grain-consuming regions (Western Region, Moscow, Ivanovo, Central Black Earth Region—all regions not scheduled to complete wholesale collectivization before fall 1931), where from 20 February to 1 May 1930 the percentages of collectivized households dropped by 46.2%, while in the priority grain-producing regions (North Caucasus, Lower and Middle Volga, Siberia), the overall decline was held to 14%.[192] When peasant departures were not the result of stormy protest and rioting, they came in the form of simple, written declarations to quit the collective. Contemporary observers pointed out that some declarations to quit were written either according to similar models or by the same hand, indicating a collective action of a different sort.[193] In the Riazan area (and again later, during the smaller 1932 exits, in the Nizhegorodskii region), peasants submitted collective declarations to quit, with their signatures formed in a circle to prevent officials from knowing who signed first and arresting supposed ringleaders.[194] And throughout the land, dekulakized peasants besieged all levels of government with complaint letters and petitions for rehabilitation and return of their property.[195]

The peasant revolt against collectivization began slowly to subside after March, although numbers of mass disturbances remained at higher levels than in January and February until June.[196] From this time into the early summer, the revolt was at least partially subsumed or perhaps redirected by a new wave of discontent arising from the aftermath of collectivization and now animated by hunger or the fear of hunger. According to OGPU reports, severe hunger and pockets of famine had appeared throughout the countryside as early as the spring of 1930. In the Lower Volga, cases of peasants swelling up from hunger were reported in the spring in Pugachevskii, Kamyshinskii, and Vol'skii *okrugs* and were attributed to a combination of the previous year's partial crop failure and the current year's excesses in collectivization and grain procurements.[197] In the Middle Volga, food difficulties were said to be especially acute in Buguruslanskii and Syzranskii *okrugs*, where there were cases of illness and even death from starvation, while in Sorochinskii *raion*, Orenburgskii *okrug*, cases of scurvy deaths due to famine were recorded.[198] Sixty percent of the population in Ostrogozhskii *okrug* in the Central Black Earth Region were said to be in dire need of food; cases of hunger-related illnesses were also reported here. According to the OGPU, food shortages, primarily among the poor, had appeared in *all* Central Black Earth *okrugs*.[199] In the North Caucasus, sharp food difficulties appeared in the Kubanskii, Armavirskii, Maikopskii, Sal'skii, Donitskii, and Stavropol'skii *okrugs*, where stomach ailments from the consumption of food surrogates and even deaths were reported. In the *stanitsa* Belorechenskaia in Labinskii *raion*, Maikopskii *okrug*, collective farmers gathered daily at meetings to demand bread, the liquidation of the collective farm, and the return of their property.[200] Siberia also confronted serious food shortages, the most severe in Rybinskii, Achinskii, Biiskii, Krasnoiarskii, Slavgorodskii, and Novosibirskii *okrugs* and Oirotskaia *oblast'*. As elsewhere, cases of illness and death due to hunger were reported. In Biiskii *okrug*, poor peasants were reportedly eating dead animals and all sorts of surrogates.[201] Hunger also made an appearance in the Ivanovo region, the Far East, Bashkiriia, Tatariia, and Crimea, to name only those areas listed by the OGPU.[202] In most of these areas, hunger was as yet limited to the poor and seems to have most often made its appearance within collective farms.[203] There is little question that these early cases of hunger were mainly, although not exclusively, a result of excessive grain requisitioning and the atrocities of collectivization.

In the Lower Volga, nine mass disturbances erupted in April over food difficulties. In one village, groups of peasants assembled daily at the *sel'sovet* demanding bread, while elsewhere in the region large crowds rioted, destroying granaries or taking food reserves by force.[204] In Bugur-uslanskii *okrug* in the Middle Volga, there were a series of disturbances over food shortages. In the village Kiriushkino, a poor peasant named Voronov said to the *sel'sovet* chairman, "[You] see that I am swelling up [from hunger]. For a week I have not seen a crumb of bread. If [you] don't give me bread I will take you by the throat—all the same I will die." In M. Buguruslan, a group of 50 women stood up at a meeting and demanded, "Give [us] bread. [If] you don't feed us, we will go and de-stroy the granary," while in Biriushkino, poor peasants laid siege to the *sel'sovet*, imploring, "If you don't give us bread, we will be forced to commit a crime." In Krasnyi Gorodok, 200 women blocked the carting out of seed grain and occupied the granary, shouting, "[You] want to kill us with hunger," and in Sof'evka, former red partisans led a crowd of 400 peasants, demanding an increase in food norms.[205] In many Siberian vil-lages suffering from food difficulties, crowds, mainly of women, besieged the *sel'sovet*s and even RIKs daily, demanding bread.[206]

Women also played a leading role in hunger riots in the Central Black Earth Region and North Caucasus. According to the OGPU, between 25 April and 10 May, mass disturbances with up to 1,448 people occurred in the Central Black Earth Region on the basis of food difficulties. In the village Kholodnoe in Skhorodnianskii *raion*, Staro-Oskol'skii *okrug*, a crowd of 300 peasants gathered at the *sel'sovet* demanding bread. When they were refused, they stormed the granary. An analogous disturbance occurred in the village Krivye Belki, where 250 women broke into the granary in search of food after their initial demands for aid were ignored. In the village Karaeshnokovo in Ol'khovatskii *raion*, Rossoshanskii *okrug*, 150 women pleaded for bread from the collective farm administration. Rebuffed, the women attacked the officials and forced them to flee for their lives.[207] Throughout the North Caucasus, groups of women, often very large in number, besieged *sel'sovet*s, demanding bread. In the village Ptich'e in Izobil'no-Tishchenskii *raion*, Stavropol'skii *okrug*, 100 women descended upon the cooperative shop intending to lynch the manager, who barely escaped. In the village Kievskoe in Krymskii *raion*, Chernomorskii *okrug*, a crowd of more than 100 people assembled at the *sel'sovet* de-manding flour and threatening to destroy the mill. In an effort to prevent the crowd from taking the food reserves, the *sel'sovet* chairman dispersed five pounds of flour per family. The next day, the village poor returned, demanding more. The crowd became violent, forcing the party cell secre-tary and a local militia man to flee, and for the next three to four hours ruled the village, combing the territory for officials and only dispersing toward evening when it became clear that all officials had disappeared.[208]

Writing from Krasnodarskii *okrug* in North Caucasus, the peasant Komarchenko told of the troubles he had seen and, unlike the OGPU, presented something of the peasant point of view on the life-or-death struggle for food in the village in the immediate aftermath of collectivization. He wrote:

> The peasants were providers, but now [they are] consumers, and all of this is due to the government. Earlier we worked with plows and horses and ate bread until we were full, now everyone is starving. . . . Right here in Gostagaevskiaia *stanitsa*, Anapskii *raion*, there was an uprising. The peasants beat up the GPU, [the] crowd took [their] rifles, and when soldiers came, then [they] cried at them, "give [us] freedom" and for ten days soldiers stood among us. . . . The peasants say that we are dying. [If they] do not give bread, their stomachs will swell, and we will swell from hunger. . . . [A]nd when we did not have enough bread, we went to the soviet and [they] told us to buy on the market and we will tell you when you come to us "to take bread" that there will be murder, there will be uprisings.[209]

Komarchenko could not have foreseen how hollow his threat would ring in later months and years as procurement-engendered famine consumed the countryside, taking millions of lives and dealing the peasantry a blow even more merciless than collectivization.

March fever gradually died down in most of the country by the summer of 1930. Apart from the brigands (discussed in the next section) that made an appearance in some areas in the early 1930s, collective forms of active resistance were limited mainly to the first stage of wholesale collectivization. Exceptions were demonstrations and riots sparked by hunger or the fear of hunger. Several reports, for instance, note attacks on granaries.[210] And in the village Bashkatov in Oboianskii *raion* in the Central Black Earth Region, in August 1931 a crowd of peasants (estimated at between 50 and 150 people), armed with pitchforks and clubs, attempted to block the requisitioning of the village's grain; other villages in the *raion* followed Bashkatov's example.[211] Mass disturbances also broke out in early February 1931 in the Lower Volga villages of Soliano-Zaimishcha, Chernyi Iar, and Kamennyi Iar, with demands for bread and manufactured goods. The disturbances here erupted in response to a RIK order to stop issuing bread and manufactured goods to anyone outside the collective farm, under the pretext "he who does not work [in the collective farm], does not eat."[212] Occasionally, riots broke out over collectivization, but much less frequently than in 1930. According to the OGPU, though, "kulaks and antisoviet elements" were calling on peasants to organize mass disturbances in the Central Black Earth Region, arguing that "the previous years' rebellion had prevented the final destruction of the peasantry." To demonstrate its point, the OGPU recorded the following peasant statements: "We had better do to them [the government] what [we did] last year"; "They are forcing us to use the seed reserves to plant collectively, but we know what to do. Nothing happened last spring, nothing will happen now"; "It begins again from the beginning, but we are learned, were we a bit better organized last year, we then would have done away with this construction of collective farms." [213]

Some evidence also indicates very occasional episodes of mass disturbances during the 1932–33 famine. Fedor Belov wrote that during the famine peasants banded together in groups of thirty to forty in the collective farm he later chaired, defending themselves with sticks and knives, in an attempt to protect the little grain remaining to them. [214] A "kulak *vystuplenie*" was reported in Kotel'nicheskii *raion*, Nizhegorodskii-Gor'kovskii *krai* (region) in March or April 1932, resulting in several murders and assaults and the destruction of a number of official buildings. [215] The historian V. V. Kondrashin, a Russian expert on the famine, concluded that cases of mass resistance during the famine were exceptions due to well-founded peasant fear. Kondrashin does, however, record several disturbances, including one in the Volga village Krasnyi Kliuch in Rtishchevskii *raion* in which the peasants combined forces to take back the collective farm's grain from the warehouse before it could be delivered to the state. [216]

The March fever of 1930 represented the last real wave of mass active resistance by peasants in Russia, the final open, collective act in the peasant civil war against Soviet power. The peasant revolt of 1929–30 was tied directly to the state's efforts at socialist transformation and, in particular, collectivization, dekulakization, and atheization. When the next big push for all-out collectivization came in fall 1930, the peasantry was already too exhausted by food shortages and state repression to continue active collective resistance. By fall, the reality and finality of collectivization was much clearer than it had been in the winter of 1929–30. And the state made fewer mistakes; it too had learned a lesson. In the second wave of dekulakization, *all* peasants classified as kulaks would be subject to resettlement; no longer would kulaks be divided into categories with some allowed to remain in their homes. [217] The entire operation of collectivization and dekulakization would be more orderly, more conspiratorial, although no less tragic to its subject population. Most peasants would choose, by necessity, desperation, and fatigue, to live within the system, channeling their protest into other forms. Those who did not, fled to the cities or faced slow economic ruin in the heavily taxed and ever-shrinking private sector of agriculture. Or they fled into the woods, the last refuge of freedom, to live the outlaw existence of a free peasant.

Brigandage

Brigands and brigandage were a phenomenon of the collectivization and immediate postcollectivization years in Soviet Russia. Bands, bandits, banditry—the Soviet terminology—represented another collective form of active resistance, another response from the peasant repertoire of popular protest. Brigands were roving bands of the dispossessed, marauders intent on vengeance when warranted and on taking what they needed and what they wanted as they rode into populated areas. Brigandage was stranger neither to Russia nor to other peasant cultures.[218] The most recent and serious episode of Russian brigandage occurred in the civil war period, and, although the 1920s were in the main years of calm, there were occasional flareups of banditry in the 1920s in untamed and thinly populated regions of Eastern Siberia and Central Asia.[219] Brigandage rose again with collectivization as lawlessness came down from on high and as some peasants followed the age-old traditional and now desperate escape route into the forest.

Soviet power, following the same steps as other ruling powers before it, used terms such as "bandits" and "banditry" to criminalize and therefore depoliticize the existence and activities of these groups made up of, by and large, young peasant men. And, in fact, some of their activity could be narrowly construed as criminal and a part of their number was apparently made up of criminal elements. In Siberia, the capital of brigandage, at the end of the 1920s there were approximately 9,000 exiled criminals who had managed to escape into the wood and to join up with bandits, due to the lack of control and supervision in Siberian exile.[220] In the second half of 1929, Siberian courts sentenced 157 band members to be executed; of these, 119 were said to be "thief-recidivists."[221] The bands, however, also included peasants—runaway kulaks or peasants labeled as kulaks, kulaks escaped from their places of exile or detention, and peasants opposed to Soviet power. According to one report, approximately 50% of the members of Siberian bands operating in Tomskii and Slavgorodskii *okrugs* were kulaks, that is, peasants unreconciled to Soviet reality.[222] Fugitive kulaks were reportedly organizing bands in Chumakovskii *raion* in Western Siberia in 1931, and in the Moscow Region in 1934 peasants escaped from exile were said to be active in bands of thieves.[223] Kulak-peasant participation in bands elsewhere was also reported to be high.[224] Peasants therefore made up a large but indeterminate contingent within the bands. A term such as "criminal," moreover, should be viewed as relative and at times interchangeable with "kulak" in those socially fluid and judicially malleable times. "Escapees from detention" could be peasants; kulaks could be criminals; peasants and kulaks were interchangeable; and a man could be branded a bandit if, as Eric Hobsbawm has written of other such phenomena, "he does something which is not regarded as criminal by his local conventions, but is so regarded by the state or the local rulers."[225] In other words, banditry should not be dismissed as a Soviet invention because of political semantics or as a criminal activity, but should instead be explored as another form of popular resistance rooted in a peasant tradition of dissent.

Although information on brigandage is scanty, it is clear that it assumed threatening dimensions in Siberia, which, as early as November

1929, was declared "unsafe due to banditry." Even prior to November, a special commission had been formed to lead the struggle with brigandage.[226] Four hundred fifty-six bands were said to be active in Siberia in 1929, and 880 were reported in Western Siberia in the first nine months of 1930.[227] By the end of 1930, 537 bands of brigands had been "liquidated" in Western Siberia.[228] Although Siberia appears to have been the center of Russian brigandage, brigands were also reported to be active in the Western Region, Moscow Region, Astrakhan, North Caucasus, and the Far East in the first half of the 1930s.[229]

Most Soviet reports claimed that the major activity of the bands was theft, generally occurring in organized raids on collective or state farms, and sometimes involving arson.[230] This response was predictable, and echoed official diagnoses of peasant banditry from other times and places, where, according to one student of the subject, "[T]he authorities . . . invariably mistook rebellion for robbery."[231] One Russian historian wrote that people were afraid to go out at night because of brigandage in and around the village Irkutskoe in Krasnoiarskii *okrug*, Siberia, in 1929.[232] In 1929, the village of Mikhailovka in Tomskii *okrug* was burned to the ground by a band of marauders who murdered the *sel'sovet* chairman in the process.[233] A heavily armed band active in Malo-Peshchovskii *raion*, Tomskii *okrug*, Siberia, hid in the forests by day and made forays into villages at night to pillage and burn in the course of 1929. This band reportedly set 60 fires, threatened peasants not to go to meetings, and was responsible for two murders.[234] The émigré newspaper *Vestnik krest'ianskoi Rossii* in 1931 quoted a Tersk *oblast* party committee secretary who said that the majority of bandits in his area were Red army deserters with families nearby; the secretary also claimed that the bands were responsible for many cases of murders of officials and activists.[235] Finally, one of the most famous and dangerous bands was led by Kochkin, and operated in the Irkutsk region in the late 1920s. The Kochkin band attacked and plundered collective farms in Irkutskii and Usol'skii *raions*, and supposedly terrorized peasants dubbed Kochkin the "black tsar."[236]

Not all Soviet observers confined their analysis of brigandage to theft and criminal gangsterism. Murders and assaults of Soviet officials, the tendency for bands to attack collective and state farms, and the parallel upsurge in banditry and socialist transformation all present a certain kind of circumstantial evidence pointing in another direction. This direction was clearly indicated in a mid-February 1930 North Caucasus regional party committee circular letter on collectivization in ethnic minority areas. The circular warned the national *oblast* party committees to stop "naked dekulakization" (dekulakization without collectivization) or more peasants would flee into the mountains and join the bandits.[237] In a June 1929 letter highly critical of the state's taxation and forced requisitioning policies in the Don and Lower Volga generally, the Soviet writer Mikhail Sholokhov argued angrily that political gangs were emerging as peasants were brutalized by the agents of Soviet power. According to Sholokhov, there was "a lot of combustible material" available for absorption into the gangs.[238] The Russian historians N. Ia. Gushchin and V. A. Il'inykh also argued that Siberian brigands were becoming increasingly politicized by the state's collectivization campaigns.[239]

The dual nature of the bands' activities, criminal and political, is typical of brigandage. Hobsbawm wrote of banditry as "a rather primitive form of organized social protest."[240] According to Hobsbawm, banditry arises in times of social turmoil when the traditional order is under attack. In the Soviet case, the bands were filled by sociopolitical outcasts, whether kulaks, peasants dubbed kulaks, or criminals from the lower orders. Mostly young males, the brigands were marginalized figures who had been disenfranchised by the system and, in the case of runaway peasants, declared outlaws before committing any crime. Once in the woods, these young, dispossessed peasants were absorbed into a criminal subculture. Their guerrilla activities derived from a blend of survival tactics and vengeance. Brigandage during collectivization became an atavistic protest against the new order and its institutions, which had expelled from its midst the young peasants who became brigands. Too little is known of the relations between the bandits and the local population to determine whether any of them played the traditional role of Robin Hood and the outlaw hero. But surely some peasants secretly rejoiced with news of the bands' exploits when those exploits were aimed at Soviet power and found solace in the emerging legends of the "black tsar" and other dangerous peasants. Whatever the case may be, that bands of brigands managed to terrorize large parts of Siberia and other parts of the countryside testifies to the endurance of popular forms of resistance in the peasant struggle against collectivization.

Conclusion

March fever—the peasant revolt of 1929–30—was a collective act of desperation and resistance. Open rebellion is never the norm in peasant resistance, and constitutes a rare and daring flash of peasant anger. For peasants, or any subordinate people, to rise up in collective violence requires either monumental brutality or monumental dismissal by governing elites. In the case of collectivization, active collective resistance was but a small, however dramatic and significant, chapter in the history of peasant protest and politics under Stalin. In the short term, it played a key role in shaping the dynamics of central policy, eventually bringing the state to its knees in March 1930 and igniting a scapegoating campaign against the collectivization cadres, who were now branded "dizzy" or fanatical for what was once described as success.[241] In the long term, however, peasant revolt in Soviet Russia, like peasant revolt in all too many other parts of the world, only succeeded in contributing to the increasing centralization and repressive nature of the state.[242] It fed into the civil war culture of the First Five-Year Plan revolution, fueling further the militarization of society, reinforcing the barracks socialism of Stalinism, and enhancing the atmosphere of enemies omnipresent. The countryside, like the nation as a whole, would be transformed into a siege state, an enormous staging ground for the amassing and training of legions of troops loyal to the state's apparatus of repression.

The peasant rebellion of 1930 was not only suppressed by arms and defused by political obfuscation, it was lost to history in the long decades of Soviet silence and censorship and Western condescension and totalitarian model-dominated Sovietology.[243] It is a chapter of Soviet history, of peasant history, worthy of rehabilitation and continued exploration beyond what can be offered here. The importance of the topic is not simply in the fact of a mighty and widespread struggle against the Stalinist state, but in the light it sheds upon a peasant culture of resistance. The protest of the time was a function of a longer tradition of peasant dissent, a popular culture of protest known to and lived by Russian peasants and peasants in general. It is in this sense that the peasant revolt must be viewed as more than a chapter in the history of resistance; it was a fundamental part of the history of the peasantry, for this episode epitomized the peasant civil war against Soviet power, a peasant war in all its manifestations.

6

"We Let the Women Do the Talking": *Bab'i Bunty* and the Anatomy of Peasant Revolt

"We dared not speak at meetings. If we said anything that the organizers didn't like, they abused us, called us *koolacks* [*sic*], and even threatened to put us in prison."

"We let the women do the talking," cried a voice from the back of the crowd.

"They did that in every village, just let the women talk."

"And how they did talk!"

"They went on day and night. The organizers had not a chance."

"If the organizer tried to stop them they made such a din that he had to call off the meeting."

"What is there to be proud of in that?" broke in another *kolkhoznik*.

"Plenty of reason for us," screamed a middle-aged woman with a baby. "Our men folk," she complained . . . , "had cold feet, so we decided that we'd do something on our own account."

—Maurice Hindus, *Red Bread*

"The revolution began with the *baba,* and with the *baba* it shall end."

—overheard at a *babii bunt*

Bab'i bunty were a specific type of peasant riot. They were the most prominent symptom of March fever and best exemplified the forms and rituals of peasant rebellion during collectivization. The term *bab'i bunty* may be translated literally as "women's riots," yet this translation does not begin to do justice to its specific cultural and historical evocations. *Babii* (singular adjective) is a colloquial expression for women that refers in particular to country women with country ways. The *baba* (singular noun) is most often perceived as illiterate, ignorant (in the broader sense of *nekul'turnaia*), superstitious, a rumor-monger, and, in general, given to irrational outbursts of hysteria. The *baba* might best be seen as a color-ful combination of the American "hag," "fishwife," and "woman driver" all cast in a peasant mold. The element of stereotype is evident. Accordingly, the modifier colors and reinforces the noun that follows. A *bunt* (singular noun) is a spontaneous, uncontrolled, and uncontrollable explosion of peasant opposition to authority. It is a riot, seemingly aimless, unpredictable, and always dangerous. A *babii bunt*, then, is a women's riot characterized by female hysteria, irrational behavior, unorganized protest, rage, and violence.

Such, in any case, were the denotation and connotation of the term as used by party leaders, local officials and other observers. Rarely, if ever, were *bab'i bunty* described or evaluated in political or ideological terms. Instead, they were the most malignant feature of the disease borne by March fever. Their causes were generally attributed to the contagion of male agitators, the kulaks and *podkulachniki,* who supposedly exploited the irrational hysteria of the *baba* for their own counterrevolutionary ends, or else blamed on the mistakes of cadres who succumbed to "dizziness from success." *Bab'i bunty* were tolerated to a far greater extent than similar protests led by peasant men. They were also dealt with less harshly in cases when criminal charges ensued. The *baba* was not perceived as the fairer sex but as the darker sector of the already dark peasant masses. Consequently, like an unruly child or a butting goat, she was not held directly responsible for her actions, even in cases when she was subject to reprimand or punishment.

Officials' perceptions of peasant actions are generally based on assumptions, in this case highly ideological and politicized, about peasant ways and mores. As Daniel Field has demonstrated, however, peasants appear at times to have exploited official preconceptions about themselves for their own ends. In his study of postemancipation peasant disturbances, Field suggests that peasants manipulated their reputation for naive monarchism as a means of deflecting punishment and as a rationalization for confrontations with officials who, according to peasants, were violating the will of the tsar.[1] Such dissembling before power in order to mask subversive acts is a traditional peasant tactic in rebellious confrontations with authority.[2] Peasant women may have had an additional advantage in their encounters with Soviet power. Not only could they play on official images of the peasantry as dark mass or the peasant as ideological friend or foe, depending upon social status, they could also call upon the culturally generalized image of what Natalie Zemon Davis in her studies of early modern France has labeled the "disorderly woman,"

> a[n] image that could operate . . . to sanction riot and political disobedience for both men and women in a society that allowed the lower orders few formal means of protest . . . [s]he [the disorderly woman] was not accountable for what she did. Given over to the sway of her lower passions, she was not responsible for her actions.[3]

If, indeed, the *baba* bore some resemblance to the disorderly woman of other times and cultures, then it may well be that *bab'i bunty* belied the official depiction of peasant women's protest and were not as irrational as they appeared to outside observers. In much the same way that the *causes* of mass disturbances were rooted in "generic" sources of peasant discontent, their predominant *form*, the *babii bunt*, and its rituals were also drawn from a peasant culture of resistance.

"A little misunderstanding"

In 1933, when Stalin called for a cow in every peasant household (partly to placate collective farm women and partly to mask the famine), he acknowledged the opposition of peasant women to collectivization by remarking that, "Of course, not long ago Soviet power had a little misunderstanding with collective farm women. This business was about cows."[4] The "business about cows" became a national phenomenon in the late 1920s and early 1930s, evolving well beyond the confines of the "little misunderstanding."

A Central Committee report of late 1929 noted that women provided the main support for "kulak insurrection."[5] Top secret briefing papers for Stalin, Molotov, and other key leaders on collectivization in the winter of 1930 reported that, "[i]n all kulak disturbances [*vystupleniia*] *the extraordinary activity of women* is evident—a circumstance sufficiently serious to draw to your attention."[6] These conclusions were echoed in the provinces. In the North Caucasus, where women were said to be the *zastrel'shchiki* (leaders) of resistance,[7] a regional party committee circular letter of 18 February 1930 on excesses in collectivization noted that the widespread and threatening unrest in the villages was centered among women.[8] A Middle Volga regional party committee decree of 11 March 1930 on excesses in the Penza area also singled out women in its discussion of unrest, pointing to a large number of *bab'i bunty*.[9] In 1929, 486 mass disturbances (from a total of 1,307) were made up exclusively of women, with an additional 67 consisting primarily of women. In 1930, 3,712 mass disturbances (from a total of 13,754) were made up almost exclusively of women, and in all remaining cases, women constituted either a majority or a significant proportion of the participants.[10] When the nation's leaders met at the Sixteenth Party Congress in June and July 1930, speakers frankly admitted the key role women had played in collective farm disturbances. Lazar Kaganovich, a Politburo member and one of Stalin's closest aids, said "We know that in connection with the excesses in the collective farm movement, women in the countryside in many cases played the most 'advanced' role in the reaction against the collective farm."[11] Andreev, first secretary of the important North Caucasus regional party committee, seconded Kaganovich, labeling women the "vanguard" in the protests against collectivization.[12]

The Communist party explained the "vanguard" role of women in the protest against collectivization by reference to what was considered to be the low cultural and political level of peasant women, the "incorrect approach" of rural officials to the volatile women, and, finally, kulak and *podkulachnik* exploitation of the women's irrational fears and potential for mass hysteria. The party's response to women's protest was different from its response to male peasant protest, which was inevitably labeled kulak opposition and dealt with by increasing the level of repression. Although repressive measures were not always excluded, the party instead emphasized a more "correct" approach to peasant women. A correct approach in this instance was a euphemism for ending the arbitrary violence—the excesses—of collectivization. The party had also stressed the importance of political work among peasant women, beginning from the time of the grain procurement crisis when the potential dangers of female-led opposition to Soviet policy first became apparent.[13] Such work had at least two objectives. First, the party sought to "educate" women by expanding political indoctrination among them. Second, the party attempted to draw more women into active involvement in the political and administrative life of the village through participation in the women's delegate meetings and soviet elections, and membership in local soviets, collective farm boards, and the Communist party. During the years of collectivization, there was a gradual, but noticable, improvement in such efforts.[14] The party's emphasis on work among women was predicated on the official assumption that women's protest was apolitical, a function of their backwardness and therefore politically curable.

It was for that reason that the party's efforts to educate peasant women were largely ineffective in quelling resistance during collectivization. Although the co-optation and advancement into soviet and party work of women, especially younger women, would have a relatively more positive effect in the mid- and later 1930s, these measures failed to address, let alone alter, the egregious policies and practices that were at the root of women's protest—indeed, the protest of *all* peasants—against the collective farm system. Moreover, the party's contradictory demands for a correct approach to peasant women on the part of rural officials and the correct implementation of its own brutal policies made it highly unlikely that the barbaric, civil-war style of rural officials would or could be tempered. As a consequence, the party was unable to quiet the fears of peasant women or to prevent the wave of *bab'i bunty* that erupted in the countryside.

Kulak *agitprop* and *petit bourgeois* instincts

Official reasoning claimed that the kulak was the chief culprit behind *bab'i bunty*. Accordingly, because she was bereft of political consciousness and agency, the *baba* easily succumbed to the influence of the kulak, *podkulachnik*, and omnipresent kulak spirit pervading the countryside at this time. In the words of an OGPU official, "kulak anticollective farm agitation *flows* among the backward female masses of the village."[15] According to another OGPU official, "The most active participants in disturbances are primarily women who act under the influence of kulak agitation."[16]

The kulak's supposed success was based on the "low *kulturnost'* of women" and the "excesses" of overly enthusiastic local officials.[17] The *baba*, moreover, was said to be a means to an end: the kulak used her to get to the men, all in the aim of counterrevolution.[18]

It was the kulak *agitprop*,[19] or rumor mill, that cynically manipulated the backwardness of peasant women and artfully exploited the mistakes of local officials. Kulak *agitprop* capitalized on the *baba's* ignorance by forecasting the end of the world and moral decadence in the collective farm. It also played upon her "petit-bourgeois instincts," supposedly stronger than those of male peasants (excepting, of course, the kulak) and the material source of her counterrevolutionary malleability. Petit-bourgeois instincts mostly pertained to concerns centering on the domestic economy, subsistence issues, and family, concerns that could only be instinctual, given the *baba's* low *kulturnost'*. They also included matters of "superstition"—that is, issues relating to the church, priest, and religion. While this official version of the nature of women's resistance was not entirely lacking in substance, women's protest engendered by the policies of collectivization was not irrational and seldom the manifestation of instinct.

Peasant women's opposition came as a direct response to the implementation of the state's destructive policies. The OGPU, which sometimes stepped partly aside from the official version of *bab'i bunty* in its classified documentation, analyzed the causation behind women's mass disturbances in 1930. According to its observations, in the first half of the year, 1,154 women's revolts were centered around the collective farm, 778 arose on religious grounds, 422 concerned the defense of the dekulakized, and 336 derived from food difficulties. In the second half of the year, 36% of women's revolts were over grain requisitioning, 20% in defense of the dekulakized, 12% on religious grounds, 10.7% due to food difficulties, 10% connected to collectivization, and the rest, miscellaneous.[20] The causes of women's protest were roughly similar to the causes of peasant rebellion in general, reflecting no more and no less than the paramount concerns of peasant politics during collectivization.[21]

Women protested vehemently against the threat that collectivization posed to the economic survival of their families and village communities. Throughout the countryside, women struggled to prevent the economic ruin of their households. The requisitioning of grain and seed reserves during collectivization presented an especially grave danger to subsistence, serving as important sources of unrest among peasant women. In V. Irmyshskii *raion*, Barnaul'skii *okrug*, Siberia, for example, crowds of women demonstrated continually, sometimes day and night, against requisitioning in the spring of 1929.[22] In 1930, in the village Tuluzakovka in Penzenskii *okrug* in the Middle Volga, a group of 70 women blocked the removal of the seed reserves, threatening to massacre an OGPU plenipotentiary if need be, while in Rybinskii *raion*, in Mordovskaia *oblast'*, at least three *bab'i bunty* erupted over the socialization of seed grain.[23] In the village Sokolov and elsewhere in Kamenskii *raion,* Kamenskii *okrug,* Siberia, crowds of women broke into collective farm granaries and took back their seed grain by force in the winter and spring of 1930.[24]

Peasant women struggled with equal determination against the socialization of domestic livestock. In the North Caucasus *stanitsa* Staro-Shcherbinskaia in Eiskii *raion,* the women fought back attempts to socialize the livestock, biting the hands of the stablemen who held the animals' reins while their children pelted the collectivizers with stones.[25] In the Ukrainian village Mikhailovka in Sinel'nikovskii *raion,* an inspector arrived only to find that the women were nowhere to be seen. He was told later that they slept in the cowsheds in fear of the cows being taken.[26] The socialization of domestic livestock directly threatened peasant women. A peasant woman's economic position within the household was based largely on the care and cultivation of domestic livestock.[27] The loss of a dairy cow, moreover, could mean that peasant children would be without milk.[28]

Women understood clearly what collectivization portended, not limiting their protest to grain requisitioning and the socialization of domestic livestock. In January 1930 in Belotserkovskii and Korostenskii *okrugs* in Ukraine, groups of from 50 to 500 women went into the fields to block the land reform that sometimes preceded the organization of a collective farm. In the village of Shevchenko and elsewhere in the Khar'kov area, women broke up meetings dedicated to land reform and collective farm construction, shouting "[We] will not go into the collective. [We] were not and will not be slaves."[29] In late 1929 in the village of Mordov in Bugul'minskii canton in Tatariia, women broke up a collectivization meeting and called their own meeting, at which they passed a decree categorically refusing to join the collective farm.[30] Three hundred women angered by the organization of a collective farm in the village Elzhoszernoe in Ul'ianovskii *okrug,* Middle Volga, broke into the *sel'sovet* and beat up their local officials, while in the village Salovka in Buguruslanskii *okrug,* 100 women demonstrated against the collective farm, refusing to disperse until arrests were made.[31] And everywhere women were in the forefront after March, when peasants quit the collective farms in droves, taking back their property by force and chasing officials out of the village.

In the aftermath of the winter 1930 collectivization campaign, *bab'i bunty* broke out over the increasing food difficulties experienced in the collective farms, especially among poor peasants. In the Mavrinskii collective farm in Dergachevskii *raion,* Central Black Earth Region, 40 women paraded with red flags, demanding the distribution of twenty *puds* per person of the newly threshed grain.[32] (A *pud* is approximately 36 pounds.) Six mass disturbances, composed mainly of women, occurred in Buguruslanskii *okrug* in the Middle Volga in spring 1930 as crowds of up to 400 people attacked *sel'sovets* and RIKs, demanding bread and attempting to storm the buildings.[33] *Bab'i bunty* over food difficulties erupted throughout the North Caucasus in the spring and early summer of 1930. In many parts of the region, women, especially poor women, besieged *sel'sovets*, pleading, "Give us bread." In the village Znamenka in Slavogorodskii *okrug*, 20 women gathered at the *raion* party committee office, demanding bread. When they received no response, they moved on to the RIK chairman's office, where they refused to leave until they were given bread: "We got nowhere with this scoundrel [the RIK chairman] by peaceful means, [we] will all go to the [soviet] officials' homes and take bread from those who have it."[34] In the village Ptich'e in Izobil'no Tish-chenskii *raion*, Stavropol'skii *okrug*, 100 women descended upon the co-operative shop with plans to carry out a *samosud* against its manager, while in the *stanitsa* Novo-Titarovskaia in Kubanskii *okrug*, 200 women threatened to destroy the cooperative shop and murder its chairman. In A.-Tuzlovskii village, Shakhtinsko-Donetskii *okrug*, women called an ille-gal meeting at which they decreed "to propose that the *rai[on]* center immediately dispatch . . . the essential quantity of grain for food. In case of refusal to send the grain, to distribute [grain] from the emergency seed grain." In their desperation, the women of one Osetian village went so far as to threaten to burn down a grain elevator if their demands for bread were not met, arguing that their children were wasting away from hunger.[35]

Women's protest over collective farms, the socialization of livestock, grain requisitioning, and food difficulties raises most clearly the issue of what Soviet power derisively labeled the petit-bourgeois instincts of peas-ant women. While instinct may have played some role, women's opposi-tion to the destruction of peasant farming was motivated largely by a set of rational interests revolving around subsistence and survival, the family, and the household economy. It was natural for women to take the lead in such protest, given their central role in the domestic economy. Like the women who led bread riots in England and France in earlier centuries and in many other parts of the world into the modern era, peasant women in the Soviet Union assumed the initiative in resisting policies and practices that threatened their families' existence and encroached directly on their sphere of labor and life.[36] Such protest, moreover, reflected the most vital and central concerns of the peasantry as a whole. Motivated in their resis-tance by a subsistence ethic that taught peasants that experimentation could be dangerous, peasant women would be sadly vindicated when the Soviet "experiment" in socialized agriculture led to catastrophic disaster in 1932–33.

Women's fears extended well beyond the material domain. Peasant women found their basic belief system under attack as the collective farm brought with it the destruction of the church, a wholesale assault on reli-gious beliefs, and a revolution in the everyday spiritual world of the peas-antry. Women were active in demonstrations against church closings, bell removals, and the arrests of priests. In a Middle Volga village, for in-stance, peasant women led the protest against the arrest of their priest, organizing three separate meetings at which demands were put forth for his release.[37] In Sukhinshevskii *okrug* in the Western Region, the closing of churches and the removal of icons led to what the sources labeled a "mass movement" in defense of the church, supposedly under the slogan "The Roman pope supports us, all the world is behind us, all the world is against Soviet power, [and] in the spring there will be war." Women led the revolt, gathering daily at the Bariatinskii and other RIKs to present their demands in crowds that soon grew to 400 people.[38] Unrest in the Catholic Kamenskii canton in the Volga German Republic at the end of December 1929 was stirred up by rumors of church closings and soon led to an uprising reportedly inspired by the slogan "For faith and God, against the collective farm." The revolt began in the village of Keller, where rumors spread of the impending arrest of the priest and the closing of the church. The believers organized a guard at the church and the priest's home, and the ringing of the church bell was to be the signal of the approach of the authorities. In early January, illegal meetings were held in a number of villages in the canton, where, according to official sources, the farmers decided "to use the women" to fight the collective farm. In Keller, crowds of women took back their property and released arrested peasants. The revolt spread to four other villages. From the beginning, the *sel'sovet* was paralyzed and the village run by leaders of the revolt.[39]

Women were fierce in their defense of the church. Some sense of this, although obviously distorted through the official lens, can be gleaned in the unpublished letter of an official writing from the Ukrainian village of Mikhailovka in the Poltava area. He wrote, "Men and women gathered and ran to the church as to a fire in order to defend the church. . . . Some women acted like beasts and went against the authority of the village [government] in order to defend the church." The women who "acted like beasts" succeeded, however, in keeping the church open.[40] Peasant women were the upholders of religion within the village and household, and they played an important lay role in the church as deaconesses, caretakers, and loyal parishioners, so it was natural that the assaults on the church would affect them most acutely. Rather than irrational beasts acting on instinct, they acted out of a devotion to their faith and church, convinced that the collective farm was the apotheosis of evil and a blasphemy before God. In defending the church, moreover, women were defending their community, because the former, perhaps more than any other village institution, signified the wholeness and unity of the latter.

The same notions of community animated peasant women in their defense of relatives, neighbors, and friends who faced expropriation and deportation as kulaks. Throughout the countryside, women bravely stood up to the officials and activists who carried out dekulakization. In a series of Crimean villages, for example, women organized demonstrations against the deportations. When the deportations finally began, the women of the district accompanied their ill-fated neighbors for some five kilometers beyond the village, in tears, cursing Soviet power.[41] And in a Russian village in Bashkiriia, one Anna Borisevich [*sic*] convinced thirty other women to walk out of a meeting in support of the families of those who had been stripped of their civil rights.[42] Peasant women defended their neighbors out of a sense of community and of justice. The importance of justice was magnified in a world suddenly turned on its head, as became tragically clear in a *babii bunt* in the Ukrainian village of Kiselevka in Lebedinskii *raion* in June 1931. Kiselevka was engaged in the cultivation of strawberries, and due to low requisitioning prices the state's procurement plan had only been fulfilled by 80%. The local officials consequently set up a checkpoint to prevent black market trade in strawberries. On 24 June, the guard stopped a middle peasant who had refused to surrender his strawberries, arguing that he personally had fulfilled his procurement obligations. The guard shot him and his horse, gravely wounding the man. As soon as word spread about the brutal and unprovoked assault, a group of 150 women gathered. They first went to the school in search of the teacher activist, then to the collective farm chairman's home, and finally to the *sel'sovet*, where anger boiled over into a riot as the women shouted, "Sov[iet] power kills people for berries. This [will happen] to all of us."[43]

Women's protest over church, neighbors, and family did not derive from instinct; rather, it was legitimate and rational, and based on universal peasant concerns derived from a peasant moral economy and political consciousness. And just as women were capable of reasoned objections to the collective farm, they were also able to initiate and organize reasoned and peaceful protest. In an Eletskii *okrug* village in the Central Black Earth Region, after the publication of Stalin's "Dizziness from Success," women led demonstrations against the collective farm, parading with black flags.[44] In another Central Black Earth village, women simply boycotted meetings when the collective farm organizer refused to allow peasants to express their opinions.[45] In a Lipetskii *raion* village meeting (also in the Central Black Earth Region), the women were so incensed by official policies and actions that they brought meetings to an impasse by raising their hands unanimously against all measures proposed by the officials, regardless of their content.[46] In the village of Goluboko in the Leningrad Region, the women took the initiative in organizing a meeting at which they passed a decree "To reject [all] measures of the party and Soviet power."[47] In these cases, women attempted to exert their will without resorting to violence. The problem with nonviolent protest, however, was that it was so rarely heard during collectivization. It was instead ignored or crushed by the weight of repression, or pushed by provocation into violence. It is for that reason, rather than any supposed irrational or hysterical nature, that women in the end turned most frequently to the *babii bunt*.

Bab'i bunty

Bab'i bunty were depicted as spontaneous outbursts of mass hysteria marked by indiscriminate violence, disorder, and a cacophony of high–pitched voices all screaming demands at once. Angry women assembled before the rural soviet were "milling crowds." The presence of children and babes-in-arms imparted an unreasoned and unreasonable air to the scene, throwing some officials off their guard and confounding others. The silent gathering of the village men off in the distance unnerved and terrified. A general din of shouts, curses, and threats filled the air, serving as the auditory context for the women's approach to Soviet power. Those officials who dared meet the women found themselves jostled, pushed, and crushed within the folds of the enveloping crowd. The foolhardy among them who thought to chase away this *baba* rage with jokes or soothing and patronizing words were rebuffed with full-fisted blows from strongly hewn female working hands. Wiser officials, or those who knew something of village women, hid out or ran away, waiting for the *babii bunt* to run out of steam or the men to take control of their women. Most women's riots fizzled out—generally without the use of repressive force—when the women attained their goals. The women were seldom held responsible for their behavior, thanks to official perceptions of the basis of their actions, as well as the embarrassment of male officials incapable of controlling disorderly women. The *bab'i bunty* thus accomplished their ends and the state held strong in its perceptions of peasant women's protest.

The official depiction of the *babii bunt* was captured concisely in a most illuminating case of a women's riot in the village Belovka in Chistopol canton in Tatariia in August 1929. The cause of the *babii bunt* in Belovka was a *sel'sovet* decision to introduce a five-field system of crop rotation in the village and to carry out a redistribution of peasant lands, most probably preliminary to the formation of a collective farm. Behind the *babii bunt*, according to the official description of the case, loomed the "local kulaks" and, in particular, the insidious figure of one Sergei Fomin, the "kulak" miller. The case report read: "As a result of kulak agitation among the dark, illiterate peasant women, a crowd of one hundred people . . . strenuously demanded the repeal of the decree on the introduction of the five-field system." Despite warnings to disperse, the crowd, "supported by the general din," continued its protest, knocking to the ground and beating a rural soviet member. At this point, other soviet activists entered the fray and, according to the report, prevented the crowd from realizing its presumed intentions of beating the activist senseless. The case was heard before the regional court, which prosecuted the ten most active women and the miller Fomin, who was described as the "ideological instigator" of the disturbance. Fomin, who was also charged with setting fire to the rural soviet secretary's house, was prosecuted separately, according to "special consideration." The women, prosecuted under Article 59 (2) of the penal code for mass disturbances, received sentences of imprisonment with strict isolation ranging from two to three years.

The Belovka case was reexamined by the Supreme Court in January 1930, at which time the decision of the regional court was overturned. The Supreme Court held Fomin *exclusively* responsible for the women's actions, describing him as the "ideological inspiration," the "ideological leader," and the main "culprit" in the disturbance. Fomin's "counterrevolutionary organizational role" in the protest was the "actual root" of the *babii bunt* and, according to the Supreme Court, the regional court had failed to discern this fact clearly enough. In addition, the Supreme Court accused the rural soviet of Belovka of insufficient preparatory work among women, something that could have mitigated the effects of Fomin's propaganda. Finally, the sentences of the women, all described as illiterate middle and lower-middle peasants, and representative of the "most backward part of the peasantry" (i.e., women), were lessened to forced labor within the village for periods ranging from six months to one year. The purpose of the sentences was to serve as a warning and an educational measure rather than as mere punishment.[48]

This case is instructive in illuminating official views of and reactions to peasant women's protest. In Belovka, the women were viewed as no more than naive dupes of the local kulaks, as figurative battering rams against Soviet power. The soviet's failure to work among the women and prepare them for the new policy transformed them into ammunition that the kulak could fire at the Soviet regime. However, the Belovka case may not tell the whole story of the *bab'i bunty*. Petro Grigorenko, in his memoirs, described the *bab'i bunty* as a kind of "tactic." The women would initiate opposition to the collective farm or other policies and the men would remain on the sidelines until the local activists attempted to quell the disorder. At that point, the more vulnerable peasant men could safely enter the fray as chivalrous defenders of wives, mothers, and daughters rather than as antisoviet *podkulachniki*.[49] Descriptions of *bab'i bunty* by officials in the field offer confirmation of Grigorenko's findings and appear to belie the official image as presented in the Belovka case.

A riot that occurred in the village of Lebedevka in Kursk at the Budennyi collective farm may serve as an example. A 25,000er named Dobychin, serving as a plenipotentiary for collectivization, arrived in the collective farm on 7 March 1930. Dobychin soon called a meeting of the peasant women, at which he was met with extreme hostility. The women cried, "We do not want a collective farm" and "You want to derail the *muzhik*." Dobychin responded, "We will not hold such types in the collective farm, good riddance . . . sleep it off and you'll see that we will let the poor peasant derail him who made you drunk and sent you here." Dobychin's words enraged the women, and led to a general uproar and an assault on the worker. The women, with one Praskov'ia Avdiushenko in the lead, approached the stage where the worker stood. Praskov'ia said to Dobychin, "Ah well, come nearer to us." She then grabbed him by his collar and dragged him off the stage. Dobychin somehow managed to escape, but the unrest continued and even escalated when the church watchman's wife began to ring the church bell. At that point, the male peasants entered the fray, joining the women in seizing their recently socialized livestock and preparing a collective declaration to quit the farm.

This disturbance, like many others, was not suppressed, but simply ended with the collapse of the collective farm.[50]

A similar case was described by the worker Zamiatin, who was among those workers recruited from the city soviets in early 1930 to work in the *sel'sovets*. Zamiatin depicted the situation faced by the 25,000er Klinov. Zamiatin said that the approach to Klinov's village resembled an "armed camp"; on his way, he saw a sign nailed to a bridge that read: "Vas'ka [Klinov] you scum, get out. We will break your legs." When he arrived, Zamiatin found the village alive with rumors of the approach of a band of riders who were coming to kill all the Communists and collective farmers. In this village, dekulakization had already been implemented but the kulaks had not yet been exiled. This omission, according to Zamiatin, had led to the existing crisis. With Zamiatin's arrival, Klinov set about preparing for the exile of the kulaks. He began by removing the church bell. The heads of kulak families were then exiled, and all went well until one of the exiled kulaks escaped and returned home to announce that the other kulaks would soon be coming back to seek vengeance. This news led to the decision to exile the remaining members of the kulak families. The announcement of this decision led to an uproar in the village. In an attempt to forestall this action, the peasant women blocked the entrances of the huts of families slated for deportation. Several days later, the women also led the opposition to the attempt to cart away the village's grain by blocking entry to the granary. This action led to a *babii bunt*, followed quickly by a general free-for-all in which all the peasants participated, many armed with pitchforks. The disturbance was suppressed by the militia, which was called in after all of the peasants had joined the rebellion.[51]

In both of these cases, peasant women were responsible for initiating the resistance and were soon joined by the peasant men in a general village riot. In a classic depiction of a *babii bunt* in a Cossack village in Sholokhov's *Virgin Soil Upturned*, the Cossack men stood at the back of the crowd of women urging them on when they attacked the chairman of the *sel'sovet*. Here, the women led the attack on the grain warehouse "with the silent approval of the men folk at the back." And while the women were dragging the collective farm chairman through the village, the men broke the locks of the grain warehouse and seized their grain.[52] The women served both as initiators and decoys in this incident.

In the village of Belogolovoe in Zhukovskii *raion*, Brianskii *okrug*, Western Region, a decision to remove the church bell (supposedly taken by a general village assembly and the RIK) touched off a *babii bunt*. On 13 January 1930, eight local activists arrived at the church to take down the bell. Before they could complete their work, a group of women, armed with stakes, stormed the church, beating up the activists and bringing their work to a halt. On the next day, following the church service, the priest held a meeting to condemn the illegal activities of the local authorities and to collect money to send a petitioner off to Moscow to complain. The meeting was closed to all activists and the church bell was to sound the alert in case of trouble. On 15 January, the RIK sent in a plenipotentiary to enforce its decision to remove the bell. As soon as the plenipotentiary was sighted, the tocsin rang out and women, along with a smaller number of men, came pouring into the streets. The crowd assaulted the official, driving him out of the village and thus, for the time being, saving their bell. On the next day, 600 people arrived from neighboring villages to join the Belogolovoe peasants in a gathering of the faithful. Predictably, the OGPU blamed the kulak and the church council for the disturbances in this village. The resistance of the village's women, however, was notable for the persistence and determination it demonstrated, as well as the fact that very few male participants were involved in the protests.[53]

In the *bab'i bunty* in Karasukskii *raion*, Slavgorodskii *okrug*, Siberia, the men, in fact, stayed home. The rioting in this *raion* began on the eve of collectivization, over the issue of grain requisitioning. In April 1928, at meetings of poor peasants, villagers demanded an explanation from the state of how the people would feed themselves following the draconian requisitions. In May, some 120 women gathered at the *raion* center's soviet executive committee office demanding bread. They succeeded in forcing the RIK chairman to distribute grain to them. Once word got out about this event, the unrest was carried back to the villages. In six different villages, the women seized the grain from the cooperative granaries. The crowds involved in the *bab'i bunty* sometimes included as many as 200 women. According to the official postmortem on the disturbances, very few of the demonstrators actually needed bread. Rather, the blame was placed, predictably, on kulak instigation and the incorrect actions of local officials who by arresting some of the women in the early stages of the unrest supposedly provoked the others. In the Karasukskii riots, the village men stayed home (it was Sunday). According to the official report, the men neither objected to the women's actions nor participated in the rioting. Instead, they "silently supported the disturbances," saying "the *babas* are protesting, nothing will happen to them, they won't be punished."[54]

In some *bab'i bunty*, peasant men played no role at all, suggesting that women's protest was often much more than a simple ruse or front for male or general peasant rebelliousness. In the village of Blagoveshchensk in Pervomaiskii *raion*, Mariupol'skii *okrug*, Ukraine, a *babii bunt* broke out on 24 April 1930 over the arrest of a peasant named Gakh who was the chairman of the church council. Three hundred women stormed the *sel'sovet*, demanding the keys to the church and the liberation of Gakh. The women arrested Naumenko, the *sel'sovet* chairman, forced him to sit in a wooden cart, and wheeled him to Gakh's house. There, they taunted him with threats of a *samosud* if he refused to sign an order releasing Gakh. The women also arrested the party cell secretary, who received the same treatment as Naumenko. The women spat in the officials' eyes, calling them "bandits, thieves, and white guards," all the time threatening to kill them on the spot. OGPU officials arrived in the nick of time to liberate the officials, but the women continued to gather every day for the next five days, escalating their demands to include the dismantling of the collective farm and the return of the kulaks' property.[55]

A *babii bunt* that broke out in the village of Butovska in Klintsovskii *raion*, Western Region, was also made up exclusively of women. Early on the morning of 3 March 1930, the tocsin was sounded, bringing the women of the village out in what the report notes was an "organized fashion." The women marched off to the *sel'sovet*, demanding that a meeting with officials be called. The soviet officials refused to meet with the women. At that point, the women dispatched one of their contingent to the neighboring village to bring back (a presumably friendly) cooperative chairman. When the chairman arrived, a meeting with the soviet officials was called. At the meeting, the women demanded that the collective farm be dismantled, raising such a din, with shouts of "down with the collective farm!", that the officials closed the meeting. The next morning, 300 women again called on the *sel'sovet*, some armed with pitchforks, demanding a meeting. When their demand was refused, the crowd broke into the *sel'sovet* and passed their own decree dissolving the collective farm. They also elected a new *sel'sovet* consisting exclusively of women. The new *sel'sovet* secretary, labeled the daughter of a kulak in the official report, donned men's clothing and rechristened herself Vasilii Vasil'evich Antonenko in a reversal of gender and power that, however rare in its form, symbolically mirrored the overturn of government that had just taken place. The next day, the women got rid of the former soviet officials, shouting "we don't need you" and "we are all mutinying." Although the report notes that the officials fled to their homes to hide, there is no indication of how the *bunt* ended or what the consequences were for its participants. The Butovska *bunt* did, however, spark other *bab'i bunty* in the *raion*, including one in the village of Gorchaka. In Butovska, the village men were nowhere to be seen. Here the women were not only the leading force of rebellion, but also displayed a degree of organization, persistence, and, in their elections of a new local government, political awareness not expected from supposedly backward *babas*. Despite the facts of the case, it is important to note that the official report concluded that in Butovska and elsewhere in the *raion*, the organized nature of the *bab'i bunty*, the seeming pattern of events, suggested planning by someone (most certainly male) "hiding behind the backs of poor and middle peasant women."[56]

A *babii bunt* that occurred in the village Tankeevka in Spasskii canton, Tatariia, revealed a level of organization and political consciousness similar to that of the Butovska incident. Here women led the protest against the decision to turn the church into a "cultural center" and melt the bell down for the purchase of a tractor. With cries of "We don't need tractors or collective farms" and "We won't give up the bell," the women attacked and beat the *sel'sovet* members. After thus disposing of the local government, they organized a meeting and elected their own government.

Interestingly enough, the official report on the incident made no claim to outside or male leadership of the protest, instead labeling the apparent female ringleader a *kulachka*, or woman kulak, and thereby providing a rare example of the "kulakization" of female protest.[57]

Events in the Lower Volga village of Boltunovka also demonstrated a degree of organization not expected according to official stereotypes. Here the *babii bunt* began because of the state's attempt to dispatch the village's recently requisitioned grain. At 8:00 A.M. on 20 September 1929, a crowd of women converged from all ends of the village at the point from where the grain was to leave. According to the report, poor peasant women had organized the *bunt* in advance, knocking on all the hut windows and warning women to come to the demonstration or face a three-ruble fine.[58] Ultimately, the protest failed because the women did not manage to show up all at once. The report, written by Leningrad workers, blamed the *bunt* neither on the women nor on kulaks, but on corrupt and rude *okrug* plenipotentiaries. This conclusion thus shifted blame to *other* officials, ones, moreover, who were often involved in power conflicts with worker brigades, thereby continuing to rationalize and depoliticize women's protest by redirecting agency and causation.[59]

A series of *bab'i bunty* that broke out in response to dekulakization demonstrate further the determination and initiative of village women. In the village Verkhnii Ikorets in Bobrovskii *raion*, Ostrogozhskii *okrug*, Central Black Earth Region, a *babii bunt* occurred on 10 February 1930 as officials attempted to carry out dekulakization. A crowd of 200 women and children pelted officials with snowballs and stones, eventually forcing them to cease their activities. All through the night, groups of from five to ten women each sat vigil and guard at the homes of peasant families that had been labeled kulak. Two days later, a detachment of forty armed Communists and militia entered the village only to be met by a crowd of 600 women, apparently ready for them, who, with shouts of "hurrah," drove back the intruders. The women then moved on the *sel'sovet* where they endeavored to put an end to the collective farm and take back their seed grain.[60] In two Western Siberian villages, the women also took the initiative in defending their neighbors. In the village Petrovka in Cherlak-skii *raion*, forty women prevented the exile of two kulaks, hiding kulak children in their homes and threatening to beat up the RIK plenipotentiary. The women argued that "We have no kulaks, they [were] incorrectly deprived of their legal rights." In Rozhdestvenskaia village, in Kargatskii *raion*, a crowd of women gathered after hearing the cries of their neighbor Liakhov who "categorically refused to leave" with the dekulakization brigade. The women hid Liakhov's children and placed Liakhov under their personal protection. When officials returned later to try again to take Liakhov, a crowd of seventy women blocked his exile, shouting "[We] will not let [you] take him" and "The plenipotentiaries should be beaten." At the same time, other women went from hut to hut gathering signatures for a petition in support of Liakhov. In the end, the women turned their wrath against the collective farm and took back their property by force.[61] Each of these incidents involved a certain amount of organization and none can be characterized as anything but reasonable in intent.

Even the most violent and seemingly irrational displays of women's anger reveal elements of prior planning or, at the least, ritualized behavior indicating that women were not simply engaged in hysterical, uncontrollable outbursts. In the village of Krivozer'e in Romodanovskii *raion*, Mordovskii *oblast'*, for example, a crowd of 200 women converged at the *sel'sovet*, demanding to be released from the collective farm. They reassembled at the same place the next day, only this time the crowd had grown to 400 and the women were demanding that the poor peasants vacate the kulaks' homes or else see their children slaughtered. The angry crowd then threatened the local activists with murder and chased them into a nearby building. There, the crowd, seemingly out of control, broke the window and attempted to force entry into the house. Despite the wildly violent nature of this revolt, the women of Krivozer'e had prearranged signals with the women of two neighboring villages, who had participated in the *bunt*. The signal for the neighboring village women to come to Krivozer'e was the waving of a red shawl.[62] A women's revolt in the village Kareli in Morshanskii *raion*, Tambovskii *okrug*, Central Black Earth Region, also showed signs of forethought as well as certain rituals of revolt. On 12 January 1930, a youth meeting decided to close the church and transform it into a school. On the 13th, several women ran into the street, crying "*karaul*" (in this instance meaning "help" or "danger"), which, like the church bell, had the effect of a war cry, bringing other women out into the street with the same cry on their lips. Several hundred women gathered at the consumer shop, where they discussed the plans to close the church, and placed the blame for this decision on the local school teacher. The crowd then decided to call out some of the young people who had been at the meeting, yelling "*na rasprava*" (roughly, "come out for punishment"), a frequent cry in village riots. When the youth failed to show, the crowd broke into their homes, armed with hatchets and stakes. The crowd soon grew to 500 people and, with this, decided to march on the teacher's house. The teacher wisely vanished, and the crowd proceeded to the church, beating the wife of a local Communist on the way. The revolt ended when a *raion* plenipotentiary met with the women and promised them that no one would close the church. Even in this seemingly frenzied revolt, it should be noted that the women, whether by tradition or design, raised the conventional war cries and, moreover, managed to stop at the priest's house for his blessing on their way to the church.[63]

These cases demonstrate that peasant women were capable of acting independently in opposing the policies of Soviet power, with or without their men's aid and support. They also reveal some rudimentary degree of organization and political sense. In classified documents, the OGPU claimed that women's revolts were frequently distinguished by a high degree of organization and persistence, and noted several cases in which women organized systems of patrols and pickets to guard kulaks and their property.[64] That peasant women sometimes arrived at protests armed with pitchforks, stakes, knives, and other weapons provides further evidence of reasoned intent and organization behind the rebellions.[65] And in some instances, peasant men were even said to have actively opposed their wives' actions. In the mostly Baptist village of Novosrednyi in the Stavropol'skii region, for example, a *babii bunt* broke out in late 1929. Here the peasants viewed the collective farm as a threat to their livelihood, and all sorts of rumors flew concerning the socialization of children and the introduction of an eighty-meter blanket. When women from a neighboring village sent word that they had taken back their recently socialized livestock, the women of Novosrednyi went, *en masse*, many with children in hand, to the collective farm office to demand the return of their animals. The collective farm officials telephoned the *raion* party committee for instructions and were told, according to the account later written by a local official, that the use of repression was forbidden. The local officials then attempted to talk to the 200 women gathered. In response, the crowd became angrier, and when someone shouted, "*Babas* [go] for the horses," the women attacked the stables and reclaimed their horses. Reportedly, many of the husbands resisted, ordering their wives to return the horses with the reasoning that "I do not want to answer for you." That night, a collective farm meeting was called. The men sat silently while the women claimed full responsibility for their actions, adding "We don't need your collective farm!" Of course, the possibility remains that the men (and women) were claiming male innocence to avoid more serious repercussions. Regardless, the events in Novosrednyi show clearly that women were capable of protest independent of male participation.[66] In a village in the Don, a mass disturbance following the publication of the Central Committee's March decree on excesses also showed signs of male reluctance to engage the powers that be. Here, women called a meeting to rail against the collective farm. They occupied the collective farm buildings and arrested the collective farm chairman, spitting in his eyes and threatening to beat him. Their husbands were at work in the field during the disturbance, but returned home to attempt to "calm" their wives as soon as they heard of the revolt. The sincerity of the men's opposition cannot be determined for certain, but it is clear that the initial revolt was initiated independently by women.[67]

Bab'i bunty, however, should not be narrowly construed as women's protest. With or without the support and participation of male peasants, they represented village resistance as a whole, serving as perhaps the dominant mode of active protest in the peasant culture of resistance during collectivization. And contrary to official images or depictions, they were in fact highly ritualized acts in which the women took center stage both as directors and actors. *Bab'i bunty* followed a relatively stylized scenario in which all peasants, not just the women, had a defined role, with the village serving as their backdrop and peasant stereotypes as their props.[68]

Bab'i bunty frequently involved a kind of peasant battle formation that was both functional and ornamental. While the peasant men generally distanced themselves from the demonstration by standing off to the side, the women came to the fore, often with children in tow.[69] The presence of men could be a defensive gesture—the men could easily come to the women's defense in the event of violence—or could serve as intimidation. Children were there both as shields and as reminders to officials of the humanity of the situation they were confronting. The dominance of women was thought to be a possible deterrent to violence or, failing that, a less ostensibly politicized mode of confrontation with Soviet power. The battle formation and the roles thus implied were less consciously construed than a part of the popular culture of resistance that had developed over time as a way to confront power.[70]

By physically distancing themselves, peasant men were at the same time politically distancing themselves from the women's seditious acts and all possible and probable consequences. Both men and women were aware of the dangers of male involvement in protests against the state and appear to have formed a kind of alliance centered on the protection of males. This was likely the case in Novosrednyi when, after the *bunt*, the women insisted on claiming full responsibility for their actions.[71] In the German village Zonnental', Krapotkinskii *raion*, North Caucasus, the women "categorically forbade" the men to come anywhere near the crowd, telling them, "This is our women's business. Don't you interfere."[72] In the Karasukskii riots, the alliance was even articulated by men who claimed in regard to the women's protest that "nothing will happen to them, they won't be punished."[73] And in the Lower Volga, women assumed the "vanguard" in revolt under the pretext that "women will not be touched."[74]

Off the record, the OGPU clearly understood at least some of the dynamics of women's protest, arguing that men tended to stay to the side in most disturbances for fear of incurring the harsh punishments meted out to kulaks. The men then "allowed" the women to take the lead with the understanding that "women can [do] anything, nothing will [happen] to women, they carry less responsibility." For instance, the OGPU reported that in the village Antonovka in Bugskii *raion* in Ukraine, women proclaimed, "We fear no one, we were already at the GPU, and they did nothing [to us] and will do [nothing]." And in the village Krasnoe in Nikolo-Pestrovskii *raion*, Middle Volga, women said, "Women [*baby*] don't give [them] the bell, nothing will happen to us for this." According to the OGPU, it was the "condescending relations of the punitive organs to women . . . that enable[d] the strengthening of opinion about the invulnerability [*beznakazannost'*] of women." And in fact, if OGPU sources are to be trusted, armed force was used in only seven cases to put down a *babii bunt* (five times in Ukraine, and once each in the Central

Black Earth Region and North Caucasus). OGPU data indicate that 68% of *bab'i bunty* were "liquidated" by persuasion, 15.5% through the satisfaction of the rebels' demands, and only 14% through the arrests of leaders and the most active participants, thus providing some justification for opinions regarding the reduced vulnerability of women to repression.[75]

In *bab'i bunty*, then, men tended to stand to the side, as far as that was possible. In nonviolent protest, they did the same. Artfully dissimulating, peasant men played upon the dominant images of the *baba* to opt out of the collective farm or other unwanted measures. For example, according to the report of a workers' brigade in the Tambov area, in the Central Black Earth Region, the men did not go to the meetings on collectivization, but sent the women instead. When asked why, they replied, "They [the women] are equal now, as they decide so we will agree."[76] The 25,000er Gruzdev was told by one peasant, "My wife does not want to socialize our cow, so I cannot do this," and a Moscow area peasant told officials that he was willing to join the collective farm, but that he was afraid because his wife had confused him.[77] Peasant men in the Odessa area told officials, "We will not go into the [collective farm] because [our] wives won't let us" while in the village Borka in Osterskii *raion*, Chernogovskii *okrug*, the majority of poor peasants reportedly refused to join the collective farm, claiming that their wives would not agree to their membership.[78] One observer noted that the men often appeared ready to join a collective farm, but would procrastinate by saying that they needed "to consult with the *baba*."[79] It was both easier and safer for a peasant man to claim that he could not join a collective farm because his wife would not let him.

The women played along. In many parts of the countryside, women told officials that they would not join the collective farm and that if their husbands did they would divorce them.[80] In a North Caucasus village, women warned an official that, "If our husbands join the collective farm, we will not let them [come] home."[81] In the *stanitsa* Vladimirskaia in Stavropol'skii *okrug*, North Caucasus, 150 women gathered at the *sel'sovet*, demanding divorces and divisions of property because they did not want to be in the collective farm, while their husbands purportedly would not give up their memberships. Elsewhere in the *okrug*, women demanded that their husbands be taken off membership lists of collective farms or face divorce.[82] In some areas, women were reported to show up at official meetings and, by force or pretext, drag their husbands away.[83] In a village in Tatariia, peasant women stormed a men's meeting on collectivization in late 1929. They led their husbands away by the hand and then returned to beat up one of the presiding officials.[84] This is not to say that there were not cases when men and women did differ over the issue of collectivization without ruse or pretext. Officials sometimes noted that the men were far more cooperative than the women. In one village, a woman organizer wrote that the "men are very conscious and help in work," while the women were "backward,"[85] and Hindus and others have provided cases of seemingly genuine marital strife over the collective farm.[86] Moreover, in areas where male peasants participated heavily in seasonal out-migration, women appear to have had the upper hand in village affairs. A former peasant soldier living in emigration after World War II told a Harvard interviewer in the 1950s:

> The women played an active role against the collective farm. The men were in general passive. The woman's role especially in the central areas was to work the land and to take care of the house. There was more or less of a matriarchy here. The men left for the city to work for wages. . . . The women told the men what to do. In Smolensk in 1931, our troops were stationed here. In one village, the women decided to call a meeting and destroy the collective farm. There were meetings all over. I remember in the town of Dubrovka near Smolensk the women decided to give out seed for sowing, the men took no part in this. They kept away. The chairman of the collective farm first laughed at this "women's nonsense" and then when the women got down to cases and it seemed that they were really serious about it he had to call in the troops.[87]

Whether the women were in charge or opposed their husbands, what is clear is that many men and women recognized male vulnerability and the far greater leverage that peasant women had in protesting against state policies. This recognition came out in the form of everyday dissimulation, and dissimulation writ large on the canvas of the *bab'i bunty*. Dissimulation thus became a part of the ritual, a characterization assumed by the actors for the benefit of their audience.

The presence of children at *bab'i bunty* also served a purpose. Their presence might have suggested to officials that protest was peaceful, or served as a cordon to protect adult women from retaliation as they approached the object of their protest. The use of children may also have been intended to humanize the situation, to remind often brutal officials that they were dealing with people, with families. In a village in the Middle Volga, it was the women who, with children in hand, came out to talk to collective farm organizers as they went from hut to hut cajoling peasants to sign up.[88] In a hungry village in Kazakhstan in the fall of 1930, women took their children in silent protest to the home of the resident 25,000er. As he sat at his table eating his dinner, the women and children surrounded his hut, staring and knocking on his door and windows.[89] In some parts of the country, rumor sanctioned or, depending upon perspective, rationalized the presence of children at women's protest. In a Kuban village, the word was that pregnant and nursing women could act without culpability. Here, some women were even said to have borrowed other people's children when they went to meetings. Officials naturally attributed the rumor to the local kulak who supposedly referred to a nonexistent law to back the rumor.[90] Hindus also quoted a peasant woman who said about women's protest: "Many of us came with our babies on purpose because we knew that the laws about women with babies would prevent their touching us."[91] Whether or not these women actually believed in the existence of such a law or appealed to an idealized version of "law," they clearly *used* the rumor of the law to their own ends.[92] Dissimulation once again assumed center stage in the production of *bab'i bunty*.

The peasant "battle formation" was but one dimension of the ritual of *bab'i bunty*. The church bell also played a key role. A village's bell was much more than an ornament or a simple device for calling peasants to the church. The bell had great significance, serving as a tocsin in emergencies and a symbol of the idea of community.[93] Many a riot erupted precisely over the issue of the state's removal of the bell (whether to melt it down for its precious metals or to punish the village by removing one of its cultural symbols), and in so doing illuminated through village unity in revolt the community meaning of the bell. The bell was also a revolutionary herald, its peals sounding a call to arms at the onset of *bab'i bunty* and peasant rebellion.[94]

The bell, however, was only the most important of an entire supporting cast of auditory actors. Officials encountering a *bunt* not only confronted the pounding ringing of the tocsin, they also were assaulted by a veritable women's orchestra of shouts and curses, including the ritual cries of *karaul* and *rasprava*, as well as calls for a *samosud*. The "noise protest," not unlike that sometimes practiced at meetings, served to confuse, disorient, and vocally disarm Soviet power, preventing it from exercising its voice of power. The noise, in a sense, allowed the women to take the upper hand from the outset. Their male adversaries, while possibly adept in speech-making, were not practiced in having to raise their voice above a provocative din. The women were able to move the confrontation to their own "turf" through their vocal artistry, for surely the craft of interruption, shouting down, and irrational cacophony (as it seemed) was in the peasant woman's sphere of talents. The milling, pushing, and density of the female crowd then merely reinforced the threat and power of what appeared to officials to be a hysterical and dangerous mob of *babas*.

All of this constituted the first scene of the play. In the next, the women made their approach to Soviet power. Most often, they went to the *sel'sovet*, sometimes even assaulting the building, as in the example of a Smolensk village in which the women smashed up the offices and tore up a portrait of Kalinin.[95] In some cases, the women beat up, sometimes quite seriously, the local officials until they no longer put up resistance. If necessary, the men could more or less safely enter the picture at this point if it became necessary to "defend" the women. Most of the time, though, the agents of Soviet power hid or ran away as soon as the women's crowd began to threaten.[96] Once the women had rid themselves of their main adversaries, they turned to the next stage of the revolt.

The resolution of the *babii bunt* occurred as the women endeavored to accomplish the goals of their revolt. These generally related to such explosive issues as church closings and bell removals, dekulakization and deportations, grain requisitioning, livestock and seed socialization, and the formation of a collective farm. Women sometimes could do little more than physically block access (in the event of church closings, bell removals, and deportations) or, on their own initiative, unofficially reverse official decrees. Or they could chase away deportation escort guards and collective farm organizers.[97] They were most effective, however, when their object was to reclaim socialized property or dissolve the collective farm. In these cases, the women, on their own or in union with the men, would storm the collective stables or granary where their property was stored and tear up the collective farm charter.[98] The revolt often ended with the resolution of the issue that had started it, although on occasion, as we have seen, the women could go so far as to form a new local government.[99]

The epilogue of a *babii bunt* usually did not include the use of state force. In most cases (and these still seemed to be rare), repression was limited to the judicial branch of government. When charges ensued, a few of the local male "kulaks" or outspoken (again, male) peasants were scapegoated, and the women either received a minor penalty or none at all. Women seem not to have generally been prosecuted under Article 58 of the penal code for counterrevolutionary crimes in cases when *bunty* ended in court actions; in reports of court cases in *Sudebnaia praktika* (case supplement to *Sovetskaia iustitsiia*, the journal of the RSFSR People's Commissariat of Justice) in 1930 and 1931, only men appear as defendants in such cases prosecuted under Article 58. The main refrain in the epilogue of *bab'i bunty* was "We are backward." And as the women repented of their backwardness, the state charged them with little more than the same. This conspiracy of stereotypes was illustrated cleverly at a peasant meeting in the village Kozlovka in the Western Region. The meeting passed a resolution condemning *their* women's riot, which had resulted in the destruction of the collective stables. The meeting pledged its honor not to allow such an incident to recur and, while asking the OGPU to take all necessary measures, also requested it not to arrest the poor and middle peasant women who participated in the *bunt* due to their "lack of consciousness."[100] A chorus of *mea culpa* generally brought the curtain down on the *bab'i bunty*, thus ending the spectacle of village revolt.

Bab'i bunty, then, were relatively ritualized performances in which villagers played parts that were customary and familiar to insiders and outsiders alike. Role playing and dissimulation were integral to the performance, as were the aspects of hysteria, disorder, and spontaneity. Women were ritual bearers as well as leaders in revolt. The *bab'i bunty* began in response to specific policies and were never aimless but always goal-oriented, whether the object of revolt was a church closing, dekulakization, or the formation of a collective farm. Both content and form were rational, and at times there was even a relatively high level of organization and political awareness behind the tumult. *Bab'i bunty* were, moreover, doubly subversive in that they not only directly challenged state power, but inverted traditional gender roles and therefore the patriarchal hierarchy of the village *and* state. The *babii bunt* was perhaps the most successful "enabling mode"[101] of peasant mass disturbances during collectivization; it was appealing to peasants because of the protection it accorded male peasants (and therefore the whole village in economic terms and by association) by conforming to official images of dark masses, disorderly women, and kulak and *podkulachnik* agitation and propaganda.

Conclusion

Peasant women, in league with peasant men, exploited the dominant images of the *baba* for their own ends. Making use of a Soviet version of Davis's "disorderly woman,"[102] peasant women took advantage of the leverage and protection provided to them by misconceived images of their actions formed by outsiders with little or no real knowledge of peasant ways. The Soviet construction of the *baba* placed gender (and all it implied) at center stage while denuding peasant women of any class attributes. By virtue of her gender and classlessness, the Soviet *baba* was denied political consciousness and agency. She was therefore and by definition incapable of political protest, given that in the Soviet context politics and, by implication, political protest could occur only in conjunction with and by derivation from class. Peasant women played into their expected roles. This tactic was a part of a peasant popular culture of resistance and exemplified the public transcript of peasant protest wherein, in rebellious encounters with dominant classes, "the public performance of the subordinate will . . . be shaped to appeal to the expectations of the powerful."[103]

If the *bab'i bunty* were more than they appeared to be, is it possible that the official image of them was a political construct of another sort? That is, is it possible that the state too had an unofficial agenda that was better served by maintaining a public posture toward *bab'i bunty* that was contrary to reality? In *Rebels in the Name of the Tsar*, Field suggested that the "myth of the tsar" (i.e., a feigned naive monarchism) was as useful to the Tsarist government during postemancipation peasant disturbances as it was to the peasantry. The myth of the tsar was based on the "myth of the peasant" as backward and loyal, and rebellious only when misguided or exploited by outsiders. These myths, according to Field, provided the regime with a rationalization for any social or political problems leading to peasant disturbances. In other words, both tsar and peasant may have participated in a deception meant to defuse and depoliticize rebellion.[104]

The myth of the peasant may have lingered into the Soviet period in more ways than one. Accordingly, the degree of state condescension may have been in direct proportion to the threat posed. Official depictions of *bab'i bunty* and peasant women's protest could have been utilized in order to minimize the true nature and extent of the opposition engendered by collectivization. In its most classified documentation, the OGPU, after all, appears to have understood many of the ramifications of *bab'i bunty*, even though it continued to blame the kulak for their instigation and to deny peasant women agency in their protests (see above). The public facade on *bab'i bunty* and the classless nature of the *baba* served a particularly useful purpose in explaining why and how village protest drew in poor and middle peasants, offering a ready rationalization for the contradictions of the class struggle in the village, for the state's failure to capture the support of its supposed poor and middle peasant allies among the peasantry. Moreover, by allowing the women relatively more leeway for protest, the state may have hoped that it could restrain the surely more dangerous protest of peasant men for, as the author Mikhail Sholokhov wrote to Stalin in 1932, if the men entered the picture, "the business ended in murder."[105] That the state understood, despite official images, the full ramifications of women's protest is also apparent in the disappearance of the *baba* in Stalinist political art in the first half of the 1930s. Victoria Bonnell has written that "[t]he new world of the village depicted by Stalinist posters effaced virtually all aspects of the traditional peasant woman, her culture, her way of life."[106] This disappearance, however, may have derived not only from the state's antipathy to the *baba* as a cultural symbol of backwardness, but also from the state's fear of and hostility toward the peasant woman as symbol and primary agent of collective, active peasant resistance to collectivization.

Bab'i bunty do not appear to have continued in any significant way beyond the season of March fever. Nevertheless, during collectivization, *bab'i bunty* and women's protest proved the most effective and widespread form of peasant collective action against the state, playing a key role in forcing the state's temporary retreat in the spring of 1930 and subsequently ensuring a more cautious approach to peasant issues that were centered on the household, family, and belief. Peasant women played a leading role in the resistance to collectivization, defending their interests and demonstrating a degree of organization and conscious political opposition rarely acknowledged. Their determined resistance, moreover, had more than a degree of prescience to it, something of which Solzhenitsyn reminds us through the words of Ivan Denisovich:

> The thing Shukhov [Ivan Denisovich] didn't get at all was what his wife wrote about how not a single new member had come to the kolkhoz since the war. All the youngsters were getting out as best they could—to factories in the towns or to the peat fields. Half the kolkhozniks had not come back after the war, and those who had wouldn't have anything to do with the kolkhoz—they lived there but earned their money somewhere outside. The only men in the kolkhoz were the gang boss, Zakhar Vasilyevich, and the carpenter, Tikhon, who was eighty-four, had married not long ago, and even had children already. The real work in the kolkhoz was done by the same women who'd been there since the start, in 1930.[107]

And it was precisely those women who had fought so hard against collectivization and whose interests, life, and culture were most at stake in the peasant civil war against Soviet power.

7

On the Sly: Everyday Forms of Resistance in the Collective Farm, 1930 and Beyond

Now, Comrade Stalin, answer please,
That people may stop wrangling:
Will there at last be calm and peace,
An end to this new-fangling?

Our life's gone bust
And all's gone bust,
All wrecked in mortal strife
We're moving sure—I don't protest—
Toward a happy life.

Yes, I agree quite willingly
That life will soon be fine,
Yet I've a personal request
To you, if you don't mind.

This, Comrade Stalin's what I ask—
It wouldn't do much harm—
Just leave me as I am a while—
Me and my little farm.

And tell them all that so-and-so
In all the realm alone
Be left—let no one trouble him,
His farmyard and his home.
                    —Alexander Tvardovsky, "Land of Muravia"

"Put the axe behind your back; the forester is about"
                    —Alexander Pushkin, *The Captain's Daughter*

By the end of 1930, peasant resistance began to enter into a new stage of activity. Peasant resistance—by definition, *kulak* resistance—operated under the official rubric of *tikhaia sapa*. Translated idiomatically as "on the sly," *tikhaia sapa* literally means a quiet or stealthful undermining or weakening of foundations. Like much of the jargon of the time, the term is military in its derivation and connotation. Stalinist rhetoric claimed that the kulak had changed tactics. Now, he (and he remained formally mostly *he*) "penetrated" the collective farm and its leadership in order to engage in "sabotage" from within. His activity was "cloaked"—he acted through poor and middle peasants, especially "backward elements" like women, or in "collusion" with local officials. The time had passed when the kulak protested openly at meetings, called the collective farm Antichrist, or organized *bab'i bunty*.[1] His main theater of operations was said to have become the collective farm and his mission was subversion.

Collectivization had in fact arrived at a new phase. The overwhelming repressive powers of the state made active forms of resistance at most short-lived possibilities, limited mainly to the chaos and explosive rage of 1930. Active resistance in any case is seldom a primary or even a widely used tool of peasant resistance, except in highly volatile times when desperation and anger clash momentarily with their source of origin. In ordinary and extraordinary times, peasants more often learn to adapt, dissimulate, and resist through quieter, less confrontational paths. In the aftermath of the collectivization campaigns, the state and peasantry entered into a stalemate. Gradually, the myriad battalions of urban Communists, officials, and workers receded, leaving the state to govern the countryside from the towns, through a system of plenipotentiary rule, periodic grain foraging campaigns, and peasant home rule. The peasantry began to settle uncomfortably into a new order. Passive resistance, *tikhaia sapa* in result, if not always intention, became the peasantry's primary defense, centered around survival and subsistence and born of hunger, desperation, and enmity.

The new moral economy

Everyday forms of resistance are a vital component in the peasant culture of resistance. This mode of resistance constitutes "the prosaic but constant struggle between the peasantry and those who seek to extract labor, food, taxes, rents, and interest from them" and may take the shape of refusal to work, foot dragging, dissimulation, pilfering, flight, or sabotage.[2] In Russia, everyday forms of resistance were deeply ingrained coping mechanisms in the life and labor of the peasantry from the earliest days of serfdom right up to the revolution. Such stratagems did not disappear in 1917, but resurfaced during the civil war and in the 1920s when peasants faced new challenges from new overlords.

By the late 1920s, everyday forms of resistance were practiced on a wide scale, as peasants sought to evade or lessen the blows of ever-increasing tax burdens and grain levies. In the face of disadvantageous and artificially low grain pricing, many peasants diverted their labor to more profitable enterprise in livestock, industrial crops, and even *samogon*.[3] As socially discriminatory policies began to drastically affect taxation and grain requisitions, some peasants turned to subterfuge in an attempt to hide or alter their socioeconomic status. Through illegal land sales, fictional divisions of properties, "adoptions" (*usynovlenie*) of hired hands, and bribery of local officials to obtain false documentation of politically acceptable social status, peasants endeavored to transform themselves from officially designated kulaks to middle or poor peasants.[4] These stratagems carried through into the collectivization era (and sometimes beyond) as did such practices as the formation of so-called "false collective farms" (*lzhekolkhozy*)[5]—generally associations of relatives, *otrub* or *khutor* neighbors, or wealthier peasants—and the more dramatic actions associated with self-dekulakization and *razbazarivanie*.[6]

Everyday forms of resistance became paramount by late 1930 and especially in the aftermath of collectivization. Peasants learned not only that they could not challenge the state directly, but that they would be forced to live within the oppressive confines of an entirely new regimen. After 1930 and most especially during the famine years of 1932–33, resistance became inextricably tied in to issues of subsistence and hunger. Peasants faced an "economy of scarcity"[7] through much of the 1930s that would compel them to adapt in order to survive.

The economy of scarcity was an inevitable outcome of the new collective farm system. It could not have been otherwise given the state's total disregard for peasant subsistence; the unceasing, rapacious levies of agricultural produce; and the chaos and mismanagement that characterized collective farming in the early 1930s. In the collective farm, the peasantry found itself reduced to a status not wholly dissimilar from that of serf days. Individually and collectively, collective farmers were expected to fulfill an enormous and onerous variety of obligations to the state. Not only were they forced to turn over a large percentage of their agricultural produce to the state, they also had to render in-kind payments to the MTS and fulfill a host of burdensome labor obligations to state and local authorities.[8] In January 1933, some attempt was made to regularize and stabilize state procurements through the introduction of a predictable fixed requisition quota and the *zakupki* (a supposedly one-time purchase of grain, and later, other products, at rates higher than requisitioning prices after the fulfillment of the state's main requisitions), but the state more often observed its new measures in the breach, as well as almost guaranteeing continued draconian levies through the introduction of decentralized requisitioning (conducted by local officials, officials from nearby urban centers, and myriad others) and by basing requisitioning norms on the infamous "biological yield," which grossly exaggerated harvests by measuring their dimensions while still unharvested in the field.[9]

Once a collective farm had fulfilled its requisition quotas, paid the MTS, set aside a reserve supply of seed for the next sowing season, and covered any necessary operating costs, what little remained of the harvest was to be divided among the members of the farm. The method of division was far from clear in 1930 and complicated in any case by a scarcity of rural bookkeepers and accountants. Remuneration was always *supposed* to be based on the type and amount of labor performed by an individual, but in the early days of collective farming it more often assumed in practice the customary forms of payment according to the number of "eaters" or workers in a family. The labor-day system (*trudoden'*) competed with a factorylike wage system for official recognition in the first half of 1930, though neither went far beyond the paper stage of implementation. It was only in mid-1931 that the labor-day system emerged triumphant and gradually began to be implemented in fact.[10] The labor day was a complicated system of accounting in which "the number of units of work performed by a collective farmer are recorded, and after the harvest the available collective farm income, in money and in kind, is distributed among the collective farmers in proportion to the number of units recorded for each farmer."[11] Labor-day units of work had varying values according to the type of work performed, skilled or unskilled. And, although rarely officially acknowledged and never sanctioned, many collective farms paid women and sometimes youth less than adult male workers.[12]

After the collective farm had fulfilled all of its official obligations, very little was left for distribution (in the form of labor days) and certainly not enough to sustain peasant families. Most collective farmers necessarily were forced to provide for their families through cultivation of private plots. While the status of the private plot was not definitively established in law until the publication of the 1935 Model Collective Farm Statute, most collective farmers managed to maintain a plot of land for personal cultivation and increasingly the state recognized its necessity for rural and urban consumption alike. From May 1932, collective farms and collective farmers were allowed to sell surplus produce from these plots on a heavily regulated market once all obligations to the state had been fulfilled. Although private traders and middlemen were strictly prohibited and the operations of the market were subjected to frequent interference, peasant income and consumption came to depend heavily on private plot and surplus marketings.[13] According to reports from the early years of the collective farms, formerly middle peasants continued to fare somewhat better than formerly poor peasants in the collective farms at least in part because of the more advantageous and greater productive capacity of the middle peasantry's private plot.[14]

The dwindling number of peasants who remained outside the collective farm system (the *edinolichniki*) fared worse, facing exorbitant tax and requisition demands and, if categorized as kulaks, a "firm" tax (*tverdie zadaniia*) that could be economically disabling. They worked the poorest arable fields and were subjected to several forced state purchases of livestock.[15] Furthermore, those peasants who quit the collective farm after the March 1930 retreat never managed to recoup their losses, given the frequently unfair land divisions practiced and the difficulties connected to forcing local officials to return what usually amounted to the basic means of production and working capital of the new collective farms.[16] The resulting hostility between those who remained and those who left contributed further to the marginal position of private farmers.[17] From late 1930, state-mandated economic repression was the primary mechanism for pushing the remaining private farmers into collective farms or off the land completely.

In and out of the collective farm, peasants lived within an economy of scarcity. Industrial and state aggrandizement took place at their expense. The continuing export of grain in conjunction with poor harvests, low productivity, and a disastrous decline in livestock all contributed to the pauperization of the countryside. Peasant consumption and access to manufactured goods fell precipitously in the first half of the 1930s. As early as spring 1930, many peasants—mainly the poor with their fewer resources and reserves—faced hunger and sometimes even death by starvation or (more often) famine-related illnesses.[18] The nadir of peasant consumption came in 1932–33, when a devastating famine struck, hitting Ukraine, North Caucasus, and Kazakhstan particularly mercilessly, but also extending through much of the rest of the nation. The famine, easily anticipated but hardly planned, was the result of the state's brutal requisitions, the chaos of collectivization, and a political culture in which peasants had little or no value as human beings.[19] Some 4 to 5 million people perished in those years.[20]

The economy of scarcity gave rise to a new moral economy among the peasantry. The term "moral economy" is used to denote popular conceptions of what is economically fair and legitimate based on customary notions of "social norms and obligations."[21] The moral economy centers largely around a subsistence ethic, regulating what is just. The new moral economy evolved directly from the new collective farm order and consequent economy of scarcity, altering peasant notions of fair play in living and working in the collective farm system, and deriving from a radically altered state perception of economic justice that contrasted sharply with the peasantry's sense of the grain as their own. In the collectivized countryside, notions of moral economy underlay and legitimated peasant modes of adaptation and strategies of survival.

Everyday forms of resistance were a tool of the moral economy, used to ensure subsistence and to sustain life. The intentions or motivations behind the exploitation of such forms of resistance are largely hidden from the historian's view, but most probably and logically derived from some indivisible combination of resistance, hunger, and despair. The struggle for subsistence, for survival, surely took precedence over the *political* act of resistance in these years. Yet the results were implicitly acts of resistance, *if only according to official definition and perception*. In the context of Stalinist political culture, any effort by the peasantry to defend itself economically and attempt to maintain a living level of subsistence became implicitly an act of resistance, tantamount to a criminal act, sabotage, and even treason.

Official definitions of the enemy—in this case, the kulak—were carried to their illogical extremes in the early and mid-1930s as the state attempted to bridle the peasantry, crushing any remaining signs of independence. Earlier pretensions to class and social definitions were by 1931 entirely eclipsed by Manichaean Stalinist images of the peasantry. Peasants were either "for the collective farm" or they were kulaks. The same type of classification was applied to whole collective farms during the famine, as a consequence of which entire villages were deported, generally for failure to fulfill requisitions.[22] Despite the "elimination of the kulak as a class" and the formal cessation of mass peasant deportations in mid-July 1931,[23] local officials were warned not to lower their vigilance. Stalin considered the country to be at war. In response to a letter from Sholokhov protesting atrocities in the Don, he dropped any reference to social categorizations and spoke simply about "cultivators":

> But . . . the honorable cultivators of your region, and not only your region, committed sabotage and were quite willing to leave the workers and the Red Army without grain. The fact that the sabotage was silent and apparently gentle (no blood was spilt) does not change the fact that the honorable cultivators in reality were making a "silent" war against Soviet power. War by starvation, my dear comrade Sholokhov.[24]

Actions continued to determine class or, more accurately, enemy status. The "kulak mood," of which Lenin wrote over a decade earlier, had not disappeared from the countryside. After 1930, many collective farmers were accused of failing to remove "the kulak within themselves" and to adjust to the new system of socialized property.[25] "Kulak instinct" was "internalized" by middle and even poor peasants. And in 1932–33, the kulak became "he who steals socialist property,"[26] when the state accused the peasantry of engaging in wholesale theft. The notorious law of 7 August 1932, "On Guarding the Property of State Enterprises, Collective Farms, and Cooperatives and the Strengthening of Socialist Property," declared those who stole or traded illegally to be "enemies of the people."[27] In this context of an all-out war with the peasantry, any action, the result of which could be construed as resistance, became just that, regardless of intention, motivation, or even cause. There was no room for neutrality.[28]

In the collective farm

On the eve of wholesale collectivization, at the November 1929 Central Committee plenum, Molotov declaimed from the rostrum that "You must always have before your eyes the factory" when approaching issues of collective farm organization.[29] During collectivization, a war was waged over alternative cultures of work. In 1930, the state sought to impose an industrial regimen of labor in the village through the division of labor, the institution of piecework and the labor day, strict labor discipline, socialist competition and shock work, and a variety of other, often far-fetched utopian schemes.[30] Although the attempt to "industrialize" the collective farm was largely abandoned in 1931, the state's ultimate goal remained the destruction or, at the least, radical alteration of peasant work culture in the effort to conquer and control peasant production. This revolution within a revolution inevitably clashed with time-proven peasant rhythms of life and labor and formed the backdrop for the struggles that would be waged within the new moral economy.

Labor discipline was a widely used expression connoting the industrial discipline of the factory and was in theory an inherent aspect of the ideal proletarian. It assumed a militarized taint in the civil war and especially during the Stalin revolution. Such obedience, expected but rarely attained, on the collective farms in the early 1930s, became an important official rallying cry amid the chaos of the new rural order. As collective farmers, peasants were expected to manifest labor discipline in their work, arriving and leaving on time, displaying a "conscious" relationship to tools, machinery, and draft animals, working in harmony within their labor brigades, and attentively following the orders of collective farm leaders.

From the start, however, peasants were accused of exhibiting "low labor discipline"—tardiness, skipping work, foot dragging, performing at inadequate levels of capacity, and so on.[31] In spring 1931, many collective farms succeeded in mobilizing only one- to two-thirds of their labor for field work.[32] By 1934, Sheboldaev, at that time party secretary of Azovsko-Chernomorskii Region, was able to point to minimal improvement in labor discipline, noting that in 1931 collective farmers in North Caucasus earned on average only 139 labor days per year; in 1932, 140; and in 1933, more than 200 although some 15% of the region's households continued to earn less than 100 labor days in 1933.[33] In collective farms in Ust'-Labinskii *raion*, North Caucasus, only about one-third of the labor force worked in the spring and early summer of 1930, with conditions tending to be worse on extremely large collective farms.[34] According to party leaders, such an "unconscious" attitude to labor characterized much of the country's collective farm force and was caused by a combination of continued kulak influences and survivals of the low *kul'turnost'* and petit-bourgeois nature of the peasantry.

Collective farmers had little of value besides their labor after 1930. As a consequence and regardless of actual intention, refusal to work and foot dragging were intrinsic acts of sabotage to a state resolved to extract *all* sources of value from the countryside. The failure to show up at work, especially in peak agricultural seasons, could spell disaster for collective farms and the state. Absenteeism appears to have been endemic in the early and mid-1930s. In 1930, in the North Caucasus *stanitsa* of Dolzhanskaia in the Don, 167 of 1,310 households flat out refused to work. In the *stanitsa* Shcherbinovskaia at about the same time, 31.2% of households failed to go out to work.[35] In late 1930 in the North Caucasus collective farm, Onward to Socialism, approximately 50% of the work force failed to show up for work, while in the nearby Il'ych's Memory collective farm, 100 households were expelled for not working.[36] In the Lower and Middle

Volga, there were reports of mass occurrences of collective farmers refusing to work in 1930.[37] Low labor discipline and absenteeism were reported
throughout Novo-Annenskii *raion*, Khoperskii *okrug*, Lower Volga in late
1930; in the Budenets collective farm, for example, up to 30% of the
work force would not go out to work.[38] In the months from October 1930
to April 1931, about one-third of all peasants expelled from collective
farms nationally were expelled for violations of labor discipline.[39] These
figures are surely underestimates for, as one study concluded in late 1930,
a collective farm only knew whether someone was not coming to work if
he or she "systematically" failed to show up.[40]

Refusal to work was at the extreme end of a spectrum of peasant
adaptive strategies that most often resulted in simple foot dragging and a
low qualitative level of work performance. Foot dragging was a culturally
acceptable peasant response to oppression since it could be as easily explained away as peasant slothfulness as resistance depending on political
exigency and who was doing the explaining. Foot dragging could be a
highly effective method of conserving labor as well as an expression of a
peasant's attitude toward work. Solzhenitsyn captured some of the latter
sentiment in the character of his peasant camp inmate Shukhov in *One
Day in the Life of Ivan Denisovich:*

> Shukhov quickly finished up the job. There's work and work. It's like the
> two ends of a stick. If you're working for human beings, then do a real job
> of it, but if you work for dopes, then you just go through the motions.[41]

Many peasants saw their labor wasted. Others may have soon realized, as
a former Tolstoyan peasant put it, that all that really mattered to the new
bosses was fulfilling plans as quickly as possible:

> We women in the collective farm went out to tie up the rye. Well, I tied it
> the way I had always tied it before, in big sheaves, tight and clean; and the
> next day I looked and saw my name on the black list and the other women's
> name on the red one. Then I began to watch how those who were on the red
> list worked, and I myself started working like that—any old way, just so it
> is as fast and as much as possible, with a bit of lying to the brigade leader
> about the output when it comes time to count the sheaves. Then I looked,
> and there was my name on the red list![42]

There were few incentives for peasants to work hard on the collective
farms, and in fact more than a few disincentives.

A study of collective farms in the Urals in late 1930 reported that in
all cases labor discipline was lower on the collective farm than it had been
under communal land tenure when peasants worked their own allotments
of land. The study concluded that there was no stimulus for improved
labor productivity.[43] The lack of material incentives to foster labor discipline was and continued to be throughout Soviet history a central reason
for the low productivity of collective farmers. In collective farms where
surplus produce was divided equally among eaters or laborers after all

state obligations had been fulfilled, there was hardly enough, if anything at all, to go around. The complicated labor-day system, in which payments to collective farmers were generally made once per year (generally in November or December), also failed to offer much in the way of incentive to hungry, exhausted peasants. Despite its intended purpose—to reward laborers according to the quantity and type of work fulfilled—many peasants initially were unable (or claimed to be unable) to understand a system in which a labor day did not equal an actual day and had generally nothing to do with the quality of work performed let alone to benefit from the theoretical incentives built into the system.[44] The inability to understand was surely promoted by low remuneration norms for labor days, an issue much bemoaned by collective farmers.[45] Although some attempt was made in the early 1930s to use advances to reward laborers, collective farmers simply had their pay reduced by the amount of the advance when the end of the year came. Privileged access to manufactured goods and honorific rewards, such as shock worker or (later) Stakhanovite titles, or mention on the "red board" of honor had some appeal, but only when manufactured goods were available or when peasants (mostly youth) saw some merit in nonmaterial incentives.

Underlying the difficulties of remuneration was the low output of most collective farms and the severe exactions of the state, which ensured not only low labor discipline but also, in many cases, hunger. There was a logical correlation between hunger and refusal to work or foot dragging on the job. As early as May 1930, intense "food difficulties" in parts of Crimea led to as many as 40% to 70% of collective farmers (depending upon the farm) refusing to work, as they pled, "We are not leaving the collective farm, but [we] cannot work, [there is] no food [and] no physical strength."[46] Wherever there was hunger in 1930,[47] there were reports of low labor discipline. In Novosibirskii *okrug* in Siberia, for example, hunger led to work stoppages in a series of collective farms.[48] Labor discipline reached its nadir during the famine. In late 1932 and early 1933, there were reports of entire brigades refusing to work in collective farms in Ukraine and North Caucasus.[49] Similar reports surfaced elsewhere in the country during those years. In Siberia, where crop failure and hunger appeared somewhat later, refusal to work was a frequent phenomenon. Here, 67.5% of all peasants expelled from collective farms in the second quarter of 1935 were expelled for not going to work.[50] Hunger and exhaustion were primary disincentives to work, disabling collective farmers and collective farms alike. Hunger merged with a "kulak mood" in facilitating what the state continued to insist publicly was kulak sabotage rather than a state-induced famine.

The element of resistance, nonetheless, was not wholly absent from issues of poor labor discipline arising from hunger and disincentive to work. Peasants sometimes tried to explain or justify their labor actions with reference to the injustices of the new order. In April 1931, for example, one peasant agitated for a work stoppage, telling his fellow collective farmers, "you work for the communists who take your bread and send it abroad," while in 1933 Ekaterina Mol'neva, who refused to work and hid away a store of grain, defiantly told her tormentors, "Better that you bring me to court, but I will not work for you, you devils."[51] In some cases, work stoppages amounted to undeclared strikes. In Crimea in 1930, over one-half of the work force of one collective farm refused to work until their socialized property was returned.[52] At about the same time, peasants in Rossoshanskii *okrug*, Central Black Earth Region, were dissatisfied with the unfinished resolution of property settlements following the March 1930 retreat. These peasants collected hundreds of signatures for a protest petition, sent a petitioner off to Moscow, and refused to work until issues were settled.[53] In September 1930, in the Lower Volga village of Akhtuba in Balandinskii *raion*, a collective farm brigade struck over the nonpayment of promised manufactured goods and attempted unsuccessfully to persuade other brigades to join them.[54] Elsewhere, there were reports of collective farmers requesting bribes to work.[55] Women remained active participants in labor action. In February 1931, the women of the Uplonovskii collective farm in Il'inskii *raion*, Western Region, went on strike, putting a halt to the processing of flax.[56] In the Middle Volga, women took part in a series of undeclared strikes in June 1931. According to the OGPU, here there were also "mass cases" of women collective farmers feigning illness to avoid work. Some 700 collective farm women reportedly descended upon the Sorochinskii hospital on 4 June 1931 with declarations of illness. The medical staff differed, claiming that 96% of the women were "absolutely healthy."[57] In each of these cases, an element of explicit resistance is evident in the actions of the collective farmers, even allowing for a set of more complex motivations behind the actions.

Socioeconomics also may have played some more specific role in labor discipline problems in the first half of the 1930s. There is evidence to suggest that poor peasants were more vulnerable to labor indiscipline in the collective farm than middle peasants. While some poor peasants continued to be labeled shirkers and sluggards by their neighbors, hunger and material resources figured more importantly in poor peasants' work habits. In parts of the Volga German Republic, for example, collective farm studies claimed that only middle peasants worked while the poor complained that they needed clothes and food to work.[58] In 1930 and 1931, hunger as yet mainly struck formerly poor peasants who, in the collective farms, had far fewer resources than their middle peasant neighbors to fall back upon.[59] It would therefore be logical to suggest that the poor may have made up a relatively large percentage of labor discipline problems prior to the 1932–33 famine, at which time class would no longer determine hunger. Poor peasants faced other obstacles in the early collective farms as well. In the early 1930s, there were cases in which poor peasants were kept off the leading organs of collective farms, given inferior work assignments, and even prevented from joining collective farms because they had so little of a material nature to contribute.[60] The growing economy of scarcity, as well as the relative withdrawal of outside forces from the everyday activities of the collective farm after 1930, may well have contributed to the emergence (or return) of internal village hostilities based on inequality. Such tensions along with the precarious economic position of many poor peasants were likely contributing factors to labor indiscipline.

Gender played at least a tangential part in labor indiscipline as well. Several late 1930 reports from the Collective Farm Scientific Research Institute concluded that male labor was used more effectively than female labor.[61] Throughout the countryside at this time, the state attempted to employ women fully in agricultural production. The effectiveness of the state's program depended upon regional peculiarities. Where women worked alongside the men in all types of field work or where women in fact dominated field work due to men's participation in *otkhodnichestvo*, problems of labor discipline may have been further exacerbated by inequalities in pay rates for men and women, leading to women's greater participation on the household's private plot, where fruits and vegetables, areas of cultivation closest to women's traditional domain, tended to prevail.[62] In some regions, however, domestic or craft work was said to interfere partially with women's work in the fields. In the Orenburg area, for example, 15% to 20% of women's working time was spent in making "Orenburg shawls." Here, "according to old traditions," women did not participate in most phases of field work.[63] In attempting to alter the rhythm of women's labor on the collective farm, the state confronted not only a general peasant work culture, but the sometimes significant gender divisions of labor at work in agriculture.

The state's attempts to transform peasant work culture were aided by force as well as new labor regimens. The state instituted an entire catalogue of penalties matching various kinds of labor infractions. In January 1933, the system of fines and expulsions that had been used recklessly and randomly all along to punish indiscipline was legalized. For refusal to work or perform a specific assignment, a collective farmer received a fine of five labor days for the first infraction and expulsion from the collective farm for the second.[64] At the same time, the state instituted political watchdogs in the form of the MTS *politotdels* which were intended (among other tasks) to supervise labor on the collective farms.[65] Despite this decree and others, some months later in 1934, 23% of the members of a single collective farm in Danilovskii *raion*, in the Stalingrad area, were fined for refusing to work, and as late as 1937 and 1938, 15.1% and 5.1%, respectively, of able-bodied collective farmers failed to earn a single labor day in the Northwestern Region.[66]

Labor discipline was not the only point of contention between collective farmers and the state. Forms of remuneration raised intense controversy in the early collective farms. Varying types of remuneration based on piecework competed with what the state considered to be wage-leveling schemes (*uravnilovka*) implemented locally. From the peasant perspective "wage leveling" could be viewed as a more egalitarian system of compensation than the labor day. Consequently, in many parts of the country, divisions of collective farm surplus (after all obligations to the state had been fulfilled) occurred on a per eater or, less frequently, per worker basis. Such a system was tacitly accepted by the state through much of 1930. Thereafter, the state conducted a vigorous campaign to install the uniform labor day.[67] Nonetheless, per-eater systems continued to exist through at least the first half of the 1930s in many areas. Throughout the North Caucasus, there were reports of per-eater divisions of the harvest.[68] One collective farm in this region distributed bread per eater in late 1930, arguing that otherwise not everyone would have enough to eat.[69] Research on the Leningrad Region in fall 1930 and spring 1931 revealed that most collective farmers "agitated" for distribution per eater, while per-eater systems persisted in Siberia and Middle Volga at this same time.[70] In Belorussia in late 1930, peasants were said to dislike piecework and therefore used it infrequently; here advances at least were distributed according to need.[71] By the fall of 1931, per-eater systems were somewhat less common, but continued to exist in pockets throughout the countryside.[72] In 1932 and 1933, for example, there were reports of per-eater systems being used in the Western Region and elsewhere.[73] Even as late as 1936, following the publication of the 1935 Model Collective Farm Statute, many collective farms determined the size of private plots according to a per-eater system.[74] Divisions of the harvest per eater occurred naturally in the collective farm, a continuation of similar principles in communal land tenure that were intended ideally as subsistence insurance, a customary survival strategy for the community, and as a way in which to strengthen community cohesion.[75]

Where per-eater systems were not in use, some collective farmers attempted to manipulate labor-day payments either as a way to avoid work in the collective farm or in an effort to earn the requisite number of labor days per year. Some collective farm chairmen even allowed peasants to sell their labor days to other peasants.[76] The sale of labor days continued at least through the first half of the 1930s; in one area labor days were sold at the rate of five rubles per day.[77] In other cases, labor-day payments were "exaggerated" in an attempt to increase the level of collective farmers' income, something the state condemned as a "self-seeking" (*rvacheskii*) tendency.[78] These tactics, like per-eater schemes, were a part of a peasant strategy of survival, implicitly acts of resistance within the new moral economy.

Property constituted another tool of survival within the collective farm. Private property continued to exist in the collective farm, in altered forms and initially subject to arbitrary confiscation. The private plot, the final dimensions of which were not confirmed until the 1935 Model Collective Farm Statute,[79] provided peasants with much of their food and personal income. It was, in fact, vital to the survival of the peasant family and legal market sales, not to mention to the continued existence of a black market which in and of itself constituted a major symbol of resistance. Each peasant household had a right to a private plot, even if only one household member actually belonged to the collective farm.[80] Some households practiced fictitious divisions of extended families either while in the collective farm or upon entry in order to increase the size of private holdings.[81] After the 1935 Statute, many peasant families expanded their holdings at the expense of collective farm lands.[82] In one *raion*, the acreage of private plots was actually larger than that of socialized land.[83] Until the more repressive legislation of the immediate prewar years, the state appears to have tacitly tolerated such aggrandizement by sheer and perhaps intentional oversight, while peasants manipulated the uses of their private plots as an everyday form of resistance arising from the struggle to survive.

Some collective farmers and even collective farm leaders engaged in another type of property manipulation as a survival mechanism. They illegally rented or sold lands. In Evdokimovskii *sel'sovet*, Azovo-Chernomorskii *krai* in 1934, for example, one collective farmer rented his private plot in exchange for a half of his tenant's harvest. Another sold outright his private plot for 1,000 rubles.[84] Illegal land sales often occurred under the cover of the legal sale of buildings attached to the land. Because private plots were generally adjacent to peasant homes, the land would constitute a hidden sale along with the house.[85] As late as 1937, in the Central Black Earth Region, there were cases of collective farms renting out land to collective and private farmers, as well as continued cases of land sales cloaked by the purchase of buildings.[86]

Dissimulation was also employed in the preservation of other forms of property and property relations. In the early 1930s—whether by artful design or because of the dearth of collective barns and stables—socialized livestock sometimes continued to live with former owners.[87] In other cases, collective farmers illicitly used socialized draft power on their private plots, sometimes with, sometimes without the sanction of collective farm leaders.[88] In some regions, interesting stratagems were applied in the use of new brigade systems of labor. In *khutor* areas in Belorussia, collective farm brigades often consisted of individual families, with the heads of households serving as brigadiers.[89] In a series of collective farms in Ozurgetskii *raion*, Georgia, individual collective farm households were assigned to work particular parcels of land—generally the same land they worked prior to collectivization.[90] A report by the relatively sympathetic Collective Farm Scientific Research Institute in late 1930 argued that, unlike in the Middle and Lower Volga, the *stodvorka* system (a system where work assignments are given to individual households) was not used in Ust'-Labinskii *raion*, North Caucasus, because it was thought to encourage "individualism." Here "healthy" requests for the use of the *stodvorka* arose from the collective farmers themselves.[91] Throughout the 1930s, but most especially in the early 1930s, many collective farms remained at least in part "nominal" collectives—a continuation of the "paper collective farms" of 1930—masking over enduring survivals of private and communal farming, including strip farming and heavy concentration on private plots, as would be the case in other countries with state-imposed collectivization.[92]

The state could choose to portray dissimulation and property manipulation as surviving manifestations of "petit-bourgeois instinct" or as sabotage, depending on the politics of the moment. Less frequently was it willing to make the same allowances for actual damage to collective farm property. Accusations of wrecking—intentional machine-breaking and damage to crops and livestock—were endemic in the early 1930s. In late 1930, in the Central Black Earth Region, a report surfaced claiming that iron had been thrown into a thresher.[93] At the same time in the Middle Volga, there were reports of "kulaks" pouring sand into tractors and littering fields with pieces of metal in order to break machinery.[94] These types of accusations were classic, to the point of stereotype, and formed the skeletal scenario of rural wrecking. Data for the USSR as a whole in 1931 puts the number of intentional machine breakages on collective farms at 2,250, or 14.9% of all cases of "enemy assaults" on collective farms.[95] In Siberia in that year, there were reportedly 399 cases of machine-breaking, while partial statistics for the Moscow Region from the end of 1930 to mid-May 1931 note only 20 cases.[96] Reports of machine-breaking continued into later years, echoing in the industrial sector and the show trials of the Great Purges.[97] With enmity grafted onto cultural shock, it is likely that there was a combination of accidental breakage based on inexperience with new kinds of machinery and damage based on a more purposeful negligence and intent to harm. The state, however, chose to characterize machine-breaking as wrecking. A resolution from a joint Central Committee–Central Control Commission plenum described the sabotage and wrecking in the collective farm sector of the early 1930s as tantamount to a new Shakhty Affair,[98] and called for wreckers and aliens to be exposed and a new "Bolshevik" cadre to be developed.[99] The MTS *politotdels* arose as a response to this plenum and led what amounted to an all-out offensive on collective farm leadership. Interestingly enough, many of the *politotdel* officials proved more understanding of rural realities than the central authorities in Moscow, as was evidenced, for example, in a November 1933 report from a *politotdel* official in the Ivanovo region, who concluded that damage to MTS machinery occurred as a result of collective farmers' grievances over the vast sums paid for its use and complaints that manual labor was more effective.[100]

The *razbazarivanie* of livestock also continued into the first half of the 1930s. According to *Kolkhoztsentr* data, in 1931, 7.4% of all cases of assaults on collective farms consisted of damage to socialized livestock, some 1,100 cases in all.[101] These cases represented the tip of the iceberg of what the state considered sabotage and what included not only the slaughter and illegal sale of livestock, but inadequate and negligent care.

As in 1929–30, there was a direct correlation between state action and *razbazarivanie*. In 1931–32, there were a series of forced purchases of livestock from the dwindling private sector along with, in 1931, a renewed campaign within the collective farms aimed at further socialization of what little livestock remained in the private possession of collective farmers. The result of this offensive was a new round of *razbazarivanie* reminiscent of 1929–30.[102] According to Soviet sources, the general number of draft animals in the collective farm declined by 16.8% in 1932.[103] The *razbazarivanie* of this period was further accentuated by the mass famine raging through the countryside. There was no food for people and no fodder for livestock. In some areas, local officials illicitly gave collective farmers permission to slaughter livestock for consumption or sale on the market.[104] In Vladimirskii *raion*, in the Ivanovo region, according to data from December 1931, as many as 85% to 90% of dairy cows were slaughtered.[105] Although the Communist party did order a retreat from further forced livestock socialization in March 1932, official sources continued to insist that "kulaks" were simply using "food difficulties" as an excuse for the criminal neglect of livestock.[106] According to a report on the Lower Volga from this period, which noted that "of course an insufficiency of bread does occur" among about 5% of collective farmers:

> Comrade Iakovlev [Commissar of Agriculture] asked a question about horses at the [collective farm] meeting . . . they are fed poorly. They [the collective farmers] say—"horses! We ourselves eat poorly." . . . When you put any question to the kulak and *podkulachnik* he tries to confuse it with the issue of crop failure, the issue of food.[107]

In the eyes of the state, horses came before peasants, who were automatically relabeled "kulak and *podkulachnik*" in this report. Peasant hunger was a manifestation of "self-seeking" tendencies, while fodder shortages for livestock were a far more serious matter. The state accused collective farmers of practicing all sorts of sadistic cruelties in their attempts to sabotage socialized livestock, especially ʻhorses. Borrowing sometimes from the scenario of wrecking, accusations of feeding horses glass and nails, cutting out horses' tongues, and simple neglect of livestock were regularly reported. In one case in the North Caucasus Budennyi collective farm in Millerovskii *raion*, where 120 of 450 horses died in a six-month period, the state made charges of mismanagement and sabotage when it discovered that (among other problems) the farm's livestock brigade consisted of members of the local intelligentsia.[108] Even more than in the case of machine-breaking, it is likely that accusations of sabotage were efforts at scapegoating collective farmers for the almost inevitable problems in animal husbandry in the midst of famine and mass socialization.

A collective farmer's ultimate statement of resistance, as in 1929–30, was simply to quit the collective farm, temporarily or permanently. In the fall of 1931 and spring of 1932, collective farmers' resignations became a mass phenomenon. In the first half of 1932, the number of collectivized households in the RSFSR declined from 10,506,500 to 9,135,200.[109] In the Middle Volga, the percentage of collectivized households dropped from 82.5% to 76.6% in 1932.[110] Between 1 November 1931 and March 1932, 37,000 households quit collective farms in the North Caucasus.[111] Mass departures were reported elsewhere in the country, including Ukraine, Lower Volga, Central Black Earth Region, and Western Region.[112] In some areas, entire collective farms collapsed.[113] Although mismanagement and chaos in collective farms as well as ever-present official "excesses" played a role, famine was the primary reason for the 1932 exodus. According to Danilov, in 1931 and 1932, collective farmers from Siberia, the Lower and Middle Volga, North Caucasus, Ukraine, and Kazakhstan sometimes left for cities and new mass construction sites in entire villages as a result of the famine.[114] Some 220,000 peasants from Ukraine, Central Black Earth Region, North Caucasus, and Lower Volga left their homes at this time, migrating to other regions in search of food until forcibly being returned in spring 1933.[115] In Western Region in 1932, and perhaps elsewhere, artificial mergers of collective farms in order to increase acreage actually resulted in the collapse of collective farms, eventually forcing the regional party committee to order the cessation of mergers in July 1932.[116] In parts of Dagestan, rumors that the policy of collectivization was to be discarded led to an exodus from the region's collective farms.[117] Here and elsewhere, the partial restoration of the market in May 1932 may have sparked a wave of rumors regarding the collective farms' imminent demise, and prompted departures. In Western Siberia, mass exits continued into 1935 as a result of crop failures and food shortages. Many of the peasants who quit collective farms were reportedly those who had fled to Siberia in search of food from other regions of the country in 1933.[118] Here, as elsewhere, those who quit the collective farms often left permanently for work in the cities.[119] Others, no doubt, soon returned, voluntarily or not, to the collective farms as they saw their options depleted. Although collective farm resignations continued on an individual basis in later years, this mass exodus was to be the last such phenomenon until the war. Motivated largely by hunger and the absolute futility of working in the collective farm, this last great prewar departure was an implicit act of resistance that derived from traditional peasant practices of flight in the face of oppression.

The days of blazing gunfights with kulaks were largely over. The state now faced the far more serious and arduous task of transforming a culture and entire way of life—and not at gunpoint but on a tractor. The state confronted a largely resistant culture, a peasantry not easily moved to change in the best of times. Brute repression, starvation, criminal mismanagement, and radically alien approaches to work rendered the new collective farm peasantry nearly intractable. The state was the main force responsible for the breakdown in peasant labor and traditional rhythms of work. The peasantry struggled to survive by assuming a largely defensive posture based on the exploitation of everyday forms of resistance—shirking work, foot dragging, wage leveling, dissimulation, sabotage, and flight. The state's real opponent in the effort "to organizationally and economically strengthen" the collective farm system, to use the official jargon, was neither kulak and *podkulachnik* nor any of the host of "backward elements," but instead a peasant culture of life and labor that naturally repelled much of what the state sought to impose by force, expending its main energies in efforts to survive.

"Self-seeking tendencies" and the grain struggle

When the state labeled peasant attempts at subsistence "self-seeking" tendencies while in effect condemning the countryside to starvation, it disfigured the terms of the peasant moral economy, turning most peasants and many local officials into "saboteurs" and "thieves" in their attempts to eke out a minimal existence within the economy of scarcity. A Tolstoyan peasant whose commune was dissolved and forcibly transformed into a collective farm recalled:

> We women became thieves; all our lives depended on theft. There were no men and we had to raise our children and feed them. There was no common dining room, as there had been in the commune, and they paid us two hundred grams of bad grain for a labor-day of work—just try to live on that! So you swipe whatever you can. When you come home from work, you walk off with a potato, a beet, a cabbage depending on where you work, and then at night you sneak off to the piles in the vegetable garden. And you have to feed the cow, too—she's the main provider for the family. All day from dawn to dusk on collective-farm work, and then in your "free" time you're cooking and washing and getting feed for the cow. You wake up your boy at night and go through the deep snow with his sled to the threshing floor, and look all around like a thief to see if you can bring back a little chaff or straw. That's how we lived.[120]

Most peasants, especially those women, children, and elderly people who stole furtively into the fields at night to clip off spikes of grain—the so-called "barbers" (*parikmakhery*) of Soviet press parlance—would not have viewed their activities as resistance. They were, instead, struggling for survival, which, however perversely, became in the inverted moral–political cosmos of the Stalinist order a kind of resistance in and of itself, state treason in the new order.

Pilfering—outright theft, to the state—was widespread in the collective farms from the very beginning of their existence.[121] In the early 1930s, a family's fate often depended on the scraps and bits that could be salvaged from fields and barns and secreted home. The state viewed pilfering as a constituent element of the "on-the-sly" activities of the kulak, who, it was said, continued to exert his influence on women and other backward elements to wreak havoc. According to *Sovetskaia iustitsiia*, the theft of socialist property was on the rise in the early 1930s. Between August and December 1931 and August and December 1932, such theft had increased fivefold in Western Siberia, fourfold in the Urals, and by one and one-half times in the Moscow Region.[122] The largest percentage of theft occurred in collective farms.[123] The director of a Siberian state farm used the familiar and pathological "epidemic" to describe the state of affairs already in late 1931 and early 1932:

> This epidemic, in my opinion, has gone beyond the point where we can fight it by ordinary means. Literally there is not a day when there are not two–three cases [where we] apprehend neighboring peasants with stolen grain. Under the pretext of gathering corn, they go into the hayricks and gather grain.[124]

"Ordinary means" were soon superseded by extraordinary measures, when on 7 August 1932 the state published its vicious law on the protection of socialist property that condemned "thieves" to not less than ten years' incarceration or execution.[125] According to recent and surely incomplete studies, some 55,000 peasants were convicted under this law in just the first five months of its existence. More than 2,000 of them received the death penalty, which was subsequently carried out in about one-half of the cases.[126] Legal authorities described the initial implementation of the new law (August through November 1932) as "liberal" and "right opportunist" and cited evidence that only a little over 50% of all cases tried under this law were subsequently confirmed by higher courts. The law was implemented much more harshly in 1933, with as many as 103,400 people convicted, and gradually lost momentum thereafter.[127] Operating in the foreground of the famine, the law constituted a second offensive against the peasant, as harshly and senselessly punitive as dekulakization. The problem with the law (as with dekulakization) was that it was almost universally applicable. As a Siberian peasant named Karpenko charged earlier with grain theft said, "If you convict me, then [you will] have to convict everyone because everyone steals grain."[128] In the definitions of the new law, thieves were now "enemies of the people."[129] Accordingly and within the context of famine, the majority of the peasantry had become traitors.

The thieves of socialist property were hungry peasants, willing to risk incarceration and even death by execution to feed themselves and their families. According to data on 20,000 peasants convicted in the first five months after the law of 7 August was enacted, 15% were kulaks, 32% collective farmers, and 50% private farmers still outside the collective farm system.[130] Even if the figure of 15% for kulaks could be trusted, the official class enemy would still remain in a decided minority among pilferers.[131] In 1932, theft often was committed by groups of peasants; by 1933, most thieves acted alone.[132] More than half of all collective farm property stolen consisted of uncollected grain from the fields. This was the work of the "barbers" and testified not only to the obvious motivation of hunger behind the act but also to the inability or even unwillingness of starving peasants to harvest fully the collective farm fields.[133] The private farmers who made up 50% of the peasants convicted under the law acted according to similar motivations, having lost much of their property and livelihood to punitive taxation, exorbitant requisition demands, and, in some cases, the *de facto* expropriation of properties that occurred as a result of leaving the collective farm after March 1930.

Women and children were responsible for a large portion of collective farm theft. Predictably, official sources claimed that the kulak was behind their actions, sending them out to steal.[134] These officially guileless thieves, however, needed no prompting besides hunger and desperation. Reports suggest that as many as one-third of all thieves may have been women with young families.[135] For example, in one case, two women (one, a 28-year-old with three children) received ten-year sentences for the pilfering of a total of four kilograms of grain.[136] In another case, two wives of exiled kulaks, left to fend for themselves, were convicted under the 7 August law for simply cutting off the tops of spikes of grain.[137] The children who pilfered also stole for themselves and their families, and were possibly used because they were thought to attract less attention or less culpability, or, alternately, were acting on their own under circumstances in which they were forced to assume the tremendous burden of their own or their family's subsistence. In two Moscow Region *raions*, for example, children made up the majority of persons convicted of theft.[138] In some areas, subsequently convicted children had pretended to be collecting mushrooms while actually gathering grain from agricultural machinery in the fields.[139] Collective farms, as a whole, sometimes demonstrated complicity when they assigned children, elderly people, and even blind or deaf peasants to night guard duties at the granaries, seemingly to facilitate theft.[140] In the Kuban collective farm Bolshevik, one-fifth of the membership was expelled for theft in 1932–33, a proportion that was likely emblematic for the region as a whole if not much of the country.[141]

Theft reached such huge dimensions that some peasants began to steal from each other. "Mass theft" of collective farmers' "private property" reportedly occurred in the Lower Volga, North Caucasus, and elsewhere.[142] Many collective farmers were said to be afraid to leave their homes for field work in fear of burglary.[143] In the final months of 1933, the situation had deteriorated to the point that cases of *samosud* over thieves were reported in parts of the countryside. In one example, peasants beat two collective farmers for stealing a few potatoes.[144] In another case, collective farm officials and a collective farm member with the same surname of the accused, possibly her husband, carried out a ritual *samosud* over a collective farm woman. For stealing some potatoes, they paraded her, covered in ink, in front of the entire collective farm membership and then locked her up in a cellar.[145] The new moral economy transformed peasants into thieves; the famine and economy of scarcity led some to turn on each other for a crust of bread.

In many parts of the country, theft occurred in collusion with local, especially collective farm, officials who, by this time, were mainly peasants according to their social origin. This was part of what the state labeled *mestnichestvo* (loosely, local interests) in the best of cases and wrecking, sabotage, or kulak penetration of officialdom in most others. The introduction of the *politotdel* in the MTS and state farms in 1933 came primarily in response to the perception that local officialdom could not be trusted.[146] Although such theft could be actual embezzlement, in many cases, especially during the famine, local officials, like their constituencies, were attempting to resist the incursions of the center and to defend local interests and stay alive. One collective farm chairman reportedly told his superiors, "We do not recognize you, and the grain is ours and we will distribute it as we please."[147] Much of local sabotage amounted to no more than the attempt to challenge requisitioning quotas as unrealistic and too high. Already in 1931, collective farm officials who resisted requisitions could be charged under Articles 109, 111, and 112 of the penal code for abuse or neglect of their office.[148] Nonetheless, in Ukraine and North Caucasus in particular but not exclusively, collective farm and *raion* officials argued that local requisitioning quotas were unrealistic.[149] In a collective farm in Tikhoretskii *raion* in North Caucasus, the collective farm leaders simply distributed all the grain among starving collective farmers and then falsified their records.[150] The chairman of the Trudovik collective farm in the Kostroma area announced at a general collective farm assembly, "Our plan is fulfilled by 50% and this is enough." He concluded that it was impossible to fulfill the plan any further.[151] In the Western Region, a Communist named Bonadykin bravely resisted requisitions, informing outside officials, simply, "I will not permit [you] to infringe on collective farm property."[152]

Many collective farm leaders and even *raion* officials attempted to secure at least a minimal subsistence for collective farmers. Collective farms often sought to establish grain reserves to provide support for non–able-bodied farmers, the very young and the very old as well as to put something aside for insurance against disaster.[153] In October 1931, the state issued a decree forbidding collective farms to establish grain reserves before requisitions were fulfilled.[154] The state claimed that collective farms were concerned first and foremost with their own "consumerist" or "self-seeking" tendencies to the detriment of grain for export, and food for workers and Red army soldiers.[155] *Kolkhoztsentr* plenipotentiary Aristov complained bitterly in the fall of 1931 that some North Caucasus collective farms thought about fulfilling state plans only after guaranteeing themselves with bread and their livestock with fodder.[156] The chairman of the New Labor collective farm in Crimea refused to hand over his farm's grain surplus, instead wisely retaining a reserve of fifty *puds* for every two collective farm inhabitants. His act was characterized as sabotage.[157] The state labeled any attempt to establish grain reserves as "fundomania,"[158] sensing in these efforts sabotage and subterfuge in the interests of the peasants and, as necessary corollary, against the state.

The state claimed that kulaks were circulating the highly "offensive" slogan of "first grain to ourselves, and then to the government."[159] Kulaks supposedly had "penetrated" collective farms and, most especially, collective farm administrations in their attempts to subvert the system from within by establishing the priority of peasant subsistence. In North Caucasus, Kuban in particular, Ukraine, and other parts of the country, the state argued that local and *raion* officialdom had "merged" with kulakdom, spreading talk of grain shortages and food difficulties.[160] Such "mergers" were somewhere in the background of the massive purges of rural officialdom conducted in 1932 and 1933.[161] Collective farms in fact made use of a wide array of stratagems to try to keep some grain in the village. Some collective farms withheld parts of their grain surplus, falsified grain balances, or underestimated harvest yields.[162] Others practiced accounting and bookkeeping tricks, maintaining two sets of books or simply not recording all of their assets.[163] There were official complaints that collective farm officials often "exaggerated" or falsified payment norms for labor days, made use of "dead souls" to inflate consumption norms, or implemented per-eater principles of income distribution to ensure a minimal level of subsistence.[164] Collective farms also could illicitly authorize private market sales *before* requisition quotas were fulfilled.[165] Some collective farms simply "gave" all the grain to hungry collective farmers, thus engaging directly in what the state called the *razbazarivanie* of grain.[166]

Subterfuge and deception continued beyond the collective farm, at the grain elevators and the railroad depots where grain was collected for the state. Both collective farms and private farmers alike occasionally managed to obtain fraudulent documents certifying that they had fulfilled their grain obligations to the state.[167] There were also reports of manipulation of scales, hidden grain under railroad car floors (presumably more to the benefit of railroad workers), and even the theft of entire train wagons of grain.[168] Some of these incidents occurred as late as 1934 and 1935 when officially theft was said to be in decline.[169] In these cases and others involving collective farms, local officials committed what had come to be defined as treason by putting "local interests" (sometimes a euphemism for peasant survival) above the national interest.[170]

With or without the collusion of local officials, collective farmers continued to resist the requisitions in the first half of the 1930s, though far less frequently than in the late 1920s. Still in the fall of 1930, there were cases of collective farmers setting conditions for turning over their grain, such as the receipt of manufactured goods or, more frequently, the satisfaction of subsistence needs first.[171] Peasants, private and collective farm alike, tried to hide away food supplies; there were even entire collective farms that jointly attempted to conceal grain.[172] In 1931 in Ol'khovskii *raion*, Lower Volga, there were cases of collective farm women blocking the carting away of their grain.[173] In a village in Tatariia, peasants expressed their sentiments about requisitioning with the mock execution of a chicken, which was left hanging with a sign attached to it reading, "because she did not fulfill the contract for eggs. [Because she] cannot produce as much as the government demands."[174] Russian historian I. E. Zelenin writes that in 1932 and 1933 there was mass dissatisfaction among peasants, especially in North Caucasus and Ukraine, as peasants refused to go out to work and spoke out against requisition quotas at collective farm meetings.[175] According to V. V. Kondrashin, a leading expert on the famine, there was very little active resistance during this time, although it was not totally unheard of, mainly because peasants were afraid. The basic, though infrequent, forms of protest were stealthful attacks on grain transports from the village, the dismantling of bridges, and the infrequent riot.[176] Peasants sometimes tried to obstruct grain from going to the elevators, and as late as 1935 a Cheliabinsk collective farm made up of former Red partisans reportedly announced, "We fought for Soviet power, we don't have to give grain to the government."[177] In Teplo-Ogarevskii *raion* in Kareliia in 1934, all of the *raion*'s collective farms protested the exorbitant demands made on their harvests. At the collective farm, Red October, a collective farm with 200 households, everyone voted against fulfilling the plan. The meeting lasted throughout the night and next day. The collective farm only complied after the authorities began to arrest its members for "speculation."[178] When the 1935 Model Collective Farm Statute finally arrived for discussion, the peasants of one collective farm crossed out the clauses relating to the fulfillment of government obligations, presumably under the mistaken assumption that the statute implied some kind of mutual agreement.[179]

In the immediate aftermath of collectivization, the grain struggle between state and peasantry assumed the attributes of a war between colonizer and colonized. What the state labeled *tikhaia sapa* was in fact a subaltern people's desperate effort at survival in the midst of famine, assisted at times by local officials whose actions derived from a combination of brave resistance and natural self-interest. The state response was massive repression, rivaling that of dekulakization and flooding the *Gulag* with new waves of peasants and rural officials. The repression was so clearly excessive that the state would issue several amnesties in 1935 in an attempt to offset at least partially the tremendous damage of the wholesale arrests of these years.[180] Peasant resistance to the plunder of their lives and labor took the form of customary strategies for survival. Yet in the collapse of "labor discipline," the wholesale pilfering of "socialist" property, and especially the theft that manifested itself among peasants themselves, there were signs of cultural breakdown and dislocation as the new order began to take shape.

Postscript: self-defense and self-destruction

Peasant resistance continued to be animated by community norms and constraints after collectivization. As the urban detachments of Soviet power gradually receded, peasants struggled not only with the state, but increasingly among themselves over issues of justice, retribution, and economic self-preservation. The collective farm, like the village commune before it, became an arena of internal conflict and tension. The state probably hinted at this development when it warned against the "idealization" of the collective farm and bemoaned the ever-lingering kulak mood in the countryside. With the "elimination of the kulak as a class," the socioeconomic roots of class struggle should have disappeared. The economy of scarcity, however, dictated not only continued inequalities within (and between) collective farms, but fierce competition around matters of subsistence. The community began to turn in on itself in the harsh environment of the economy of scarcity, expelling not only those who violated community standards of collectivism and fairness, but also those whose existence was or could be construed to be alien, peripheral, or marginal to the community. Self-defense and self-destruction competed in shaping the new collective farm community.

The politics of collectivization played on in the village throughout the 1930s. Peasant activists continued to be individuals despised and resented for violating community ideals of collectivism. Activists who had participated directly in collectivization and dekulakization often lived amid hostile neighbors, who well remembered earlier suffering, and a portion of expropriated kulaks who still lived in or near the village and served as perpetual troublemakers ("agitators") according to the state.[181] Terms like "kolkhoznik" (collective farmer) and "communar" could be used as insults depending upon their source of origin.[182] Cases of retribution and false denunciation aimed against the peasant activists of collectivization surfaced in the press in these years.[183] An activist responsible for the 1928 prosecution of kulaks who supposedly beat him and killed his brother found himself persecuted by his neighbors and, ironically, assessed a firm tax as a kulak in 1931. The father of one of the convicted kulaks of 1928 reportedly influenced his friend, the *sel'sovet* chairman, to "unmask" the former activist.[184] In another case, a *sel'korka* denounced local officials for associating with kulaks, even going so far as to stage a criminal act to implicate them. In the end, the court found that the *sel'korka* was the daughter of a peasant who had been expelled from the collective farm and the lover of a dekulakized peasant. The local officials were the same activists who had carried out these repressive operations earlier.[185] In these cases, peasants not only sought revenge, but in doing so appropriated and manipulated the language of their oppressors. Through the first half of the 1930s, in addition to some seemingly genuine exposes of wrongdoing, peasants poured hundred of denunciations into the press, reporting kulak penetration of collective farm administrations, kulak sabotage, and other nefarious activities by kulaks in disguise.[186] Muckraking and false denunciation (political or otherwise) had apparently already become by 1931 a major enterprise of rural courts (*sel'sudy*), accounting in most regions of the country for some portion of the 20% to 30% of all court cases defined as slander and insult cases.[187] Such denunciations are probably impossible to untangle in search of the truth. Truth, however, was as relative a concept as class in the postcollectivization countryside and until local studies of *sel'sud* cases and denunciation letters are pursued it will suffice to suggest that state labels probably became powerful weapons of internal politics for collective farmers on either side of the barricades as memory and long-simmering tensions motivated a denouement in individual collectivization family histories.

It was not only the activists of collectivization who could find themselves beyond the pale of peasant society. New styles of activists, often young and often female, who chose loyalty to the collective farm over the community could find themselves subject to the enmity of their neighbors for breaking ranks. Laborers who excelled, shock workers (*udarniki*), and later Stakhanovites were often treated as a version of strikebreakers for outdoing their neighbors and ingratiating themselves with the authorities, generally for material reward, but sometimes for the brief adulation accorded them, or as a matter of duty and belief. The term *udarnik*, came to replace *bedniak* (poor peasant) as a term of abuse in some places. For example, according to an MTS *politotdel* official in Kuban:

> one collective farm woman in tears complained to a *politotdel* representative that they [the other collective farmers] insulted her, calling her an *udarnitsa* [female form of *udarnik*]. She assured [them] that she worked conscientiously, but for some reason they insulted her, giving her the name of *udarnitsa*. She threatened to quit work if they did not stop these insults.[188]

In another case, a young male peasant claimed to be a "secret *udarnik*," not wishing for anyone to know of his status and devotion to work.[189] Women activists were particular targets of peasant wrath, receiving treatment ranging from curses to arson of their homes and murder. A Lower Volga newspaper report from 1934 noted that women activists were often abused by husbands who were "shamed" by their wives' work. Rumors also spread that women shock workers who had to sleep temporarily away at the fields during peak work seasons were promiscuous.[190] In the mid-1930s, collective farm women Stakhanovites faced persecution, beatings, and even rape by relatives and fellow collective farmers who resented their activities.[191] A woman activist risked doubly violating village norms by breaking ranks not only with her community but with the subordinate role expected of her by other peasants.

If stepping out of ranks could spell danger to new activists and disunity among neighbors, distinction by punishment could be equally destabilizing to community norms. In the Kuban, for example, quarrels broke out in the collective farms when individuals found their names placed on the "black board" of shame for poor work. Here, peasants complained that such a practice violated the principle of neighborly (*dobrososedskie*) relations.[192] In the same way, some village communities continued to defend and support peasants who earlier had been punished as kulaks. Escapes from the special kulak settlements where peasants were exiled were far from uncommon. Between September and November 1931, alone, over 37,000 escapes were reported, many of them ending in "tragedy."[193] In 1932, 207,010 peasants reportedly escaped, while in 1933 and 1934 the number of escapes remained high at 215,856 and 87,617 respectively.[194] The fugitives often attempted to reach their native villages.[195] News of returned kulaks sometimes surfaced in the press as they were targeted or scapegoated as thieves and resentenced or returned to their places of exile.[196] Their former neighbors frequently attempted to shelter them or feed them, all the while maintaining an unarticulated conspiracy of secrecy around their return, entailing great personal risk.[197] In still other cases, peasants stepped forward to defend neighbors unjustly accused as kulaks and threatened with expulsion from the collective farm.[198] Under greatly changed circumstances, a sense of the village as community lingered on beyond the trauma of collectivization. Whether it was adulation or admonition, collective farmers resented the practices of the new order that would set neighbor against neighbor, raising or lowering one at the expense or shame of all. They therefore employed both repressive and defensive measures aimed at monitoring and seeking to exert some semblance of control over internal village dynamics.

The effort to maintain unity and community may have turned into a search for homogeneity and cohesion through leveling within the economy of scarcity. Difference within the village setting became glaring as peasants, no longer faced with everyday intrusions and constant, direct violence from the common enemy, struggled to survive, experiencing hardship after hardship. The policing of internal unity, normally a customary aspect of villages and small communities, could turn into a quest for homogenization as peasants turned against villagers who were distinguished in one way or another from their neighbors. Prominent among the victims of repression in the immediate postcollectivization years were a cast of "outsiders" and marginal peoples, traditionally suspect or scorned in peasant societies, but only actively persecuted in times of great social stress.[199] *Byvshie liudi*, elements closely tied in the popular mind to the prerevolutionary regime such as landowners, traders, shop keepers, clergy, village and *volost'* elders, Tsarist officers, and prerevolutionary policemen, came under fierce attack from above and, in all probability, from below. A number of categories of *byvshie liudi* were traditional objects of peasant antipathy and, in the context of famine and desolation, were likely candidates for scapegoating and persecution as peasant social memory fueled postcollectivization politics similar to the struggles with collectivization activists.[200] Other outsiders or semi-outsiders, such as seasonal workers, artisans, and members of the rural intelligentsia, also appeared disproportionately among the victims of rural repression at this time. These categories of rural inhabitants generally had access to outside earnings as well as the right to a parcel of land and other privileges from the collective farm if they or a member of their household was a collective farm member. At the same time, they were not necessarily required to fulfill the same labor requirements as their neighbors. Within an economy of scarcity, such seeming privileges could have easily set these households above the rest in the eyes of the community, making a seeming mockery of norms of fairness and egalitarianism to starving peasants, and violating the new moral economy. According to community standards, these rural inhabitants failed to do their "fair share" of labor in the collective farm while depleting what little resources there were on the same basis as regular collective farm laborers.[201] In much the same way, economically or socially marginal households could suffer for failure to fulfill their fair share of the burdens of the collective farm while drawing on its limited resources. Poor households led by single women, wives of conscripted soldiers, widows, the elderly and invalids, often appeared among those singled out for persecution locally, but like other outsiders later reprieved by higher authorities. Although some collective farms tried to set aside a reserve fund for non-able-bodied peasants of all categories,[202] it appears likely that most older communal mechanisms for maintaining the village's less fortunate broke down as the countryside underwent transformation, and the non-able-bodied and the weak came to be seen as living violations of the new moral economy.[203]

Those peasants who remained outside of the collective farm system, the *edinolichniki* or private farmers, became the ultimate official outsiders in the new collectivized countryside. For the state, private farmers were often tantamount to kulaks or, at best, *podkulachniki*. For collective farmers, they presented something far more complex. At times, like returned kulaks, they remained members of the community. Sometimes, in fact, only one member of a household belonged to the collective farm—for that was all that was required to maintain most collective farm privileges—making the private farmer not only a member of the community but a member of the family. Some practiced a kind of temporary, seasonal membership in the collective farm in order to avoid the taxes on private farmers that were levied at defined times of the year.[204] At other times, these kinds of subterfuges, as well as the perilous state of the national and local economy, forced collective farms to become defensive bulwarks to lessen the burden of the times and to try to maintain a certain level of subsistence for its members. Under these circumstances, there could be hostility between peasants who were members of the collective farm and peasants who were not. In some cases, especially in the famine years, collective farms refused petitions from peasants to join or rejoin the collectives.[205] In other cases, more onerous requirements were placed in the way of prospective new members, a practice condemned in Moscow. In the Central Black Earth Region, Middle Volga, Siberia, and elsewhere, there were cases of collective farms refusing entry to peasants who had no inventory or requiring them to purchase a horse before entry.[206] The private farmer faced a double bind, squeezed by state and collective farm peasantry alike. In the context of the collectivized countryside, *edinolich-*

nik became a new status, alien to the state and, at times, to the collective farm peasantry as well.

Homogenization collided with notions of community in the collective farm, recalling that village collectivism in reality was never more than an ideal against which to view difference and to oppose outside attempts to divide the community. The centrifugal and centripetal forces acting upon the new collective farm community represented a contradiction more apparent than real, for both of these opposing forces, alternately strengthening and weakening the bonds of community, had similar derivations and consequences. The trauma of collectivization, the desperation of hunger and competition for scarce material resources, and the violence of the times dictated a blend of community resistance based on self-defensive and self-destructive strategies all aimed at survival and leading in the direction of, although never quite arriving at, homogenization. Like the precollective farm village, the collectivized community did not become a cohesive collectivity, egalitarian and undifferentiated. Pressures from within and from without the collective farm shaped new sociopolitical configurations, new kinds of stratification. As the community re-formed itself, new, frequently changing elites emerged around the collective farm administration that would dominate a rank and file further subdivided by skill, earnings, family size, and family network. Community conflicts around self-preservation and homogenization operated alongside this more modern hierarchy. Repression and cultural rupture lay behind the internecine divisions of the early 1930s, while other aspects of peasant culture endured at the same time to strengthen the bonds and ideals of community. The result was a hybrid society. The memory and politics of collectivization became ensconced in the fabric of postcollectivization village interrelational dynamics.

Conclusion

The preamble to the 1935 Model Collective Farm Statute evokes the ritualized vows and cadences of an oath of allegiance. Collective farmers promised "to guarantee a full victory over poverty and darkness, over the backwardness of small-scale private farming; to create high productivity of labor and to guarantee in that way the best life for collective farmers."[207] The preamble concluded with a less-than-rousing pledge of loyalty:

> The collective farm path, the path of socialism, is the only correct path for the laboring peasantry. Members of [collective farm] artels must strengthen their artels, work honestly, divide collective farm revenue according to labor, guard socialized property, take care of collective farm goods, take care of tractors and machinery, establish good care of the horses, fulfill the tasks of their worker-peasant government—and thus make their collective farms Bolshevik and all collective farmers rich [*zazhitochnye*].[208]

Here, in brief, was the Communist recipe for the Stalin revolution in the countryside and the "socialist transformation" of the peasantry. The underside of the recipe, however, represented a Communist wish and a dream as much as a catalogue of cures for each and every one of the chronic ailments of the collective farm order of the first half of the 1930s.

To attain its wish or effect a cure, the Communist party included in the new statute a series of compromises to reflect the intractable and ongoing reality of peasant ways and the imperative of reaching an accord with those realities. The 1935 statute granted the land to collective farms in perpetuity (*navechno*), a promise intended less as the threat of serfdom many peasants perceived it to be than as a guarantee of future stability in land relations. Private plots in defined dimensions were fully legalized, and collective farmers' private property—homes, domestic livestock, barns and sheds, household necessities, and tools and implements for use on the private plot—was minutely detailed and ensured inviolability. Collective farmers were even promised the use of collective farm horses for their personal needs—at a price—and recited the exact rules for collective farm expulsions.[209] By 1935, many of these features had already (*de facto* or otherwise) become a part of most collective farms, so that, to a large extent, the state was merely accepting a *fait accompli*. And already in spring 1932 and again in early 1933, the state had taken several hard steps backward when it authorized a limited collective farm trade and acknowledged the importance of more precise definitions of collective farm obligations.[210] This is not to say that the state would not subsequently routinely violate its own ordinances, nor to say that the state in any way voluntarily accepted some kind of peasant dictate.[211] Rather, the state was forced to accept a certain fixed reality dictated by cynical self-interest and to settle in the end for "just" taking grain from its peasant colony, ceasing to push its revolutionary-colonizing mission on its subjects, or at least doing so with a much-diminished ardor and vigor.

However obliquely, the 1935 Model Collective Farm Statute testified to the strength and sustainability of peasant culture and tradition in the face of an onslaught of Communist modernity and brute force. The peasantry did not emerge in any sense of the word "triumphant" from its ordeal. The death and destruction wrought by collectivization, famine, and cultural trauma in the first half of the 1930s had already dealt an enormous blow to the peasantry. Yet the peasantry's continued resistance, whether in the act of subsistence or protest, revealed the cohesiveness and durability of the peasantry as an autonomous social formation—sometimes in spite of, sometimes because of the state's offensive. Passive and everyday forms of resistance, traditional mechanisms of peasant survival and peasant politics, preceded, accompanied, and continued well beyond collectivization and the famine to the present day, chronically undermining the foundations of socialized agriculture. Collectivization ultimately resulted in the victory of the state, but it was a Pyrrhic victory. Collectivization was entrenched, and the peasant rebellion of 1929–30 was not to be repeated, but the civil war continued. Two fundamentally different cultures at odds with one another entered into the deadlocked quagmire of colony and colonizer.

Conclusion

Eugenia Ginzburg begins her classic memoir with the unforgettable sentence, "The year 1937 began, to all intents and purposes, at the end of 1934—to be exact, on the first of December."[1] That was the date of the assassination of Leningrad party leader, S. M. Kirov, an event which many see as the spark to the Great Purge.[2] Doubtless, there was a longer prehistory behind the terrible repression of the late 1930s. Solzhenitsyn cites the Bolshevik revolution as the foundation stone of Stalinism, while others posit prerevolutionary historical traditions or the "formative experience" of the Russian Civil War.[3] One could as easily look to 1930 and the bloody destruction and chaos of collectivization for the source, a source, of Stalin's terror. As much as the revolution and civil war, collectivization molded a generation of Communists whose "baptism of fire" came in the violence of 1930. Those who survived the experience with their faith in Communism intact came to see the world in the stark binary oppositions so characteristic of Stalinism, the Manichaean world that divided into Red and White, friend and foe, revolution and counterrevolution. And while the mind-set of 1937 may have been at least partially shaped in 1930, so too was its physical incarnation, the apparatus of repression that would set to work cleansing the nation of enemies. The OGPU, later NKVD, perfected its operations at this time, multiplying and subdividing into the most refined specializations as it confronted the enormous tasks of dekulakization, mass deportations, and the administration of the vast expanses of the kulak diaspora, both in the "special settlements" and within the nation's industrial empire. The experience the state gained in crushing peasant rebellion during collectivization surely lies somewhere in the background of 1937 and later acts of atrocity.

The impact of collectivization on the evolution of the Stalinist state was distinctive only in the degree of subsequent barbarism. The most significant effect of peasant revolt cross-culturally is, all too often, to enhance the centralizing and repressive nature of the state.[4] Peasant rebellion was bound to fail. Yet to conclude the obvious is to obscure the essence. The very fact of a peasant rebellion against the Stalinist state during collectivization, as well as the manifold reasons for its failure, tells a story of singular meaning about the peasantry and the state, and the hybrid agricultural system that would come out of the cultural clash between the two.

Collectivization encapsulated the original fault lines of the Bolshevik revolution, between a minority class in whose name the Communists professed to rule and the majority peasantry whose very reality appeared to block the revolution. Stalin's collectivization was an attempt to eliminate the fault line, to solve the accursed peasant problem by force, to create a socialist society and economy from above. It was a campaign of domination that aimed at nothing less than the internal colonization of the peasantry. Collectivization would ensure a steady flow of grain to the state. It would also enable Soviet power to subjugate the peasantry through the imposition of administrative and political controls and forced acculturation into the dominant culture. Although the Communist party publicly proclaimed collectivization to be "socialist transformation," it was in reality a war of cultures, a virtual civil war between state and peasantry.

Collectivization posed a profound threat to the peasant way of life. Peasants of every social strata responded to this threat by uniting as a culture—in a very real sense, as a class—in defense of their families, beliefs, communities, and livelihood, and overcoming their ordinary and multiple differences. Peasant resistance was rooted in peasant culture rather than in any specific social stratum and drew upon a repository of traditional devices native to that culture. It was shaped by an agency and political consciousness that derived from reasoned concerns centered largely on issues of justice and subsistence, and supplemented by retribution, anger, and desperation. Its forms were customary, pragmatic, and flexible, adapted to fit each situation and threat. Peasant culture lived on in peasant resistance.

The peasant vision of collectivization was most clearly distilled through the world of rumor. Collectivization rumors were draped in the language of apocalypse. The Soviet state was said to be the Antichrist, initiating his rule on earth through the collective farm. Warnings of retribution, war, and invasion called to mind the horsemen of apocalyptic tradition. Omnipresent tales of moral abomination in the collective farm called forth the unholy triad of Communism-Antichrist-sexual depravity. The peasant association of collectivization and enserfment, although not necessarily apocalyptic, used serfdom as a metaphor for evil, a secular, social apocalypse that, when tied to collectivization, transformed Communists into present-day landlords and made a mockery of the revolution. Rumors served as political metaphor and parable, turning the world upside down through the creation of an alternative universe of symbolic inversion, and thereby delegitimizing the existing order of things—the collective farms, collectivization, and the Soviet state. Rumors were also a kind of collective vision, a mental projection, in this case a projection of the political world of the peasantry. More than any other form of popular resistance, rumors encapsulated and allegorized collectivization as civil war.

Peasants turned to violence only as a last resort. In the meantime, in an attempt to blunt the force of the state's offensive, peasants made use of a vast array of self-help strategies. The most vivid and dangerous form of self-help was *razbazarivanie*, or the "squandering" of livestock and other property through destruction and sale, and considered to be the epitome of peasant "darkness" and savagery. As protest, sabotage, or a way to liquefy assets, *razbazarivanie* enabled peasants to gird themselves against the economic perils of the new order. For some peasants, those labeled kulaks, *razbazarivanie* was one method among many of socioeconomic transfiguration, or "self-dekulakization." Self-dekulakization embraced other stratagems as well, including flight from the countryside. Both *razbazarivanie* and self-dekulakization fed directly into the escalating frenzy of collectivization and dekulakization in early 1930.

Peasant communities also engaged in a more direct self-help when they banded together to protect members subject to repression under the kulak label. The refrain "We have no kulaks here" was heard throughout the countryside as every peasant learned that the kulak label, instead of dividing them, served as the great equalizer once it was clear that it was *peasant* interests as a whole that were on the line and that *anyone* could be a kulak. Support or defense of "kulaks" was dangerous and subject to interpretation by the state as a counterrevolutionary activity. When all else failed, peasants turned to their most traditional of defenses—writing letters and petitions to higher authorities. They wrote on behalf of themselves and others, individually and collectively, and they made use of the traditional myth of a benevolent central authority in their attempts to seek redress.

Peasant self-help may be viewed as a specific form of implicit resistance. Although often cloaked in *muzhik* vestments, it was neither irrational nor the emanation of some dark side of the peasantry. It was, rather, logical, political, and humane. Acts of self-help could be direct and clear protest. Or peasants could try to mute the political import of their actions by playing the parts of *muzhiki* and *baby*, dissembling, or appropriating dominant modes of discourse. In this way, the *form* as well as the *content* of peasant protest derived from a culture of resistance common to Russian peasants and, indeed, all peasants. These acts of self-help, like rumors, served to demonstrate to the state the political solidarity and cohesion of the peasantry in defense of its interests.

Peasant terror further reinforced cohesion and amplified the culture of civil war so prominently featured in collectivization. It was generally animated by customary norms of justice, retribution, and community, and masked by disguise, dissimulation, anonymity, and an escape route of double meanings. Peasants manipulated official images of *muzhik* psychology, dissembling before power and sovietizing their actions to fit the crime. Terror was first a threat to any member of the community who had broken or was aiming to break ranks with the village collective and to any official who believed violence against the community could occur without cost. It was second a form of retribution levied on those who had helped to carry out Soviet policies, especially dekulakization, against the community, and in so doing had violated traditional community norms or ideals of cohesion. The extreme coercive pressure of the outside authorities appears to have reinforced a new and repressive attempt by peasants to maintain village unity and insularity in the face of all odds. More than any other form of resistance, terror illuminated the civil war within the civil war that pitted a minority of peasant activists against the community.

Collective action was, like terror, a form of active resistance used by peasants in their attempts to ward off the blows of forced grain requisitioning, collectivization, dekulakization, and atheization. Collective action drew directly upon the strength and cohesion of the community, requiring its collective will and participation. It assumed many different forms, among which protest at meetings with officials, riots, insurrections, and brigandage were most prominent. When peasants took part in collective action, they did not simply erupt into frenzied and violent madness, as official reports claimed, but aimed their protest at specific targets with specific goals in mind, demonstrating a rebel consciousness rooted in peasant interests. Peasant collective action, moreover, assumed traditional forms long a part of the peasant repertoire of rebellion, often appearing as a kind of ritual of resistance.

The hallmark of collective action was the *babii bunt*. Women led the resistance to church closings, deportations of kulaks, and the socialization of livestock. Rumor had it at this time that "[they] will not touch the women," "they" referring to the authorities.[5] Whether peasant women and men actually believed this rumor, pretended to believe it, or used it to mobilize more credulous neighbors is perhaps besides the point, for, whatever the case, the rumor *worked*. Peasant women were not as politically vulnerable as their male counterparts and they took advantage of this fact. The Communist party described the *bab'i bunty* as irrational, spontaneous outbursts of women's hysteria and always denied women agency in these protests, attributing blame to the kulak, priest, or male *podkulachnik*. The official construction of the *baba* placed gender (and all that that implied) at center stage, while denuding peasant women of any attributes of class. By virtue of gender and classlessness, the Soviet *baba* was denied political consciousness and agency. She was therefore by definition incapable of political protest. Peasant women, in league with peasant men, exploited these images of themselves for their own ends and led the protest against collectivization. Ironically, the central role of women in collective action may have played directly into the hands of the state by enabling it to dismiss peasant protest as primarily the acts of "dark," "uncultured" women, led astray by kulaks or the "excesses" of local officials. But in the short term, *bab'i bunty* played a major role in forcing the state into its temporary retreat of March 1930.

Passive resistance was the final peasant response to collectivization. It

was a response that continued long beyond the campaigns of collectivization, to endure to the present day as the only viable peasant mechanism
for expressing protest, however muted, against an essentially unjust system. Endemic in collective farming were such typical peasant acts of passive resistance as foot dragging, shirking work, negligence, theft, and dissembling. Peasants also adapted their resistance to the collective farm
system by developing responses specific to socialized agriculture, like the
creation of family collective farms or family work brigades, the maintenance of strip farming and the old borders (*mezhi*) within the collective
farm, struggles over the forms of labor payment, the expansion of the
private plot at the expense of collective land, and so on. The staying power
of many forms of traditional agricultural organization and production
within the collective farm was a direct result of what Soviet officials
viewed as peasant obstinacy and backwardness, but what is better understood as the result of everyday forms of peasant resistance. Passive resistance served as a powerful agent in forcing the state to modify and adapt
some of its most coercive policies. The state's victory over the peasantry
in the collectivization contest was more apparent than real, given the
maintenance of peasant tradition within the context of socialized agriculture. Peasant passive resistance, working in combination with an oppressive, overly centralized, poorly managed, and underfunded system of collective farming, played a key role in hobbling Soviet agriculture and
hindering its further development and modernization.

The peasant rebellion against collectivization was the most serious
episode in popular resistance experienced by the Soviet state after the
Russian Civil War. In 1930, more than two million peasants took part in
13,754 mass disturbances. In 1929 and 1930, the OGPU recorded 22,887
"terrorists acts" aimed at local officials and peasant activists, more than
1,100 of them murders.[6] Peasant resistance played an important, if often
unintended, role in the complex and contradictory development of collectivization, alternately provoking the state into further repression or pushing it into temporary retreat, while all the time serving as a key prop in
the civil war atmosphere of the Stalin revolution. The very strength of a
peasant culture of resistance, however, played no small part in the ultimate failure of peasant rebellion. The community-based nature of the
peasant politics of collectivization, the localism of revolt, the absence of
organized structures of resistance, and the isolation of peasant rebels from
other sources of support all contributed to the archaisms of peasant politics, the brevity of active forms of resistance, and the ease with which the
state attained dominance over the countryside.

In the end, peasant rebels were no match for the vast police powers
of the state, and, like most other peasant rebellions, this one was destined
to fail. The main element in the peasantry's defeat was state repression.
Millions of peasants were arrested, imprisoned, deported, or executed in
the years of collectivization. The state dismantled existing authority structures in the village, removing and replacing traditional elites. The econ-

omy of scarcity complemented state repression, first robbing peasants of their grain and then depriving millions of their lives in the famine that followed collectivization. Repression and a one-sided war of attrition effectively silenced peasant rebels.

Yet repression alone could not and did not end peasant resistance; nor could it have served as the *only* mechanism of control in the long term. For reasons of sheer necessity, the state would largely give up its revolutionary–missionary aspirations in the countryside, choosing, pragmatically and cynically, to exert its domination over the peasantry through the control of vital resources, most especially grain. Plans for the elimination of differences between town and countryside fell to the wayside as reasons of state asserted themselves and the last of the ideals of 1917 crumbled. The peasant household continued to be the mainstay of the peasant—if not collective farm—economy, and homes, domestic livestock, barns, sheds, and household necessities were deemed peasants' private property. The private plot and the limited collective farm market remained alongside socialized agriculture to guarantee a minimum subsistence for collective farmers and to supplement the nation's consumer needs. Peasants were co-opted into positions of authority, and over the next decades, the state gradually extended more of its admittedly paltry benefits from the urban to the rural sector. The Soviet agricultural system became a hybrid system, based on peasant private plots and collective farms, all in the service of the state, but also offering the peasantry something in the exchange.

In the long term, the social by-products of industrialization and urbanization proved as efficacious in securing peasant acquiescence as the brute repression of collectivization. Continued outmigration and permanent resettlement in cities of males and young people spread extended families between town and village, bringing peasant culture to the town and fixing in place urban bridges to the village more firmly than ever before. Education, military service, and improved transportation and communication facilitated a certain degree of sovietization in the countryside, or, at the very least, some homogenization across the urban divide.

The Stalinist state and the collective farm system triumphed in the end, but their triumph did not spell the end of peasant culture or a popular culture of resistance. The peasantry reemerged, not unchanged to be sure, from within socialized agriculture. Passive resistance and other weapons of the weak became endemic mechanisms of coping and survival for the peasantry within the collective farm. Agriculture stagnated, becoming the Achilles' heel of the Soviet economy, a ceaseless reminder of the ironies of the "proletarian revolution" in peasant Russia. Like the peasant commune before it, the collective farm became a bulwark against change and as much a subsistence shelter for peasants as a control mechanism for the state. Over time, the collective farm became the quintessential risk-aversion guarantor that peasants had always sought. Socioeconomic leveling, a basic subsistence, and some degree of cultural independence, demographic isolation, and feminization of the village maintained and even strengthened certain aspects of village culture and tradition.[7] The constant and historic insecurity of peasant life would ironically bond the peasant to the collective farm.

To the extent that it was possible, peasants made the collective farm their own. State attempts at decollectivization in the first half of the 1990s provide ample evidence for this. Decollectivization was blocked by a peasantry grown accustomed to the collective farm. This seeming intransigence was less the result of backwardness, or a "serf mentality," as some interpreters would see it,[8] than a simple continuity of peasant needs, values, and ways of living. Decollectivization, moreover, demonstrated continuity with earlier state efforts to remold and modernize the peasantry. Its implementation was top down, relying on some measure of force (although nothing like that of the Stalinist state), and revealed all the usual elements of the cultural manipulation and imperialism of modernization. Peasants responded to decollectivization with skepticism and hostility, having molded the collective farm at least partially to their own needs.[9]

Collectivization was a Pyrrhic victory, achieved at great cost and human tragedy. In the name of Communist gods, utopian visions, and a modernizing ethos transformed by Stalinism, the Soviet state attempted depeasantization, a kind of cultural genocide, against a peasantry that only too starkly reflected the realities of a Russia based in an agrarian economy and society resistant to the Communist experiment. Long after collectivization, a peasantry, in some sense of the word, would remain, sometimes embittered and most of the time engaged in a continuing and undeclared war based on the constant and manifold employment of the devices of everyday forms of resistance on the collective farm. As it confronted the peasantry across the cultural divide, the revolution would founder in the very countryside it sought to transform, evolving into the repressive and bloody contours of Stalinism, and reminding us once again that the October Revolution and the Stalinist industrial and military infrastructure of the USSR were, from the start, built upon a peasant foundation inadequate to sustain a proletarian revolution and too weak to maintain its country's superpower status into the late twentieth century. The peasantry lost the battle against the collective farm, but endured as a cultural entity in spite of, perhaps because of, the Soviet order. The peasant rebellion against collectivization was an act of lasting significance for the story it tells of peasant politics, revolution, and the Stalinist state, and for its reminder of the bravery, dignity, and humanity of a people who struggled against overwhelming odds to resist, protest, survive, and preserve some degree of autonomy within the oppressive confines of Stalinism.

Notes

Introduction

1. See chap. 1.

2. The idea of "depeasantization" is not exclusive to Soviet Communists. Proponents of modernization theory assumed "depeasantization" to be an integral phase of "modernization."

3. *RGAE*, f. 7486, op. 37, d. 122, p. 154; f. 7486, op. 37, d. 49, p. 56. (Vareikis added to his statement: "however, we have not managed to discover this network.")

4. "Blank spots" was a term frequently used in the early phases of the Gorbachev era to describe areas of history previously neglected or falsified.

5. The two major political studies of collectivization are by R. W. Davies, *The Socialist Offensive: The Collectivisation of Soviet Agriculture, 1929–1930* (Cambridge, Mass., 1980); and Moshe Lewin, *Russian Peasants and Soviet Power: A Study of Collectivization*, tr. Irene Nove (New York, 1975).

6. *Stalin's Peasants: Resistance and Survival in the Russian Village after Collectivization* (New York, 1994), p. 48. She minimizes peasant resistance against collectivization to "wailing and lamentations and all manner of passive and furtive resistance."

7. See discussions in David Moon, *Russian Peasants and Tsarist Legislation on the Eve of Reform: Interaction between Peasants and Officialdom* (London, 1992), p. 2; Elizabeth J. Perry, "Rural Violence in Socialist China," *The China Quarterly*, no. 2 (1985), p. 414; Terrence Ranger, "Peasant Consciousness: Culture and Conflict in Zimbabwe," in Teodor Shanin, ed., *Peasants and Peasant Societies*, 2nd ed. (Oxford, 1987), p. 312; James C. Scott, *The Moral Economy of the Peasant: Rebellion and Subsistence in Southeast Asia* (New Haven, 1976), p. 145.

8. See Lewin, *Russian Peasants*, esp. chaps. 2, 3.

9. See Teodor Shanin, *Defining Peasants* (Oxford, 1990), pp. 23–7.

10. See, for example, Kazimierz Dobrowolski, "Peasant Traditional Culture," in Shanin, ed., *Peasants*, p. 272, who writes that "the individuals who deviated from the commonly accepted pattern of behaviour obtaining within their respective classes or groups [among the peasantry] met with such repressive measures as ridicule, reproach, moral censure, ostracism or even the application of official legal sanctions."

11. On "outsiders," see Teodor Shanin, *Russia as a 'Developing Society'*, vol. 1 of *The Roots of Otherness: Russia's Turn of Century*, 2 vols. (New Haven, 1985), p. 83–5.

12. For example, *ibid.*, pp. 83–4; Hamza Alavi, "Peasant Classes and Primordial Loyalties," *Journal of Peasant Studies*, vol. 1, no. 1 (Oct. 1973), pp. 46–8; and Yves-Marie Berce, *History of Peasant Revolts: The Social Origins of Rebellion in Early Modern France*, tr. Amanda Whitmore (Ithaca, 1990), p. 342.

13. See Eugene D. Genovese, *From Rebellion to Revolution: Afro-American Slave Revolts in the Making of the New World* (New York, 1981), pp. 59–60, who notes the "special hatred reserved for traitors" in slave revolts in the Americas.

14. There were sometimes wide variations in calculations and definitions of peasant strata, as well as regional variations in the size of specific groupings. For a range of calculations concerning wealthy peasants, see Moshe Lewin, "Who Was the Soviet Kulak?" in *The Making of the Soviet System* (New York, 1985), p. 122.

15. Eric R. Wolf, *Peasant Wars of the Twentieth Century* (New York, 1969), pp. 291–3. On leveling, see Shanin, *Defining Peasants*, pp. 124–5.

16. Y. Taniuchi, *The Village Gathering in Russia in the Mid-1920s*, University of Birmingham Soviet and East European Monographs, no. 1 (Birmingham, UK, 1968), p. 23. On the fate of the peasant commune after 1917, see also Dorothy Atkinson, *The End of the Russian Land Commune, 1905–1930* (Stanford, 1983); V. P. Danilov, *Sovetskaia dokolkhoznaia derevnia*, 2 vols. (Moscow, 1977–79); and D. J. Male, *Russian Peasant Organisation before Collectivization* (Cambridge, 1971).

17. See especially the argument developed by Barbara Evans Clements, in "The Effects of the Civil War on Women and Family Relations," in Diane P. Koenker, William G. Rosenberg, and Ronald Grigor Suny, eds., *Party, State, and Society in the Russian Civil War: Explorations in Social History* (Bloomington, 1989), pp. 105–22. See also Beatrice Farnsworth and Lynne Viola, eds., *Russian Peasant Women* (New York, 1992), pp. 3–4; Orlando Figes, *Peasant Russia, Civil War* (Oxford, 1989), pp. 70, 101–2, 154–5; Teodor Shanin, *The Awkward Class* (Oxford, 1972), esp. chap. 8.

18. See especially the fine works of Ben Eklof, *Russian Peasant Schools* (Berkeley, 1986); Stephen P. Frank, *Criminality, Cultural Conflict, and Justice in Rural Russia, 1856–1914* (forthcoming); and Christine D. Worobec, *Peasant Russia: Family and Community in the Post-Emancipation Period* (Princeton, 1991).

19. See, e.g., the discussion in Jeffrey Brooks, "The Breakdown in Production and Distribution of Printed Material, 1917–1927," in Abbot Gleason, Peter Kenez, and Richard Stites, eds., *Bolshevik Culture* (Bloomington, 1985), pp. 151–74.

20. Shanin, "Peasantry as a Class," in Shanin, ed., *Peasants*, p. 329.

21. Clifford Geertz, *The Interpretation of Cultures* (New York, 1973), pp. 5, 12.

22. Robert Redfield, *Peasant Society and Culture* (Chicago, 1956), p. 25.

23. See Barrington Moore, Jr., *Social Origins of Dictatorship and Democracy: Lord and Peasant in the Making of the Modern World* (Boston, 1967), p. 471; and Charles Tilly, Louise Tilly, and Richard Tilly, *The Rebellious Century, 1830–1930* (Cambridge, 1975), p. 85, on the importance of popular conceptions of justice.

24. See Scott, *Moral Economy*, p. 3.

25. Ranger, "Peasant Consciousness," p. 313.

26. See Tilly et al., *Rebellious Century*, p. 46.

27. On symbolic inversion, see David Underdown, *Revel, Riot, and Rebellion: Popular Politics and Culture in England, 1603–1660* (Oxford, 1985), p. 111; Le Roy Ladurie, *Carnival at Romans*, tr. Mary Feeney (New York, 1980), pp. 189–92, 316; T. V. Sathyamurthy, "Indian Peasant Historiography," *Journal of Peasant Studies*, vol. 18, no. 1 (Oct. 1990), pp. 111–2, 119; James C. Scott, *Domination and the Arts of Resistance: Hidden Transcripts* (New Haven, 1990), p. 44.

28. See Tilly et al., *Rebellious Century*, pp. 50–1, for definitions and classifications of types of violence according to "competitive," "reactive," and "proactive" forms. Also see James Scott, "Hegemony and the Peasantry," *Politics and Society*, vol. 7, no. 3 (1977), p. 271, on peasants' struggles "to restore and defend customary rights" rather than create a new order.

29. See the excellent article by Matthew Schneer, "A Peasant Community During Russia's First Revolution," *Slavic Review*, vol. 53, no. 1 (spring 1994), pp. 105–6, for a discussion of some of the significant issues and literature relating to the question of state-peasant interaction in 1905.

30. David Warren Sabean, *Power in the Blood: Popular Culture and Village Discourse in Early Modern Germany* (Cambridge, 1984), pp. 2–3.

31. Hannah Arendt, *The Origins of Totalitarianism* (New York, 1973), pp. 311–26; Lewin, *Making of the Soviet System*, chaps. 9, 11, 12.

Chapter 1

1. Mikhail Kalinin used this expression at the First All-Union Conference of Marxist Agronomists. See *Trudy pervoi vsesoiuznoi konferentsii agrarnikov-marksistov*, vol. 1 (Moscow, 1930), pp. 97–8. Also see *Proletarii*, 24 Jan. 1930, p. 1.

2. Scott, *Domination*, pp. xii, 13–14.

3. *Ibid.*, p. xii.

4. On class and the Communists' relation to the working class, see Sheila Fitzpatrick, "The Bolsheviks' Dilemma: Class, Culture, and Politics in the Early Soviet Years," *Slavic Review*, vol. 47, no. 4 (Dec. 1988).

5. See Esther Kingston-Mann, "Breaking the Silence," in Kingston-Mann and Timothy Mixter, eds., *Peasant Economy, Culture, and Politics of European Russia, 1800–1921* (Princeton, 1991), pp. 5–7, for a discussion of Marxist approaches to the peasantry.

6. The contradiction is only apparent. While theory held to determinism, practice tended toward voluntarism. Russian Marxists from Plekhanov had faith that once they mastered the "blueprint of history," they could then exert their will in moving it along its predetermined course. For example, see G. Plekhanov, "On the Question of the Individual's Role in History," *Selected Philosophical Works* (Moscow, 1976), pp. 283–316.

7. V. I. Lenin, *Polnoe sobranie sochinenii*, 5th ed., 55 vols. (Moscow, 1958–66), vol. 37, p. 40. (Hereafter *PSS*.)

8. Lenin had realized the political centrality of the peasantry in revolution in the course of the 1905 Revolution. See Esther Kingston-Mann, *Lenin and the Problem of Marxist Peasant Revolution* (New York, 1983), chaps. 5–6.

9. Lenin, *PSS*, vol. 35, p. 102.

10. L. Kritsman, *Proletarskaia revoliutsiia v derevne* (Moscow-Leningrad,

1929), pp. 6–9. Lenin would admit this dual dimension of the 1917 Revolution in one of his last articles, "Our Revolution." See Lenin, *PSS*, vol. 45, pp. 378–82.

11. Figes, *Peasant Russia*, esp. chap. 3.

12. See Lars T. Lih, *Bread and Authority in Russia, 1914–1921* (Berkeley, 1990).

13. See Figes, *Peasant Russia*, pp. 188–99, for further discussion regarding the *kombedy*.

14. Lenin, *PSS*, vol. 36, p. 316.

15. *Ibid.*

16. *Ibid.*, vol. 37, p. 16.

17. *Ibid.*, vol. 37, pp. 39–42.

18. *Ibid.*, vol. 38, p. 9.

19. *Ibid.*, vol. 38, p.14.

20. *Ibid.*, vol. 39, p. 123. (*Muzhik* is a pejorative for peasant.)

21. *Ibid.*, vol. 39, p. 154.

22. *Ibid.*, vol. 39, p. 277.

23. *Ibid.*, vol. 43, p. 58.

24. *Ibid.*, vol. 43, p. 59.

25. *Ibid.*, vol. 45, p. 77.

26. *Ibid.*, vol. 43, pp. 60–61.

27. *Ibid.*, vol. 45, pp. 369–77, 389–406.

28. *Ibid.*, vol. 45, p. 372.

29. Especially in the key year of 1928. See Lewin, *Russian Peasants*.

30. Lenin, *PSS*, vol. 42, p. 159.

31. See Stephen F. Cohen, *Bukharin and the Bolshevik Revolution*, rev. ed. (New York, 1980), chap. 6.

32. For information on the pervasive nature of war rumors at this time, see *RTsKhIDNI*, f. 17, op. 85, d. 289, pp. 2–14, 17–36.

33. For a discussion of the literature, see Chris Ward, *Stalin's Russia* (London, 1993), pp. 56–9.

34. I. Stalin, *Sochineniia*, 13 vols. (Moscow, 1946–52), vol. 11, pp. 1, 3.

35. This was a consistent theme in Stalin's writing and speeches through the 1920s, articulated most clearly in "K voprosam Leninizma," *ibid.*, vol. 8, p. 27.

36. *Ibid.*, vol. 8, pp. 142–3.

37. *Ibid.*, vol. 10, p. 259.

38. *Ibid.*, vol. 12, pp. 45–7.

39. *Ibid.*, vol. 11, p. 95.

40. *Ibid.*, vol. 11, p. 162.

41. *Ibid.*, vol. 12, pp. 40–1.

42. *Ibid.*, vol. 12, p. 54.

43. *Ibid.*, vol. 12, p. 171.

44. *Ibid.*, vol. 12, p. 149.

45. *Ibid.*, vol. 13, p. 41.

46. *Ibid.*, vol. 12, pp. 162–4.

47. *Ibid.*, vol. 12, p. 132.

48. *XV s"ezd VKP (b). Sten. otchet*, 2 vols. (Moscow, 1961–62), vol. 2, p. 1419.

49. Davies, *Socialist Offensive*, pp. 112, 147.

50. *Ibid.*, p. 442.

51. M. A. Vyltsan, N. A. Ivnitskii, Iu. A. Poliakov, "Nekotorye problemy

istorii kollektivizatsii v SSSR," *Voprosy istorii,* no. 3 (1965), pp. 4–7; Lewin, *Russian Peasants,* chap. 15.

52. *RGAE,* f. 260, op. 1, d. 6, pp. 163–4.

53. Lynne Viola, *The Best Sons of the Fatherland: Workers in the Vanguard of Soviet Collectivization* (New York, 1987), chap. 1.

54. *RTsKhIDNI,* f. 17, op. 2, d. 441, vol. 1: pp. 32, 69–70, 72, 104; vol. 2: 3–18, 33, 40, 42, 50, 56, 61, 64–72.

55. *RGAE,* f. 7486, op. 37, d. 40, pp. 231–230, 220, 217–13, 55–54. (Some *dela* from this archive are numbered backward.)

56. The legislation is in *KPSS v rezoliutsiiakh i resheniiakh s"ezdov, konferentsii i plenumov TsK,* 7th ed., part II (Moscow, 1953), pp. 544–7. For Stalin's injunction regarding the Commissariat of Agriculture (which is noted in the published legislation), see *RGAE,* f. 7486, op. 37, d. 40, p. 233. (*Kolkhoztsentr* had already issued its own decree of 10 December 1929, calling for extremely high rates of livestock socialization. See chap. 3 below.) Stalin's reference to the "elimination of the kulak as a class" at the Conference of Marxist Agronomists, is in Stalin, *Sochineniia,* vol. 12, p. 169. For further information on Stalin's revisions of the Commission's work, see N. A. Ivnitskii, "Istoriia podgotovki postanovleniia TsK VKP(b) o tempakh kollektivizatsii sel'skogo khoziaistva ot 5 ianvaria 1930 g.," *Istochnikovedenie istorii sovetskogo obshchestva,* vyp. 1 (Moscow, 1964), pp. 274–5; and *Pis'ma I. V. Stalina V. M. Molotovu, 1925–1936 gg.* (Moscow, 1995), pp. 171–3, where Stalin writes that the Commission's project is "unsuitable" [*nepodkhodiashchii*].

57. Davies, *Socialist Offensive,* pp. 442–3.

58. For further information, see Lynne Viola, "The Campaign to Eliminate the Kulak as a Class, Winter 1929–1930: A Reevaluation of the Legislation," *Slavic Review,* vol. 45, no. 3 (fall 1986), pp. 503–524.

59. For the central directives on dekulakization, see *RGAE,* f. 7486, op. 37, d. 78, pp. 97–89, 3–1; f. 7486, op. 37, d. 138, pp. 4–2. The main directives have been published in *Neizvestnaia Rossiia. XX vek,* 4 vols. to date (Moscow, 1992–94), vol. 1, pp. 189, 237–50; and *Istoricheskii arkhiv,* no. 4 (1994), pp. 147–52.

60. Davies, *Socialist Offensive,* pp. 442–3.

61. *RGAE,* f. 7446, op. 5, d. 87, p. 2.

62. For example, see *ibid.,* f. 7486, op. 37, d. 78, p. 63.

63. *Ibid.,* f. 7486, op. 37, d. 122, p. 174.

64. See chap. 2 of this book.

65. Stalin, *Sochineniia,* vol. 12, pp. 191–99.

66. Davies, *Socialist Offensive,* pp. 442–3.

67. *Pravda,* 16 Sept. 1988, p. 3; V. N. Zemskov, "Spetsposelentsy (po dokumentatsii NKVD-MVD SSSR)," *Sotsiologicheskie issledovaniia,* no. 11 (1990), p. 3. Also see *RTsKhIDNI,* f. 17, op. 120, d. 52, pp. 20–21, for other (slightly lower) data. The number of families exiled in 1931 was higher than in 1930, probably at least in part because the three-category division of kulaks was no longer in use in 1931. (See *Neizvestnaia Rossiia,* vol. 1, p. 257.) The number of people, mainly "kulaks," receiving sentences of execution in 1930 was 20,201; in 1931, 10,651. See V. P. Popov, "Gosudarstvennyi terror v sovetskoi Rossii. 1923–1953 gg.," *Otechestvennye arkhivy,* no. 2 (1992), pp. 28–9.

68. *RTsKhIDNI,* f. 17, op. 120, d. 52, pp. 69–70, 73, 80–5, 119–20, 186, 189–98; *RGAE,* f. 5675, op. 1, d. 23a, pp. 60, 50–48, 21.

69. Zemskov, "Spetsposelentsy," p. 6.

70. See Figes, *Peasant Russia*.

71. V. G. Tan-Bogoraz, ed., *Staryi i novyi byt* (Leningrad, 1924), pp. 91–2.

72. F. Kretov, *Derevnia posle revoliutsii* (Moscow, 1925), p. 25.

73. *Krest'iane o sovetskoi vlasti* (Moscow-Leningrad, 1929), pp. 157–8, 160–1, 188–90.

74. See *RTsKhIDNI*, f. 17, op. 85, d. 289, pp. 17, 66. All through the 1920s, peasants called for the formation of a "peasant union" to protect the rights of peasants. See *ibid.*, p. 94.

75. *Metallist*, no. 6 (14 Feb. 1929), p. 25; *Dokumenty svidetel'stvuiut: Iz istorii derevni nakanune i v khode kollektivizatsii, 1927–1932 gg.*, eds. V. P. Danilov and N. A. Ivnitskii (hereafter *DS*) (Moscow, 1989), pp. 237–8; Anna Louise Strong, *The Soviets Conquer Wheat* (New York, 1931), p. 30.

76. See chap. 2 for further information on the apocalyptic mood of the peasantry.

77. Maxim Gorky, "On the Russian Peasantry," *Journal of Peasant Studies*, vol. 4, no. 1 (Oct. 1976), pp. 13, 17–22.

78. *Ibid.*, p. 24.

79. *Ibid.*, p. 23.

80. *Ibid.*, p. 24.

81. *Ibid.*, pp. 25–6.

82. See Cathy A. Frierson, *Peasant Icons: Representations of Rural People in Late Nineteenth Century Russia* (New York, 1993), for a description of these earlier generalizations. Stephen Frank provides an illuminating discussion of pre-revolutionary "reform" and "modernization" discourse on the peasantry in "Confronting the Domestic Other: Rural Popular Culture and Its Enemies in Fin-de-Siecle Russia," in Stephen P. Frank and Mark D. Steinberg, eds., *Cultures in Flux: Lower-Class Values, Practices, and Resistance in Late Imperial Russia* (Princeton, 1994), pp. 74–107.

83. Stalin, *Sochineniia*, vol. 12, p. 149.

84. See chap. 6 for further information on women's protest and male responsibility.

85. See chap. 3; and Matt F. Oja, "*Traktorizatsiia* as Cultural Conflict, 1929–1933," *Russian Review*, vol. 51, no. 3 (July 1992), pp. 343–62.

86. Lenin, *PSS*, vol. 37, p. 39.

87. F. Panferov, *Brusski* (New York, n.d. [written from 1928 to 1937]), pp. 104–5.

88. Petro G. Grigorenko, *Memoirs*, tr. Thomas P. Whitney (New York, 1982), p. 216.

89. *Voprosy shefstva*, no. 2 (Feb. 1926), p. 1.

90. For example, see Ia. Burov, *Derevnia na perelome (god raboty v derevne)* (Moscow-Leningrad, 1926), pp. 39–40.

91. *Sovetskaia iustitsiia* (hereafter *SIu*), no. 9 (30 March 1931), p. 2; A. I. Ermolaev, *Kollektivizatsiia i klassovaia bor'ba v Leningradskoi oblasti* (Moscow-Leningrad, 1931), pp. 7–8.

92. See above.

93. Viola, *Best Sons*, p. 131.

94. An OGPU report from February 1930 made reference to "*bedniak* [poor peasant]*-podkulachniki*" and "*seredniak* [middle peasant]*-podkulachniki*." See *RGAE*, f. 7486, op. 37, d. 131, p. 49.

95. On the latter point, see Lynne Viola, "The Second Coming: Class Ene-

mies in the Soviet Countryside, 1927–1935," in J. Arch Getty and Roberta T. Manning, eds., *Stalinist Terror: New Perspectives* (Cambridge, 1993), pp. 73, 77–81.

96. Lynne Viola, "The Peasants' Kulak: Social Identities and Moral Economy in the Soviet Countryside in the 1920s," in V. P. Danilov and Roberta T. Manning, eds., *Collectivization and the Soviet Countryside* (forthcoming).

97. See Lewin, *The Making of the Soviet System*, pp. 121–41, for discussion of this issue.

98. Kari Bronaugh, "Graphic Propaganda and the Revolutionary Laugh: Political Cartoons in *Pravda* and *Prozhektor*, 1923–33," unpubl. ms.

99. See, for example, *RGAE*, f. 7486, op. 37, d. 61, p. 113; f. 260, op. 1, d. 6, p. 39.

100. Viola, "Second Coming," in Getty and Manning, eds., *Stalinist Terror*, p. 79.

101. S. Leikin, "Krest'ianka v klassovoi bor'be," in V. Ulasevich, ed., *Zhenshchina v kolkhoze* (Moscow, 1930), p. 28.

102. Lenin, *PSS*, vol. 37, pp. 39–42.

103. Maurice Hindus, *Red Bread: Collectivization in a Russian Village* (Bloomington, 1988), p. 5.

104. See Lynne Viola, "'L'ivresse du success': les cadres russes et le pouvoir sovietique durant les campagnes de collectivisation de l'agriculture," *Revue des etudes slaves*, vol. 64, no. 1 (1992), pp. 75–101, for a discussion of the dynamics of "dizziness" in the countryside during collectivization.

105. Mikhail Sholokhov, *Virgin Soil Upturned*, tr. Robert Daglish (Moscow, 1981), vol. 1, p. 85.

106. *Proletarii*, 24 Jan. 1930, p. 1.

107. *Zaria vostoka*, 25 May 1930, p. 2; *XIV vserossiiskii s"ezd sovetov. Sten. otchet* (Moscow, 1929), Biulleten' no. 9, pp. 28–29.

108. Georges Agabekov, *OGPU: The Russian Secret Terror*, (New York, 1931), p. 7.

109. *XVI s"ezd VKP(b). Sten. otchet* (Moscow-Leningrad, 1930), pp. 352, 360.

110. T. A. Liapina, ed., "Iz istorii Tambovskoi derevni nachala 30-kh godov," *Sovetskie arkhivy*, no. 6 (1991), p. 48.

111. See John Putnam Demos, *Entertaining Satan: Witchcraft and the Culture of Early New England* (New York, 1982), p. 13, for a discussion of projection in relation to witch hunts.

112. Scott, *Domination*, p. xi.

113. *RGAE*, f. 7486, op. 37, d. 78, p. 90. The Politburo decree is published in *Istoricheskii arkhiv*, no. 4 (1994), pp. 147–52. The OGPU decree from 2 Feb. includes priests among those to be dekulakized. See *Neizvestnaia Rossiia*, vol. 1, p. 238–9.

114. On mass icon burnings, see *RGAE*, f. 7486, op. 37, d. 91, p. 2.

115. *Ibid.*, f. 7486, op. 37, d. 119, p. 14.

116. *Ibid.*, f. 260, op. 1, d. 6, p. 176. (The author of this critical report asked, "Are these not the morals of Shchedrin's heroes?")

117. For example, see M. Golubykh, *Kazach'ia derevnia* (Moscow-Leningrad, 1930), pp. 230–5; Hindus, *Red Bread*, pp. 39–44; Tan-Bogoraz, *Staryi i novyi byt*, p. 48.

118. Berce, *History of Peasant Revolts*, p. 40. See also p. 314, for the re-

moval of bells as punishment for village resistance. Such removals also occurred after Russian village revolts. See chap. 5.

119. *Zapadnyi oblastnoi komitet VKP (b). Sten. otchet 2-i oblastnoi partkonferentsii* (Moscow-Smolensk, 1931), p. 165.

120. Pope Pius XI called for a world-wide day of prayer, to be held on 16 March 1930, on behalf of the persecuted believers of Russia. This action led Stalin to suspend temporarily the antireligious campaign, according to Roy Medvedev, *Let History Judge*, tr. George Shriver (New York, 1989), pp. 229–30.

121. *GARF*, f. 5457, op. 14, d. 135, p. 106.

122. *GARF*, f. 374, op. 9, d. 398, p. 680. See also the document in Nicolas Werth and Gael Moullec, *Rapports secrets sovietiques, 1921–1991: La societe Russe dans les documents confidentiels* (Paris, 1994), pp. 288–91, on Moscow Region church closings and reopenings.

123. Medvedev, *Let History Judge*, p. 230.

124. *Politicheskii i trudovoi pod"em rabochego klassa SSSR (1928–29 gg.). Sb. dokumentov* (Moscow, 1956), p. 543.

125. Davies, *Socialist Offensive*, pp. 227–8.

126. See Viola, "Second Coming," in Getty and Manning, eds., *Stalinist Terror*, pp. 88–90, on the repression of craftsmen.

127. M. M. Gromyko, "Traditional Norms of Behavior and Forms of Interaction of Nineteenth-Century Russian Peasants," in Marjorie Mandelstam Balzer, ed., *Russian Traditional Culture* (Armonk, N.Y., 1992), p. 227.

128. *Neizvestnaia Rossiia*, vol. 1, p. 238–9.

129. See Viola, "Second Coming," in Getty and Manning, eds., *Stalinist Terror*, pp. 70–4, 81–90, for a discussion of the repression that struck local "notables," outsiders, and others.

130. See *Kollektivizatsiia sel'skogo khoziaistva na Severnom Kavkaze* (hereafter, *KSK*) (Krasnodar, 1972), p. 233, for a January 1930 women's conference in Stavropol'skii *okrug* at which the "flowering" of *znakharstvo* and midwifery was condemned. Also see V. G. Tan-Bogoraz, ed., *Komsomol v derevne: ocherki* (Moscow-Leningrad, 1926), pp. 131, 133. For a general discussion of Soviet attempts to take women's health care out of the private domain of midwife and community, see Elizabeth Waters, "Teaching Mothercraft in Postrevolutionary Russia," *Australian Slavonic and East European Studies*, vol. 1, no. 2 (1987), pp. 29–56.

131. See *Neizvestnaia Rossiia*, vol. 2, pp. 337–48, for further, documentary information on the use of church bells for state economic purposes.

132. *Krest'ianskaia pravda*, 16 Aug. 1929, p. 2; 23 Aug. 1929, p. 3.

133. Hindus, *Red Bread*, p. 187. See also Richard Stites, "Bolshevik Ritual Building in the 1920s," in Sheila Fitzpatrick, Alexander Rabinowitch, and Richard Stites, eds., *Russia in the Era of NEP* (Bloomington, 1991), p. 298; and N. S. Polishchuk, "U istokov sovetskikh prazdnikov," *Sovetskaia etnografiia*, no. 6 (1987), pp. 3–15.

134. Viola, *Best Sons*, pp. 160–2.

135. For example, see V. Kavraiskii and I. Khamarmer, *Uroki klassovoi bor'by: itogi vyborov sovetov Sibiri 1928–29* (Novosibirsk, 1929), p. 78.

136. L. P. Egorova, "Klassovaia bor'ba v Zapadnosibirskoi derevne v khode khlebozagotovital'nykh kampanii (1928–1930 gg.)," *Osushchestvlenie agrarnoi politiki KPSS v Sibiri i na Dal'nom vostoke* (Tomsk, 1986), p. 33. The case is also cited in A. P. Ugrovatov, "Bor'ba kommunistov organov iustitsii Sibiri s kulaches-

tvom v khlebozagotovitel'nuiu kampaniiu 1929/30 gg.," *Deiatel'nost' partiinykh organizatsii Sibiri po sotsialisticheskomu preobrazovaniiu i razvitiiu derevni* (Novosibirsk, 1982), p. 96.

137. *Kollektivizatsiia sel'skogo khoziaistva Tsentral'nogo Promyshlennogo raiona* (hereafter, *KTsPO*) (Riazan, 1971), p. 361.

138. *RGAE*, f. 260, op. 1, d. 13, p. 20. (Most commissions remained active only "on paper.")

139. See, for example, the discussion and examples in Ia. Shafir, *Gazeta i derevnia*, 2nd ed. (Moscow-Leningrad, 1924), pp. 27–30; and A. Selishchev, *Iazyk revoliutsionnoi epokhi* (Moscow, 1928), pp. 210–18.

140. Anna Larina, *Nezabyvaemoe* (Moscow, 1989), p. 209.

141. *KTsPO*, p. 408.

142. In Khoper *okrug*, Lower Volga, a collective farm received the name "Death to Kulaks." (*RGAE*, f. 7486, op. 37, d. 101, p. 49.) Other interesting collective farm names included: "Stepan Razin," "Dream of the Revolution," "Art," "Truth," "Sacco and Vanzetti," "Collective Farm in the Name of the Paris Commune," "Lenin's Corner," "Lenin's Work," "Lenin's Spark," "The OGPU Collective Farm," and so on. (*RGAE*, f. 7486, op. 37, d. 40, p. 98.)

143. Victoria E. Bonnell, "The Peasant Woman in Stalinist Political Art of the 1930s," *American Historical Review*, vol. 98, no. 1 (Feb. 1993), pp. 67–8.

144. *Ibid.*, pp. 67–8, 78–9.

Chapter 2

1. Alexander Pushkin, *The Captain's Daughter* (New York, 1978), p. 107.

2. See Anand A. Yang, "A Conversation of Rumors: The Language of Popular *Mentalities* in Late Nineteenth-Century Colonial India," *Journal of Social History*, vol. 21 (spring 1987), p. 485.

3. On rumors and fear, see Sathyamurthy, "Indian Peasant Historiography," p. 124; Georges Lefebvre, *The Great Fear of 1789: Rural Panic in Revolutionary France*, tr. J. White (London, 1973); and Eric Hobsbawm and George Rude, *Captain Swing: A Social History of the Great English Agricultural Uprising of 1830* (New York, 1975), pp. 198–200, 215.

4. On the use of sanctions to maintain unity among subordinate groups, see Scott, *Domination*, p. 27.

5. See John Berger, "The Vision of a Peasant," in Shanin, ed., *Peasants*, p. 282, who writes in regard to peasant mentality that "A closeness to what is unpredictable, invisible, uncontrollable and cyclic predisposes the mind to a religious interpretation of the world."

6. See Shafir, *Gazeta*, p. 99, for a contemporary view of the insight provided by rumors. For a psychoanalytic view of rumors, see C. G. Jung, *Flying Saucers: A Modern Myth of Things Seen in the Skies*, tr. R.F.C. Hull (Princeton, 1978), pp. 13–4, 18, 23. Also see the analysis of meanings of popular prophecy in Ottavia Niccoli, *Prophecy and People in Renaissance Italy*, tr. L. G. Cochrane (Princeton, 1990).

7. Sathyamurthy, "Indian Peasant Historiography," pp. 125–6.

8. See chap. 1.

9. For a view which stresses the specifically Russian nature of this type of thinking, see Nicolas Berdyaev, *The Russian Idea* (New York, 1948).

10. Amos Funkenstein, "A Schedule for the End of the World: The Origins

and Persistence of the Apocalyptic Mentality," in Saul Friedlander et al., eds., *Visions of Apocalypse: End or Rebirth?* (New York, 1985), p. 62; and Thomas A. Kselman, *Miracles and Prophecies in Nineteenth-Century France* (New Brunswick, N.J., 1983), pp. 80–83.

11. Norman Cohn, *The Pursuit of the Millennium* (London, 1957), p. 22; Saul Friedlander, "Introduction," in Friedlander et al., eds., *Visions*, p. 5. See also James C. Scott, *Weapons of the Weak: Everyday Forms of Peasant Resistance* (New Haven, 1985), p. 332; and James J. Donnelly, Jr., "Pastorini and Captain Rock: Millenarianism and Sectarianism in the Rockite Movement of 1821–24," in Samuel Clark and James J. Donnelly, Jr., eds., *Irish Peasants: Violence and Political Unrest, 1780–1914* (Manchester, 1983), p. 104.

12. Cohn, *Pursuit*, pp. 22, 41–2, 82–3, 127–8; also see Bernard Capp on Renaissance England, in "The Political Dimension of Apocalyptic Thought," in C. A. Patrides and Joseph Wittreich, eds., *The Apocalypse in English Renaissance Thought and Literature* (Manchester, 1984), pp. 93–124.

13. Michael Cherniavsky, "The Old Believers and the New Religion," in Michael Cherniavsky, ed., *The Structure of Russian History* (New York, 1970), pp. 140–88; and K. V. Chistov, *Russkie narodnye sotsial'no-utopicheskie legendy XVII–XIX vv.* (Moscow, 1967), pp. 99–112.

14. Saul Friedlander, "Themes of Decline and End in Nineteenth-Century Western Imagination," in Friedlander et al., eds., *Visions*, pp. 62–62, 71. Also see Kselman, *Miracles*, chap. 3.

15. See Boris Shragin and Albert Todd, eds., *Landmarks*, tr. Marian Schwartz (New York, 1977).

16. For discussions of this period, see David M. Bethea, *The Shape of Apocalypse in Modern Russian Fiction* (Princeton, 1989); James H. Billington, *The Icon and the Axe* (New York, 1970), pp. 474–518; and Bernice Glatzer Rosenthal, "Eschatology and the Appeal of Revolution," *California Slavic Studies*, vol. 11 (1980), pp. 105–39.

17. Blok's poem "The Twelve" is an excellent representation of this mixture of revolutionary and apocalyptic themes, as are Bely's novels *The Silver Dove* and *Saint Petersburg*. Similar undertones inform memoirs by Victor Shklovsky, *A Sentimental Journey: Memoirs, 1917–1922*, tr. Richard Sheldon (Ithaca, 1984); and Sergei Mstislavskii, *Five Days Which Transformed Russia*, tr. Elizabeth Kristofovich Zelensky (Bloomington, 1988).

18. V. P. Danilov, "Dinamika naseleniia SSSR za 1917–1929 gg.," in *Arkheograficheskii ezhegodnik za 1968 god* (Moscow, 1970), pp. 245–6.

19. "Black Repartition" denoted the peasant dream of a general redivision of all the lands.

20. See D. P. Rozit, *Partiia i sovety v derevne* (Moscow, 1925), pp. 12–17; D. P. Rozit, *Proverka raboty nizovogo apparata v derevne* (Moscow, 1926), p. 59; N. Rosnitskii, *Polgoda v derevne* (Penza, 1925), pp. 158–9, 165–6; V. Kavraiskii and I. Nusinov, *Klassy i klassovaia bor'ba v sovremennoi derevne*, 2nd ed. (Novosibirsk, 1929), pp. 143–5, 154; *Litso Donskoi derevni k 1925 g.*, pp. 40–1; A. Luzhin and M. Rezunov, *Nizovoi sovetskii apparat* (Moscow, 1929), p. 150.

21. For examples, see P. Fedin, *Klassovaia bor'ba v derevne* (Voronezh, 1929), pp. 5–12; A. Gagarin, *Khoziaistvo, zhizn' i nastroeniia derevni* (Moscow and Leningrad, 1925), p. 28; M. Golubykh, *Ocherki glukhoi derevni* (Moscow, 1926), p. 71; N. G. Komarov, *Litso klassovogo vraga* (Leningrad, 1929), pp. 30–2, 44–6; *Litso Donskoi derevni*, pp. 29–31, 40–1.

22. This problem is illustrated in *Derevnia pri NEP'e: kogo schitat' kulakom, kogo—truzhenikom, chto govoriat ob etom krest'iane?* (Moscow, 1924). Also see Ia. Iakovlev, *Derevnia kak ona est'*, 2nd ed. (Moscow, 1923), pp. 12–13; and Rosnitskii, *Polgoda*, pp. 25–9.

23. E. A. Ivanova, "Bor'ba s kulachestvom v khode stroitel'stva kollektivnykh form khoziaistva v derevne (Tiumenskii okrug)," *Uch. zap. Mogilevskogo gos. ped. instituta*, vyp. II (1955), p. 108.

24. I. Sh. Frenkel', "Bor'ba s kulachestvom v Kurskoi gubernii vo vremia khlebozagotovitel'nykh kampanii 1928 i 1929 gg.," *Uch. zap. Kurskogo ped. instituta*, vyp. VI (1957), p. 40.

25. See Alexei Velidov, "The 'Decree' on the Nationalization of Women: The Story of a Mystification," *Moscow News*, nos. 8–9 (1990), p. 13.

26. Selishchev, *Iazyk*, p. 215.

27. Ia. Dorofeev, *Derevnia Moskovskoi gubernii* (Moscow, 1923), p. 44.

28. Brooks, "Breakdown in Production and Distribution of Printed Material," in Gleason et al., eds., *Bolshevik Culture*, pp. 153, 165.

29. Shafir, *Gazeta*, passim; Dorofeev, *Derevnia*, pp. 42–3; Golubykh, *Ocherki*, pp. 50, 52. Also see occasional evidence in Tan-Bogoraz, *Staryi i novyi byt*, pp. 53–7; and Tan-Bogoraz, *Revoliutsiia v derevne*, pt. I (Moscow-Leningrad, 1924), pp. 73–6, although it should be noted that Tan and his collaborators generally saw a *decline* in superstitions among the peasants they observed. See also Lewin, "Grappling with Stalinism, " in *Making of the Soviet System*, p. 298.

30. A. M. Bol'shakov, *Derevnia, 1917–27* (Moscow, 1927), p. 332; A. Evdokimov, *Kolkhozy v klassovykh boiakh* (Leningrad, 1930), p. 19; *Litso Donskoi derevni*, p. 165; Rozit, *Partiia*, p. 85; Tan-Bogoraz, *Komsomol*, pp. 16–7.

31. Tan-Bogoraz, *Komsomol*, p. 16.

32. The use of *chastushki* to mock tradition and to present social criticism was a continuation from the prerevolutionary period. See Stephen P. Frank, "Simple Folk, Savage Customs? Youth, Sociability, and the Dynamics of Culture in Rural Russia, 1856–1914," *Journal of Social History*, vol. 25, no. 4 (1992), pp. 723–4.

33. Tan-Bogaraz, *Staryi i novyi byt*, p. 49.

34. Tan-Bogoraz, *Komsomol*, p. 71. The rhyming pun is lost in translation. The *chastushka* reads: "Ded Nikita bogomol,/Chasto v tserkvi molitsia,/On boitsia,/Chto syn ego okomsomolitsia." A variation on this *chastushka* read: "Kak u tetki Akuliny,/Staroi bogomolochki,/Vnuchki Pan'ka, Tan'ka, San'ka, Man'ka—/Komsomolochki."

35. Bol'shakov, *Derevnia*, p. 336. ("Takikh shpionerov-pionerov nam ne nado.")

36. A. Evdokimov, *V bor'be za molodezh'* (Leningrad, 1929), p. 41; E. L. Fertaup, *Nizovoi sovetskii apparat i derevnia Urala* (Sverdlovsk, 1925), p. 115; *Litso Donskoi derevni*, p. 186.

37. Tan-Bogoraz, *Komsomol*, p. 188. In *Why I Escaped* (New York, nd), pp. 149–52, the emigre Peter Pirogov recalled, in a similar fashion, how he feared his father's reaction when he became a pioneer.

38. N. Lagovier, *O samosudakh* (Moscow-Leningrad, 1927), p. 4. Clashing cultures in the prerevolutionary period led the educated public to similar conclusions about the rise of hooliganism at the turn of the century. See Frank, "Confronting the Domestic Other," pp. 74–107.

39. For examples, see Gagarin, *Khoziaistvo*, p. 93; Golubykh, *Ocherki*, pp.

48–52, 69–71; Lagovier, *O samosudakh*, p. 4; *Litso Donskoi derevni*, pp. 115–6. Also note Lewin's conclusion in "Rural Society in Twentieth-Century Russia," in *Making of the Soviet System*, p. 55.

40. Tan-Bogoraz, *Staryi i novyi byt*, p. 122. This quote is from the following *chastushka*: "Komissary cherti,/Net na vas i smerti,/Vy by okoleli,/My by ne zhaleli."

41. *Dvoeverie* originally referred to that mixture of paganism and Christianity that characterized the peasants' faith.

42. Burov, *Derevnia*, pp. 76–7; Komarov, *Litso*, p. 24.

43. Tan-Bogoraz, *Staryi i novyi byt*, pp. 55–7.

44. Rosnitskii, *Polgoda*, p. 171.

45. Komarov, *Litso*, pp. 54–55.

46. Bol'shakov, *Derevnia*, p. 412. Also see A. Bol'shakov, *Kommuna Kudrova* (Leningrad, 1930), p. 147; and Richard Stites, *Revolutionary Dreams* (New York, 1989), pp. 111–4, for information on new Communist rituals.

47. A. Angarov, *Klassovaia bor'ba v derevne i sel'sovet* (Moscow, 1929), p. 21.

48. Golubykh, *Kazach'ia*, pp. 230–5; Hindus, *Red Bread*, pp. 40–4, 191; Tan-Bogoraz, *Staryi i novyi byt*, p. 48.

49. According to Evdokimov, *V bor'be za molodezh'*, pp. 46–8, three-fourths of the Skoptsy were castrated after the Revolution, thereby indicating (according to the author) an increase in membership (but little potential for organic renewal). An increase in membership among Molokane is noted in *Saratovskaia partiinaia organizatsiia v gody sotsialisticheskoi industrializatsii strany i podgotovki sploshnoi kollektivizatsii sel'skogo khoziaistva (1926–1929 gg.)* (Saratov, 1960), pp. 237–8.

50. A. Dolotov, *Tserkov' i sektantstvo v Sibiri* (Novosibirsk, 1930), pp. 3–4, 77–8; Gagarin, *Khoziaistvo*, pp. 85–9; A. Iartsev, *Sekta evangel'skikh khristian*, 2nd ed. (Moscow, 1928), pp. 8–9, 11; *Saratovskaia partiinaia organizatsiia*, pp. 237–8.

51. Evdokimov, *V bor'be za molodezh'*, pp. 27–9.

52. Dolotov, *Tserkov*, pp. 77, 114.

53. Evdokimov, *V bor'be za molodezh'*, p. 41.

54. Dolotov, *Tserkov*, pp. 60, 68–9.

55. *Ibid.*, pp. 54, 56–7, 69, 73. In the Don, several cases were reported of Old Believer families who would not allow their children to visit the reading hut or Komsomol cell (*Litso Donskoi derevni*, pp. 117–8). However, most contemporary commentators noted a decline in the number of Old Believers after the Revolution. (Dolotov, *Tserkov*, p. 73; Rosnitskii, *Polgoda*, p. 224).

56. See Cohn, *Pursuit*, pp. 77–80; and Kselman, *Miracles*, pp. 135–6, 138, on the relationship between apocalyptic thinking and anti–Semitism.

57. Dolotov, *Tserkov*, p. 68.

58. Rozit, *Proverka*, p. 85.

59. On cases of anti-Semitism in the village, see Evdokimov, *Kolkhozy*, p. 34; and Evdokimov, *V bor'be za molodezh'*, pp. 5, 59. Angarov, *Klassovaia bor'ba*, p. 13, also makes note of rural anti-Semitism.

60. Cohn, *Pursuit*, pp. 77–80; Kselman, *Miracles*, pp. 135–6, 138.

61. See Kselman, *Miracles*, pp. 59, 77, on how prophecies and healing cults helped nineteenth-century French peasants make sense of the chaos and flux in their world by appealing to traditional ways of understanding.

62. For cases of renewed icons, see *Bednota*, 8 Jan. 1924, p. 2; 11 Jan. 1924, p. 1; *Sudebnaia praktika* (hereafter *SP*), no. 6 (29 March 1929), p. 15; Shafir, *Gazeta*, pp. 114–5; and Dolotov, *Tserkov*, p. 48.

63. Tan-Bogoraz, *Revoliutsiia*, pt. II, p. 7.

64. Golubykh, *Kazach'ia*, p. 232.

65. V. G. Tan-Bogoraz, ed., *Obnovlennaia derevnia* (Leningrad, 1925), p. 86. When they heard this rumor, the peasant men in the village apparently were skeptical, but the women believed and planned an expedition to "check the accuracy" of the rumor.

66. Dolotov, *Tserkov*, p. 45; Shafir, *Gazeta*, p. 105.

67. Dolotov, *Tserkov*, pp. 43–4.

68. *Ibid.*, pp. 47–8.

69. Kselman, *Miracles*, p. 49.

70. Shafir, *Gazeta*, pp. 107–110, 114.

71. Tan-Bogoraz, *Revoliutsiia*, pt. I, p. 8.

72. Dolotov, *Tserkov*, pp. 46–7.

73. Scott, "Hegemony," p. 284.

74. Eric R. Wolf, "On Peasant Rebellions," in Shanin, ed., *Peasants*, p. 373.

75. Shafir, *Gazeta*, pp. 99, 117; *Saratovskaia partiinaia organizatsiia*, p. 104; Frenkel', "Bor'ba s kulachestvom v Kurskoi gubernii," p. 39. Also see V. V. Kondrashin, "Golod 1932–1933 godov v derevniakh Povolzh'ia," *Voprosy istorii*, no. 6 (1991), p. 180, for famine-era rumors telling peasants that the famine was organized to get the people to give up their gold and other valuables to the state hard currency exchange in order to get food.

76. For example, see R. N. Kireev, "K voprosu ob istoricheskoi neizbezhnosti likvidatsii kulachestva kak klassa (po materialam Iuzhnogo Zaural'ia)," *Voprosy agrarnoi istorii Urala i Zapadnoi Sibiri* (Kurgan, 1971), p. 232.

77. *RGAE*, f. 7446, op. 5, d. 87, p. 12. For the mid-1920s, see Kretov, *Derevnia*, pp. 26–7.

78. *RTsKhIDNI*, f. 78, op. 1, d. 358, p. 72.

79. Kireev, "K voprosu," p. 232.

80. *Kollektivizatsiia i razvitie sel'skogo khoziaistva na Kubani* (Hereafter, *KK*) (Krasnodar, 1981), pp. 113–5; *RGAE*, f. 7446, op. 5, d. 87, p. 12; *Sotsialisticheskoe pereustroistvo sel'skogo khoziaistva Moldavskoi ASSR* (Kishinev, 1964), p. 281.

81. See the typology in Lynne Viola, "Guide to Document Series on Collectivization," in Sheila Fitzpatrick and Lynne Viola, eds., *A Researcher's Guide to Sources on Soviet Social History in the 1930s* (Armonk, N.Y., 1990).

82. For examples, see N. A. Ivnitskii, ed., "Dokladnaia zapiska Kolkhoztsentra v TsK VKP (b) o kolkhoznom stroitel'stve v 1928–1929 gg.," *Materialy po istorii SSSR: dokumenty po istorii sovetskogo obshchestva*, 7 vols. (Moscow, 1955–59), vol. 7, p. 245; A. Karavaev and A. Sosnovskii, *Krasnopolianskii gigant* (Moscow, 1929), pp. 71–2, 85; G. Timofeev, *Mezha umerla: Krasnopolianskii raion sploshnoi kollektivizatsii* (Moscow, 1930), p. 77; Leikin, "Krest'ianka," pp. 27–8; O. M. Gribkova and M. E. Lepekhina, eds., "Uchastie rabochikh-metallistov v kolkhoznom stroitel'stve vesnoi 1930," *Istoricheskii arkhiv*, no. 2 (1955), pp. 48–9; *Bol'shevik*, no. 13 (15 July 1930), p. 68; *Kollektivist*, nos. 15–6 (Aug. 1930), p. 2.

83. "Sovetskaia vlast' ne ot boga, a ot antikhrista." L. Erikhonov, *Kulak pered sudom*, (Samara, 1929), pp. 42–3.

84. M. N. Chernomorskii, ed., "Rol' rabochikh brigad v bor'be za sploshnuiu kollektivizatsii v Tambovskoi derevne," *Materialy*, vol. 1, p. 380; Fedin, *Klassovaia bor'ba*, pp. 58, 60; *Kollektivizatsiia sel'skogo khoziaistva v Severo-Zapadnom raione* (hereafter, *KSZ*) (Leningrad, 1970), pp. 162–3; Timofeev, *Mezha umerla*, pp. 17, 20–1.

85. N. V. Elizarov, *Likvidatsiia kulachestva kak klassa* (Moscow-Leningrad, 1930), pp. 68–9; Erikhonov, *Kulak pered sudom*, pp. 51–3; Evdokimov, *Kolkhozy*, p. 34; *Istoriia kollektivizatsiia sel'skogo khoziaistva Urala* (hereafter, *IU*) (Perm, 1983), pp. 115–6; *KSZ*, pp. 162–3.

86. *RGAE*, f. 7486, op. 37, d. 61, p. 109.

87. *KSZ*, p. 91; Leikin, "Krest'ianka," pp. 41–2; Lynne Viola, "Notes on the Background of Soviet Collectivisation: Metal Worker Brigades in the Countryside, Autumn 1929," *Soviet Studies*, vol. 36, no. 2 (April 1984), p. 213.

88. *RGAE*, f. 7486, op. 37, d. 61, pp. 113–12, 110.

89. *KK*, pp. 52–3.

90. Ivnitskii, ed., "Dokladnaia zapiska," p. 242. The expression "Bartholomew's Night massacre" appears to be synonymous today with pogrom or massacre in the Russian vernacular. One may surmise that the expression had the same meaning among peasants in the 1920s and 1930s. (My thanks to Donald Van Atta for pointing this out.)

91. *KTsPO*, p. 336.

92. Karavaev and Sosnovskii, *Krasnopolianskii gigant*, p. 72; I. I. Ivanov, "Likvidatsiia v Chuvashii kulachestva kak klassa," in *Istoriia i kul'tura Chuvashskoi ASSR* (Cheboksary, 1971), vyp. 1, pp. 208–9.

93. *GARF*, f. 5469, op. 13, d. 123, pp. 78–91.

94. *RGAE*, f. 7446, op. 5, d. 87, p. 11.

95. *Ibid.*, f. 7486, op. 37, d. 131, p. 157.

96. *Ibid.*, f. 7486, op. 37, d. 193, pp. 129, 69.

97. For example, L. P. Egorova, "K voprosu o kontrrevoliutsionnoi deiatel'nosti kulachestva v Zapadnoi Sibiri v 1928–1929 gg.," in *Sbornik rabot aspirantov kafedry istorii KPSS* (Tomsk, 1974), vol. 11, pp. 96–7; Frenkel', "Bor'ba s kulachestvom v Kurskoi gubernii," p. 39; Shafir, *Gazeta*, pp. 25, 45, 115–6. A special meeting was required in the remote village of Beliaevka in the Urals to convince peasants that mid-1920s rumors about war were not true. See Golubykh, *Ocherki*, p. 43. See also the reports based on OGPU information about the panicky mood in the countryside surrounding war rumors in 1927, in *RTsKhIDNI*, f. 17, op. 85, d. 289, pp. 2–14, 17–36.

98. *DS*, p. 454; Erikhonov, *Kulak pered sudom*, pp. 42–3; Evdokimov, *Kolkhozy*, p. 33; *Istoriia kolektivizatsii sil's'kogo gospodarstva Ukrains'koi RSR* (Kiev, 1965), vol. 2, p. 545; N. A. Ivnitskii, *Klassovaia bor'ba v derevne i likvidatsiia kulachestva kak klassa* (Moscow, 1972), p. 106; Karavaev and Sosnovskii, *Krasnopolianskii gigant*, p. 71; *Kollektivizatsiia sel'skogo khoziaistva Iakutskoi ASSR* (Iakutsk, 1978), pp. 92–3; *KTsPO*, pp. 399–400; *KSZ*, pp. 75–6; *Kollektivizatstiia sel'skogo khoziaistva v Zapadnom raione* (hereafter, *KZ*) (Smolensk, 1968), pp. 256, 386–7; *Sotsialisticheskoe pereustroistvo sel'skogo khoziaistva Moldavskoi*, p. 281 (here it was rumored that the Romanians would invade); Timofeev, *Mezha umerla*, p. 82; Ugrovatov, "Bor'ba," p. 85.

99. Evdokimov, *Kolkhozy*, p. 33; *KTsPO*, pp. 398–9; *RGAE*, f. 7486, op. 37, d. 131, p. 34; *GARF*, f. 5457, op. 14, d. 114, p. 26; *Nizhevolzhskii kolkhoznik*, nos. 15–6 (Aug. 1931), pp. 38–40; Lynne Viola, "Bab'i Bunty and Peasant

Women's Protest During Collectivization," *Russian Review*, vol. 45, no. 1 (1986), p. 31.

100. *RGAE*, f. 260, op. 1, d. 6, p. 38.

101. Velidov, "Decree on the Nationalization of Women," p. 13.

102. Viola, "Bab'i bunty," pp. 31–2.

103. *RGAE*, f. 7486, op. 37, d. 131, p. 34; f. 7486, op. 37, d. 102, p. 56; *Kollektivizatsiia sel'skogo khoziaistva Bashkirskoi ASSR* (Ufa, 1980), p. 79; *KTsPO*, pp. 398–9.

104. *RGAE*, f. 260, op. 1, d. 6, p. 50.

105. Leikin, "Krest'ianka," p. 30. This rumor also circulated in the Middle Volga (see *RGAE*, f. 7446, op. 5, d. 87, p. 12), although here rumor had it that the women were being sent to China because of a supposed dearth of Chinese women. News of the creation of day-care centers and an overnight day care called a "children's city" (*detskii gorod*) may have inspired these rumors (see D. Katsenel'baum, "Zhenshchina v kolkhoze," in Ulasevich, ed., *Zhenshchina*, p. 104). In the commune "Kolos," all children did actually live together in a children's home (see A. Sokolov, *Kommuna 'Kolos'* [Moscow-Leningrad, 1929], pp. 67–8). See Viola, "Bab'i bunty," p. 31, for other cases when rumors seemingly of the absurd were inspired by actual events.

106. Karavaev and Sosnovskii, *Krasnopolianskii gigant*, p. 84.

107. Evdokimov, *Kolkhozy*, pp. 27–8.

108. Viola, "Bab'i bunty," p. 30.

109. M. E. Kolesova, "Kollektivizatsiia i krest'ianstvo v zerkale pisem 25–tysiachnikov," *Sovetskie arkhivy*, no. 3 (1991), p. 77.

110. *RGAE*, f. 7446, op. 5, d. 87, p. 12.

111. *Ibid.*, f. 7486, op. 37, d. 61, p. 45.

112. *Ibid.*, f. 7486, op. 37, d. 192, p. 383.

113. *Ibid.*, f. 7486, op. 37, d. 192, p. 422.

114. *Ibid.*, f. 7486, op. 37, d. 192, p. 422.

115. Evdokimov, *Kolkhozy*, p. 27.

116. *KTsPO*, pp. 398–9; *KZ*, p. 256; *RGAE*, f. 7486, op. 37, d. 91, p. 5; f. 7486, op. 37, d. 61, p. 113; f. 7486, op. 37, d. 131, p. 50; f. 7486, op. 37, d. 193, p. 69; and *KK*, pp. 73–5.

117. *RGAE*, f. 7486, op. 37, d. 49, p. 44; d. 61, p. 73.

118. *Ibid.*, f. 7486, op. 37, d. 61, p. 131.

119. *Ibid.*, f. 7486, op. 37, d. 193, p. 69; *Istoriia kolektivizatsii sil's'kogo gospodarstva Ukrains'koi RSR*, vol. 2, p. 545; *KK*, pp. 73–5; *KZ*, pp. 386–7.

120. See, for example, Timofeev, *Mezha umerla*, p. 82.

121. For a different view, taking more literally peasant references to serfdom, see Fitzpatrick, *Stalin's Peasants*, pp. 68–9.

122. Bethea, *Shape of Apocalypse*, pp. 47, 53.

123. On this linkage, see Niccoli, *Prophecy and People*, pp. 131, 134–6.

124. Sathyamurthy, "Indian Peasant Historiography," p. 119.

125. See Wolf, "On Peasant Rebellions," in Shanin, ed., *Peasants*, p. 373, who writes that "Peasant anarchism and an apocalyptic vision of the world, together, provide the ideological fuel that drives the rebellious peasantry."

126. Angarov, *Klassovaia bor'ba*, p. 19; Ermolaev, *Kollektivizatsiia*, p. 48; *SIu*, no. 6 (28 Feb. 1930), pp. 5–6.

127. On women transmitting rumors, see Ermolaev, *Kollektivizatsiia*, p. 48; and Viola, "Bab'i Bunty," pp. 28–33.

128. On marginal rural inhabitants and rumors, see Elizarov, *Likvidatsiia*, p. 68; Evdokimov, *Kolkhozy*, pp. 31, 34; Leikin, "Krest'ianka," p. 28.

129. Aleksandr I. Solzhenitsyn, *The Gulag Archipelago*, tr. Thomas P. Whitney (New York, 1975), vol. 2, p. 103.

130. Kolesova, "Kollektivizatsiia i krest'ianstvo," p. 83.

131. *RGAE*, f. 7486, op. 37, d. 102, pp. 53.

132. *Ibid.*, f. 7486, op. 37, d. 102, p. 56.

133. Leikin, "Krest'ianka," pp. 41–2; also see *Kollektivizatsiia sel'skogo khoziaistva v Nizhegorodskom-Gor'kovskom krae* (hereafter *KNG*) (Kirov, 1985), p. 142; and Karavaev and Sosnovskii, *Krasnopolianskii gigant*, pp. 71–2.

134. *The Penal Code of the RSFSR* (London, 1934), pp. 25, 50. (It is not clear how often this article was used, but its use is suggested in Erikhonov, *Kulak pered sudom*, p. 34; as well as in *Proletarii* [14 Jan. 1930], p. 1, where the Moscow Regional Procurator [in an article entitled, "Last Warning: For Counterrevolutionary Agitation We Will Shoot"] called for the application of this article to any kulak spreading rumors.)

135. Angarov, *Klassovaia bor'ba*, p. 14. The rhyme is lost in translation. The original is: "Traktor pashet gluboko,/Zemli sokhnut./Skoro vse kolkhozniki/ S golodu podokhnut."

136. Evdokimov, *Kolkhozy*, pp. 34–5. (Quoted in part)

137. Kavraiskii and Khamarmer, *Uroki*, p. 22.

138. *Put trudovykh pobed* (hereafter, *PTP*) (Volgograd, 1967), pp. 270–5; *KNG*, p. 142.

139. *GARF*, f. 5469, op. 13, d. 123, pp. 28–40.

140. Dolotov, *Tserkov*, p. 43.

141. Cohn, *Pursuit*, pp. 41–2, 82–3, 127–8; Kselman, *Miracles*, p. 65.

142. It is not without interest to note that Peter Burke has suggested that the story of Christ of the Second Coming may actually have served as the prototype for the stories of the return of dead rulers which figured so largely in cases of popular pretenders to the throne. See his *Popular Culture in Early Modern Europe* (New York, 1978), pp. 152–3. The surfacing of the idea of the Second Coming in the Soviet countryside may have been partly determined by the demise of naive monarchism, although there are occasional references to the appearance of a Romanov. (These references, however, were more frequently encountered among aristocratic circles in the emigration than among Russian peasants.)

143. On the ferment and constant debate over collectivization in the villages, see Hindus, *Red Bread*, pp. 22–32, 166–83.

144. See also chap. 4.

145. *RGAE*, f. 7446, op. 5, d. 87, p. 23; V. A. Demeshkin, "Voprosy klassovoi bor'by v Zapadnosibirskoi derevne nakanune i v khode kollektivizatsii i ikh osveshchenie v sovetskoi istoricheskoi literature," *Sbornik rabot aspirantov kafedry istorii KPSS*, vyp. 13 (Tomsk, 1975), p. 115.

146. *RGAE*, f. 7446, op. 5, d. 39, p. 15.

147. *Kollektivist*, nos. 15–6 (Aug. 1930), p. 2.

148. Daniel Field, *Rebels in the Name of the Tsar* (Boston, 1976).

149. See Viola, "Bab'i Bunty," pp. 38–42, and chap. 6 below.

150. This aspect of apocalyptic rumors—i.e., their function as a religious justification for rebellion—is consistent with earlier patterns of peasant rebellion in prerevolutionary Russia. Legends of "tsar deliverers" (one of several basic themes in peasant protest) served as a "sanction" for struggle against the ruling

tsar. See Chistov, *Russkie narodnye sotsial'no-utopicheskie legendy*, p. 233.

151. Ladurie, *Carnival*, p. 316.

152. See Michael Adas, *Prophets of Rebellion: Millenarian Protest Movements against the European Colonial Order* (Chapel Hill, N.C., 1979), p. 81, for a discussion of the role which the absence of alternative modes of expression, political organizations, and methods played in the peasant turn to millenarian modes of expression.

Chapter 3

1. Scott, *Weapons*, p. xvi.

2. Isaac Deutscher, *Stalin*, 2nd ed. (New York, 1977), p. 325.

3. *XVI s"ezd*, p. 579.

4. *Ibid.*, p. 633.

5. *Ibid.*, p. 634.

6. N. Ia. Gushchin and V. A. Il'inykh, *Klassovaia bor'ba v Sibirskoi derevne 1920-e—seredina 1930-kh gg.* (Novosibirsk, 1987), p. 213; *Istoriia kollektivizatsii sel'skogo khoziaistva v Vostochnoi Sibiri* (hereafter, *IVS*) (Irkutsk, 1979), p. 17. Also see *RGAE*, f. 7486, op. 37, d. 131, p. 108.

7. *KZ*, p. 309.

8. *RGAE*, f. 7446, op. 5, d. 87, p. 35.

9. Ivnitskii, *Klassovaia bor'ba*, pp. 122–4.

10. *RGAE*, f. 7486, op. 37, d. 61, p. 37.

11. *Ibid.*, f. 7486, op. 37, d. 61, p. 25.

12. Viola, "Campaign," pp. 508–11; and *Proletarii*, 14 Jan. 1930, p. 1.

13. N. A. Ivnitskii, *Kollektivizatsiia sel'skogo khoziaistva v SSSR* (Moscow, 1988), p. 9; G. I. Shmelov, "Ne smet' komandovat'!" *Oktiabr'*, no. 2 (Feb. 1988), pp. 9–10.

14. *KZ*, p. 227.

15. *RGAE*, f. 7486, op. 37, d. 40, p. 233. The more cautious recommendations of the commission are in *RGAE*, f. 7486, op. 37, d. 40, pp. 217–12. See also Ivnitskii, "Istoriia," pp. 274–5; N. I. Nemakov, *Kommunisticheskaia partiia— organizator massovogo kolkhoznogo dvizheniia* (Moscow, 1966), pp. 100–1.

16. *KPSS v rezoliutsiiakh*, pp. 544–7.

17. Stalin, *Sochineniia*, vol. 12, pp. 191–9. The Central Committee decree of 14 March 1930 is in *KPSS v rezoliutsiiakh*, pp. 548–51.

18. Viola, "Campaign," p. 507.

19. *Ibid.*, pp. 506–12. The TsIK-SNK decree of 1 February 1930 and accompanying secret instructions are published in *Spetspereselentsy v Zapadnoi Sibiri, 1930–vesna 1931 g.*, ed. V. P. Danilov and S. A. Krasil'nikov (Novosibirsk, 1992), pp. 20–25. See also chap. 1.

20. *Sobranie zakonov i rasporiazhenii raboche-krest'ianskogo pravitel'stva SSSR*, no. 6 (13 Feb. 1930), pp. 137–8; *Sobranie uzakonenii i rasporiazhenii raboche-krest'ianskogo pravitel'stva RSFSR*, no. 3 (10 Feb. 1930), pp. 39–40.

21. *IVS*, pp. 118–9; *Na leninskom puti* (Ivanovo-Voznesensk obkom VKP[b]), no. 12 (28 Sept. 1929), p. 21.

22. *SIu*, no. 19 (10 July 1930), p. 31; *Istoriia kolkhoznogo prava: Sbornik zakonodatel'nykh materialov SSSR i RSFSR, 1917–1958 gg.*, 2 vols. (Moscow, 1959), vol. 1, pp. 189–90. Regional authorities followed suit with their own decrees forbidding the slaughter of certain types of livestock. See, for example, *Kol-*

lektivizatsiia sel'skogo khoziaistva v Srednem Povolzh'e (hereafter, *KSP*) (Kuiby-shev, 1970), pp. 215–18.

23. I. Vareikis, *O sploshnoi kollektivizatsii i likvidatsii kulachestva kak klassa* (Voronezh, 1930), p. 25.

24. *Molot*, 14 Jan. 1930, p. 2.

25. *SIu*, nos. 24–25 (10–20 Sept. 1930), p. 6. Also see V. K. Medvedev, *Krutoi povorot* (Saratov, 1961), p. 110.

26. *RGAE*, f. 7486, op. 37, d. 78, p. 74.

27. *RTsKhIDNI*, f. 17, op. 32, d. 184, p. 45.

28. For example, see Stalin, *Sochineniia*, vol. 11, pp. 4–5.

29. Jerzy F. Karcz, "Thoughts on the Grain Problem," *Soviet Studies*, vol. 18, no. 4 (April 1967), pp. 409–12, 414–5, 421–2.

30. See Davies, *Socialist Offensive*, pp. 44–5.

31. *RGAE*, f. 7486, op. 37, d. 77, p. 55.

32. *Ibid.*, f. 7486, op. 37, d. 193, pp. 126–16, 82.

33. For example, see *XVI s'ezd*, p. 634; *KSK*, pp. 217–8; and Gushchin and Il'inykh, *Klassovaia bor'ba*, p. 212.

34. *RGAE*, f. 7486, op. 37, d. 77, p. 57.

35. *Ibid.*, f. 7486, op. 37, d. 61, p. 74.

36. *Ibid.*, f. 7486, op. 37, d. 61, p. 129.

37. *Ibid.*, f. 7446, op. 5, d. 87, p. 38. It is also likely that in MTS regions, collectivization was more advanced; *razbazarivanie* may have been more pro-nounced as a consequence.

38. *Ibid.*, f. 7486, op. 37, d. 40, p. 214.

39. *XVI s"ezd*, p. 633.

40. Hindus, *Red Bread*, pp. 165–6.

41. *RGAE*, f. 7486, op. 37, d. 193, p. 27.

42. *Ibid.*, f. 7486, op. 37, d. 61, p. 49.

43. *Ibid.*, f. 7486, op. 37, d. 61, p. 129.

44. *Kollektivizatsiia sel'skogo khoziaistva v Tsentral'no-Chernozemnoi ob-lasti* (hereafter, *KTsChO*) (Voronezh, 1978), p. 123.

45. Pirogov, *Why I Escaped*, pp. 192–4, 206–8.

46. *RGAE*, f. 7486, op. 37, d. 61, pp. 55–4; Timofeev, *Mezha umerla*, p. 57. Some peasants sold their livestock to pay off debts before entering the collec-tive farm. See *RGAE*, f. 7486, op. 37, d. 61, pp. 41, 38.

47. *RGAE*, f. 7486, op. 37, d. 133, p. 151; f. 7486, op. 37, d. 77, p. 57.

48. *Ibid.*, f. 7486, op. 37, d. 77, p. 56.

49. *Molot*, 7 Jan. 1930, p. 5.

50. *RGAE*, f. 7446, op. 5, d. 87, p. 38–9.

51. *Ibid.*, f. 7486, op. 37, d. 61, p. 75.

52. *Proletarii*, 8 Jan. 1930, p. 1.

53. *RGAE*, f. 7446, op. 5, d. 87, p. 36.

54. *Ibid.*, f. 7486, op. 37, d. 193, p. 23.

55. *SP*, no. 3 (28 Feb. 1930), p. 19.

56. *SIu*, no. 2 (20 Jan. 1930), p. 4.

57. *RGAE*, f. 7446, op. 5, d. 23, pp. 29–30; *KSK*, p. 226; *RGAE*, f. 7486, op. 37, d. 61, p. 74. In the Kuban, insurance premiums for horses paid from 30 to 40 rubles, thus doubling current market value. (*RGAE*, f. 7486, op. 37, d. 61, p. 74) That peasants continued to use this stratagem is clear from an RSFSR Commissariat of Finance circular of mid-to late 1932, published in *SIu*, no. 28 (10

Oct. 1932), p. 21, which forbade insurance payments for livestock that died as a result of neglect or "squandering."

58. *RGAE*, f. 7446, op. 5, d. 87, p. 10.

59. *Ibid.*, f. 7446, op. 2, d. 135, p. 1; f. 7446, op. 5, d. 39, p. 156; *Bol'shevik*, no. 6 (31 March 1930), p. 23; *SIu*, no. 29 (30 Oct. 1930), pp. 3–4.

60. M. L. Bogdenko, ed., "Uchastie sovkhozov v sotsialisticheskoi perestroike derevne v 1929–1930 gg.," *Materialy*, vol. 7, p. 314.

61. *RGAE*, f. 7446, op. 5, d. 87, p. 4.

62. *Bol'shevik*, no. 6 (31 March 1930), p. 23.

63. *RGAE*, f. 7446, op. 2, d. 38, p. 25.

64. *Ibid.*, f. 7486, op. 37, d. 121, p. 1.

65. I. P. Ikonnikova and A. P. Ugrovatov, "Stalinskaia repetitsiia nastupleniia na krest'ianstvo," *Voprosy istorii KPSS*, no. 1 (1991), pp. 77–8; also see *Krest'ianskii iurist*, (hereafter, *KIu*), no. 2 (31 Jan. 1928), pp. 1–2.

66. Hindus, *Red Bread*, p. 196.

67. *RGAE*, f. 7446, op. 14, d. 187, p. 22.

68. *SIu*, no. 9 (30 March 1932), pp. 9–12; no. 24 (30 Aug. 1932), pp. 25–8; *Kollektivizatsiia sel'skogo khoziaistva v Severnom raione* (hereafter, *KS*) (Vologda, 1964), p. 25.

69. V. P. Danilov, "Glava piataia: Kollektivizatsiia sel'skogo khoziastva v SSSR," *Istoriia SSSR*, no. 5 (1990), p. 15; I. Ia. Trifonov, *Likvidatsiia ekspluatatorskikh klassov v SSSR* (Moscow, 1975), p. 265; *DS*, pp. 24–5.

70. Lewin, *Making of the Soviet System*, p. 140; also see Ivnitskii, *Klassovaia bor'ba*, p. 59.

71. Trifonov, *Likvidatsiia*, p. 265.

72. V. A. Sidorov, "Likvidatsiia v SSSR kulachestva kak klassa," *Voprosy istorii*, no. 7 (1968), pp. 25–6.

73. Ivnitskii, *Klassovaia bor'ba*, pp. 59–60.

74. Trifonov, *Likvidatsiia*, p. 265.

75. N. Ia. Gushchin, "Klassovaia bor'ba v sibirskoi derevne nakanune i v gody massovoi kollektivizatsii," in *Problemy sotsial'no-ekonomicheskogo razvitiia sovetskoi derevni* (Vologda, 1975), p. 48.

76. Ivnitskii, *Kollektivizatsiia*, p. 16; *DS*, p. 46; V. P. Danilov, "U kolkhoznogo nachalo," *Sovetskaia Rossiia*, 11 Oct. 1987, p. 4.

77. N. Ia. Gushchin, "Likvidatsiia kulachestva kak klassa v sibirskoi derevne," *Sotsial'naia struktura naseleniia Sibiri* (Novosibirsk, 1970), p. 130.

78. *RGAE*, f. 7446, op. 5, d. 23, p. 28.

79. *GARF*, f. 5469, op. 13, d. 123, pp. 78–91.

80. *PTP*, p. 233.

81. A. K. Azizian, *Arenda zemli i bor'ba s kulakom* (Moscow-Leningrad, 1929), p. 71; Kavraiskii and Khamarmer, *Uroki*, p. 7.

82. *SP*, no. 10 (30 July 1930), pp. 3–5; *SIu*, no. 39 (10 Oct. 1929), pp. 908–9; no. 40 (17 Oct. 1929), pp. 950–2; no. 41 (24 Oct. 1929), pp. 959–61; no. 49 (17 Dec. 1929), pp. 1147–9.

83. *SP*, no. 10 (30 July 1930), pp. 3–4.

84. *RGAE*, f. 7446, op. 5, d. 19, p. 3. Given current shortages of building materials and structures for collective and official uses, it is not surprising to find cases of Soviet institutions buying "kulak buildings."

85. Kavraiskii and Khamarmer, *Uroki*, p. 7.

86. Liapina, "Iz istorii Tambovskoi derevni," pp. 47–8.

87. Ermolaev, *Kollektivizatsiia*, p. 56; Leikin, "Krest'ianka," pp. 42–3.

88. *Derevenskii iurist* (hereafter, *DIu*), no. 15 (Aug. 1934), p. 12. The organization of false collective farms may have served as another stratagem in these years to avoid the kulak label. Numerous reports claimed they were organized on the basis of networks of relatives and, especially, networks of *khutors*. See, for examples, *KIu*, no. 17 (15 Sept. 1928), p. 14; and no. 8 (30 April 1929), pp. 13–14, on religious collectives; *KIu*, no. 13 (15 July 1929), p. 13; Bol'shakov, *Kommuna Kudrova*, p. 16; and *XVII s"ezd VKP (b). Sten. otchet* (Moscow, 1934), p. 217, on family networks within collectives. On false collectives in general, see Lynne Viola, "The Case of Krasnyi Meliorator," *Soviet Studies*, vol. 38, no. 4 (Oct. 1986), pp. 508–529.

89. *RGAE*, f. 7486, op. 37, d. 193, p. 61.

90. For example, see *KSK*, pp. 274–5.

91. Iu. V. Arutiunian, "Kollektivizatsiia sel'skogo khoziaistva i vysvobozhdenie rabochei sily dlia promyshlennosti," in *Formirovanie i razvitie sovetskogo rabochego klassa* (Moscow, 1964), p. 111. In *Stalin's Peasants*, p. 80, Fitzpatrick writes that 12 million peasants left for the towns during the First Five-Year Plan.

92. F. A. Karevskii, "Likvidatsiia kulachestva kak klassa v Srednem Povolzh'e," *Istoricheskie zapiski*, vol. 80 (1967), pp. 100–1; *Problemy agrarnoi istorii sovetskogo obshchestva* (Moscow, 1971), p. 210.

93. Merle Fainsod, *Smolensk Under Soviet Rule* (Cambridge, Mass., 1958), p. 245. See also *KZ*, p. 283, on rates of *otkhodnichestvo*.

94. Gushchin, "Likvidatsiia," P. 130; Gushchin and Il'inykh, *Klassovaia bor'ba*, p. 213.

95. *RGAE*, f. 7486, op. 37, d. 61, p. 72.

96. *Ibid.*, f. 7486, op. 37, d. 49, p. 78.

97. Gushchin and Il'inykh, *Klassovaia bor'ba*, p. 213.

98. *RGAE*, f. 7446, op. 5, d. 87, p. 13.

99. *Ibid.*

100. David L. Hoffmann, "Moving to Moscow: Patterns of Peasant In-Migration During the First Five-Year Plan," *Slavic Review*, vol. 50, no. 4 (Winter 1991), pp. 847–57; and David L. Hoffmann, *Peasant Metropolis: Social Identities in Moscow, 1929–1941* (Ithaca, 1994), pp. 54–63.

101. V. P. Danilov, "Krest'ianskii otkhod na promysly v 1920-kh godakh," *Istoricheskie zapiski*, vol. 94 (1974), p. 113.

102. K. M. Shuvaev, *Staraia i novaia derevnia* (Moscow, 1937), p. 48.

103. *RGAE*, f. 7446, op. 5, d. 87, p. 29.

104. *Ibid.*, f. 7486, op. 37, d. 193, p. 99; f. 7486, op. 37, d. 49, p. 104; f. 7486, op. 37, d. 131, pp. 148–7. Throughout the country, there were cases of *otkhodniki* being expelled from their trade unions for refusing to enter collective farms. Presumably, this repressive (and illegal) measure may have been an additional incentive for *otkhodniki* to give up their land holdings. See *RGAE*, f. 7446, op. 5, d. 19, p. 32.

105. Egorova, "Klassovaia bor'ba," pp. 31–2.

106. *RGAE*, f. 7486, op. 37, d. 131, p. 42.

107. Sekretno-Politicheskii otdel OGPU, "Dokladnaia zapiska o formakh i dinamike klassovoi bor'by v derevne v 1930 gody," p. 58. (This document is from the project *The Tragedy of the Soviet Countryside*, 5 vols., eds. V. P. Danilov, R. T. Manning, and L. Viola. Forthcoming.)

108. *DS*, p. 324; *RGAE*, f. 7486, op. 37, d. 78, pp. 86–3.

109. *RGAE*, f. 7486, op. 37, d. 138, p. 44. Maxim Litvinov, Commissar of Foreign Affairs, was beseiged with letters from foreign governments and private citizens (especially German) demanding that the Soviet Union respect the rights of "foreign" peasants. Although the citizenship of these peasants as "foreign" seems far from clear, Litvinov appears to have made many interventions on their behalf, arguing the need to observe international legal norms and "the extremely difficult situation" of his commissariat in regard to this issue. See, for examples, his letter to Stalin of 18 February 1930 and his letter to Iakovlev of 2 February 1930, in *RGAE*, f. 7486, op. 37, d. 138, pp. 46, 40. Also see *Neizvestnaia Rossiia*, vol. 2, pp. 324–36.

110. "Dokladnaia zapiska o formakh i dinamike klassovoi bor'by," p. 58.

111. Pirogov, *Why I Escaped*, p. 206.

112. *KSK*, p. 267.

113. Fitzpatrick, *Stalin's Peasants*, p. 81; Hoffmann, *Peasant Metropolis*, pp. 42–5.

114. Fitzpatrick, *Stalin's Peasants*, p. 81.

115. *RGAE*, f. 7446, op. 5, d. 87, p. 25; also see *Bol'shevik*, no. 6 (31 March 1930), p. 23.

116. *GARF*, f. 374, op. 9, d. 398, p. 598–9.

117. *RGAE*, f. 7446, op. 5, d. 19, p. 2.

118. On bribery to alter socioeconomic status, see *SIu*, no. 10 (10 April 1930), pp. 4–5; no. 7 (15 April 1937), pp. 34–5; *KIu*, no. 2 (Jan. 1931), p. 11; *DIu*, no. 18 (Sept. 1931), p. 8; no. 3 (Feb. 1933), p. 13; no. 2 (Jan. 1934), p. 12; no. 17 (Sept. 1934), pp. 13–4.

119. Ivan Tvardovskii, "Stranitsy perezhitogo," *Iunost'*, no. 3 (1988), pp. 23, 27.

120. Bella Ulanovskaia, "Voluntary Seclusion: The Life of a Lonely Old Woman in a Deserted Village," *Russian Review*, vol. 51, no. 2 (April 1992), p. 202.

121. *Ibid.*, pp. 198–203.

122. Aleksandr I. Solzhenitsyn, *The Gulag Archipelago*, tr. Harry Willetts (New York, 1978), vol. 3, p. 366. See the remarkable story of one Old Believer family that fled "the world," the state, and collectivization in the 1930s, only to resurface decades later, in Vasily Peskov, *Lost in the Taiga*, tr. Marian Schwartz (New York, 1994).

123. *RGAE*, f. 7446, op. 5, d. 87, p. 21; also see *ibid.*, p. 30.

124. *Ibid.*, f. 7486, op. 37, d. 49, p. 52.

125. Fainsod, *Smolensk*, p. 246.

126. *RGAE*, f. 7486, op. 37, d. 78, p. 25.

127. *Iz istorii raskulachivaniia v Karelii, 1930–1931: Dokumenty i materialy* (Petrozavodsk, 1991), p. 20.

128. *RGAE*, f. 7486, op. 37, d. 93, p. 105. Also see the 4 February 1930 "Secret Instructions" of TsIK-SNK on dekulakization in *Neizvestnaia Rossiia*, vol. 1, p. 247.

129. *GARF*, f. 374, op. 9, d. 398, p. 598.

130. *SIu*, nos. 24–5 (10–20 Sept. 1930), p. 6.

131. *Krest'ianstvo Sibiri v period stroitel'stva sotsializma (1917–1937 gg.)* (Novosibirsk, 1983), pp. 261–2; Gushchin, "Likvidatsiia," p. 131; Viola, "Campaign," p. 510, n. 30.

132. *KS*, p. 275.

133. *PTP*, p. 210.

134. *RGAE*, f. 7486, op. 37, d. 122, p. 77.

135. *KZ*, pp. 357–61.

136. See chap. 1.

137. See Ranger, "Peasant Consciousness," in Shanin, ed., *Peasants*, p. 312, for discussion of the importance of community in peasant political consciousness in the recent literature on peasantries.

138. Hindus, *Red Bread*, pp. 255–6.

139. Ivnitskii, "Dokladnaia zapiska," p. 242.

140. *KK*, pp. 47–8.

141. *IU*, p. 94.

142. *RGAE*, f. 7486, op. 37, d. 78, p. 72. The phrase "Soviet kulak" may have been the *Pravda* correspondent's invention.

143. *KSP*, pp. 627–8.

144. For example, see *Metallist*, no. 11 (21 March 1929), p. 5; *Derevenskii kommunist*, no. 2 (22 Jan. 1929), pp. 38–9; *Litsom k derevne*, no. 2 (Oct. 1928), pp. 1–3; Komarov, *Litso*, p. 31.

145. *Derevenskii kommunist*, no. 21 (14 Nov. 1929), p. 22; Fedin, *Klassovaia bor'ba*, pp. 6–7.

146. *DS*, pp. 231, 238.

147. *Bol'shevik*, no. 13 (15 July 1930), p. 72.

148. A. Gozhanskii, *V razvernutoe nastuplenie na kulaka* (Leningrad, 1931), p. 21.

149. *RGAE*, f. 7486, op. 37, d. 122, p. 79; f. 7486, op. 37, d. 193, p. 72; Elizarov, *Likvidatsiia*, pp. 47–8; Ivnitskii, "Dokladnaia zapiska," p. 243; *Sotsialisticheskoe pereustroistvo sel'skogo khoziaistva Moldavskoi*, p. 402.

150. *RGAE*, f. 7486, op. 37, d. 131, p. 61.

151. *Ibid.*, f. 260, op. 1, d. 6, p. 39.

152. *Ibid.*, f. 7486, op. 37, d. 78, p. 77.

153. Leikin, "Krest'ianka," p. 44.

154. *RGAE*, f. 7486, op. 37, d. 122, p. 77.

155. Valerii Vasil'ev, "Krest'ianskie vosstaniia na Ukraine, 1929–1930 gody," *Svobodnaia mysl'*, no. 9 (1992), p. 75.

156. *RGAE*, f. 7486, op. 37, d. 193, p. 72. Also see *RGAE*, f. 7486, op. 37, d. 122, p. 154.

157. *Ibid.*, f. 7486, op. 37, d. 131, p. 158.

158. *Ibid.*

159. See chaps. 4 and 5.

160. Tvardovskii, "Stranitsy perezhitogo," pp. 12–3.

161. *GARF*, f. 374, op. 9, d. 398, p. 147. Also see *RGAE*, f. 7446, op. 5, d. 29, p. 2, for a report on poor peasants providing friendly aid to kulaks.

162. *RGAE*, f. 7446, op. 5, d. 87, p. 17.

163. Fedor Belov, *The History of a Collective Farm* (New York, 1955), p. 6.

164. William Edgerton, ed., *Memoirs of Peasant Tolstoyans in Soviet Russia* (Bloomington, 1993), p. 61.

165. *KTsPO*, pp. 443–4.

166. For example, see Vareikis' report in Werth and Moullec, *Rapports secrets sovietiques*, p. 122.

167. For example, *Slu*, no. 18 (25–30 June 1931), p. 31; *Sel'skokhoziaistvennaia gazeta*, 8 Dec. 1929, p. 3.

168. *RGAE*, f. 260, op. 1, d. 6, p. 38; f. 7486, op. 37, d. 131, p. 180.

169. *SIu*, no. 2 (20 Jan. 1931), pp. 9–10.

170. This was the case in Sibiria (Gushchin, "Klassovaia bor'ba," pp. 55–6); and a central decree in *Neizvestnaia Rossiia*, vol. 1, p. 257, suggests that it was the case nationally.

171. *RGAE*, f. 7446, op. 16, d. 77, p. 20; f. 7486, op. 37, d. 49, p. 112; f. 7486, op. 37, d. 192, p. 416; Elizarov, *Likvidatsiia*, p. 73; *GARF*, f. 5469, op. 13, d. 123, pp. 78–91.

172. *RGAE*, f. 7486, op. 37, d. 61, p. 134.

173. Solzhenityn, *Gulag*, vol. 2, p. 477.

174. G. Kh. Ryklin, *Kak sovetskaia pechat' pomagaet krest'ianinu* (Moscow-Leningrad, 1926), pp. 29–31. Also see *Istoricheskii arkhiv*, no. 4 (1994), pp. 82–3.

175. "'Velikii perelom' v derevne," *Izvestiia Sibirskogo otdeleniia AN SSSR: seriia istorii, filologii i filosofii*, vyp. 1 (1989), p. 10; Ivnitskii, *Kollektivizatsiia*, p. 10.

176. *RGAE*, f. 7446, op. 5, d. 88, pp. 16, 18–20, 25–27.

177. *SIu*, no. 20 (20 July 1930), p. 21.

178. Gushchin, "Likvidatsiia," p. 131.

179. *SIu*, no. 21 (30 July 1930), p. 19.

180. Fainsod, *Smolensk*, pp. 180–1.

181. *RTsKhIDNI*, f. 17, op. 120, d. 26, pp. 1–10; *Istoriia krest'ianstva SSSR*, 4 vols. (Moscow, 1986), vol. 2, p. 216; Hindus, *Red Bread*, pp. 255–6. According to information in *RTsKhIDNI*, the commission on rehabilitation was divided over the number of incorrect deportations. While Bergavinov thought the figure of ten per cent to be an exaggeration, Tolmachev and Eremin considered it impossible to judge precisely the number of mistaken exiles, noting that in some areas of the North as many as 60% of deportations were incorrect.

182. *SIu*, no. 15 (30 May 1930), p. 2.

183. *RGAE*, f. 7446, op. 5, d. 88, pp. 64–5.

184. *Current Digest of the Soviet Press*, vol. 39, no. 33 (1987), p. 10; also in *DS*, pp. 232–5.

185. *RGAE*, f. 7446, op. 5, d. 88, p. 32.

186. *Ibid.*, p. 1.

187. *Ibid.*, f. 7446, op. 5, d. 88, p. 23.

188. *Ibid.*, p. 66.

189. *Ibid.*, f. 7486, op. 37, d. 102, p. 49.

190. *Ibid.*, p. 63.

191. *RGAE*, f. 7446, op. 5, d. 88, p. 67.

192. *Ibid.*, pp. 58–9.

193. *DS*, pp. 170–1.

194. *Ibid.*, pp. 227–30.

195. *RGAE*, f. 7446, op. 5, d. 88, pp. 43–4.

196. *Ibid.*, f. 7446, op. 5, d. 87, p. 33.

197. *Ibid.*, f. 7446, op. 5, d. 88, p. 53.

198. *Ibid.*, f. 7446, op. 5, d. 88, pp. 55–7.

199. For example, see *ibid.*, f. 7446, op. 5, d. 88, pp. 11–15.

200. A published source for these types of letters are the columns, variously labeled *"Nam pishut"* or *"Signaly aktiva,"* in *Krest'ianskii* (later *Derevenskii*) *iurist*, 1928–35.

201. In *Stalin's Peasants* (p. 257), Fitzpatrick writes that most peasant letters

were individually penned, rather than collective compositions in the post-collectivization 1930s. On village deportations, see A. Radin and L. Shaumian, *Za chto zhiteli stanitsy Poltavskoi vyseliaiutsia s Kubani v severnye kraia* (Rostov n/ Donu, 1932); *KSK*, p. 32.

202. For information about peasant complaints, see *SIu*, no. 22 (Sept. 1934), p. 19; no. 24 (Sept. 1934), pp. 4–5; no. 5 (Feb. 1936), pp 9–10; and *DIu*, nos. 3–4 (Feb. 1932), p. 28; no. 9 (May 1934), pp. 13–4; no. 16 (Aug. 1934), p. 14; no. 18 (Sept. 1934), p. 2.

Chapter 4

1. On similar interactions between state and societal violence in other societies, see Douglas Hay, "Time, Inequality, and Law's Violence," in Austin Sarat and Thomas R. Kearns, eds., *Law's Violence* (Ann Arbor, 1992), pp. 141–74.

2. On the centrality of justice in popular violence, see Moore, *Social Origins*, p. 471; and Tilly et al., *Rebellious Century*, p. 85.

3. Fainsod, *Smolensk*, p. 241.

4. I. I. Alekseenko, "Rabochie-dvadtsatipiatitysiachniki—provodniki politiki kommunisticheskoi partii v kolkhoznom stroitel'stve," *K sorokaletiiu velikoi oktiabr'skoi sotsialisticheskoi revoliutsii* (Krasnoiarsk, 1957), p. 425.

5. *GARF*, f. 5469, op. 13, d. 122, pp. 152–4.

6. "Dokladnaia zapiska o formakh i dinamike klassovoi bor'by," p. 40. Compare these figures with those of earlier years. According to OGPU data, the number of terrorist cases in the countryside in 1924 was 339; in 1925, 902; in 1926, 711; and in the first eight months of 1927, 580. The total for the period from January 1924 to September 1927 was 2,532. See *RTsKhIDNI*, f. 17, op. 85, d. 289, p. 75 (Table 1).

7. "Dokladnaia zapiska o formakh i dinamike klassovoi bor'by," p. 38.

8. This information was conveyed to me by V. P. Danilov on the basis of his work in the State Archive of the Ministry of Security for *The Tragedy of the Russian Countryside* project. In all of 1926, there were 110 murders attributed to kulak terror, and in 1927, 44. (Other types of terror were largely negligible in these earlier years.) See *RTsKhIDNI*, f. 17, op. 85, d. 289, p. 77 (Table 4–3).

9. For an interesting and detailed analysis of interpretive problems in police (and especially political police) sources, see R. C. Cobb, *The Police and the People: French Popular Protest, 1789–1820* (Oxford, 1970), part I.

10. The resolution is dated 21 March 1930. *Iz istorii raskulachivaniia v Karelii*, p. 58.

11. *SIu*, nos. 22–3 (10–20 Aug. 1930), p. 16. For discussion of misclassification of counterrevolutionary crimes and terror, see *SIu*, no. 16 (10 June 1930), pp. 27–8; nos. 22–3 (10–20 Aug. 1930), p. 11; no. 18 (25–30 June 1931), pp. 31–3; no. 3 (30 Jan. 1932), p. 25; *SP*, no. 5 (10 Apr. 1930), pp. 4–6; no. 8 (10 June 1930), p. 12.

12. "Dokladnaia zapiska o formakh i dinamike klassovoi bor'by," pp. 76–7.

13. See David Christian, *"Living Water": Vodka and Russian Society on the Eve of Emancipation* (Oxford, 1990), for a discussion of the role of drinking in peasant society.

14. "Dokladnaia zapiska o formakh i dinamike klassovoi bor'by," p. 38.

15. *Istoriia kolkhoznogo prava*, vol. 1, pp. 151–2.

16. For information on attacks on activists' families, see "Dokladnaia zapiska o formakh i dinamike klassovoi bor'by," p. 81.

17. Fainsod, *Smolensk*, p. 241.

18. *DS*, p. 297; *KZ*, p. 223. Also see *SIu*, no. 6 (28 Feb. 1930), p. 8, for legal data confirming this pattern (179 attacks against lower soviet officials; 105 against activists).

19. *KTsChO*, pp. 57–8.

20. *Ibid.*, pp. 74–6. See also *Iz istorii raskulachivaniia v Karelii*, p. 109.

21. I. Ia. Trifonov, *Ocherki istorii klassovoi bor'by v SSSR v gody NEPa* (Moscow, 1960), p. 206.

22. *SIu*, no. 3 (30 Jan. 1932), p. 23.

23. On the 25,000ers, see Viola, *Best Sons*, p. 159; on teachers, see *XIV Vserossiiskii s"ezd sovetov. Sten. otchet*, Biulleten' no. 14, p. 42; Trifonov, *Ocherki*, p. 207 (who reports 152 terrorists acts against teachers from August 1928 to May 1929, including 11 murders, 19 attempted murders, and 19 beatings); and V. R. Veselov, "Rol' i mesto pedagogicheskoi intelligentsii v bor'be za utverzhdenie kolkhoznogo stroia v derevne," *Iz istorii partiinykh organizatsii Verkhnego Povolzh'ia*, vyp. 38 (Iaroslavl, 1974), p. 28.

24. *KSK*, p. 738, n. 59.

25. On stereotyped images of kulaks in Soviet political cartoons, see Bronaugh, "Graphic Propaganda."

26. Egorova, "K voprosu," p. 112. Also see *KTsChO*, p. 76, which divides terrorists active in May and June 1929 into the following: 163 kulak-zazhitochnye, 25 middle peasants, and 8 poor peasants. Data on the social composition of terrorists in Kareliia is published in *Iz istorii raskulachivaniia v Karelii*, p. 109. Here, in the second half of 1929, terrorists included 19 kulaks, 5 zazhitochnye and *lishentsy*, 9 middle peasants, and 2 poor peasants. In the first half of 1930, the composition of terrorists remained roughly the same, the primary difference being a breakdown between "inspirers" and "executors" of terror.

27. *SIu*, no. 6 (28 Feb. 1930), p. 9.

28. "Dokladnaia zapiska o formakh i dinamike klassovoi bor'by," p. 72.

29. *Ibid.*

30. See Fainsod, *Smolensk*, p. 241, for a similar qualification.

31. See E. P. Thompson, "The Crime of Anonymity," in Douglas Hay et al., *Albion's Fatal Tree: Crime and Society in Eighteenth Century England* (London, 1975), pp. 255.

32. "Dokladnaia zapiska o formakh i dinamike klassovoi bor'by," pp. 43–4, 74.

33. *SP*, no. 16 (21 Dec. 1930), p. 14. On the specific articles of the penal code, see *Penal Code*, pp. 24–5, 34–5.

34. "Dokladnaia zapiska o formakh i dinamike klassovoi bor'by," p. 44. See also Thompson, "Crime of Anonymity," pp. 284–5, on the difficulties of detecting and convicting the authors of anonymous letters.

35. Statistics on threats are poor, but for some very partial information, see *DS*, p. 246; and Fedin, *Klassovaia bor'ba*, p. 12. For evidence that threats did intimidate some activists, see *RGAE*, f. 7486, op. 37, d. 122, p. 104; and *RTsKhIDNI*, f. 17, op. 85, d. 354, p. 12.

36. *KNG*, p. 102.

37. *RTsKhIDNI*, f. 17, op. 32, d. 184, p. 28.

38. *RGAE*, f. 7486, op. 37, d. 61, p. 126.
39. *Ibid.*, f. 7446, op. 5, d. 87, p. 23.
40. *IU*, p. 107. Also see the case reported in *Litsom k derevne*, nos. 23–4 (Dec. 1930), p. 34.
41. *GARF*, f. 374, op. 9, d. 398, p. 491.
42. *Ibid.*, f. 5469, op. 13, d. 123, pp. 28–40.
43. *DIu*, no. 17 (Sept. 1934), pp. 11–2.
44. "Dokladnaia zapiska o formakh i dinamike klassovoi bor'by," pp. 91–2.
45. *Ibid.*, p. 90.
46. *Ibid.*, p. 90.
47. *Ibid.*, pp. 90–1.
48. *Ibid.*, p. 91. Also see other examples in *ibid.*, pp. 90–4.
49. *Ibid.*
50. *Ibid.*
51. *Ibid.*, pp. 92–3.
52. *Ibid.*, p. 92.
53. *Ibid.*, pp. 90–94.
54. On the use of arson to settle village accounts, see Gagarin, *Khoziaistvo*, p. 39. On peasant arsonists elsewhere, see Hobsbawm and Rude, *Captain Swing*, p. 98.
55. Edgerton, *Memoirs of Peasant Tolstoyans*, p. 19.
56. *SIu*, no. 4 (10 Feb. 1931), p. 24. Alternately, peasant witnesses may have been pressured into turning an actual arson into an ordinary fire.
57. *DS*, p. 246.
58. "Dokladnaia zapiska o formakh i dinamike klassovoi bor'by," pp. 42, 71. See Table 4–3 for a monthly breakdown of arsons in 1930.
59. *RGAE*, f. 7446, op. 5, d. 39, p. 3; *Kollektivizatsiia sel'skogo khoziaistva Zapadnoi Sibiri* (hereafter, *KZS*) (Tomsk, 1972), p. 197. OGPU figures give the slightly lower figure of 339 arsons. See Table 4–3.
60. *RGAE*, f. 7446, op. 14, d. 187, p. 22.
61. *DS*, pp. 173–4; Ivnitskii, *Klassovaia bor'ba*, p. 121; *KTsPO*, p. 258; *KSZ*, p. 110; *Na Leninskom puti* (Novosibirsk), nos. 13–4 (31 July 1928), p. 17; *RGAE*, f. 7446, op. 5, d. 39, p. 75.
62. *KTsPO*, pp. 240–1.
63. Ivnitskii, "Dokladnaia zapiska," p. 245; Timofeev, *Mezha umerla*, pp. 77–8.
64. *KK*, pp. 54–5; *KNG*, pp. 121–2. Also see below on *samosud*.
65. *KIu*, no. 3 (15 Feb. 1929), p. 10.
66. Erikhonov, *Kulak pered sudom*, pp. 51–3.
67. *Iz istorii kollektivizatsii sel'skogo khoziaistva Riazanskoi oblasti* (hereafter, *IR*) (Riazan, 1962), p. 177; *KSK*, pp. 274–5, 384, 391; *KTsPO*, p. 443; *KZ*, p. 276; *Saratovskaia partiinaia organizatsiia v period nastupleniia sotsializma po vsemu frontu: Sozdanie kolkhoznogo stroia* (Saratov, 1961), pp. 115–6; *RGAE*, f. 7446, op. 5, d. 87, pp. 12, 24; f. 7446, op. 16, d. 77, pp. 30–1; f. 7486, op. 37, d. 61, p. 132.
68. "Dokladnaia zapiska o formakh i dinamike klassovoi bor'by v derevne," p. 43.
69. *SIu*, no. 5 (20 Feb. 1931), p. 9; *RGAE*, f. 7446, op. 5, d. 87, p. 24; *GARF*, f. 5469, op. 13, d. 122, p. 142.
70. "Dokladnaia zapiska o formakh i dinamike klassovoi bor'by," pp. 79–80.

71. M. Gorkii et al., eds., *Belomor* (New York, 1935), p. 176.

72. *SIu*, no. 14 (20 May 1932), p. 38. For other cases, see *KZ*, pp. 387–8; *SIu*, no. 2 (20 Jan. 1932), p. 10; *KIu*, no. 4 (Feb. 1931), p. 15; and *Zavershenie kollektivizatsii sel'skogo khoziaistva i organizatsionno-khoziaistvennoe ukreplenie kolkhozov Belorusskoi SSR. Sb. dokumentov i materialov* (Minsk, 1985), pp. 98–9.

73. The quote in the preceding heading is in *KTsPO*, pp. 244–6.

74. *KSK*, p. 738, n. 59; also see p. 221.

75. See below, and cases in *KZS*, pp. 94–5; *GARF*, f. 5469, op. 13, d. 122, pp. 66–8; f. 5469, op. 13, d. 123, p. 17.

76. Angarov, *Klassovaia bor'ba*, p. 13; *DS*, pp. 236–7, 240; Fedin, *Klassovaia bor'ba*, p. 22.

77. *DS*, p. 240.

78. *Ibid.*, pp. 243–5; *IU*, pp. 73–5.

79. *IU*, pp. 73–5, 116–8.

80. *DS*, pp. 245–6.

81. *RTsKhIDNI*, f. 17, op. 3, d. 761, p. 17.

82. "Dokladnaia zapiska o formakh i dinamike klassovoi bor'by," p. 38.

83. *KSK*, pp. 218–9.

84. *RGAE*, f. 7446, op. 16, d. 77, p. 30.

85. *Ibid.*, f. 7486, op. 37, d. 78, p. 87.

86. "Dokladnaia zapiska o formakh i dinamike klassovoi bor'by," p. 77.

87. *Ibid.*, p. 64.

88. *KZS*, pp. 94–5. Also see Gushchin, "Iz istorii," p. 83, who claims she was brutally tortured before her death.

89. *IU*, p. 119.

90. *RGAE*, f. 3983, op. 5, d. 93, p. 9.

91. For a discussion of *samosud* in prerevolutionary Russia, see Stephen P. Frank, "Popular Justice, Community, and Culture Among the Russian Peasantry, 1870–1900," in Ben Eklof and Stephen P. Frank, eds., *The World of the Russian Peasant* (Boston, 1990). According to Frank, the most brutal forms of *samosud* were reserved for outsiders in prerevolutionary Russia. This dynamic appears to have changed during collectivization when activists implicitly became outsiders. For further information on *samosud* in the Soviet period, see Lagovier, *O samosudakh*.

92. *KIu*, no. 12 (30 Jan. 1928), p. 13.

93. Ivanova, "Bor'ba," p. 115.

94. Gushchin, "Iz istorii," p. 84.

95. *KZS*, pp. 163–4.

96. *KNG*, pp. 121–2.

97. Elizarev, *Likvidatsiia*, p. 75; Ermolaev, *Kollektivizatsiia*, p. 50; *KTsPO*, pp. 244–6; *KIu*, no. 18 (30 Sept. 1928), pp. 13–4; no. 2 (31 Jan. 1929), p. 11; *RGAE*, f. 7446, op. 5, d. 51, p. 26.

98. See Frank, "Popular Justice." Frank defines *samosud* in much broader terms than I am able to do here. I use mainly cases of lynching under the heading of *samosud*.

99. Scott, *Domination*, p. 151. Also Berce, *History of Peasant Revolts*, p. 219, on the popular culture of riots.

100. *RGAE*, f. 7446, op. 14, d. 187, p. 22.

101. For example, *KTsPO*, p. 646; *SIu*, no. 3 (Jan. 1936), p. 5; no. 13 (May

1936), pp. 3, 7–8; and on women, see Roberta T. Manning, "Women in the Soviet Countryside on the Eve of World War II, 1935–1940," in Farnsworth and Viola, eds., *Russian Peasant Women*, pp. 216–22.

102. *DIu*, no. 7 (May 1933), p. 12; no. 9 (July 1933), p. 16; *Iu*, pp. 142, 160–1, 180; *KNG*, p. 209; *Saratovskaia partiinaia organizatsiia v gody bor'by za zavershenie sotsialisticheskoi rekonstruktsii narodnogo khoziaistva* (Saratov, 1963), p. 22; *SIu*, no. 8 (20 Mar. 1932), p. 33; no. 16 (1934), p. 12; no. 9 (Mar. 1935), p. 17; no. 17 (15 June 1936), p. 25.

103. *DIu*, no. 12 (Oct. 1933), p. 13; no. 9 (May 1934), pp. 8–9.

104. *Ibid.*, no. 10 (May 1935), pp. 2–7.

105. *Ibid.*, no. 10 (May 1932), p. 14.

106. *SIu*, no. 30 (Nov. 1934), p. 11.

107. *XVI s"ezd*, p. 226.

108. Scott, *Domination*, pp. xii.

109. See Sathyamurthy, "Indian Peasant Historiography," pp. 121–3, for a discussion of peasant techniques of enforcing solidarity in struggles with authorities, and the harsh penalties used against peasant collaborators.

110. Aleksandr I. Solzhenitsyn, *The Gulag Archipelago*, tr. Thomas P. Whitney (New York, 1973), vol. 1, p. 387.

Chapter 5

1. Mikhail Karavai, *Politotdel* (Moscow, 1934), p. 5.

2. On solidarity as "contagion" in the official perception of subaltern revolt, see Sathyamurthy, "Indian Peasant Historiography," p. 120.

3. Ivnitskii, "Dokladnaia zapiska," p. 245.

4. *RTsKhIDNI*, f. 17, op. 3, d. 761, p. 17.

5. Olga A. Narkiewicz, *Making of the Soviet State Apparatus* (Manchester, 1970), p. 198.

6. See the discussion in Davies, *Socialist Offensive*, pp. 158–9, 161, 173. See also *RTsKhIDNI*, f. 17, op. 2, d. 441 (2 vols.), for the transcript of the November 1929 Plenum.

7. Ivnitskii, *Kollektivizatsiia*, p. 10.

8. *PTP*, p. 215.

9. For the impact of collectivization on the morale of peasant soldiers, see E. H. Carr, *Foundations of a Planned Economy*, (London, 1978), vol. 2, pp. 330–1; *Vestnik krest'ianskoi Rossii*, no. 7 (Dec. 1930), pp. 9–10; and V. I. Varenov, *Pomoshch' Krasnoi armii v razvitii kolkhoznogo stroitel'stva, 1929–1933 gg.* (Moscow, 1978), pp. 40–7. Although the Red army was in fact used in quelling peasant revolt, there were apparently attempts, probably based on fears of instability within the ranks, to limit its role in suppressing village disturbances. An OGPU directive of 2 Feb. 1930 instructed that the army was to be used only in extreme situations or in circumstances where there were not enough OGPU troops, in which case only "trustworthy" soldiers screened by the OGPU were to be employed. See *Neizvestnaia Rossiia*, vol. 1, p. 242.

10. *DS*, pp. 387, 390; also cited in I. E. Zelenin, "Osushchestvlenie politiki 'likvidatsii kulachestva kak klassa' (osen' 1930–1932 gg.)," *Istoriia SSSR*, no. 6 (1990), p. 47, n. 4.

11. Stalin, *Sochineniia*, vol. 12, pp. 191–9.

12. *DS*, pp. 36–7.

13. This definition comes from the OGPU. See "Dokladnaia zapiska o formakh i dinamike klassovoi bor'by," p. 41.

14. *Ibid.*, p. 38.

15. *Ibid.*, p. 38.

16. *Ibid.*, p. 63, 68.

17. Ivnitskii, *Klassovaia bor'ba*, pp. 258, 277; also see *KNG*, pp. 202–3; and Kondrashin, "Golod," p. 180, for some examples of famine-era acts of collective (active) resistance.

18. "Dokladnaia zapiska o formakh i dinamike klassovoi bor'by," pp. 40, 69.

19. These figures were relayed to me by V. P. Danilov on the basis of his work in the State Archive of the Ministry of Security for *The Tragedy of the Russian Countryside* project.

20. Villages with the largest populations were located in the Central Black Earth Region, Middle and Lower Volga, North Caucasus, and Ukraine, where population size was approximately 400 people (80 households). Villages in the Western Region, Belorussia, Urals, and Central Industrial Region tended to have populations of less than 200 people. See V. P. Danilov, "Sel'skoe naselenie soiuza SSR nakanune kollektivizatsii," *Istoricheskie zapiski*, no. 74 (1963), pp. 68–71.

21. "Dokladnaia zapiska o formakh i dinamike klassovoi bor'by," p. 70.

22. *Ibid.*, p. 65.

23. Karevskii, "Likvidatsiia," pp. 89–90.

24. "Dokladnaia zapiska o formakh i dinamike klassovoi bor'by," p. 101.

25. Trifonov, *Likvidatsiia*, p. 303; *Istoriia krest'ianstva SSSR* (Moscow, 1978), vol. 2, p. 103.

26. V. P. Danilov et al., *Sovetskoe krest'ianstvo* (Moscow, 1973), p. 281; Sidorov, "Likvidatsiia," pp. 24, 31–2.

27. Trifonov, *Ocherki*, p. 233; Medvedev, *Krutoi povorot*, p. 108.

28. N. A. Ivnitskii, "Klassovaia bor'ba v derevne v period podgotovki i provedeniia kollektivizatsii sel'skogo khoziaistva," *Problemy agrarnoi istorii* (Minsk, 1978), p. 150.

29. Gushchin and Il'inykh, *Klassovaia bor'ba*, p. 214; and Gushchin, "Likvidatsiia," p. 122.

30. *Spetspereselentsy*, pp. 48–9.

31. *RGAE*, f. 7486, op. 37, d. 78, pp. 86–83.

32. *GARF*, f. 374, op. 9, d. 398, p. 247.

33. "Dokladnaia zapiska o formakh i dinamike klassovoi bor'by," p. 56; also see p. 47.

34. *Ibid.*, p. 100.

35. *GARF*, f. 5469, op. 13, d. 122, p. 143. Also see *RGAE*, f. 7486, op. 37, d. 61, p. 110.

36. "Dokladnaia zapiska o formakh i dinamike klassovoi bor'by," pp. 101–2.

37. *Vestnik krest'ianskoi Rossii*, no. 7 (Dec. 1930), p. 11; no. 8 (Jan. 1931), pp. 9–12; nos. 13–4 (June-July 1931), pp. 11–5; no. 9 (Sept. 1932), p. 4.

38. G. E. Sokolov, "Nekotorye voprosy sotsial'noi politiki partii na sele pri perekhode ot vosstanovleniia k rekonstruktsii narodnogo khoziaistva (1924–1927 gg.)," *KPSS v bor'be za pobedu i uprochenie sotsializma* (Moscow, 1986), p. 152; *DS*, p. 17; James Hughes, *Stalin, Siberia and the Crisis of the New Economic Policy* (Cambridge, 1991), p. 45, on petitions for a peasant union; and Egorova, "K voprosu," p. 100. On calls for a peasant union in 1929 and 1930, see Angarov, *Klassovaia bor'ba*, p. 13; *Bol'shevik*, no. 13 (15 July 1930), p. 72.

39. Angarov, *Klassovaia bor'ba*, p. 13; *RGAE*, f. 7486, op. 37, d. 49, p. 110.

40. *KNG*, p. 142; Leikin, "Krest'ianka," pp. 41–2; Kavraiskii and Khamarmer, *Uroki*, p. 21; Karavaev and Sosnovskii, *Krasnopolianskii gigant*, pp. 71–2; I. D. Eingorn, "Religioznye organizatsii protiv massovogo kolkhoznogo dvizheniia v Zapadnoi Sibiri," *Trudy Tomskogo gos. univ.*, tom 190, pp. 288–9; *GARF*, f. 5469, op. 13, d. 122, pp. 152–4.

41. *RGAE*, f. 7486, op. 37, d. 91, p. 4.

42. *Ibid.*, f. 7486, op. 37, d. 131, p. 52.

43. See, for examples, *ibid.*, f. 7486, op. 37, d. 102, pp. 58, 55; f. 7486, op. 37, d. 61, p. 110; f. 7486, op. 37, d. 91, p. 7; *RTsKhIDNI*, f. 17, op. 85, d. 355, p. 2; f. 17, op. 85, d. 354, p. 10.

44. *RGAE*, f. 7486, op. 37, d. 61, p. 110.

45. *Ibid.*, f. 7486, op. 37, d. 91, p. 4.

46. *Ibid.*, f. 7486, op. 37, d. 91, p. 6.

47. See chap. 6; and *RGAE*, f. 7486, op. 37, d. 91, p. 6; f. 7486, op. 37, d. 61, p. 132.

48. *RGAE*, f. 7486, op. 37, d. 91, p. 6.

49. *Ibid.*, f. 7486, op. 37, d. 131, p. 34.

50. *Ibid.*, f. 7486, op. 37, d. 49, p. 44.

51. For comparison: On the civil war, Figes, *Peasant Russia*, chap. 7; and Mikhail Frenkin, *Tragediia krest'ianskikh vosstanii v Rossii, 1918–1921 gg.* (Jerusalem, 1987), pp. 82, 84. On the 1905 Revolution, Roberta Manning, *The Crisis of the Old Order in Russia* (Princeton, 1982), p. 141; and Teodor Shanin, *Russia, 1905–07: Revolution as a Moment of Truth*, vol. 2 of *The Roots of Otherness* (New Haven, 1986), chap. 3. And finally, see Geroid Tanquary Robinson, *Rural Russia Under the Old Regime* (Berkeley, 1969), p. 86, on peasant riots in 1861.

52. See, for example, what the OGPU had to say about certain of these categories, in "Dokladnaia zapiska o formakh i dinamike klassovoi bor'by," pp. 47, 55. Also see *RGAE*, f. 7486, op. 37, d. 122, pp. 33, 35.

53. "Turf" is borrowed from Timothy Mixter's article, "The Hiring Market as Workers' Turf," in Kingston-Mann and Mixter, eds., *Peasant Economy*, pp. 294–340.

54. For example, *RGAE*, f. 7446, op. 5, d. 87, pp. 4, 17; f. 7446, op. 5, d. 88, p. 32; f. 7486, op. 37, d. 61, pp. 114–3; f. 7486, op. 37, d. 131, pp. 55, 33; f. 7486, op. 37, d. 119, p. 14; f. 7486, op. 37, d. 192, pp. 76–5. "Solovki" refers to the Solovetskii islands, the home of a desolate and forbidding concentration camp after 1917.

55. Solzhenitsyn, *Gulag*, vol. 1, p. 509.

56. For example, *RGAE*, f. 7446, op. 5, d. 87, p. 4.

57. *Ibid.*, f. 7446, op. 5, d. 23, p. 29.

58. *GARF*, f. 374, op. 9, d. 398, p. 146.

59. *RGAE*, f. 7486, op. 37, d. 122, pp. 181–80.

60. *Ibid.*, f. 7446, op. 5, d. 23, p. 29.

61. Miron Dolot, *Execution by Hunger* (New York, 1985), pp. 16–23.

62. *KSK*, pp. 532–3.

63. G. Furman, *Kak pomogali kolkhozam 25-tysiachniki* (Moscow, 1930), p. 23; Viola, *Best Sons*, pp. 162–4.

64. Leikin, "Krest'ianka," p. 32.

65. *RGAE*, f. 7446, op. 5, d. 87, p. 24.

66. *Ibid.*, f. 7486, op. 37, d. 131, pp. 46–5.

67. Vasil'ev, "Krest'ianskie vosstaniia na Ukraine," p. 76.
68. For example, *GARF*, f. 5469, op. 13, d. 122, pp. 152–4; *DS*, p. 244.
69. *RGAE*, f. 7486, op. 37, d. 122, p. 78.
70. Hindus, *Red Bread*, pp. 45–7.
71. *Ibid., passim.*
72. *RGAE*, f. 7446, op. 5, d. 87, p. 11.
73. Leikin, "Krest'ianka," pp. 30–2.
74. R. Belbei, *Za ili protiv* (Moscow, 1930), pp. 50–5.
75. For example, *DS*, p. 244.
76. E. J. Hobsbawm, "Peasants and Politics," *Journal of Peasant Studies*, vol. 1, no. 1 (Oct. 1973), p. 13.
77. For example, *GARF*, f. 5469, op. 13, d. 122, pp. 152–4; *RGAE*, f. 7486, op. 37, d. 61, pp. 73–2, 56; *KSZ*, pp. 162–3.
78. *RGAE*, f. 7486, op. 37, d. 61, p. 49.
79. *GARF*, f. 374, op. 9, d. 398, p. 481.
80. *RGAE*, f. 7486, op. 37, d. 102, p. 47.
81. *Ibid.*, f. 7486, op. 37, d. 61, p. 82.
82. *Ibid.*, f. 7486, op. 37, d. 61, pp. 95–3; f. 7486, op. 37, d. 131, p. 47.
83. *Ibid.*, f. 7486, op. 36, d. 131, p. 47. (Decrees are from February 1930.)
84. *Ibid.*, f. 7446, op. 5, d. 87, pp. 23–4; f. 7486, op. 37, d. 61, pp. 95–3, 45; f. 7486, op. 37, d. 131, pp. 180, 52; f. 7486, op. 37, d. 119, pp. 99–8, 11; f. 7486, op. 37, d. 193, p. 129; *RTsKhIDNI*, f. 17, op. 85, d. 355, p. 2; *Spetspereselentsy v Zapadnoi Sibiri*, p. 167; *IR*, pp. 125–6; *KTsPO*, pp. 240–2; *KS*, p. 146; *KZ*, pp. 191–3; *Saratovskaia partiinaia organizatsiia v period nastupleniia sotsializma po vsemu frontu*, p. 108; *DS*, pp. 244–5.
85. *GARF*, f. 374, op. 9, d. 398, p. 598.
86. *RGAE*, f. 7446, op. 5, d. 39, p. 17.
87. See Figes, *Peasant Russia*, pp. 324–34, on the Chapany uprisings.
88. *RGAE*, f. 7486, op. 37, d. 131, pp. 49–8.
89. *Ibid.*, f. 7486, op. 37, d. 61, p. 115.
90. *GARF*, f. 5469, op. 13, d. 123, p. 17.
91. *RGAE*, f. 7446, op. 5, d. 87, p. 24; *Litsom k derevne*, no. 6 (March 1930), p. 16.
92. *RGAE*, f. 7486, op. 37, d. 61, pp. 45–4.
93. *KSZ*, p. 79.
94. *RGAE*, f. 7446, op. 5, d. 87, p. 10.
95. *Ibid.*, f. 7486, op. 37, d. 131, p. 49.
96. *Ibid.*, f. 7486, op. 37, d. 131, p. 48.
97. *Ibid.*, f. 7486, op. 37, d. 131, p. 46.
98. *RTsKhIDNI*, f. 78, op. 1, d. 358, pp. 122–33.
99. *RGAE*, f. 7486, op. 37, d. 122, p. 239.
100. Ivnitskii, "Klassovaia bor'ba," p. 148; Ivnitskii, *Klassovaia bor'ba*, p. 98; Trifonov, *Ocherki*, p. 201; N. Ia. Gushchin, "Iz istorii klassovoi bor'by v Sibirskoi derevne v 1928–29 gg.," *Izvestiia Sibirskogo otdeleniia AN SSSR*, no. 1, vyp. 1 (Jan. 1967), p. 82; *IU*, pp. 73–5; and *Istoriia krest'ianstva SSSR*, vol. 2, p. 100.
101. For example, *GARF*, f. 374, op. 9, d. 398, pp. 405, 598; *RGAE*, f. 7446, op. 5, d. 87, p. 12.
102. *RGAE*, f. 7486, op. 37, d. 61, p. 108.
103. *Ibid.*, f. 7486, op. 37, d. 102, p. 58.

104. Scott, *Domination*, p. 118. Also see chap. 1 of this book.

105. Alexander Pushkin, *The Captain's Daughter* (New York, 1978), p. 106.

106. The intimidation aspects of riots are discussed in Underdown, *Revel, Riot, and Rebellion*, p. 118.

107. "Dokladnaia zapiska o formakh i dinamike klassovoi bor'by," p. 70.

108. *Ibid.*, pp. 77–8; *RTsKhIDNI*, f. 17, op. 85, d. 355, p. 2.

109. "Dokladnaia zapiska o formakh i dinamike klassovoi bor'by," p. 61; Vasil'ev, "Krest'ianskie vosstaniia na Ukraine," pp. 74, 76.

110. "Dokladnaia zapiska o formakh i dinamike klassovoi bor'by," pp. 41, 70. (Armed forces suppressed 108 mass disturbances in February, 807 in March, and 56 in April.) The relatively scant use of the army was probably based on a combination of inadequate resources and fears of disloyalty. Although most evidence on pacification of revolts is still unavailable, a valuable document on Ukrainian peasant rebellion in February and March 1930 gives some insightful information on casualties and arrests. On the basis of information from 13 *okrugs* pacified in this period, there were 107 casualties (including 43 deaths) on the government side and 147 casualties (including 58 deaths) on the opposing side. The data for the "opposing side" is, even according to the official source, underestimated, given the ability of peasants to hide and shelter the wounded. Further, from 1 February to 15 March, 25,000 peasants were arrested in these *okrugs* for "counterrevolutionary kulak activity" (of which 656 were shot, 3,673 imprisoned in concentration camps, and 5,580 subject to internal exile). *RTsKhIDNI*, f. 85, op. 1c, d. 118, pp. 48–9.

111. Ikonnikova and Ugrovatov, "Stalinskaia repetitsiia," p. 79.

112. *RTsKhIDNI*, f. 17, op. 85, d. 355, pp. 1, 3.

113. *Ibid.*, p. 1.

114. Vasil'ev, "Krest'ianskie vosstaniia na Ukraine," p. 71.

115. *Ibid.*, p. 72.

116. *RGAE*, f. 7486, op. 37, d. 49, p. 111.

117. *RTsKhIDNI*, f. 17, op. 85, d. 355, p. 2.

118. *Ibid.*

119. *Ibid.*

120. For example, *KS*, pp. 123–5.

121. Egorova, "K voprosu," p. 104.

122. Ivnitskii, *Klassovaia bor'ba*, p. 101.

123. See Table 5–2.

124. "Dokladnaia zapiska o formakh i dinamike klassovoi bor'by," pp. 67, 69.

125. Vasil'ev, "Krest'ianskie vosstaniia na Ukraine," pp. 71–74, 76; *RTsKhIDNI*, f. 85, op. 1c, d. 118, p. 43.

126. See Eric R. Wolf, "On Peasant Rebellions," in Shanin, ed., *Peasants*, p. 372; and Terry Martin, "Language and Terror: Soviet Language Reform and Reaction," *Midwestern Colloquium on Modern Russian History*, University of Toronto, fall 1994, which points to nationalism as a "mobilizing factor" in revolt.

127. Vasil'ev, "Krest'ianskie vosstaniia na Ukraine," p. 75.

128. "Dokladnaia zapiska o formakh i dinamike klassovoi bor'by," pp. 92, 94.

129. Ukrainian leaders Kosior and Chubar' explicitly linked nationality and the "kulak question" at the November 1929 plenum. See *RTsKhIDNI*, f. 17, op. 2, d. 441, vyp. 2, pp. 72, 89.

130. See Table 5–4.

131. "Dokladnaia zapiska o formakh i dinamike klassovoi bor'by," pp. 67, 69.

132. *Istoriia KPSS*, tom 4, kniga 2-aia (Moscow, 1971), p. 185; *Kollektivi-*

zatsiia sel'skogo khoziaistva Turkmenskoi SSR, vol. 2 (Ashkhabad, 1968), pp. 274–5, 340–1, 358, 635:n.27; A. Nuritov, "K voprosu o kharakture i formakh klassovoi bor'by v Uzbekskom kishlake (1932–1934 godu)," *Nauchnye trudy aspirantov Tashkentskogo gos. univ.,* vyp. 207 (Tashkent, 1962), p. 232.

133. *GARF,* f. 5457, op. 14, d. 112, p. 220.

134. The *basmachi* were members of a nationalist movement in Central Asia, who continued to resist Soviet power well beyond the official end of the civil war. The *bai* were the wealthy, upper stratum of Central Asia's agricultural class before the revolution; the term acquired some of the attributes of "kulak" in the 1920s.

135. *RTsKhIDNI,* f. 85, op. 1c, d. 118, p. 43.

136. *RGAE,* f. 7486, op. 37, d. 122, p. 54.

137. "Dokladnaia zapiska o formakh i dinamike klassovoi bor'by," p. 84.

138. *RGAE,* f. 7486, op. 37, d. 122, p. 54; Vasil'ev, "Krest'ianskie vosstaniia na Ukraine," p. 77. On 13 November 1929, the Ukrainian government passed a resolution to exile "socially dangerous elements" (criminals, bandits, arsonists, *byvshie liudi,* and those with "links to kulaks," presumably including kulaks) from its border areas. (*RGAE,* f. 5675, op. 1, d. 23a, pp. 44–1). Further, during collectivization, thousands of demobilized soldiers and their families were settled in key border areas. (See *RGAE,* f. 5675, op. 1, d. 23a.)

139. Trifonov, *Likvidatsiia,* pp. 303–4; for percentages of collectivized households, see Davies, *Socialist Offensive,* vol. 1, pp. 109, 133.

140. "Dokladnaia zapiska o formakh i dinamike klassovoi bor'by," p. 69.

141. See Table 5–4.

142. *RGAE,* f. 7486, op. 37, d. 102, p. 49.

143. *Ibid.,* f. 7486, op. 37, d. 131, p. 45.

144. "Dokladnaia zapiska o formakh i dinamike klassovoi bor'by," pp. 85–6.

145. *RGAE,* f. 7486, op. 37, d. 122, p. 103.

146. *PTP,* pp. 18, 236–46, 269–70, 283.

147. *Ibid.,* pp. 270–5.

148. "Dokladnaia zapiska o formakh i dinamike klassovoi bor'by," pp. 83–4. For a slightly different version, see *PTP,* pp. 270–5. In this version, the peasants of Vladimirovka seize all government buildings, arrest local officials and activists, and cut the telegraph and telephone link-ups to the *raion* center. Saratov sends in the cavalry, but not before the uprising has run its course.

149. *RTsKhIDNI,* f. 17, op. 21, d. 3763, pp. 50–52.

150. "Dokladnaia zapiska o formakh i dinamike klassovoi bor'by," pp. 67, 69.

151. *RGAE,* f. 7486, op. 37, d. 61, p. 70.

152. Slightly different versions of the revolt are in *RGAE,* f. 7486, op. 37, d. 131, p. 33; and P. G. Chernopitskii, *Na velikom perelome* (Rostov n/Donu, 1965), pp. 101–4. On the destruction of livestock in this area, see A. P. Finarov, "K voprosu o likvidatsii kulachestva kak klassa i sud'ba byvshikh kulakov v SSSR," *Istoriia sovetskogo krest'ianstva i kolkhoznogo stroitel'stva v SSSR* (Moscow, 1963), p. 275. Also see M. Ia. Levina and E. N. Oskolkov, "Iz istorii kollektivizatsii sel'skogo khoziaistva na Severnom Kavkaze," in *Arkhivy po obshchestvennym naukam* (Rostov-na-Donu, 1970), p. 174, for reference to another large uprising in Taganrogskii *raion,* Donskii *okrug* in the same region.

153. *RGAE,* f. 7486, op. 37, d. 122, pp. 35, 33.

154. "Dokladnaia zapiska o formakh i dinamike klassovoi bor'by," pp. 84–5.

155. *Ibid.,* p. 85.

156. *Istoriia KPSS*, p. 54; Gushchin, "Klassovaia bor'ba," pp. 50–1; "Dokladnaia zapiska o formakh i dinamike klassovoi bor'by," p. 69.

157. "Dokladnaia zapiska o formakh i dinamike klassovoi bor'by," p. 69.

158. *Spetspereselentsy*, pp. 124–8, 166.

159. Gushchin, "Likvidatsiia," pp. 133–4; V. N. Burkov, "Derevenskie partiinye organizatsii Zapadnoi Sibiri v bor'be za razvertyvanie sploshnoi kollektivizatsii i likvidatsiiu kulachestva kak klassa (konets 1929–vesna 1930 gg.)," *Uch. zapiski Tomskogo gos. univ.*, no. 56 (1965–6), p. 50.

160. "Dokladnaia zapiska o formakh i dinamike klassovoi bor'by," p. 82.

161. *RGAE*, f. 7486, op. 37, d. 101, p. 39.

162. Finarov, "K voprosu,", pp. 274–5.

163. Burkov, "Derevenskie partiinye organizatsii," p. 50; I. I. Iakovlev, "Iz istorii dvadtsatipiatitysiachnikov na Altae v pervoi polovine 1930 goda," *Nekotorye voprosy istorii KPSS* (Barnaul, 1973), pp. 71–2; Gushchin and Il'inykh, *Klassovaia bor'ba*, p. 215; *Spetspereselentsy*, pp. 59–60.

164. The percentages of collectivized households in the Central Black Earth Region rose from 40.5% in January 1930 to 83.3% in March. See Davies, *Socialist Offensive*, vol. 1, p. 442.

165. "Dokladnaia zapiska o formakh i dinamike klassovoi bor'by," pp. 67, 69.

166. *RGAE*, f. 7486, op. 37, d. 49, p. 111; and Sidorov, "Likvidatsiia," p. 25.

167. "Dokladnaia zapiska o formakh i dinamike klassovoi bor'by," p. 69.

168. *RGAE*, f. 7486, op. 37, d. 49, pp. 110–11; N. Mikhailov and N. Teptsov, "Chrezvychaishchina," *Rodina*, no. 8 (1989), p. 32.

169. Danilov, "Sel'skoe naselenie," pp. 68–71.

170. *RGAE*, f. 7486, op. 37, d. 49, p. 110.

171. "Dokladnaia zapiska o formakh i dinamike klassovoi bor'by," p. 82.

172. *RGAE*, f. 7486, op. 37, d. 102, p. 60.

173. *DS*, pp. 313–4.

174. Here, percentages of collectivized households rose from 14.3% in January to 74.2% in March. Davies, *Socialist Offensive*, vol. 1, p. 442.

175. Cohen, *Bukharin*, p. 330; Trifonov, *Likvidatsiia*, p. 303; "Dokladnaia zapiska o formakh i dinamike klassovoi bor'by," p. 69.

176. "Dokladnaia zapiska o formakh i dinamike klassovoi bor'by," pp. 67, 69; Danilov, "Sel'skoe naselenie," pp. 68–71.

177. Mikhailov and Teptsov, "Chrezvychaishchina," p. 32.

178. For example, one activist suffered the arson of his home. *GARO* (*Gosudarstvennyi arkhiv Riazanskoi oblasti*), f. r-5, op. 2, d. 5, pp. 278, 333; 403–11, 422, 677. (I am indebted to Stephen Frank for sharing this source with me.)

179. Viola, *Best Sons*, p. 125.

180. *DS*, pp. 36–7, 390–1.

181. The uncertainty and momentary illegitimacy of the central authorities was an important factor in the spread of peasant rebellion in Russia in 1905 and 1917 and in other peasant revolts in other nations as well. See John Bushnell, *Mutiny Amid Repression* (Bloomington, 1985), for Russia in 1905; and Scott, *Domination*, pp. 192–3, on peasants "testing the limits" in general.

182. *RGAE*, f. 260, op. 1, d. 6, pp. 177–8.

183. Strong, *Soviets Conquer Wheat*, pp. 92–3.

184. *PTP*, pp. 270–5.

185. *RGAE*, f. 7486, op. 37, d. 122, p. 99.

186. Strong, *Soviets Conquer Wheat*, p. 102; and, e.g., *GARF*, f. 374, op. 9,

Notes to pages 172–176

d. 418, p. 70; N. A. Ivnitskii and D. M. Ezerskii, eds., "Dvadtsatipiatitysiachniki i ikh rol' v kollektivizatsii sel'skogo khoziaistva v 1930 g.," *Materialy*, vol. 1, pp. 472–3.

187. *GARF*, f. 5469, op. 13, d. 123, pp. 78–91; *RGAE*, f. 7486, op. 37, d. 122, p. 104.

188. Burkov, "Derevenskie partiinye organizatsii," p. 63.

189. *Spetspereselentsy*, pp. 165–7.

190. It should be noted that exits from and even collapses of collective farms due to mass departures had been a feature of collectivization from January 1930 if not earlier. According to the OGPU, in the second half of February, there were mass presentations of applications to quit collective farms in almost all collective farms in Chapaevskii *raion*, Samarskii *okrug*, Middle Volga. In the North Caucasus, some 50 recently organized collective farms collapsed in early January. See *RGAE*, f. 7486, op. 37, d. 61, pp. 69, 61.

191. Viola, *Best Sons*, p. 124.

192. *RGAE*, f. 7446, op. 1, d. 143, p. 47.

193. Belbei, *Za ili protiv*, p. 27; Leikin, "Krest'ianka," p. 25; *SIu*, nos. 17–18 (30 June 1932), p. 29, for an indication that this phenomenon continued to occur later, in the 1932 exits.

194. *IR*, p. 158; *KNG*, p. 210.

195. For example, of 46,261 peasant families exiled to the North, 35,000 submitted petitions for reassessment of their status in the spring of 1930. See *Istoriia krest'ianstva SSSR*, vol. 2, p. 216.

196. See Table 5–1.

197. *RGAE*, f. 7486, op. 37, d. 131, p. 155.

198. *Ibid.*, pp. 161, 153.

199. *Ibid.*, pp. 153–1.

200. *Ibid.*, pp. 177–6.

201. *Ibid.*, pp. 192, 173.

202. *Ibid.*, pp. 188–3, 170, 151–49.

203. *Ibid.*, pp. 192, 177, 173, 153, 150.

204. *Ibid.*, pp. 155–4.

205. *Ibid.*, pp. 161, 153.

206. *Ibid.*, p. 171.

207. *Ibid.*, pp. 152–1.

208. *Ibid.*, pp. 174–3.

209. *Ibid.*, f. 7486, op. 37, d. 102, p. 216.

210. For examples, see *KSK*, p. 384; and *GARF*, f. 5457, op. 14, d. 114, pp. 18–9.

211. *RGAE*, f. 7486, op. 37, d. 192, p. 383.

212. *Ibid.*, f. 7486, op. 37, d. 193, p. 113. (Six hundred people took part in the revolt in Soliano-Zaimishcha and 100 people in each of the other village revolts.)

213. *Ibid.*, p. 98. Also see *ibid.*, p. 105, for mass disturbances in the Lower Volga.

214. Belov, *History of a Soviet Collective Farm*, p. 13.

215. *KNG*, pp. 202–3.

216. Kondrashin, "Golod," p. 180.

217. *Neizvestnaia Rossiia*, vol. 1, p. 257; Gushchin, "Klassovaia bor'ba," p. 56.

218. See E. J. Hobsbawm, *Bandits* (London, 1969); and E. J. Hobsbawm, *Social Bandits and Primitive Rebels: Studies in Archaic Forms of Social Movement in the 19th and 20th Centuries* (Glencoe, Ill., 1959).

219. For the civil war, see Figes, *Peasant Russia*, pp. 340–53. For NEP, and a December 1926 government decree declaring Siberia "unsafe due to banditry," see *DS*, p. 14.

220. Egorova, "K voprosu," pp. 116–7; also see *SIu*, no. 13 (May 1935), p. 10; and *Vnutrennie voiska v gody mirnogo sotsialisticheskogo stroitel'stva, 1922–1941 gg. Dokumenty i materialy* (Moscow, 1977), p. 296.

221. Ugrovatov, "Bor'ba," pp. 90–1.

222. Gushchin and Il'inykh, *Klassovaia bor'ba*, p. 196.

223. *Vnutrennie voiska*, p. 307; *DIu*, no. 17 (Sept. 1934), p. 12.

224. Ugrovatov, "Bor'ba," p. 86; *Vnutrennie voiska*, p. 296; Gushchin and Il'inykh, *Klassovaia bor'ba*, p. 196.

225. Hobsbawm, *Social Bandits*, p. 15.

226. Gushchin, "Likvidatsiia," p. 122; Egorova, "K voprosu," p. 118.

227. Gushchin, "Klassovaia bor'ba," pp. 50–1; Ugrovatov, "Bor'ba," p. 86; Gushchin and Il'inykh, *Klassovaia bor'ba*, p. 214.

228. Gushchin, "Klassovaia bor'ba," pp. 54–5; Zelenin, "Osushchestvlenie," p. 36.

229. Fainsod, *Smolensk*, p. 244; Sergei Maksudov, ed., *Neuslyshannye golosa: dokumenty Smolenskogo arkhiva* (Ann Arbor, 1987), p. 82; *DIu*, no. 17 (Sept. 1934), p. 12; *PTP*, pp. 270–5; *KSK*, pp. 258–9; *Iz istorii kollektivizatsii sel'skogo khoziaistva Dal'nego vostoka (1927–1937 gg.)* (Khabarovsk, 1979), p. 7; *Current Digest of the Soviet Press*, vol. 39, no. 33 (1987), p. 10.

230. For example, *DIu*, no. 17 (Sept. 1934), p. 12; Egorova, "K voprosu," pp. 115–8; Gushchin and Il'inykh, *Klassovaia bor'ba*, p. 197; Gushchin, "Iz istorii," p. 87; and see below.

231. Sathyamurthy, "Indian Peasant Historiography," p. 115.

232. Ugrovatov, "Bor'ba," p. 86.

233. Gushchin, "Iz istorii," p. 87.

234. Egorova, "K voprosu," p. 115.

235. *Vestnik krest'ianskoi Rossii*, no. 17 (Oct. 1931), pp. 10–13.

236. It is not entirely clear whether the Kochkin band was stopped in 1929 or 1930. For further information, see Trifonov, *Likvidatsiia*, p. 304; I. S. Stepichev, "Iz istorii klassovoi bor'by v Vostochnosibirskoi derevne v period podgotovki i nachala sploshnoi kollektivizatsii," in *Istoriia sovetskogo krest'ianstva i kolkhoznogo stroitel'stva v SSSR* (Moscow, 1963), p. 318; Gushchin and Il'inykh, *Klassovaia bor'ba*, p. 197.

237. *KSK*, pp. 255–9.

238. *Current Digest of the Soviet Press*, vol. 39, no. 33 (1987), p. 10.

239. Gushchin and Il'inykh, *Klassovaia bor'ba*, pp. 196–7.

240. Hobsbawm, *Social Bandits*, p. 13.

241. On the brief scapegoating campaign against rural cadres, see Viola, "'L'ivresse du succes'," pp. 95–8.

242. Scott, *Weapons*, p. xvi, makes this point, although he is mainly referring to peasants' participation in successful revolutionary movements.

243. Even Fitzpatrick, in an otherwise exceptional work, passed over this chapter in *Stalin's Peasants*.

Chapter 6

1. Field, *Rebels*, pp. 23, 209–10, 214.
2. See Scott, *Weapons*, p. xvi.
3. Natalie Zemon Davis, "Women on Top," *Society and Culture in Early Modern France* (Stanford, 1975), pp. 131, 146.
4. Stalin, *Sochineniia*, vol. 13, p. 252.
5. Ivnitskii, "Dokladnaia zapiska," p. 242.
6. *RTsKhIDNI*, f. 17, op. 85, d. 355, p. 406.
7. V. Ulasevich, "Zhenshchina na stroike sotsializma," in Ulasevich, ed., *Zhenshchina*, p. 7.
8. *KSK*, p. 263.
9. *KSP*, pp. 171–2.
10. "Dokladnaia zapiska o formakh i dinamike klassovoi bor'by," pp. 48, 68. The 1930 monthly dynamics of mass disturbances consisting primarily of women were as follows (with the total number of mass disturbances in parentheses): January—229 (402); February—379 (1,048); March—1,172 (6,528); April—550 (1,992); May—486 (1,375); June—301 (886); July—167 (618); August—105 (256); September—82 (159); October—141 (270); November—56 (129); December—44 (91).
11. *XVI s"ezd*, p. 70.
12. *Ibid.*, p. 123.
13. See *XIV vserossiiskii s"ezd sovetov. Sten. otchet*, Biulleten' no. 3, pp. 11–2; and *II sessiia VTsIK XIV sozyva. Sten. otchet* (Moscow, 1929), Biulleten' no. 7, pp. 25–8; and *KTsPO*, p. 222.
14. See, for examples, *Chto nuzhno znat' kazhdomu rabotniku kolkhoza?* (Moscow, 1930), p. 7; *Derevenskii kommunist*, no. 1 (12 Jan. 1930), p. 32; M. Kureiko, *25-tysiachniki na kolkhoznoi stroike* (Moscow-Leningrad, 1930), pp. 44–5; and the Sovnarkom draft decree. "On Measures to Secure the Entry of Women Peasants into Agricultural Cooperatives," in *RGAE*, f. 4108, op. 2, d. 336, pp. 60–1. For information on the expanding role of women in political life in the countryside, see Atkinson, *End of the Russian Land Commune*, pp. 367–8; Susan Bridger, *Women in the Soviet Countryside* (Cambridge, 1987), pp. 10–16.
15. *RGAE*, f. 7486, op 37, d. 61, p. 133. (Italics mine).
16. *Ibid.*, f. 7486, op. 37, d. 131, p. 159.
17. *Ibid.*, f. 260, op. 1, d. 6, p. 38.
18. *Ibid.*, f. 7486, op. 37, d. 61, p. 133; "Dokladnaia zapiska o formakh i dinamike klassovoi bor'by," p. 51.
19. The kulak *agitprop* received its name from the party's agitation and propaganda department, which was known popularly by the acronym *agitprop*.
20. "Dokladnaia zapiska o formakh i dinamike klassovoi bor'by," p. 49.
21. See Table 5–2.
22. *RTsKhIDNI*, f. 17, op. 85, d. 355, p. 1.
23. *RGAE*, f. 7486, op. 37, d. 131, p. 158.
24. *Ibid.*, p. 170.
25. *Ibid.*, f. 260, op. 1, d. 6, p. 39.
26. *Ibid.*, f. 3983, op. 5, d. 163, p. 59.
27. On the importance of this point, see Ulasevich, "Zhenshchina," p. 10; and *RGAE*, f. 7486, op. 37, d. 49, p. 114.
28. See, for example, Strong, *Soviets Conquer Wheat*, p. 37.

29. *RGAE,* f. 7486, op. 37, d. 61, pp. 132, 127.

30. *Ibid.,* p. 93.

31. *Ibid.,* f. 7486, op. 37, d. 131, pp. 46–5.

32. *Ibid.,* f. 7446, op. 5, d. 39, p. 201.

33. *Ibid.,* f. 7486, op. 37, d. 131, p. 153.

34. *Ibid.,* p. 170.

35. *Ibid.,* p. 174–70.

36. On women's role in bread riots, see Berce, *History of Peasant Revolts,* pp. 174–5, 262–3; Colin Lucas, "The Crowd and Politics Between *Ancien Regime* and Revolution in France," *Journal of Modern History,* vol. 60, no. 3 (Sept. 1988), pp. 422–3; George Rude, *The Crowd in the French Revolution* (New York, 1972), pp. 69, 73, 152, 182–3; E. P. Thompson, "The Moral Economy of the English Crowd in the Eighteenth Century," *Past and Present,* no. 50 (Feb. 1971), pp. 115–6; and Underdown, *Rebel, Riot and Rebellion,* pp. 111, 117. Both Berce and Rude attribute women's leading role to "biological" instinct or nonpolitical motives centering around concerns for food and family. Thompson, on the other hand, attributes women's key role in bread riots to their experience and knowledge of the market and prices.

37. *GARF,* f. 5457, op. 14, d. 135, p. 106.

38. *RGAE,* f. 7486, op. 37, d. 119, pp. 14–11.

39. *Ibid.,* f. 7486, op. 37, d. 61, pp. 105–4.

40. *Ibid.,* f. 7486, op. 37, d. 102, p. 223.

41. *GARF,* f. 374, op. 9, d. 398, p. 490.

42. *RGAE,* f. 7446, op. 5, d. 87, p. 26.

43. *Ibid.,* f. 7486, op. 37, d. 194, pp. 295–4.

44. *GARF,* f. 374, op. 9, d. 418, p. 57.

45. *RGAE,* f. 7446, op. 5, d. 23, p. 29.

46. *SIu,* no. 6 (28 Feb. 1930), pp. 5–6.

47. Evdokimov, *Kolkhozy,* pp. 25–6.

48. *SP,* no. 3 (28 Feb. 1930), pp. 11–12.

49. Grigorenko, *Memoirs,* p. 35.

50. G. I. Arsenov, *Lebedevka, selo kolkhoznoe* (Kursk, 1964), pp. 43–4.

51. S. Zamiatin, *Burnyi god. Opyt raboty piatitysiachnika v Rudnianskom raione na Nizhnei Volge* (Moscow, 1931), pp. 9–16.

52. Sholokhov, *Virgin Soil Upturned,* vol. 1, pp. 311, 316, 321.

53. "Dokladnaia zapiska o formakh i dinamike klassovoi bor'by," pp. 88–9.

54. *Na Leninskom puti* (Novosibirsk), nos. 13–4 (31 July 1928), pp. 20–2. (My thanks to Anne Rassweiler for pointing out this article to me.)

55. "Dokladnaia zapiska o formakh i dinamike klassovoi bor'by," pp. 87–8.

56. *Smolensk Archives,* WKP 261, pp. 60–1. (My thanks to Dan Healey for this source.)

57. *RGAE,* f. 7446, op. 5, d. 87, pp. 25–6. Also see *GARF,* f. 374, op. 9, d. 418, p. 77.

58. The use of a three-ruble fine also occurred in the village Petropavlovskaia in Tataria in order to force people to come to a meeting in protest of land reform. Those who refused to go to the meeting were, according to the source, dragged out by force. See *SP,* no. 3 (28 Feb. 1930), p. 11.

59. *GARF,* f. 5469, op. 13, d. 122, p. 151.

60. "Dokladnaia zapiska o formakh i dinamike klassovoi bor'by," p. 87.

61. *RGAE,* f. 7486, op. 37, d. 193, pp. 72–1.

62. "Dokladnaia zapiska o formakh i dinamike klassovoi bor'by," p. 88.

63. *Ibid.*, pp. 86–7.

64. *Ibid.*, pp. 49–50.

65. See, for examples, cases in Maksudov, *Neuslyshannye golosa*, pp. 62–4, 75–6; *II sessiia VTsIK XIV sozyva. Sten. otchet*, Biulleten' no. 7, p. 28; Kolesova, "Kollektivizatsiia i krest'ianstvo," p. 77; "Dokladnaia zapiska o formakh i dinamike klassovoi bor'by," p. 50.

66. I. K Martovitskii, "Babii bunt," in A. F. Chmyga and M. O. Levkovich, eds., *Pervaia borozda* (Moscow, 1981), pp. 174–81.

67. *RGAE*, f. 7486, op. 37, d. 122, p. 203.

68. See Scott, *Domination*, p. 151, who writes that "Over time, naturally, such modes of collective action become part and parcel of popular culture, and the riot becomes something like a scenario, albeit a dangerous one, enacted by a large repertory company whose members know the basic plot and can step into the available roles." Also see Berce, *History of Peasant Revolts*, p. 19.

69. For example, see the cases in Martovitskii, "Babii bunt," pp. 174–81; Maksudov, *Neuslyshannye golosa*, pp. 75–6; *DS*, p. 472; and *PTP*, pp. 239–44.

70. Scott, *Domination*, p. 151.

71. Martovitskii, "Babii bunt," p. 177.

72. "Dokladnaia zapiska o formakh i dinamike klassovoi bor'by," p. 50.

73. *Na Leninskom puti* (Novosibirsk), nos. 13–4 (31 July 1928), pp. 20–2.

74. "Zhenshchin ne tronut." *RGAE*, f. 7486, op. 37, d. 122, p. 103.

75. "Dokladnaia zapiska o formakh i dinamike klassovoi bor'by," pp. 50–1.

76. Chernomorskii, "Rol' rabochikh brigad," p. 325.

77. V. Denisov, *Odin iz dvadtsatipiatitysiach* (Krasnoiarsk, 1967), p. 27; *RGAE*, f. 7446, op. 5, d. 87, p. 24.

78. *RGAE*, f. 7486, op. 37, d. 61, pp. 133, 123.

79. Fedin, *Klassovaia bor'ba*, p. 70.

80. For example, *RGAE*, f. 7486, op. 37, d. 61, pp. 121, 73, 44; *KSP*, pp. 632–5.

81. *RGAE*, f. 7486, op. 37, d. 61, p. 42.

82. *Ibid.*, p. 44.

83. Fedin, *Klassovaia bor'ba*, p. 71; Kolesova, "Kollektivizatsiia i krest'ianstvo," p. 77.

84. *RGAE*, f. 7486, op. 37, d. 61, pp. 94–3.

85. Kolesova, "Kollektivizatsiia i krest'ianstvo," p. 77. Also see Fedin, *Klassovaia bor'ba*, pp. 69–70.

86. Hindus, *Red Bread*, pp. 49–50; Strong, *Soviets Conquer Wheat*, pp. 114–5; Belbei, *Za ili protiv*, p. 50. Also see *KZ*, pp. 183–4, for cases of women "categorically" refusing to enter collective farms while their husbands had already joined. The Tolstoyan, Dimitry Morgachev was firmly (and bitterly) convinced that women were alien to communal life and attributed to them a great part of the blame for the failure of some of the Tolstoyan communes. See Edgerton, *Memoirs of Peasant Tolstoyans*, pp. 138, 159.

87. *Harvard University Refugee Interview Project*, vol. 18, no. 341, pp. 5–6 ("A" schedule).

88. *KSP*, pp. 632–5.

89. *GARF*, f. 5457, op. 14, d. 114, p. 18.

90. Leikin, "Krest'ianka," pp. 29–30. Leikin describes a meeting with 300 angry women, many of whom brought infants with them, borrowed or their own.

91. Hindus, *Red Bread*, p. 170.

92. It is possible that some women may have heard of the series of directives aiming to prevent the *deportation* of pregnant women, nursing mothers, and families lacking an able-bodied male. Most of these directives, however, *appear* to have come later, in the wake of March fever as a consequence of the nightmarish chaos of the deportations and resettlements of kulak families. Moreover, they referred only to deportations, making no mention of other forms of repression like fines, in-residence forced labor, and so on. For a sample of some of these directives, see Viola, "Second Coming," in Getty and Manning, eds., *Stalinist Terror*, pp. 94–5, n. 161; and *GASO* (*Gosudarstvennyi arkhiv Sverdlovskoi oblasti*), f. 88r, op. 21, ed. khr. 63, pp. 15–16; f. 88r, op. 21, d. 51, p. 148. (I am indebted to James Harris for sharing this source with me.) It should also be noted that at least from July 1931 it was officially forbidden to deport kulak families in the absence of an able-bodied male. (See *RTsKhIDNI*, f. 17, op. 120, d. 52, p. 90.)

93. Berce, *History of Peasant Revolts*, pp. 6–7.

94. For illustrations, see *Smolensk Archives*, WKP 261, pp. 60–1; and *PTP*, pp. 239–44.

95. *Smolensk Archives*, WKP 261, pp. 60–1.

96. See the preceding cases and those in chap. 5.

97. For examples, see chap. 5. Also see Pirogov, *Why I Escaped*, pp. 166–7; *RGAE*, f. 7446, op. 5, d. 87, pp. 25–6; and Maksudov, *Neuslyshannye golosa*, pp. 57–8, for riots related to church closings or bell removals.

98. For example, Martovitskii, "Babii Bunt," pp. 174–81; L. Berson, *Vesna 1930 goda. Zapiska dvadtsatipiatitysiachnika* (Moscow, 1931), pp. 57–62; *GARF*, f. 5469, op. 13, d. 122, p. 151; *IR*, p. 158.

99. For examples, see *Smolensk Archives*, WKP 261, pp. 60–1; and *RGAE*, f. 7446, op. 5, d. 87, pp. 25–6.

100. *KZ*, pp. 266–7.

101. Scott, *Domination*, p. 151.

102. Davis, "Women on Top," pp. 131, 146.

103. Scott, *Domination*, p. 2.

104. Field, *Rebels*, pp. 2, 213–4.

105. *DS*, p. 472.

106. Bonnell, "The Peasant Woman in Stalinist Political Art," pp. 67–8.

107. Alexander Solzhenitsyn, *One Day in the Life of Ivan Denisovich*, tr. Ronald Hingley and Max Hayward (New York, 1963), p. 45.

Chapter 7

1. *SIu*, no. 30 (7 Nov. 1931), pp. 14–6. See also *ibid.*, no. 3 (30 Jan. 1932), p. 22; no. 4 (10 Feb. 1932), p. 11; no. 12 (30 Apr. 1932), pp. 13–4; no. 1 (Jan. 1933), p. 2.

2. Scott, *Weapons*, p. xvi; Forrest D. Colburn, ed., *Everyday Forms of Peasant Resistance* (Armonk, N.Y., 1989), pp. ix–x.

3. Karcz, "Thoughts on the Grain Problem," pp. 409–12, 414–5, 421–2; Ikonnikova and Ugrovatov, "Stalinskaia repetitsiia," pp. 77–8; *DIu*, no. 2 (31 Jan. 1928), pp. 1–2.

4. Gushchin, "Iz istorii," p. 85; Gozhanskii, *V razvernutoe nastuplenie*, p. 10; Kavraiskii and Khamarmer, *Uroki*, p. 7; *RGAE*, f. 7486, op. 37, d. 193, p. 61;

Azizian, *Arenda zemli*, p. 71; *KIu*, no. 7 (15 Apr. 1928), p. 5; *SP*, no. 10 (30 July 1930), pp. 3–5.

5. Viola, "Case of Krasnyi Meliorator," pp. 508–29. See also Bol'shakov, *Kommuna Kudrova*, p. 16; and *KIu*, no. 13 (15 July 1929), p. 13, for examples.

6. See chap. 3.

7. See Viola, "Second Coming," in Getty and Manning, eds., *Stalinist Terror*, p. 91.

8. See R. W. Davies, *The Soviet Collective Farm* (Cambridge, Mass., 1980), p. 29, who estimates that one-fourth of the harvest of 1930 went to the MTS.

9. See the discussions of the requisitioning mechanisms in Moshe Lewin, "'Taking Grain': Soviet Policies of Agricultural Procurements Before the War," in *Making of the Soviet System*, pp. 156–60, 170–2; and Zhores A. Medvedev, *Soviet Agriculture* (New York, 1987), pp. 106, 108.

10. Davies, *Soviet Collective Farm*, pp. 132–53; and Alec Nove, *An Economic History of the USSR* (New York, 1990), p. 171.

11. Davies, *Soviet Collective Farm*, p. 141.

12. See examples in *RGAE*, f. 260, op. 1, d. 10, p. 64; f. 260, op. 1, d. 13, pp. 75–6; f. 260, op. 1, d. 15, p. 53; *KTsPO*, p. 321; *Saratovskaia partiinaia organizatsiia v period nastupleniia sotsializma po vsemu frontu*, p. 42; Elena Kravchenko, *Krest'ianka v kolkhozakh* (Moscow, 1929), p. 30; Ulasevich, "Zhenshchina," p. 10; and P. Kaminskaia, "Organizatsiia zhenskogo truda v kolkhozakh," p. 78, in Ulasevich, ed., *Zhenshchina*.

13. Davies, *Soviet Collective Farm*, pp. 161, 169; Nove, *Economic History*, pp. 174–6.

14. For example, *RGAE*, f. 260, op. 1, d. 16, pp. 16, 82. (This conclusion may shed some light into the partial famine among poor peasants in the collective farm in 1930. See chap. 5.)

15. Nove, *Economic History*, pp. 163–5. Nove gives the following figures (p. 163) on the percentages of peasant households collectivized: 1930—23.6%; 1931—52.7%; 1932—61.5%; 1933—64.6%; 1934—71.4%; 1935—83.2%; 1936—89.6%, which illustrates the decreasing percentages of households still outside the collective farm system.

16. For example, *RGAE*, f. 260, op. 1, d. 4, p. 16.

17. *Ibid.*, f. 260, op. 1, d. 4, p. 16; f. 7446, op. 5, d. 39, pp. 26, 62, 64, 80; *Bol'shevik*, nos. 15–6 (31 Aug. 1930), p. 31; *ibid.*, nos. 23–4 (30 Dec. 1930), p. 79; *Saratovskaia partiinaia organizatsiia v period nastupleniia sotsializma po vsemu frontu*, pp. 130–1.

18. See chap. 5.

19. See Robert Conquest, *The Harvest of Sorrow* (New York, 1986), for another view.

20. The numbers of famine deaths are still not, and may never be, definitively established. For recent explorations, see Nove, "Victims of Stalinism," and Wheatcroft, "More Light," in Getty and Manning, eds., *Stalinist Terror*, pp. 262–7, 278–89.

21. Thompson, "Moral Economy," pp. 78–9. See also Scott, *Moral Economy*, p. 3.

22. Radin and Shaumian, *Za chto zhiteli stanitsy Poltavskoi vyseliaiutsia s Kubani v severnye kraia*, p. 14. See *SIu*, no. 7 (Apr. 1933), p. 7, for Krylenko's thinking on the possibility of collective farmers' "neutrality."

23. *RTsKhIDNI*, f. 17, op. 120, d. 52, pp. 66, 89–90.

24. Cited in Nove, *Economic History*, p. 166.

25. For example, Solts' speech in *Slu*, no. 10 (May 1933), p. 2.

26. *Ibid.*, no. 6 (March 1933), pp. 15–6.

27. *Istoriia kolkhoznogo prava*, vol. 1, pp. 224–5.

28. See *Slu*, no. 9 (30 March 1931), p. 2, for an interesting argument about neutrality. (Also *ibid.*, no. 7 [Apr. 1933], p. 7.)

29. *RTsKhIDNI*, f. 17, op. 2, d. 441, vyp. 2, pp. 14–5.

30. For further information, see Viola, *Best Sons*, chap. 6.

31. For example, *GARF*, f. 374, op. 9, d. 398, p. 58; *RGAE*, f. 7446, op. 16, d. 77, p. 4.

32. Lazar Volin, *A Century of Russian Agriculture* (Cambridge, Mass., 1970), p. 236.

33. *XVII s"ezd VKP(b)*, p. 149.

34. *RGAE*, f. 260, op. 1, d. 10, p. 45.

35. *Bol'shevik*, no. 13 (15 July 1930), p. 69.

36. *RGAE*, f. 260, op. 1, d. 15, p. 33.

37. *Ibid.*, f. 7486, op. 37, d. 194, p. 282; f. 7486, op. 37, d. 193, p. 47.

38. *Ibid.*, f. 260, op. 1, d. 10, p. 92.

39. *Ibid.*, f. 7446, op. 14, d. 187, pp. 32–4. (On average, 3–4 expulsions per farm.)

40. *Ibid.*, f. 260, op. 1, d. 15, p. 35.

41. Solzhenitsyn, *One Day*, p. 14.

42. Edgerton, *Memoirs of Peasant Tolstoyans*, p. 104. (The "red list" [sometimes rendered "board"] contained the names of the best workers and the "black list" those of the worst.)

43. *RGAE*, f. 260, op. 1, d. 10, p. 63.

44. *Ibid.*, f. 260, op. 1, d. 10, p. 47; f. 260, op. 1, d. 15, p. 31.

45. *Ibid.*, f. 260, op. 1, d. 10, p. 47; f. 260, op. 1, d. 13, p. 28; f. 260, op. 1, d. 15, p. 22, f. 260, op. 1, d. 16, p. 19.

46. *Ibid.*, f. 7486, op. 37, d. 131, p. 182.

47. See chap. 5.

48. *RGAE*, f. 7486, op. 37, d. 131, p. 105.

49. Zelenin, "Osushchestvlenie," p. 40; and Zelenin, "O nekotorykh 'belykh piatnakh' zavershaiushchego etapa sploshnoi kollektivizatsii," *Istoriia SSSR*, no. 2 (1989), p. 15.

50. *KZS*, pp. 267–70. (In all, 6,944 households were expelled in the second quarter of 1935.) Also see *KSP*, pp. 294, 482, for other examples of peasants refusing to work.

51. *Slu*, no. 11 (20 Apr. 1931), p. 16; no. 16 (Aug. 1933), p. 6.

52. *GARF*, f. 374, op. 9, d. 398, p. 507.

53. *RGAE*, f. 260, op. 1, d. 3, p. 4.

54. *Ibid.*, f. 7446, op. 5, d. 39, p. 159.

55. *Ibid.*, f. 7446, op. 1, d. 240, p. 50.

56. *Ibid.*, f. 7486, op. 37, d. 193, p. 88.

57. *Ibid.*, f. 7486, op. 37, d. 194, p. 282.

58. *Ibid.*, f. 260, op. 1, d. 13, p. 18.

59. See chap. 5; and *ibid.*, f. 260, op. 1, d. 16, p. 16.

60. For example, *RGAE*, f. 260, op. 1, d. 13, pp. 22, 82; f. 260, op. 1, d. 15, p. 17. (At the same time, there were cases when middle peasants were excluded

from leadership positions on the collective farms. See, for example, *RGAE*, f. 260, op. 1, d. 15, pp. 14, 16.)

61. *Ibid.*, f. 260, op. 1, d. 10, pp. 34, 45, 61–2.

62. On inequalities, see *ibid.*, f. 260, op. 1, d. 10, p. 64; f. 260, op. 1, d. 13, pp. 75–6; f. 260, op. 1, d. 15, p. 53.

63. *Ibid.*, f. 260, op. 1, d. 16, p. 114. On domestic work taking up time, see *ibid.*, f. 260, op. 1, d. 10, p. 34.

64. *SIu*, no. 1 (1934), pp. 21–2; *KSZ*, p. 409, n. 46. Expulsions were widespread as a method of discipline and punishment in the mid-1930s: 3.8% of collective farmers, more in old than newer collective farms, were expelled in 1931 (roughly one-half as "kulaks" and one-half for violations of labor norms. (*RGAE*, f. 7446, op. 14, d. 187, pp. 32–4). According to data from 1933, in 120 *raions* of the Moscow Region, 26,334 households (or 3.33% of all collective farm members) were expelled from collective farms; in several *raions*, percentages reached 10 to 12. More than one-half of all these households were eventually reinstated. (*SIu*, no. 15 [Aug. 1933], pp. 8–10). In some areas, expulsions were already related to labor needs and occurred seasonally depending upon how much surplus labor there was. (*SIu*, no. 1 [1934], pp. 21–2).

65. See Robert F. Miller, *One Hundred Thousand Tractors* (Cambridge, Mass., 1970).

66. *SIu*, no. 14, (1934), p. 4; *KSZ*, p. 395.

67. See Davies, *Soviet Collective Farm*, pp. 157–9; and F. Nakhimson, G. Roginskii, B. Sakhov, *Sud i prokuratura na okhrane proizvodstva i truda*, part II (Moscow, 1932), p. 272.

68. *RGAE*, f. 7446, op. 5, d. 51, pp. 12, 18. Also see *RGAE*, f. 260, op. 1, d. 11, p. 12.

69. *Ibid.*, f. 260, op. 1, d. 15, p. 21.

70. Ermolaev, *Kollektivizatsiia*, p. 47; *RGAE*, f. 7446, op. 5, d. 42, p. 83; *KSP*, p. 228.

71. *RGAE*, f. 260, op. 1, d. 10, pp. 32, 34.

72. Nakhimson et al., *Sud*, p. 272.

73. *KZ*, p. 426; *SIu*, no. 22 (Nov. 1933), pp. 3–4.

74. *SIu*, no. 2 (Jan. 1936), pp. 5–6.

75. See Teodor Shanin, "The Nature and Logic of the Peasant Economy," in *Defining Peasants*, pp. 123–6.

76. *RGAE*, f. 7446, op. 2, d. 216, pp. 77–8.

77. *SIu*, no. 12 (30 Apr. 1932), pp. 13–4; no. 22 (Nov. 1933), p. 4; no. 9 (March 1935), pp. 3–4.

78. *Ibid.*, no. 9 (30 March 1932), p. 14; *RGAE*, f. 7446, op. 5, d. 51, p. 18.

79. *Istoriia kolkhoznogo prava*, vol. 1, pp. 427–33.

80. *SIu*, no. 24 (Aug. 1935), pp. 3–4; no. 20 (Oct. 1937), pp. 14–5.

81. *KZ*, pp. 433, 518; *KZS*, p. 264.

82. *SIu*, no. 11 (Apr. 1935), pp. 32–3; no. 12 (Apr. 1935), p. 4; no. 14 (May 1935), p. 10; no. 24 (Aug. 1935), pp. 1–2; no. 4 (28 Feb. 1937), p. 27.

83. *Ibid.*, no. 7 (March 1935), pp. 1–4. Also see *ibid.*, no. 24 (Aug. 1935), pp. 1–2.

84. *Ibid.*, no. 11 (1934), p. 7.

85. *Ibid.*, no. 11 (Apr. 1935), pp. 32–3; no. 32 (Nov. 1935), pp. 1–3.

86. *KTsChO*, pp. 280–1. These practices were continuations of similar prac-

tices in the 1920s. See, for examples, *KIu*, no. 7 (15 Apr. 1928), p. 5; *SP*, no. 10 (30 July 1930), pp. 3–12; and Azizian, *Arenda zemli*, p. 71.

87. *RGAE*, f. 260, op. 1, d. 13, p. 38; V. I. Frolov, *God bor'by politotdela* (Arkhangel'sk, 1934), p. 6; P. I. Kushner, *The Village of Viriatino*, ed. and tr. Sula Benet (Garden City, N.Y., 1970), p. 180; *SIu*, no. 8 (20 March 1932), p. 14.

88. *SIu*, no. 2 (20 Jan. 1932), pp. 10, 23.

89. *RGAE*, f. 7446, op. 1, d. 240, p. 62.

90. *Istoriia kollektivizatsiia sel'skogo khoziaistva Gruzinskoi SSR* (Tbilisi, 1970), p. 436.

91. *RGAE*, f. 260, op. 1, d. 10, pp. 46–7.

92. For further information of a comparative nature, see Frederic L. Pryor, *The Red and the Green: The Rise and Fall of Collectivized Agriculture in Marxist Regimes* (Princeton, 1992), pp. 12–3.

93. *RGAE*, f. 7446, op. 5, d. 39, p. 183.

94. *Ibid.*, p. 156.

95. *Ibid.*, f. 7446, op. 14, d. 187, p. 22.

96. Gushchin, "Klassovaia bor'ba," p. 55; *KZS*, p. 197; *DS*, p. 38.

97. For example, *SIu*, no. 11 (June 1933), p. 4; *KSP*, p. 419; Iu. S. Borisov and D. M. Ezerskii, eds., "Dokumenty o politicheskoi i organizatsionno-khoziaistvennoi deiatel'nosti politotdelov sovkhozov v 1933–1935 gg.," *Materialy*, vol. 7, p. 388.

98. The Shakhty Affair was a contrived criminal case of "wrecking" held in 1928 and featuring industrial engineers and specialists working in the Donbass. The case was used to argue for the creation of a "proletarian cadre" of specialists, loyal to the regime.

99. *SIu*, nos. 2–3 (Jan. 1933), pp. 22–5.

100. *KTsPO*, p. 646.

101. *RGAE*, f. 7446, op. 14, d. 187, p. 22.

102. See Nove, *Economic History*, pp. 164–5; *Istoriia krest'ianstva SSSR*, vol. 2, pp. 234–5; and *Istoriia kolkhoznogo prava*, vol. 1, pp. 209–11, 212–3, 220–2, for relevant legislation. See also Table 3–1, for a statistical representation of the decline in livestock in these years.

103. *Istoriia krest'ianstva SSSR*, vol. 2, p. 235.

104. *SIu*, no. 9 (30 March 1932), pp. 9–12; no. 20 (20 July 1932), pp. 20–1.

105. *Ibid.*, no. 9 (30 March 1932), pp. 9–12.

106. *Istoriia krest'ianstva SSSR*, vol. 2, p. 235.

107. *RGAE*, f. 7446, op. 1, d. 240, p. 136.

108. *Ibid.*, f. 7446, op. 5, d. 45, p. 118. See also *SIu*, no. 11 (June 1933), pp. 6–7.

109. Vyltsan, Ivnitskii, and Poliakov, "Nekotorye problemy," p. 10.

110. *KSP*, p. 23; also see *ibid.*, p. 478, on Mordovia.

111. *RGAE*, f. 7446, op. 1, d. 240, p. 106.

112. *SIu*, no. 15 (Aug. 1933), pp. 8–10; *KZ*, pp. 368–9, 386, 419–20, 432; and Werth and Moullec, *Rapports secrets soviétiques*, p. 149.

113. For example, *KZ*, pp. 432, 664, n. 69.

114. V. P. Danilov, "Kollektivizatsiia: Kak eto bylo," *Pravda*, 16 Sept. 1988, p. 3.

115. Ivnitskii, *Kollektivizatsiia*, p. 22. See also *KZ*, p. 420; and *KZS*, pp. 268–70, for earlier, somewhat vague references to this migration.

116. *KZ*, p. 664, n. 69.

117. *Kollektivizatsiia sel'skogo khoziaistva Dagestanskoi ASSR,* vol. 2 (Makhachkala, 1976), p. 187.

118. *KZS,* pp. 268–70.

119. *Ibid.,* pp. 268–71; *KZ,* pp. 368–9; Danilov, "Kollektivizatsiia: Kak eto bylo." See also chap. 3.

120. Edgerton, *Memoirs of Peasant Tolstoyans,* p. 104.

121. For information about the widespread nature of "pilfering" already in 1930, see *RGAE,* f. 260, op. 1, d. 6, p. 172; and Fainsod, *Smolensk,* pp. 151–2, 261.

122. *SIu,* no. 2 (1934), pp. 8–11.

123. *Ibid.,* no. 1 (Jan. 1933), p. 6.

124. *Ibid.,* no. 4 (10 Feb. 1932), p. 32.

125. *Istoriia kolkhoznogo prava,* vol. 1, pp. 224–5.

126. Danilov, "Kollektivizatsiia: Kak eto bylo;" Ivnitskii, *Kollektivizatsiia,* pp. 21–2.

127. *SIu,* no. 9 (1934), p. 8; no. 13 (1934), p. 6; Popov, "Gosudarstvennyi terror," p. 26.

128. *SIu,* no. 4 (10 Feb. 1932), p. 32.

129. *Istoriia kolkhoznogo prava,* vol. 1, p. 224.

130. Ivnitskii, *Kollektivizatsiia,* pp. 21–2.

131. See also *SIu,* no. 2 (1934), pp. 8–11, in which it is claimed that 42.5% of the Northern *krai's* thieves were kulaks, 26.7% in Middle Volga, and 20% in Urals.

132. *Ibid.,* no. 16 (Aug. 1933), p. 6.

133. *Ibid.,* no. 1 (Jan. 1933), p. 6.

134. For example, *ibid.,* no. 15 (Aug. 1933), pp. 4–6.

135. *Ibid.,* no. 11 (1934), pp. 12–3.

136. *Ibid.,* no. 11 (1934), p. 2.

137. *Ibid.,* no. 16 (Aug. 1933), p. 7.

138. *Ibid.,* p. 4.

139. *Ibid.,* p. 2.

140. *Ibid.,* no. 11 (June 1933), p. 2.

141. Karavai, *Politotdel,* p. 11.

142. *SIu,* no. 15 (Aug. 1933), pp. 4–6.

143. *Ibid.,* no. 16 (Aug. 1933), p. 3; no. 21 (Nov. 1933), p. 12; no. 2 (1934), pp. 8–11.

144. *DIu,* no. 13 (Nov. 1933), p. 16.

145. *SIu,* no. 30 (Nov. 1934), p. 9.

146. For example, *ibid.,* nos. 2–3 (Jan. 1933), pp. 22–5; no. 15 (Aug. 1933), pp. 8–10.

147. *Ibid.,* no. 4 (10 Feb. 1932), p. 33. (He received a sentence of two-years incarceration.)

148. *Ibid.,* no. 21 (30 July 1931), p. 4.

149. *Ibid.,* no. 32 (30 Nov. 1932), p. 1; nos. 2–3 (Jan. 1933), pp. 22–5; *DIu,* no. 21 (Nov. 1931), pp. 2–4.

150. *SIu,* no. 32 (30 Nov. 1932), p. 1.

151. *DIu,* no. 4 (Feb. 1933), p. 11.

152. *SIu,* no. 7 (Apr. 1933), p. 21.

153. See *RGAE,* f. 260, op. 1, d. 5, p. 13; f. 260, op. 1, d. 11, p. 12; f. 260, op. 1, d. 16, p. 6.

154. Iu. A. Moshkov, *Zernovaia problema v gody sploshnoi kollektivizatsii sel'skogo khoziaistva SSSR* (Moscow, 1966), pp. 169–70.

155. *DIu*, no. 21 (Nov. 1931), pp. 2–4. Also *ibid.*, no. 20 (Nov. 1931), p. 5.

156. *RGAE*, f. 7446, op. 5, d. 51, p. 12.

157. *Ibid.*, p. 19. A *pud* equals approx. 36 pounds.

158. *SIu*, no. 22 (Nov. 1933), p. 4.

159. *Ibid.*, no. 15 (Aug. 1933), pp. 4–6.

160. E.g., *ibid.*, nos. 2–3 (Jan. 1933), pp. 28–9.

161. For further information, see Nobuo Shimotomai, "Springtime for the *Politotdel*: Local Party Organization in Crisis," *Acta Slavica Iaponica*, tomus IV (1986), pp. 11–2; Nobuo Shimotomai, "A Note on the Kuban Affair (1932–1933)," *Acta Slavica Iaponica*, tomus I (1983), pp. 45–8; Daniel Thorniley, *The Rise and Fall of the Soviet Rural Communist Party, 1927–39* (New York, 1988), pp. 112–7, 142–51.

162. *SIu*, no. 22 (Aug. 1931), p. 18; no. 16 (10 June 1932), p. 9; no. 15 (Aug. 1933), pp. 4–6; no. 16 (Aug. 1933), p. 7; no. 20 (1934), pp. 2–3; no. 1 (Jan. 1935), pp. 9–10.

163. *Ibid.*, no. 11 (20 Apr. 1931), p. 16; *Klassovaia bor'ba i prestupnost' na sovremennom etape*, vyp. I (Leningrad, 1933), p. 66. See Belov, *History of a Soviet Collective Farm*, p. 46, for similar practices in the 1940s.

164. *RGAE*, f. 7446, op. 5, d. 51, p. 18; *SIu*, no. 11 (20 Apr. 1931), p. 15; nos. 6–7 (10 March 1932), p. 6; no. 16 (10 June 1932), p. 9; no. 11 (June 1933), p. 2.

165. *SIu*, no. 21 (Nov. 1933), p. 4; no. 24 (Sept. 1934), p. 1; no. 26 (Oct. 1934), pp. 1–2.

166. *Ibid.*, no. 16 (Aug. 1933), pp. 5, 7–8.

167. *Ibid.*, no. 16 (1934), pp. 1–2; no. 20 (1934), pp. 2–3; no. 1 (Jan. 1935), pp. 9–10; *KTsPO*, p. 332.

168. *SIu*, no. 20 (1934), p. 1.

169. *Ibid.*, no. 3 (Jan. 1935), pp. 2–3.

170. *Ibid.*, no. 8 (Apr. 1933), pp. 2–5.

171. For example, *RGAE*, f. 7446, op. 16, d. 77, pp. 4, 19, 71.

172. *SIu*, nos. 6–7 (10 March 1932), pp. 7–8.

173. *RGAE*, f. 7446, op. 5, d. 51, p. 17.

174. *Ibid.*, f. 7486, op. 37, d. 122, p. 94.

175. Zelenin, "O nekotorykh 'belykh piatnakh'," p. 15.

176. Kondrashin, "Golod," p.180.

177. *SIu*, no. 11 (June 1933), p. 1; no. 13 (May 1935), pp. 1–6.

178. Arvo Tuominen, *The Bells of the Kremlin*, tr. Lily Leino (Hanover and London, 1983), pp. 117–23.

179. *KTsPO*, p. 743. (More often, peasants interpreted the clause on the "eternal [*vechnoe*] use of land" as a return to serfdom.)

180. For discussions of the law and the difficulties encountered in its implementation, see *SIu*, no. 29 (Oct. 1935), pp. 9–11; no. 3 (Jan. 1936), pp. 7–8; no. 10 (Apr. 1936), pp. 18–9; no. 5 (Feb. 1936), pp. 7–8; no. 16 (8 June 1936), pp. 4–6. The laws are published in *Sobranie zakonov*, no. 40 (11 Aug. 1933), pp. 613–4; no. 44 (4 Sept. 1935), pp. 674–5. (The amnesty covered the years 1928 to 1935.)

181. *RGAE*, f. 260, op. 1, d. 6, pp. 37–9; f. 260, op. 1, d. 11, p. 2.

182. *Ibid.*, f. 260, op. 1, d. 4, p. 16.

183. See chap. 4.

184. *SIu*, nos. 17–8 (30 June 1932), pp. 31–2.

185. *Ibid.*, no. 30 (Nov. 1934), p. 11. See also the full discussion of this case in chap. 4.

186. A good printed source for these types of documents is *Derevenskii* (earlier *Krest'ianskii*) *iurist*. The columns "Nam pishut" and "Signaly aktiva" are especially useful.

187. *SIu*, no. 29 (20 Oct. 1931), p. 18.

188. Karavai, *Politotdel*, pp. 46–7.

189. *Ibid.*

190. *Saratovskaia partiinaia organizatsiia v gody bor'by za zavershenie*, p. 79.

191. For example, *SIu*, no. 3 (Jan. 1936), p. 5; no. 12 (Apr. 1936), p. 3; no. 4 (28 Feb. 1937), p. 25; *DIu*, no. 15 (Aug. 1935), p. 9; *KTsPO*, p. 646. See also Manning, "Women," pp. 220–1.

192. Karavai, *Politotdel*, p. 41.

193. *DS*, p. 48. Also see Solzhenitsyn, *Gulag*, vol. 2, p. 392; *Vestnik krest'ianskoi Rossii*, nos. 9–10 (Feb.-March 1931), pp. 15–6.

194. Zemskov, "Spetsposelentsy," p. 6.

195. For example, *KZS*, pp. 163–4.

196. For example, *SIu*, no. 30 (30 Oct. 1932), p. 8; nos. 2–3 (Jan. 1933), pp. 28–9; no. 14 (July 1933), pp. 4–5. See also the incredible journeys of Ivan Tvardovskii in "Stranitsy perezhitogo," *Iunost'*, no. 3 (1988), pp. 11–29.

197. *SIu*, no. 27 (30 Sept. 1932), p. 23; and see chap. 3.

198. For example, *Sotsialisticheskoe pereustroistvo sel'skogo khoziaistva Moldavskoi ASSR*, p. 402.

199. Literature on the early modern European and American witch crazes is relevant here. See, for examples, H. R. Trevor-Roper, *The European Witch-Craze of the Sixteenth and Seventeenth Centuries and Other Essays* (New York, 1968), chap. 3; Joseph Klaits, *Servants of Satan* (Bloomington, 1985), esp. chap. 4; Paul Boyer and Stephen Nissenbaum, *Salem Possessed* (Cambridge, 1974); Demos, *Entertaining Satan*; Michael Kunze, *Highroad to the Stake: A Tale of Witchcraft*, tr. William E. Yuill (Chicago, 1987); Norman Cohn, *Europe's Inner Demons* (New York, 1977).

200. For a more detailed analysis, see Viola, "Second Coming," in Getty and Manning, eds., *Stalinist Terror*, pp. 70–81.

201. *Ibid.*, pp. 81–90.

202. *RGAE*, f. 260, op. 1, d. 5, p. 13; f. 260, op. 1, d. 11, p. 12; f. 260, op. 1, d. 16, p. 6.

203. Viola, "Second Coming," pp. 90–95.

204. *KZS*, p. 271.

205. For example., *RGAE*, f. 7446, op. 5, d. 39, p. 26; *Bol'shevik*, nos. 23–4 (30 Dec. 1930), p. 79; *Saratovskaia partiinaia organizatsiia v period nastupleniia*, pp. 130–1.

206. *RGAE*, f. 7446, op. 5, d. 39, pp. 62, 64; f. 7446, op. 5, d. 57, p. 16. (The practice appears to have occurred from the beginnning. See, e.g., *Molot*, 11 Feb. 1930, p. 3.)

207. *Istoriia kolkhoznogo prava*, vol. 1, p. 427.

208. *Ibid.*

209. *Ibid.*, pp. 427–30.

210. For example, see the legislation in *ibid.*, pp. 213–9, 352–3, 357–9.

211. This was in no sense of the word what Sheila Fitzpatrick has described as "negotiation" or "bargaining" between state and peasantry in *Stalin's Peasants*, pp. 7, 10.

Conclusion

1. Eugenia Semyonovna Ginzburg, *Journey into the Whirlwind*, tr. P. Stevenson and M. Hayward (New York, 1967), p. 3.

2. See J. Arch Getty, *Origins of the Great Purges* (Cambridge, 1985), pp. 207–10.

3. Solzhenitsyn, *Gulag*, esp. vol. 1. On prerevolutionary historical traditions, see Robert C. Tucker, *Stalin in Power* (New York, 1990). On the civil war, see Sheila Fitzpatrick, "The Legacy of the Civil War," in Koenker et al., eds. *Party, State, and Society*, pp. 385–98.

4. Scott, *Weapons of the Weak*, p. xvi.

5. *RGAE*, f. 7486, op. 37, d. 122, p. 103.

6. See Tables 5–1, 5–4; 4–1, 4–3.

7. For examples, see Tamara Dragadze, *Rural Families in Soviet Georgia* (New York, 1988), pp. 27, 34; and Perry, "Rural Violence in Socialist China," pp. 426–7.

8. For example, Fitzpatrick, *Stalin's Peasants*, pp. 319–20.

9. For a thoughtful discussion, see V. P. Danilov, "Agrarnaia reforma v postsovetskoi Rossii," *Kuda idet Rossiia?* (Moscow, 1994), pp. 125–36.

Glossary

baba   peasant woman (slightly pejorative)

batrak   landless rural laborer

chastushka   popular song

Kolkhoztsentr   All-Russian (later All-Union) Union of Agricultural Collectives; the primary agency in charge of the collective farm system and nominally under the jurisdiction of the Commissariat of Agriculture

kombed   committee of village poor

Komsomol   Communist Youth League

kulak   literally a "fist"; in Communist parlance, a capitalist farmer

MTS   machine-tractor station

muzhik   male peasant (slightly pejorative)

OGPU   *Ob"edinennoe gosudarstvennoe politicheskoe upravlenie* (internal security police)

okrug   county; administrative-territorial unit between the *raion* and regional levels

otkhodnik   seasonal peasant labor

peregiby   excesses

podkulachnik   kulak hireling, or literally "subkulak"

RIK   *raionnyi ispol'nitel'nyi komitet* (district-level executive committee of soviet government)

RSFSR   Russian Soviet Federative Socialist Republic

raion   district

razdel   peasant household division

samogon   moonshine

sel'kor/sel'korka   rural correspondent (male/female)

sel'sovet   lowest level of rural government

skhod   peasant assembly within the commune

smychka   worker-peasant alliance

SR   Socialist Revolutionary

starosta   peasant elder

Select Bibliography

ABBREVIATIONS

DIu	*Derevenskii iurist*
DS	*Dokumenty svidetel'stvuiut*
GARF	*Gosudarstvennyi arkhiv Rossiiskoi federatsii* (State Archive of the Russian Federation)
IR	*Iz istorii kollektivizatsii sel'skogo khoziaistva Riazanskoi oblasti*
IU	*Istoriia kollektivizatsii sel'skogo khoziaistva Urala*
IVS	*Istoriia kollektivizatsii sel'skogo khoziaistva v Vostochnoi Sibiri*
KIu	*Krest'ianskii iurist*
KK	*Kollektivizatsiia i razvitie sel'skogo khoziaistva na Kubani*
KNG	*Kollektivizatsiia sel'skogo khoziaistva v Nizhegorodskom-Gor'kovskom krae*
KS	*Kollektivizatsiia sel'skogo khoziaistva v Severnom raione*
KSK	*Kollektivizatsiia sel'skogo khoziaistva na Severnom Kavkaze*
KSP	*Kollektivizatsiia sel'skogo khoziaistva v Srednem Povolzh'e*
KSZ	*Kollektivizatsiia sel'skogo khoziaistva v Severo-Zapadnom raione*
KTsChO	*Kollektivizatsiia sel'skogo khoziaistva v Tsentral'no-Chernozemnoi oblasti*
KTsPO	*Kollektivizatsiia sel'skogo khoziaistva Tsentral'nogo Promyshlennogo raiona*
KZ	*Kollektivizatsiia sel'skogo khoziaistva v Zapadnom raione*
KZS	*Kollektivizatsiia sel'skogo khoziaistva Zapadnoi Sibiri*
PTP	*Put' trudovykh pobed*
RGAE	*Rossiiskii gosudarstvennyi arkhiv ekonomiki* (Russian State Archive of the Economy)
RTsKhIDNI	*Rossiiskii tsentr khraneniia i izucheniia dokumentov noveishei istorii* (Russian Center for the Preservation and Study of the Records of Contemporary History)
SIu	*Sovetskaia iustitsiia*
SP	*Sudebnaia praktika*

PRIMARY SOURCES

Archival Sources

Citations of archival materials are by *fond, opis', delo,* page(s) and abbreviated: f., op., d., p.

GARF (State Archive of the Russian Federation)
   fond 374 (NK RKI SSSR)
   fond 5457 (TsK soiuza tekstil'shchikov)
   fond 5469 (TsK soiuza metallistov)
RGAE (Russian State Archive of the Economy)
   fond 260 (Nauchno-issledovatel'skii kolkhoznoi institut)
   fond 3983 (Soiuz soiuzov sel'skokhoziaistvennoi kooperatsii RSFSR-SSSR)
   fond 5675 (Uchrezhdenie po rukovodstvu pereseleniem v SSSR)
   fond 7446 (Kolkhoztsentr SSSR i RSFSR)
   fond 7486 (Narkomzem SSSR)
RTsKhIDNI (Russian Center for the Preservation and Study of the Records of Contemporary History, formerly *Central Party Archive of the Institute of Marxism-Leninism)*
   fond 17 (Tsentral'nyi komitet KPSS)
   fond 78 (Mikhail Ivanovich Kalinin)
Sekretno-politicheskii otdel OGPU, "Dokladnaia zapiska o formakh i dinamike klassovoi bor'by v derevne v 1930 godu." From *The Tragedy of the Soviet Countryside.* 5 vols. Ed. V. P. Danilov, R. T. Manning, L. Viola. (Forthcoming.) (Excerpts of this document have recently been published in *Cahiers du monde Russe,* vol. 35, no. 3 [1994].)
Smolensk Archives

Russian and Soviet Periodicals

Bednota
Bol'shevik
Istoricheskii arkhiv
Kollektivist
Krest'ianskaia gazeta
Krest'ianskaia pravda
Krest'ianskii iurist/Derevenskii iurist
Litsom k derevne
Metallist
Molot
Na leninskom puti (Ivanovo-Voznesensk)
Na leninskom puti (Novosibirsk)
Nizhevolzhskii kolkhoznik
Otechestvennye arkhivy
Pravda
Proletarii
Sovetskaia etnografiia
Sotsialisticheskoe zemledelie
Sotsiologicheskie issledovaniia

Sovetskaia iustitsiia
Sovetskie arkhivy
Sudebnaia praktika
Trud
Vestnik krest'ianskoi Rossii
Voprosy istorii
Voprosy shefstva
Zaria vostoka

Published Documents, Laws, and Stenographic Reports

Bogdenko, M. L., ed. "Uchastie sovkhozov v sotsialisticheskoi perestroike derevni v 1929–30 gg." *Materialy po istorii SSSR: dokumenty po istorii sovetskogo obshchestva.* Vol. 7. Moscow, 1959.

Borisov, Iu. S., and Ezerkii, D. M., eds. "Dokumenty o politicheskoi i organizatsionno-khoziaistvennoi deiatel'nosti politotdelov sovkhozov v 1933–35 gg." *Materialy po istorii SSSR: dokumenty po istorii sovetskogo obshchestva.* Vol. 7. Moscow, 1959.

Chernomorskii, M. N., ed. "Rol' rabochikh brigad v bor'be za sploshnuiu kollektivizatsii v Tambovskoi derevne." *Materialy po istorii SSSR: dokumenty po istorii sovetskogo obshchestva.* Vol 1. Moscow, 1955.

XIV vserossiiskii s"ezd sovetov. Sten. otchet. Moscow, 1929.

Dokumenty svidetel'stvuiut: Iz istorii derevni nakanune i v khode kollektivizatsii, 1927–32 gg. Ed. V. P. Danilov and N. A. Ivnitskii. Moscow, 1989.

Gribkova, O. M., and Lepekhina, M. E., eds. "Uchastie rabochikh-metallistov v kolkhoznom stroitel'stve vesnoi 1930." *Istoricheskii arkhiv*, no. 2 (1955).

Istoriia kolektivizatsii sil's'kogo gospodarstva Ukrains'koi RSR. Vol. 2. Kiev, 1965.

Istoriia kolkhoznogo prava: Sb. zakonodatel'nykh materialov SSSR i RSFSR, 1917–1958 gg. 2 vols. Moscow, 1958–59.

Istoriia kollektivizatsii sel'skogo khoziaistva Gruzinskoi SSR. Tbilisi, 1970.

Istoriia kollektivizatsii sel'skogo khoziaistva Urala. Perm, 1983.

Istoriia kollektivizatsii sel'skogo khoziaistva v Vostochnoi Sibiri. Irkutsk, 1979.

Ivnitskii, N. A., ed. "Dokladnaia zapiska Kolkhoztsentra v TsK VKP(b) o kolkhoznom stroitel'stve v 1928–29 gg." *Materialy po istorii SSSR: dokumenty po istorii sovetskogo obshchestva.* Vol. 7. Moscow, 1959.

Iz istorii kollektivizatsii sel'skogo khoziaistva Dal'nego Vostoka. Khabarovsk, 1979.

Iz istorii kollektivizatsii sel'skogo khoziaistva Riazanskoi oblasti. Riazan, 1962.

Iz istorii raskulachivaniia v Karelii, 1930–31: dokumenty i materialy. Petrozavodsk, 1991.

Kolesova, M. E., ed. "Kollektivizatsiia i krest'ianstvo v zerkale pisem 25-tysiachnikov." *Sovetskie arkhivy*, no. 3 (1991).

Kollektivizatsiia i razvitie sel'skogo khoziaistva na Kubani. Krasnodar, 1981.

Kollektivizatsiia sel'skogo khoziaistva Bashkirskoi ASSR. Ufa, 1980.

Kollektivizatsiia sel'skogo khoziaistva Dagestanskoi ASSR. Vol. 2. Makhachkala, 1976.

Kollektivizatsiia sel'skogo khoziaistva Iakutskoi ASSR. Iakutsk, 1978.

Kollektivizatsiia sel'skogo khoziaistva na Severnom Kavkaze. Krasnodar, 1972.

Kollektivizatsiia sel'skogo khoziaistva Tsentral'nogo Promyshlennogo raiona. Riazan, 1971.

Kollektivizatsiia sel'skogo khoziaistva Turkmenskoi SSSR. Vol. 2. Ashkhabad, 1968.

Kollektivizatsiia sel'skogo khoziaistva v Nizhegorodskom-Gor'kovskom krae. Kirov, 1985.

Kollektivizatsiia sel'skogo khoziaistva v Severnom raione. Vologda, 1964.

Kollektivizatsiia sel'skogo khoziaistva v Severo-Zapadnom raione. Leningrad, 1970.

Kollektivizatsiia sel'skogo khoziaistva v Srednem Povolzh'e. Kuibyshev, 1970.

Kollektivizatsiia sel'skogo khoziaistva v Tsentral'no-Chernozemnoi oblasti. Voronezh, 1978.

Kollektivizatsiia sel'skogo khoziaistva v Zapadnom raione. Smolensk, 1968.

Kollektivizatsiia sel'skogo khoziaistva Zapadnoi Sibiri. Tomsk, 1972.

KPSS v rezoliutsiiakh i resheniiakh s"ezdov, konferentsii i plenumov TsK. 7th ed. Part II. Moscow, 1953.

Liapina, T. A., ed. "Iz istorii Tambovskoi derevni nachala 30-kh godov." *Sovetskie arkhivy,* no. 6 (1991).

Maksudov, Sergei, ed. *Neuslyshannye golosa: dokumenty Smolenskogo arkhiva.* Vol. 1. Ann Arbor, 1987.

Materialy po istorii SSSR: dokumenty po istorii sovetskogo obshchestva. 7 vols. Moscow, 1955–59.

Neizvestnaia Rossiia. XX vek. 4 vols. Moscow, 1992–4.

The Penal Code of the RSFSR (Text of 1926 with Amendments up to Dec. 1, 1932). London, 1934.

XV s"ezd VKP (b). Sten. otchet. 2 vols. Moscow, 1961–62.

Pis'ma I. V. Stalina V. M. Molotovu, 1925–1936 gg. Moscow, 1995.

Politicheskii i trudovoi pod"em rabochego klassa SSSR (1928–29 gg.). Sb. dokumentov. Moscow, 1956.

Put' trudovykh pobed. Volgograd, 1967.

Saratovskaia partiinaia organizatsiia v gody bor'by za zavershenie sotsialisticheskoi rekonstruktsii narodnogo khoziaistva. Saratov, 1963.

Saratovskaia partiinaia organizatsiia v gody sotsialisticheskoi industrializatsii strany i podgotovki sploshnoi kollektivizatsii sel'skogo khoziaistva (1926–29 gg.). Saratov, 1960.

Saratovskaia partiinaia organizatsiia v period nastupleniia sotsializma po vsemu frontu: Sozdanie kolkhoznogo stroia. Saratov, 1961.

XVII s"ezd VKP(b). Sten. otchet. Moscow, 1934.

XVI s"ezd VKP(b). Sten. otchet. Moscow-Leningrad, 1930.

Sobranie uzakonenii i rasporiazhenii raboche-krest'ianskogo pravitel'stva RSFSR.

Sobranie zakonov i rasporiazhenii raboche-krest'ianskogo pravitel'stva SSSR.

Sotsialisticheskoe pereustroistvo sel'skogo khoziaistva Moldavskoi ASSR. Kishinev, 1964.

Spetspereselentsy v Zapadnoi Sibiri, 1930-vesna 1931 g. Ed. V. P. Danilov and S. A. Krasil'nikov. Novosibirsk, 1992.

Trudy pervoi vsesoiuznoi konferentsii agrarnikov-marksistov. Vol. 1. Moscow, 1930.

Vnutrennie voiska v gody mirnogo sotsialisticheskogo stroitel'stva, 1922–41 gg. Dokumenty i materialy. Moscow, 1977.

Vtoraia sessiia VTsIK XIV sozyva. Sten. otchet. Moscow, 1929.

Werth, Nicolas, and Moullec, Gael, eds. *Rapports secrets sovietiques, 1921–1991: La societe Russe dans les documents confidentiels.* Paris, 1994.

Zapadnyi oblastnoi komitet VKP (b). Sten. otchet 2-i oblastnoi partkonferentsii. Moscow-Smolensk, 1931.

Zavershenie kollektivizatsii sel'skogo khoziaistva i organizatsionno-khoziaistvennoe ukreplenie kolkhozov Belorusskoi SSSR. Sb. dokumentov i materialov. Minsk, 1985.

Other Primary Sources

Agabekov, Georges. *OGPU: The Russian Secret Terror.* New York, 1931.

Angarov, A. *Klassovaia bor'ba v derevne i sel'sovet.* Moscow, 1929.

Azizian, A. K. *Arenda zemli i bor'ba s kulakom.* Moscow-Leningrad, 1929.

Bel'bei, R. *Za ili protiv.* Moscow, 1930.

Belov, Fedor. *The History of a Collective Farm.* New York, 1955.

Berson, L. *Vesna 1930 goda. Zapiska dvadtsatipiatitysiachnika.* Moscow, 1931.

Bol'shakov, A. M. *Derevnia, 1917–27.* Moscow, 1927.

———. *Kommuna Kudrova.* Leningrad, 1930.

Burov, Ia. *Derevnia na perelome (god raboty v derevne).* Moscow-Leningrad, 1926.

Chto nuzhno znat' kazhdomu rabotniku kolkhoza? Moscow, 1930.

Derevnia pri NEP'e: kogo schitat' kulakom, kogo—truzhenikom, chto goveriat ob etom krest'iane? Moscow, 1924.

Dolot, Miron. *Execution by Hunger.* New York, 1985.

Dolotov, A. *Tserkov' i sektantstvo v Sibiri.* Novosibirsk, 1930.

Dorofeev, Ia. *Derevnia Moskovskoi gubernii.* Moscow, 1923.

Edgerton, William, ed. *Memoirs of Peasant Tolstoyans in Soviet Russia.* Bloomington, 1993.

Elizarov, N. V. *Likvidatsiia kulachestva kak klassa.* Moscow-Leningrad, 1930.

Erikhonov, L. *Kulak pered sudom.* Samara, 1929.

Ermolaev, A. I. *Kollektivizatsiia i klassovaia bor'ba v Leningradskoi oblasti.* Moscow-Leningrad, 1931.

Evdokimov, A. *Kolkhozy v klassovykh boiakh.* Leningrad, 1930.

———. *V bor'be za molodezh': klassovaia bor'ba v derevne.* Leningrad, 1929.

Fedin, P. *Klassovaia bor'ba v derevne.* Voronezh, 1929.

Fertaup, E. L. *Nizovoi sovetskii apparat i derevnia Urala.* Sverdlovsk, 1925.

Frolov, V. I. *God bor'by politotdela.* Arkhangel'sk, 1934.

Furman, G. *Kak pomogali kolkhozam 25-tysiachniki.* Moscow, 1930.

Gagarin, A. *Khoziaistvo, zhizn' i nastroeniia derevni (po itogam obsledovaniia Pochinkovskoi volosti Smolenskoi gubernii).* Moscow-Leningrad, 1925.

Golubykh, M. *Kazach'ia derevnia.* Moscow-Leningrad, 1930.

———. *Ocherki glukhoi derevni.* Moscow, 1926.

Gorkii, M., et al., eds. *Belomor.* New York, 1935.

Gorky, Maxim. "On the Russian Peasantry." *Journal of Peasant Studies,* vol. 4, no. 1 (Oct. 1976).

Gozhanskii, A. *V razvernutoe nastuplenie na kulaka.* Leningrad, 1931.

Grigorenko, Petro G. *Memoirs.* Tr. Thomas P. Whitney. New York, 1982.

Hindus, Maurice. *Red Bread: Collectivization in a Russian Village.* Bloomington, 1988.

Iakovlev, Ia. *Derevnia kak ona est' (ocherki Nikol'skoi volosti).* 2nd ed. Moscow, 1923.

Iartsev, A. *Sekta evangel'skikh khristian.* 2nd ed. Moscow, 1928.

Karavaev, A., and Sosnovskii, A. *Krasnopolianskii gigant.* Moscow, 1929.

Karavai, Mikhail. *Politotdel.* Moscow, 1934.

Katsenel'baum, D. "Zhenshchina v kolkhoze." In *Zhenshchina v kolkhoze.* Ed. V. Ulasevich. Moscow, 1930.

Kavraiskii, V., and Khamarmer, I. *Uroki klassovoi bor'by: itogi vyborov sovetov Sibiri 1928–29.* Novosibirsk, 1929.

Kavraiskii, V., and Nusinov, I. *Klassy i klassovaia bor'ba v sovremennoi derevne.* 2nd ed. Novosibirsk, 1929.

Klassovaia bor'ba i prestupnost' na sovremennom etape. Vyp. I. Leningrad, 1933.

Komarov, N. G. *Litso klassovogo vraga: klassovaia bor'ba v derevne vo vremia perevyborov sel'skikh sovetov v 1929 godu (po materialam rabochikh shefskikh brigad).* Leningrad, 1929.

Kravchenko, Elena. *Krest'ianka v kolkhozakh.* Moscow, 1929.

Krest'iane o sovetskoi vlasti. Moscow-Leningrad, 1929.

Kretov, F. *Derevnia posle revoliutsii.* Moscow, 1925.

Kureiko, M. *25-tysiachniki na kolkhoznoi stroike.* Moscow-Leningrad, 1930.

Lagovier, N. *O samosudakh.* Moscow-Leningrad, 1927.

Leikin, S. "Krest'ianka v klassovoi bor'be." In *Zhenshchina v kolkhoze.* Ed. V. Ulasevich. Moscow, 1930.

Lenin, V. I. *Polnoe sobranie sochinenii,* 5th ed. 55 vols. Moscow, 1958–66.

Litso donskoi derevni k 1925 g. (po materialam obsledovaniia DKK i Don. RKI.) Rostov n/D, 1925.

Luzhin, A., and Rezunov, M. *Nizovoi sovetskii apparat.* Moscow, 1929.

Nakhimson, F.; Roginskii, G.; and Sakhov, B. *Sud i prokuratura na okhrane proizvodstva i truda.* Part II. Moscow, 1932.

Pirogov, Peter. *Why I Escaped.* New York, n.d.

Radin, A., and Shaumian, L. *Za chto zhiteli stanitsy poltavskoi vyseliaiutsia s Kubani v severnye kraia.* Rostov n/Donu, 1932.

Rosnitskii, N. *Polgoda v derevne: osnovnye itogi obsledovaniia 28 volostei i 32,730 krest'ianskikh khoziaistv Penzenskoi gub.* Penza, 1925.

Rozit, D. P. *Partiia i sovety v derevne.* Moscow, 1925.

———. *Proverka raboty nizovogo apparata v derevne: osnovnye itogi proverki nizovogo apparata chlenami TsKK RKP(b) v 12 uezdakh i okrugakh SSSR.* Moscow, 1926.

Ryklin, G. Kh. *Kak sovetskaia pechat' pomagaet krest'ianinu.* Moscow-Leningrad, 1926.

Selishchev, A. *Iazyk revoliutsionnoi epokhi.* Moscow, 1928.

Shafir, Ia. *Gazeta i derevnia.* 2nd ed. Moscow-Leningrad, 1924.

Shuvaev, K. M. *Staraia i novaia derevnia (materialy issledovaniia s. Novo-Zhivotinnogo i der. Mokhovatki Berezovskogo raiona, Voronezhskoi oblasti za 1901 i 1907, 1926 i 1937 gg.).* Moscow, 1937.

Sokolov, A. *Kommuna 'Kolos'.* Moscow-Leningrad, 1929.

Stalin, I. *Sochineniia.* 13 vols. Moscow, 1946–52.

Strong, Anna Louise. *The Soviets Conquer Wheat.* New York, 1931.

Tan-Bogoraz, V. G., ed. *Komsomol v derevne: ocherki.* Moscow-Leningrad, 1926.

———, ed. *Obnovlennaia derevnia.* Leningrad, 1925.

———, ed. *Revolutsiia v derevne.* Pt. I. Moscow-Leningrad, 1924.

———, ed. *Staryi i novyi byt.* Leningrad, 1924.

Timofeev, G. *Mezha umerla: Krasnopolianskii raion sploshnoi kollektivizatsii.* Moscow, 1930.

Tvardovskii, Ivan. "Stranitsy perezhitogo." *Iunost',* no. 3 (1988).

Ulasevich, V. "Zhenshchina na stroike sotsializma." *Zhenshchina v kolkhoze.* Ed. V. Ulasevich. Moscow, 1930.

Vareikis, I. *O sploshnoi kollektivizatsii i likvidatsii kulachestva kak klassa.* Voronezh, 1930.

Zamiatin, S. *Burnyi god. Opyt raboty piatitysiachnika v Rudnianskom raione na Nizhnei Volge.* Moscow, 1931.

Zhenshchina v kolkhoze. Ed. V. Ulasevich. Moscow, 1930.

SECONDARY SOURCES

Adas, Michael. *Prophets of Rebellion: Millenarian Protest Movements Against the European Colonial Order.* Chapel Hill, N.C., 1979.

Alavi, Hamza. "Peasant Classes and Primordial Loyalties." *Journal of Peasant Studies,* vol. 1, no. 1 (Oct. 1973).

Atkinson, Dorothy. *The End of the Russian Land Commune, 1905–1930.* Stanford, 1983.

Berce, Yves-Marie. *History of Peasant Revolts: The Social Origins of Rebellion in Early Modern France.* Tr. Amanda Whitmore. Ithaca, 1990.

Berger, John. "The Vision of a Peasant." In *Peasants and Peasant Society.* 2nd ed. Ed. Teodor Shanin. Oxford, 1987.

Bethea, David M. *The Shape of Apocalypse in Modern Russian Fiction.* Princeton, 1989.

Bonnell, Victoria E. "The Peasant Woman in Stalinist Political Art of the 1930s." *American Historical Review,* vol. 98, no. 1 (Feb. 1993).

Bridger, Susan. *Women in the Soviet Countryside: Women's Roles in Rural Development in the Soviet Union.* Cambridge, 1987.

Brooks, Jeffrey. "The Breakdown of Production and Distribution of Printed Material, 1917–1927." In *Bolshevik Culture.* Ed. Abbot Gleason, Peter Kenez, Richard Stites. Bloomington, 1985.

Burke, Peter. *Popular Culture in Early Modern Europe.* New York, 1978.

Bushnell, John. *Mutiny Amid Repression: Russian Soldiers in the Revolution of 1905–06.* Bloomington, 1985.

Carr, E. H. *Foundations of a Planned Economy.* Vol. 2. London, 1978.

Cherniavsky, Michael. "The Old Believers and the New Religion." In *The Structure of Russian History.* Ed. Michael Cherniavsky. New York, 1970.

Chernopitskii, P. G. *Na velikom perelome: sel'skie sovety Dona v period podgotovki i provedeniia massovoi kollektivizatsii.* Rostov, 1965.

Christian, David. *"Living Water": Vodka and Russian Society on the Eve of Emancipation.* Oxford, 1990.

Clements, Barbara Evans. "The Effects of the Civil War on Women and Family Relations." In *Party, State, and Society in the Russian Civil War: Explorations in Social History.* Ed. Diane P. Koenker, William G. Rosenberg, and Ronald Grigor Suny. Bloomington, 1989.

Cobb, R. C. *The Police and the People: French Popular Protest, 1789–1820.* Oxford, 1970.

Cohn, Norman. *Europe's Inner Demons*. New York, 1977.

———. *The Pursuit of the Millennium*. London, 1957.

Colburn, Forrest D., ed. *Everyday Forms of Peasant Resistance*. Armonk, N.Y., 1989.

Conquest, Robert. *The Harvest of Sorrow*. New York, 1986.

Danilov, V. P. "Glava piataia: kollektivizatsiia sel'skogo khoziaistva v SSSR." *Istoriia SSSR*, no. 5 (1990).

———. "Kollektivizatsiia: kak eto bylo." *Pravda*, 15 Sept. 1988.

———. "Krest'ianskii otkhod na promysly v 1920-kh godakh." *Istoricheskie zapiski*, vol. 94 (1974).

———. "Sel'skoe naselenie soiuza SSR nakanune kollektivizatsii." *Istoricheskie zapiski*, vol. 74 (1963).

———. *Sovetskaia dokolkhoznaia derevnia*. 2 vols. Moscow, 1977–79.

———, et al. *Sovetskoe krest'ianstvo: kratkii ocherk istorii (1917–70)*. 2nd ed. Moscow, 1973.

Davies, R. W. *The Socialist Offensive: The Collectivisation of Soviet Agriculture, 1929–1930*. Cambridge, Mass., 1980.

———. *The Soviet Collective Farm, 1929–30*. Cambridge, Mass., 1980.

Davis, Natalie Zemon. "Women on Top." *Society and Culture in Early Modern France*. Stanford, 1975.

Demos, John Putnam. *Entertaining Satan: Witchcraft and the Culture of Early New England*. New York, 1982.

Deutscher, Issac. *Stalin*. 2nd ed. New York, 1977.

Egorova, L. P. "K voprosu o kontrrevoliutsionnoi deiatel'nosti kulachestva v Zapadnoi Sibiri v 1928–29 gg." *Sbornik rabot aspirantov kafedry istorii KPSS*. Tomsk, 1974.

———. "Klassovaia bor'ba v Zapadnosibirskoi derevne v khode khlebozagotovital'nykh kampanii (1928–30 gg.)." *Osushchestvlenie agrarnoi politiki KPSS v Sibiri i na Dal'nom Vostoke*. Tomsk, 1986.

Eklof, Ben. *Russian Peasant Schools: Officialdom, Village Culture, and Popular Pedagogy, 1861–1914*. Berkeley, 1986.

Fainsod, Merle. *Smolensk Under Soviet Rule*. Cambridge, Mass., 1958.

Farnsworth, Beatrice, and Viola, Lynne, eds. *Russian Peasant Women*. New York, 1992.

Field, Daniel. *Rebels in the Name of the Tsar*. Boston, 1976.

Figes, Orlando. *Peasant Russia, Civil War: The Volga Countryside in Revolution, 1917–21*. Oxford, 1989.

Fitzpatrick, Sheila. *Stalin's Peasants: Resistance and Survival in the Russian Village after Collectivization*. New York, 1994.

Frierson, Cathy A. *Peasant Icons: Representations of Rural People in Late Nineteenth Century Russia*. New York, 1993.

Frank, Stephen P. "Confronting the Domestic Other: Rural Popular Culture and Its Enemies in Fin-de-Siecle Russia." In *Cultures in Flux: Lower-Class Values, Practices, and Resistance in Late Imperial Russia*. Ed. Stephen P. Frank and Mark D. Steinberg. Princeton, 1994.

———. "Popular Justice, Community, and Culture Among the Russian Peasantry, 1870–1900." In *The World of the Russian Peasant*. Ed. Ben Eklof and Stephen P. Frank. Boston, 1990.

———. "Simple Folk, Savage Customs? Youth, Sociability, and the Dynamics of

Culture in Rural Russia, 1856–1914." *Journal of Social History*, vol. 25, no. 4 (1992).

Funkenstein, Amos. "A Schedule for the End of the World: The Origins and Persistence of the Apocalyptic Mentality." In *Visions of Apocalypse: End or Rebirth?* Ed. Saul Friedlander et al. New York, 1985.

Geertz, Clifford. *The Interpretation of Cultures*. New York, 1973.

Genovese, Eugene D. *From Rebellion to Revolution: Afro-American Slave Revolts in the Making of the New World*. New York, 1981.

Getty, J. Arch, and Manning, Roberta T., eds. *Stalinist Terror: New Perspectives*. Cambridge, 1993.

Gushchin, N. Ia. "Iz istorii klassovoi bor'by v Sibirskoi derevne v 1928–29 gg." *Izvestiia Sibirskogo otdeleniia AN SSSR (seriia obshch. nauk)*, no. 1, vyp. 1 (Jan. 1967).

———. "Klassovaia bor'ba v Sibirskoi derevne nakanune i v gody massovoi kollektivizatsii." *Problemy sotsial'no-ekonomicheskogo razvitiia sovetskoi derevni*. Vologda, 1975.

———. "Likvidatsiia kulachestva kak klassa v Sibirskoi derevne." *Sotsial'naia struktura naseleniia Sibiri*. Novosibirsk, 1970.

———, and Il'inykh, V. A. *Klassovaia bor'ba v Sibirskoi derevne 1920-e—seredina 1930-kh gg.* Novosibirsk, 1987.

Hay, Douglas. "Time, Inequality, and Law's Violence." In *Law's Violence*. Ed. Austin Sarat and Thomas R. Kearns. Ann Arbor, 1992.

Hobsbawm, E. J. "Peasants and Politics." *Journal of Peasant Studies*, vol. 1, no. 1 (Oct. 1973).

———. *Social Bandits and Primitive Rebels: Studies in Archaic Forms of Social Movement in the 19th and 20th Centuries*. Glencoe, Ill., 1959.

Hobsbawm, Eric, and Rude, George. *Captain Swing: A Social History of the Great English Agricultural Uprising of 1830*. New York, 1975.

Hoffmann, David L. "Moving to Moscow: Patterns of Peasant In-Migration During the First Five-Year Plan." *Slavic Review*, vol. 50, no. 4 (winter 1991).

———. *Peasant Metropolis: Social Identities in Moscow, 1929–41*. Ithaca, 1994.

Hughes, James. *Stalin, Siberia and the Crisis of the New Economic Policy*. Cambridge, 1991.

Ikonnikova, I. P., and Ugrovatov, A. P. "Stalinskaia repetitsiia nastupleniia na krest'ianstvo." *Voprosy istorii KPSS*, no. 1 (1991).

Istoriia krest'ianstva SSSR. Vol. 2. Moscow, 1978.

Ivnitskii, N. A. "Istoriia podgotovki postanovleniia TsK VKP(b) o tempakh kollektivizatsii sel'skogo khoziaistva ot 5 ianvaria 1930 g." *Istochnikovedenie istorii sovetskogo obshchestva*. Vyp. 1. Moscow, 1964.

———. *Klassovaia bor'ba v derevne i likvidatsiia kulachestva kak klassa*. Moscow, 1972.

———. "Klassovaia bor'ba v derevne v period podgotovki i provedeniia kollektivizatsii sel'skogo khoziaistva." *Problemy agrarnoi istorii*. Chast' 2. Minsk, 1978.

———. *Kollektivizatsiia sel'skogo khoziaistva v SSSR: opyt, uroki, vyvody*. Moscow, 1988.

Jung, C. G. *Flying Saucers: A Modern Myth of Things Seen in the Skies*. Tr. R. F. C. Hull. Princeton, 1978.

Karcz, Jerzy F. "Thoughts on the Grain Problem." *Soviet Studies,* vol. 18, no. 4 (April, 1967).

Karevskii, F. A. "Likvidatsiia kulachestva kak klassa v Srednem Povolzh'e." *Istoricheskie zapiski,* vol. 80 (1967).

Kingston-Mann, Esther. *Lenin and the Problem of Marxist Peasant Revolution.* New York, 1983.

Kingston-Mann, Esther, and Mixter, Timothy, eds. *Peasant Economy, Culture, and Politics of European Russia, 1800–1921.* Princeton, 1991.

Kireev, R. N. "K voprosu ob istoricheskoi neizbezhnosti likvidatsii kulachestva kak klassa (po materialam Iuzhnogo Zaural'ia)." *Voprosy agrarnoi istorii Urala i Zapadnoi Sibiri.* Kurgan, 1971.

Kondrashin, V. V. "Golod 1932–33 godov v derevniakh Povolzh'ia." *Voprosy istorii,* no. 6 (1991).

Krest'ianstvo Sibiri v period stroitel'stva sotsializma. Novosibirsk, 1983.

Kselman, Thomas. *Miracles and Prophecies in Nineteenth-Century France.* New Brunswick, N.J., 1983.

Kushner, P. I. *The Village of Viriatino.* Ed. and tr. Sula Benet. Garden City, N.Y., 1970.

Ladurie, Emmanuel Le Roy. *Carnival at Romans.* Tr. Mary Feeney. New York, 1980.

Lefebvre, Georges. *The Great Fear of 1789: Rural Panic in Revolutionary France.* Tr. J. White. London, 1973.

Lewin, Moshe. *The Making of the Soviet System: Essays in the Social History of Interwar Russia.* New York, 1985.

———. *Russian Peasants and Soviet Power: A Study of Collectivization.* Tr. Irene Nove. New York, 1975.

Lih, Lars T. *Bread and Authority in Russia, 1914–21.* Berkeley, 1990.

Lucas, Colin. "The Crowd and Politics Between *Ancien Regime* and Revolution in France." *Journal of Modern History,* vol. 60, no. 3 (Sept. 1988).

Male, D. J. *Russian Peasant Organisation before Collectivisation.* Cambridge, 1971.

Manning, Roberta Thompson. *The Crisis of the Old Order in Russia: Gentry and Government.* Princeton, 1982.

———. "Women in the Soviet Countryside on the Eve of World War II, 1935–1940." In *Russian Peasant Women.* Ed. Beatrice Farnsworth and Lynne Viola. New York, 1992.

Martovitskii, I. K. "Babii bunt." In *Pervaia borozda.* Ed. A. F. Chmyga and M. O. Levkovich. Moscow, 1981.

Medvedev, Roy. *Let History Judge: The Origins and Consequences of Stalinism.* Tr. George Shriver. New York, 1989.

Medvedev, V. K. *Krutoi povorot: iz istorii kollektivizatsii sel'skogo khoziaistva Nizhnego Povolzh'ia.* Saratov, 1961.

Medvedev, Zhores A. *Soviet Agriculture.* New York, 1987.

Mikhailov, N., and Teptsov, N. "Chrezvychaishchina." *Rodina,* no. 8 (1989).

Miller, Robert F. *One Hundred Thousand Tractors.* Cambridge, Mass., 1970.

Mixter, Timothy. "The Hiring Market as Workers' Turf: Migrant Agricultural Laborers and the Mobilization of Collective Action in the Steppe Grainbelt of European Russia, 1853–1913." In *Peasant Economy, Culture, and Politics of European Russia.* Ed. Esther Kingston-Mann and Timothy Mixter. Princeton, 1991.

Moon, David. *Russian Peasants and Tsarist Legislation on the Eve of Reform: Interaction between Peasants and Officialdom, 1825–1855.* London, 1992.

Moore, Barrington Jr. *Social Origins of Dictatorship and Democracy: Lord and Peasant in the Making of the Modern World.* Boston, 1967.

Moshkov, Iu. A. *Zernovaia problema v gody sploshnoi kollektivizatsii sel'skogo khoziaistva SSSR.* Moscow, 1966.

Nemakov, N. I. *Kommunisticheskaia partiia—organizator massovogo kolkhoznogo dvizheniia.* Moscow, 1966.

Narkiewicz, Olga A. *The Making of the Soviet State Apparatus.* Manchester 1970.

Niccoli, Ottavia. *Prophecy and People in Renaissance Italy.* Tr. L. G. Cochrane. Princeton, 1990.

Nove, Alec. *An Economic History of the USSR.* New York, 1990.

Oja, Matt F. "*Traktorizatsiia* as Cultural Conflict, 1929–33." *Russian Review,* vol. 51, no. 3 (July 1992).

Perry, Elizabeth J. "Rural Violence in Socialist China." *The China Quarterly,* no. 2 (1985).

Polishchuk, N. S. "U istokov sovetskikh prazdnikov." *Sovetskaia etnografiia,* no. 6 (1987).

Popov, V. P. "Gosudarstvennyi terror v sovetskoi Rossii. 1923–53 gg." *Otechestvennye arkhivy,* no. 2 (1992).

Problemy agrarnoi istorii sovetskogo obshchestva: materialy nauchnoi konferentsii, 9–12 iiunia 1969 g. Moscow, 1971.

Pryor, Frederic L. *The Red and the Green: The Rise and Fall of Collectivized Agriculture in Marxist Regimes.* Princeton, 1992.

Ranger, Terrence. "Peasant Consciousness: Culture and Conflict in Zimbabwe." In *Peasants and Peasant Societies.* 2nd ed. Ed. Teodor Shanin. Oxford, 1987.

Redfield, Robert. *Peasant Society and Culture.* Chicago, 1956.

Rude, George. *The Crowd in the French Revolution.* New York, 1972.

Sabean, David Warren. *Power in the Blood: Popular Culture and Village Discourse in Early Modern Germany.* Cambridge, 1984.

Sathyamurthy, T. V. "Indian Peasant Historiography: A Critical Perspective on Ranajit Guha's Work." *Journal of Peasant Studies,* vol. 18, no. 1 (Oct. 1990).

Schneer, Matthew. "A Peasant Community During Russia's First Revolution." *Slavic Review,* vol. 53, no. 1 (spring 1994).

Scott, James C. *Domination and the Arts of Resistance: Hidden Transcripts.* New Haven, 1990.

———. "Hegemony and the Peasantry." *Politics and Society,* vol. 7, no. 3 (1977).

———. *The Moral Economy of the Peasant: Rebellion and Subsistence in Southeast Asia.* New Haven, 1976.

———. *Weapons of the Weak: Everyday Forms of Peasant Resistance.* New Haven, 1985.

Shanin, Teodor. *The Awkward Class: Political Sociology of Peasantry in a Developing Society. Russia, 1910–1925.* Oxford, 1972.

———. *Defining Peasants.* Oxford 1990.

———, ed. *Peasants and Peasant Societies.* 2nd ed. Oxford, 1987.

————. *The Roots of Otherness: Russia's Turn of Century.* 2 vols. New Haven, 1985–6.

Shimotomai, Nobuo. "A Note on the Kuban Affair (1932–33)." *Acta Slavica Iaponica.* Tomus I (1983).

————. "Springtime for the *Politotdel:* Local Party Organizations in Crisis." *Acta Slavica Iaponica.* Tomus IV (1986).

Sidorov, V. A. "Likvidatsiia v SSSR kulachestva kak klassa." *Voprosy istorii,* no. 7 (1968).

Solzhenitsyn, Aleksandr I. *The Gulag Archipelago.* Tr. Thomas P. Whitney and Harry Willetts. 3 vols. New York, 1973–78.

Stites, Richard. *Revolutionary Dreams.* New York, 1989.

Thompson, E. P. "The Crime of Anonymity." In *Albion's Fatal Tree: Crime and Society in Eighteenth Century England.* Ed. Douglas Hay et al. London, 1975.

————. "The Moral Economy of the English Crowd in the Eighteenth Century." *Past and Present,* no. 50 (Feb. 1971).

Thorniley, Daniel. *The Rise and Fall of the Soviet Rural Communist Party, 1927–39.* New York, 1988.

Tilly, Charles; Tilly, Louise; and Tilly, Richard. *The Rebellious Century, 1830–1930.* Cambridge, 1975.

Trifonov, I. Ia. *Likvidatsiia ekspluatatorskikh klassov v SSSR.* Moscow, 1975.

————. *Ocherki istorii klassovoi bor'by v SSSR v gody NEPa.* Moscow, 1960.

Ugrovatov, A. P. "Bor'ba kommunistov organov iustitsii Sibiri s kulachestvom v khlebozagotovitel'nuiu kampaniiu 1929/30 gg." *Deiatel'nost' partiinykh organizatsii Sibiri po sotsialisticheskomu preobrazovaniiu i razvitiiu derevne.* Novosibirsk, 1982.

Ulanovskaia, Bella. "Voluntary Seclusion: The Life of a Lonely Old Woman in a Deserted Village." *Russian Review,* vol. 51, no. 2 (April 1992).

Underdown, David. *Revel, Riot, and Rebellion: Popular Politics and Culture in England, 1603–1660.* Oxford, 1985.

Varenov, V. I. *Pomoshch' krasnoi armii v razvitii kolkhoznogo stroitel'stva, 1929–33 gg.* Moscow, 1978.

Vasil'ev, Valerii. "Krest'ianskie vosstaniia na Ukraine, 1929–30 gody." *Svobodnaia mysl',* no. 9 (1992).

Velidov, Alexei. "The 'Decree' on the Nationalization of Women: The Story of a Mystification." *Moscow News,* nos. 8–9 (1990).

Viola, Lynne. "Bab'i Bunty and Peasant Women's Protest During Collectivization." *Russian Review,* vol. 45, no. 1 (1986).

————. *The Best Sons of the Fatherland: Workers in the Vanguard of Soviet Collectivization.* New York, 1987.

————. "The Campaign to Eliminate the Kulak as a Class, Winter, 1929–30: A Reevaluation of the Legislation." *Slavic Review,* vol. 45, no. 3 (fall 1986).

————. "The Case of Krasnyi Meliorator *or* 'How the Kulak Grows into Socialism'." *Soviet Studies,* vol. 38, no. 4 (Oct. 1986).

————. "Guide to Document Series on Collectivization." In *A Researcher's Guide to Sources on Soviet Social History in the 1930s.* Ed. Sheila Fitzpatrick and Lynne Viola. Armonk, N.Y., 1990.

————. " 'L'ivresse du success': les cadres russes et le pouvoir sovietique durant les campagnes de collectivisation de l'agriculture." *Revue des etudes slaves,* vol. 64, no. 1 (1992).

————. "The Peasants' Kulak: Social Identities and Moral Economy in the Soviet Countryside in the 1920s." In *Collectivization and the Soviet Countryside.* Ed. V. P. Danilov and Roberta T. Manning. (Forthcoming).

————. "The Second Coming: Class Enemies in the Soviet Countryside, 1927–35." In *Stalinist Terror: New Perspectives.* Ed. J. Arch Getty and Roberta T. Manning. Cambridge, 1993.

Vyltsan, M. A.; Ivnitskii, N. A.; Poliakov, Iu. A. "Nekotorye problemy istorii kollektivizatsii v SSSR." *Voprosy istorii*, no. 3 (1965).

Ward, Chris. *Stalin's Russia.* London, 1993.

Wolf, Eric R. "On Peasant Rebellions." In *Peasants and Peasant Society.* 2nd ed. Ed. Teodor Shanin. Oxford, 1987.

————. *Peasant Wars of the Twentieth Century.* New York, 1969.

Worobec, Christine D. *Peasant Russia: Family and Community in the Post-Emancipation Period.* Princeton, 1991.

Yang, Anand A. "A Conversation of Rumors: The Language of Popular *Mentalites* in Late Nineteenth-Century Colonial India." *Journal of Social History*, vol. 21 (spring 1987).

Zelenin, I. E. "O nekotorykh 'belykh piatnakh' zavershaiushchego etapa sploshnoi kollektivizatsii." *Istoriia SSSR*, no. 2 (1989).

————. "Osushchestvlenie politiki 'likvidatsii kulachestva kak klassa' (osen' 1930–32 gg.)." *Istoriia SSSR*, no. 6 (1990).

Zemskov, V. N. "Spetsposelentsy (po dokumentatsii NKVD-MVD SSSR)." *Sotsiologicheskie issledovaniia*, no. 11 (1990).

Index

alcohol, 106–7, 127, 148–9, 151, 162–3, 265 n. 13. *See also samogon*
Andreev, A. A., 73, 183
Angarov, A., 52
anti-Semitism, 52–3, 252 nn.56, 59
apocalypse, 14, 30, 55, 60–1, 101, 145
arson, 4, 101, 112, 121–4, 266 nn. 54, 56, 58–9
  statistics, 105, 110, 122
artel, 26
artisans, 41, 229
Astrakhan, 63, 81, 86, 161–3, 171, 178
Azovskii-Chernomorskii Region, 211, 217

baba, 32–3, 43–4, 69–70, 98, 115, 150, 181–2, 184–5, 203–4, 236. *See also bab'i bunty*
bab'i bunty, 11, 113, 125, 181–204, 206, 237, 277 n. 10
  and food difficulties, 186–8
  and hunger riots, 174
  and naive monarchism, 182
Bartholomew's Night massacre, 28, 57, 254 n.90
Bauman, K. Ia, 34
Belorussia, 70, 114, 122, 126, 160, 216, 269 n. 20, 273 n. 138
Belov, Fedor, 90, 176
Berce, Yve-Marie, 39
Bonnell, Victoria E., 43, 204
bribery, 207, 214, 261 n. 118
brigands and brigandage, 133, 175–9
Budennyi, S. M., 70, 74–5

Bukharin, Nikolai, 20–2, 43, 56
Butovska, 194

carnival, 42–3, 50, 123
Central Asia, 83, 159–60, 177, 273 n. 134
Central Black Earth Region, 4, 81, 89, 93, 97, 143, 214, 217–8, 220, 230, 269 n. 20
  and arson, 122
  and collectivization, 27–9, 172, 274 n. 164
  and dekulakization, 28, 37
  and livestock, 70–1, 75
  and mass disturbances, 134, 157, 168–70, 174–5
  and meetings, 147–8, 152
  and proclamations, 118–9
  and rumors, 56–7, 59
  and self-dekulakization, 83
  and terror, 103, 111, 117, 125, 128, 130
  and women's protest, 186, 189, 195–6, 199
Central Control Commission, 218
Central Executive Committee, 92–3
charivari, 43
chastushki, 50, 63, 126, 251 n. 32
church, 49, 52, 153
  bell, 40, 42, 135, 151, 154–5, 157, 161–2, 164–5, 170, 187, 191–2, 196, 201, 248 n.131
  closures, 39–40, 135, 154–5, 157–8, 164, 187–8, 194, 248 n. 122
  and collectivization, 39–40
  councils, 27, 144–5, 193
  holidays, 42, 53, 106